Springer Textbooks in Law

Springer Textbooks in Law compiles high-quality educational content aimed at undergraduate and graduate students in all areas of law. All self-contained volumes are authored by accomplished academics and suitable for use in class as well as individual study. Many of them include chapter abstracts, definitions of technical terms, cases and self-assessment exercises, as well as recommended reading sections. This series is an invaluable resource for students and lecturers alike and spans the full range of topics in international and European law, including fundamentals of law and comparative law. Special attention is paid to current and emerging topics such as IT law, intellectual property, human rights as well as dispute resolution, mediation, arbitration – and many more.

María Julia Ochoa Jiménez
Claudia Madrid Martínez
Editors

A Private International Law for Colombia

Springer

Editors
María Julia Ochoa Jiménez
Loyola University
Sevilla, Andalucía, Spain

Claudia Madrid Martínez
University of Antioquia
Medellín, Antioquia, Colombia

ISSN 2509-999X ISSN 2510-0009 (electronic)
Springer Textbooks in Law
ISBN 978-3-032-04105-0 ISBN 978-3-032-04106-7 (eBook)
https://doi.org/10.1007/978-3-032-04106-7

This Springer imprint is published by the registered company Springer Nature Switzerland AG
The registered company address is: Gewerbestrasse 11, 6330 Cham, Switzerland

Preface

This book's approach to Colombian private international law is unique. Its main objective is to address how the most relevant issues in each of the main areas of this legal field manifest themselves in Colombia, analyzing them in a way that is both exhaustive in disciplinary terms and critically engaged.

When we set out to prepare the book, our aim was not only to support practitioners and judges in the interpretation and application of the rules currently in force, but also to help teachers, students, and researchers gain a better understanding of these kinds of rules and the discipline to which they belong. Furthermore, we have been motivated by the need to revisit such rules. Thus, the book explores the possibility of a new legislation that takes into account the most pressing challenges that private international law is facing in Colombia, situated as it is within the Latin American context, where the discipline has been historically robust. In this sense, the discussions in each chapter pay special attention to the Draft General Act on Private International Law for Colombia prepared by the *Instituto Antioqueño de Derecho Internacional Privado* (IADIP), to which some of the contributors are members.

As can be seen throughout its pages, the book comprises contributions from leading specialists in private international law with a solid knowledge of the Colombian system. We are grateful to them, as their participation has ensured the inclusion of diverse voices and expertise.

We believe we have achieved what we set out to do and are now pleased to present the book to readers. We do so in the hope that it will be of value to all those interested in understanding how private international law is conceived and set in motion in this part of the world.

The Editors

Sevilla, Spain
Medellín, Colombia

María Julia Ochoa Jiménez
Claudia Madrid Martínez

Contents

Introduction

María Julia Ochoa Jiménez

Abstract The lack of systematic studies hinders the development of private international law in Colombia. Academics, practitioners, or judges may encounter difficulties when faced with the application of the private international law rules contained in the Colombian legal system, which are scattered in various legal instruments. This volume not only systematically analyzes the technical mechanisms contained in such rules but also outlines the historical and theoretical context in which they exist. In addition, attention is given to the need for special legislation that fits Colombia's reality and takes into consideration the developments of private international law in Latin America. This volume also embodies an effort to consider some of the global challenges facing Colombian private international law today in relation to issues concerning the protection of human rights, including those of the most disadvantaged groups.

> When the gypsies came bac k, Úrsula had turned the whole population of the village against them. But curiosity was greater than fear, for that time the gypsies went about the town making a deafening noise…
>
> G García Márquez, One Hundred Years of Solitude

The first part of this text is based on a presentation about the contributions of Colombia to private international law, which I gave on the occasion of the establishment of Spanish as an official language of the Hague Conference on Private International Law and in honor of Werner Goldschmidt, organized by the School of Law, Universidad Nacional de Rosario, Argentina, July 2023.

M. J. Ochoa Jiménez (✉)
Loyola University, Sevilla, Andalucía, Spain
e-mail: mjochoa@uloyola.es

M. J. Ochoa Jiménez, C. Madrid Martínez (eds.), *A Private International Law for Colombia*, Springer Textbooks in Law,
https://doi.org/10.1007/978-3-032-04106-7_1

1 *Unde Venis*, Colombian Private International Law?

The diversity of laws is a natural and necessary fact.[1] With this assertion, Fernando Vélez began his *Programa de los Principios Generales del Derecho Internacional Privado*, which was published in 1891. In order to continue explaining what private international law is about, Velez sustained that uniformity in the details of the legislations of nations is unrealizable. And, in an attempt to adapt the name of this legal field to such reality, Vélez suggested that it should rather be called "theory of the extraterritorial authority of laws".[2]

Fernando Vélez was a professor of public and private law at the University of Antioquia in Medellin, in southwestern Colombia, during the late nineteenth and early twentieth centuries. His work can be seen within the framework of the doctrine of private international law developed in the nineteenth century, which was marked by events that took place beyond Colombia's borders. Experiences linked to the regional codification on this matter were initiated after the independence[3] with the *Tratado de Unión, Liga y Confederación Perpetua* between the Republics of Colombia, Central America, Peru, and the United Mexican States, discussed within the framework of the Amphictyonic Congress of Panama of 1826, which was preceded by the *Tratado de Liga, Unión y Confederación Perpetua* of 1822 between Peru and Colombia (which then integrated the Provinces of Venezuela, New Granada, and Ecuador).[4] Such regional codification movement took shape at the Lima Congress of 1878, the Montevideo Congress that began ten years later, and the adoption of the Bustamante Code at the beginning of the twentieth century.

In his *Principios Generales*, Velez presented his ideas about some subjects relevant to the debates that determined the pace of development of the Latin American private international at that time. Some of these ideas sound familiar even today. For instance, he stated that the theory of reciprocity "is unjust"[5] or that "it is inaccurate that foreign laws should only be applied out of courtesy",[6] an idea that he reinforced when he sustained that each country may provide for the application of foreign laws within its jurisdiction as it sees fit.[7] He further said as follows:

> in states where the legislation mandates to rule in certain cases by foreign law, the judge is obliged to provide himself *ex officio* with all the necessary means to acquire the exact knowledge of foreign law, which cannot be considered as a fact, or a document, or a pleading to be presented by the parties.[8]

---

[1] Vélez (1891, p. 3).

[2] ibid.

[3] Yepes (1930, p. 714).

[4] Parra Aranguren (1996, p. 113).

[5] Vélez (1891, p. 6).

[6] ibid., p. 3.

[7] ibid., p. 3.

[8] ibid., p. 23.

Another contribution of Velez was his interest in the dissemination of law, including private international law. Vélez said in 1905:

> It is not enough for a nation to have good laws for them to give the results that should be expected from such laws: it is necessary that, at least, the knowledge of their fundamental principles is spread in such a way that there are few individuals who do not acquire it and who are ignorant of their rights and obligations.[9]

For their part, Edmond Champeau, who was dean and professor of the Faculty of Bogotá, and Antonio José Uribe, who also taught at the University of Antioquia, explained in their *Tratado de Derecho Civil Colombiano* of 1899 that private international law mainly deals with the following questions: In the event of difficulties arising between a foreigner and a national, which will be the competent authority? Which law will be applicable by that authority?[10] To settle the matter, they stated that it is up to private international law to resolve those possible and frequent conflicts.[11] And, following the path in favor of the application of foreign law previously marked by Vélez, Uribe argued that the violation of foreign law could mean the violation of national law in two situations: by express provision of national law or by application of an international treaty binding for Colombia.[12]

Some years later, Julián Restrepo Hernández wrote that, as a scientific discipline, private international law deals with the influence of the foreign element in legal relations. Restrepo Hernández, who was a professor at the Colegio del Rosario in Bogotá, included such a definition in his book *Derecho Internacional Privado* of 1914. Furthermore, he explained that the science of private international law gives solutions that are more or less approximate to conflicts of laws and that such solutions may be included in international treaties and national laws, thus becoming positive law.[13]

Restrepo Hernández additionally expressed his desire to have a science of private international law *made in Colombia*. For him, a country that thinks and lives from abroad is a "miserable colony"[14] or a mere "satellite".[15] In this line, he thought that there was nothing as patriotic as nationalizing science,[16] and he thus criticized what he described as "the unjustifiable Frenchness of our legal theory".[17] Nevertheless, at the same time, he warns that it would be absurd that by nationalizing a science, it should be made anew. Colombian private international law was, for him, called upon to take the best foreign sources and developments and adapt them to the needs and circumstances of the country. Convinced that Colombia was prepared to receive

[9] Vélez (1905), cited by Castaño Zuluaga (2002, p. 23).

[10] Champeau and Uribe (1899, p. 16).

[11] ibid., p. 16.

[12] Uribe (1900, pp. LVIII–LIX).

[13] Restrepo Hernández (1914, p. 4).

[14] Restrepo Hernández (1917, p. 427).

[15] ibid.

[16] ibid.

[17] ibid.

many foreigners, he argued that to adequately face what their presence implied, it was necessary to study the science of private international law and meditate instead of improvising or copying ideas.[18]

Another outstanding Colombian jurist in the field of private international law was Jesús María Yepes, who in 1930 taught the first course on Latin American private international law at the Hague Academy, in which he discussed the contribution of Latin America to the development of public and private international law.[19] Yepes emphasized there the identity of values and realities that existed in the region in these legal areas and the fact that the process of codification of private international law that took place after the Congress of Lima in 1878 and the Congress of Montevideo in 1888 and 1889 laid the foundations of modern private international law, while in Europe the codification impulse materialized later, in 1893, with the first session of the Hague Conference.[20]

Although in the mid-twentieth century it is possible to identify a kind of decline in Colombian private international law doctrine, the work of Alfredo Cock Arango deserves some attention. Cock Arango, who taught private law at the University of Antioquia and other Colombian universities, proposed a formula to deal with conflicts of laws that was included in his book *Tratado de Derecho Internacional Privado*, and which had considerable acceptance among his contemporaries. The two-step formula that Cock Arango proposed was described as simple and rational.[21] Briefly, it was as follows: first, every legal act or fact is subject to the law by virtue of the rule of which it was produced; second, laws that establish rights and impose obligations that are not immediately based on legal facts or acts have no application outside the territory of the nation to which they belong.[22] Without going into the reasoning that precedes this formula or what follows from it, it is worth stressing that Cock Arango was concerned with designing a formula that aimed to be applicable to cases of conflict of laws of any kind.[23] He was thus trying to put into practice the kind of innovative spirit to which Restrepo Hernández alluded, i.e., "without resorting to any of the usual theories".[24]

The work of José Joaquín Caicedo Castilla also stands out in the Colombian private international law doctrine of the twentieth century. His *Manual de Derecho Internacional Privado* was revised and updated several times after 1939, when it was published for the first time. The book *Apuntes de Derecho Internacional Privado* by Ramón Mantilla Rey was published in 1982, where he summarized his lessons at the Universidad Nacional de Colombia. Simultaneously, several editions

[18] Restrepo Hernández (1914, p. 14).

[19] Hernández-Bretón (2009, p. 279).

[20] See also Delic (2017).

[21] Delage (1937, pp. 333–346).

[22] ibid.

[23] ibid.

[24] ibid.

of the book *Tratado de Derecho Internacional Privado* by Marco Gerardo Monroy Cabra were also published.[25]

In the following decades, the decline in the study of private international law was accentuated to a large extent as a consequence of the marginal attention that has been paid to its general theory and rules in law schools. This did not, however, prevent Colombian jurists from continuing to study some dimensions of private international law. Attention has been certainly given to the impact of some international rules and standards in the country, such as the Vienna Convention on the International Sale of Goods of 1980 and the UNIDROIT Principles of International Commercial Contracts.[26]

In addition to being scarce, recent publications on Colombian private international law frequently lack comprehensive and in-depth studies.[27] Usually, they are located at two extremes: either they refer to Colombian private international law from a very narrow and partial perspective, limiting themselves to dealing with one specific aspect of the Colombian legal system related to the field, or they do so in a too general and superficial manner.

Now, the lack of special legislation on private international law in the country has marked not only the academic realm but also legal practice. Existing regulations are scarce, lack systematic regulation, and are mostly old. Therefore, judicial decisions are not abundant either. Most of the private international rules that are currently in force in Colombia are in the Civil Code, the Code of Commerce, the General Code of Procedure Law, and in some special legislations, for example, regarding secured transactions.[28] One can find such rules also in multilateral treaties to which Colombia is a party, such as the Treaty of Montevideo of 1889 on International Civil Law and some of the treaties adopted by the Hague Conference on Private International Law and the Organization of American States.

In 1980, the Colombian President created a Review Commission of the Colombian Civil Code, which contained private international rules.[29] The review had to be conducted within one year,[30] but the deadline was extended twice.[31] Finally, the Commission submitted a draft to the Ministry of Justice in 1984.[32] However, this was not passed. Until very recently, this was the only official proposal to reform the private international law provisions included in the Civil Code, the

---

[25] Monroy Cabra (1983).

[26] In this regard, the studies by Oviedo Albán (2012a, b) are noteworthy.

[27] In English, publications are even scarcer than in Spanish. Some publications deal with very specific topics, for example, Zuleta and Rincón (2017). There are also some writings containing general descriptions (e.g., in reference books), such as Zapata Giraldo (2017).

[28] Act No. 1676 of 2013.

[29] The members of this commission were prominent Colombian jurists: Arturo Valencia Zea, José Gabino Pinzón Martínez, José Alejandro Bonivento Fernández, Luis Manrique Naranjo, Pedro Lafont Pianetta, and Gilberto Peña Castrillón.

[30] Decree No. 959, April 28, 1980.

[31] In 1980 (Decree No. 1319, May 25, 1981) and 1984 (Decree No. 0098, January 18, 1984).

[32] Review Commission (1984).

first version of which dates back to 1858.[33] In 2021, a new proposal to review the Civil Code was prepared by the National University of Colombia, with the support of the Ministry for Justice, on the basis of the aforementioned 1984 draft. After adding some modifications, a new version of this proposal was published in 2023. Nevertheless, this was not well received among academics and practitioners either.[34]

Throughout this book, special attention is paid to the proposal for special legislation on private international law that was prepared by the *Instituto Antioqueño de Derecho Internacional Privado* (IADIP) in 2021, under the title Draft General Act on Private International Law for Colombia (hereafter, "IADIP Draft").[35] This is based on a previous academic proposal prepared by José Luis Marín Fuentes,[36] one of the members of IADIP, taking into account national legislations existing in other Latin American countries, e.g., the Venezuelan Act on Private International Law, and regional codifications, e.g., the Inter-American Convention on General Rules of Private International Law, to which Colombia is a party since 1981.[37]

The IADIP Draft contains important contributions, in addition to offering a special systematic regulation on the matter. In the first place, it responds to the need to overcome the current strong territorialism. In this regard, it can be pointed out that, for example, starting from the consideration of the right of transnational access to justice, flexibility is given to the process of recognition of the effectiveness of foreign decisions, contemplating it as a summary process and attributing jurisdiction over this matter to the authority before which the effects of the respective judgment are sought to be enforced.

Other novelties include the possibility of strengthening the protection of the rights of Indigenous peoples and communities through private international law. This may be seen as today's response to the need pointed out by Restrepo Hernández more than one hundred years ago for moving Colombian private international law "from satellite to planet", preventing it from being a "miserable colony".[38] Thus, the IADIP Draft introduces a particular form of internationally mandatory rules, explicitly including those rules that protect the rights of Indigenous peoples or communities over the natural resources existing in their lands, and a special conflict rule for cases of restitution of goods that, having a cultural value for an Indigenous people or community, have unlawfully left the Colombian territory and are being returned to the country.

---

[33] The main domestic legal instrument that contains conflict provisions in Colombia is still the Civil Code of 1887. This code entails the same provisions of the Civil Code of the *Estado Soberano de Santander* from 1858, which is said to be a copy of the Civil Code of Chile of 1855 that was drafted by Andrés Bello. See Mantilla Rey (1982, p. 26).

[34] More on this in Chap. "Private International Law and Comparative Law: A Colombian Approach" of this volume.

[35] An English version of the complete text of the IADIP Draft is available at Salvadori and Boutin Icaza (2024).

[36] Marín Fuentes (2014).

[37] Act No 21 of 1981.

[38] Restrepo Hernández (1917, p. 427).

2 This Book

This book has two main characteristics that make it stand out in the existing literature on Colombian private international law. The first one is that all of its authors have devoted years of work to the themes they deal with in their respective contributions. Thus, they are not only sensitive to the potential of this legal field to meet some of the most pressing needs of the country but are also aware of the means through which this potential can be deployed. Additionally, the book offers a vision of the future of private international law in Colombia having a very specific starting point, which is the abovementioned IADIP Draft.

The book is organized into six parts, which can be thematically grouped into two. The first thematic group is quite general. It introduces some theoretical approaches that aim to offer ways to understand the larger context in which Colombian private international law arises. Part I entails three chapters that are thus devoted to introductory notions. Contemporary studies of private international law in Colombia have not so far focused on looking at this legal field in such a broad manner. The fact that this perspective has remained underexplored explains to certain extent why the studies contained in the chapters that form this first thematic group are so important and, at the same time, some of them are still in an early stage. This general contextual approach provides, in any case, a suitable framework for a more adequate and acute observation of the technical issues that will be dealt with in the rest of the book.

Part I includes Chaps. "Colombian Private International Law: Three Dimensions, One Perspective", "Private International Law and Comparative Law: A Colombian Approach", and "An Introduction to the Private International Law of the Latin American Countries Today". In the first two chapters, María Julia Ochoa Jiménez deals with two fundamental questions. The first of such questions is considered in Chap. "Colombian Private International Law: Three Dimensions, One Perspective" and relates to the national, international, and global dimensions of private international law. Such dimensions, as she argues, may determine the ways in which private international law plays the role it is called upon to play in today's world, in terms of cultural diversity or sustainable development, as well as with regard to the protection of human rights beyond the borders of states. The second fundamental question is discussed in Chap. "Private International Law and Comparative Law: A Colombian Approach" and focuses on the linkages between private international law and comparative law. The main contribution of this chapter is the examination, albeit exploratory, of the different ways in which comparative studies have been carried out in Colombian private international law by academics, judges, and legislators. This has been so far one of the least explored areas in Latin American private international law scholarship. This chapter shows a path through which we may reach a more realistic understanding of the particularities that this field has acquired in the region, where it has been in play for the last two centuries. As the chapter implies, it allows us to observe that we should not limit ourselves to the widely accepted simplistic assumption of a lack of originality in Latin American law, which includes Colombian private international law. Among other harmful effects, such an assumption has prevented us from deeper explorations and may, if we continue to accept it uncritically, continue to do so in the future. In Chap. "An Introduction to the Private International Law of the Latin American Countries Today", Eugenio Hernández-Bretón briefly introduces us to the evolution of private international law in Latin American countries. This chapter provides a valuable up-to-date overview of the national private international law codifications while referring where appropriate to the international treaties adopted in the region. A common feature of Latin American national systems is, as the author points out, that national "codifications are not contained in one single legal instrument but in a series of different bodies of law", and therefore it is their aggregate, together with international treaties in force, that forms the national legal system in the field of private international of each country. As will be discussed at length in the following parts of the book, this is particularly true also in the case of the Colombian system of private international law.

The second thematic group of the book is much more extensive than the first one. This group, which covers Parts II through VI, aims to analyze in detail the technical bases of private international law and how they are conceived and used in Colombia. Attention must be paid to the fact that currently there is no national special legislation on private international law in the country. The lack of a national special legislation on this matter has an impact on situations that entail foreign elements and, therefore, are relevant to private international law. But there is certainly a law in Colombia that contains some rules of private international law, both conflictual and material, including some procedural ones. There are even some basic rules in the field that were adopted in the nineteenth century and have remained untouched since then. Although inadequately and imperfectly, the Colombian legal system responds in some way to situations with foreign elements. The chapters that make up this second part of the book take a detailed look at how this occurs. In addition, these chapters discuss what could be done to make Colombian law more responsive to the needs posed by the different types of situations with foreign elements. In this regard, the solutions proposed in the IADIP Draft are considered when dealing with each specific subject through the chapters that compound this thematic group.

From Part II onward, the book addresses the three questions that constitute the core of private international law: (i) which country's courts must resolve the case, (ii) what law must be applied to resolve the case, and (iii) under what circumstances must the decisions by the courts of one state be recognized and executed in another state. The first issues dealt with are those related to international procedural law, which will be followed by issues related to the determination of the applicable law. There are two main reasons for this order. The first is that starting with the determination of the international competence of the country's courts logically underlies any approach to a cross-border private law case. The other reason is the scarcity of international procedural law rules in the country. As will be seen, there are practically no international procedural rules in the Colombian domestic legal system, with few exceptions such as those relating to the extraterritorial effect of foreign decisions. This latter point is included in Part II with the sole practical intention of dealing with procedural issues together, although it is a question that, logically, only arises once each specific case has been resolved and a decision, judicial or arbitral, is available.

Thus, Part II, which includes Chaps. "International Jurisdiction in Colombia", "International Judicial Cooperation in Colombia", and "Extraterritorial Effect of Judgments in Colombian Private International Law", focuses on the Colombian legal framework regarding international procedural issues. First, in Chap. "International Jurisdiction in Colombia", Claudia Madrid Martínez focuses on the study of international jurisdiction. In Colombia, there are no national rules that attribute international competence to the country's courts to decide cross-border cases in a systematic manner. As an effort to fill this loophole, an extended interpretation of some existing rules that address domestic (i.e., non-international) cases has been proposed.[39] However, such kinds of proposals do not seem plausible. Considering this, Madrid Martínez comprehensively analyzes what this situation entails and the approaches available to manage it appropriately. In Chap. "International Judicial Cooperation in Colombia", Luis Alfredo Pinilla deals with the Colombian legal framework regarding international judicial cooperation. Thus, the chapter starts by presenting the international treaties to which Colombia is a party and allows us to have a comprehensive knowledge of how international treaties and standards are put into practice at the domestic level. Chapter "Extraterritorial Effect of Judgments in Colombian Private International Law" turns to the recognition of foreign judicial decisions. Cross-border transactions and the international movement of persons give rise to a relatively frequent demand for recognition of foreign decisions in Colombia. However, a preliminary study showed that the Supreme Court of Justice[40] dismissed most of the claims. Its decisions represent, nevertheless, the most abundant jurisprudence in the field of private international law in the country. Thus, María Julia Ochoa Jiménez and José Luis Marín Fuentes examine in this chapter the main underlying issues, and the fundamental theoretical and dogmatic approaches developed by the Colombian Supreme Court of Justice about this subject matter.

The theoretical, conceptual, and technical mechanisms of private international law that must be considered by the competent authority to decide about the applicable law in a private international law case are presented and discussed in Parts III–VI.

The main topic of Part III concerns the questions that deal in a cross-cutting manner with the main issues of private international law regarding the resolution of conflict-of-law cases and the possibility of applying foreign law. Due to the strong territorial conception of private international law that can be currently found in the Colombian context,[41] this implies the need to address the preferential consideration of the *lex fori* that still prevails in the country. Part III is formed by three chapters,

[39] Guerra Hernández (2016).

[40] This subject matter is currently governed by some provisions of the General Code of Procedure Law (Articles 605–607).

[41] Samtleben (2023), Ochoa Jiménez (2019).

namely, Chaps. "Sources and Methodological Plurality of Private International Law in Colombia", "Application of Foreign Law in Colombia", and "General Institutions in Colombian Private International Law", which were drafted by Claudia Madrid Martínez. She discusses in Chap. "Sources and Methodological Plurality of Private International Law in Colombia" how the particular interconnections between international treaties and domestic laws in Colombia make it difficult to establish whether they are hierarchically organized. This chapter also explains how the different private international law methods of regulation of cross-border cases, i.e., internationally mandatory rules, substantive rules, and conflict rules, materialize in Colombian law. In Chap. "Application of Foreign Law in Colombia", Madrid Martínez deals with a key and characteristic element of private international law: the application of foreign law. This issue is itself complex from several points of view. The author unravels the technical–legal aspects, in procedural and substantive terms. Thus, the chapter delves into the procedural implications that distinguish between the treatment of foreign law as a law or as a fact and sets out the Colombian legal framework. It highlights the "mixed system" established by the Colombian Constitutional Court, in which judges and parties may intervene. In Chap. "General Institutions in Colombian Private International Law", Madrid Martínez focuses on the general private international law rules and principles to address the challenge of establishing whether a particular case must be resolved under a foreign law or, on the contrary, following the *lex fori*. It distinguishes between mechanisms that operate when foreign law applies, i.e., characterization, unknown institution, renvoi, acquired rights and adaptation, and mechanisms that prevent the application of foreign law, i.e., public policy and evasion of law.

The objective of Part IV (Chaps. "Property Rights in Colombian Private International Law" and "International Intellectual Property Contracts in Colombia: Applicable Law and Dispute Resolution") is to discuss the main rules of Colombian private international law relating to property rights. In Chap. "Property Rights in Colombian Private International Law", María Julia Ochoa Jiménez first addresses the way in which the *lex rei sitae* rule is introduced in Latin America, in general, and in Colombia, in particular. She then critically observes how this rule is established in the legal instruments currently in force in Colombia. The chapter also presents the general and special rules contained in the IADIP Draft, such as those on intellectual property, and the return of cultural property, including that property of Indigenous origin. This latter rule, which is quite innovative, leads to a more detailed consideration of the relation between private international law and the rights of Indigenous peoples and communities in Colombia. Chap. "International Intellectual Property Contracts in Colombia: Applicable Law and Dispute Resolution", for its part, turns to the rules existing in Colombian law regarding international intellectual property contracts. There, Brenda Salas observes the way in which the autonomy of the parties is recognized in relation to this subject matter, as well as the main issues involved in the determination of the applicable law to these kinds of contracts and the competent authority for conflict resolution when the parties have remained silent. This chapter also looks at the relevant rules included in the IADIP Draft.

Part V, which entails Chaps. "Natural Persons in Colombian Private International Law", "Marriage and Marital Unions in Colombian Private International Law", and "International Family Law in Colombia", addresses the main features of Colombian private international law concerning persons and family matters. In Chap. "Natural Persons in Colombian Private International Law", Laura Victoria García Matamoros examines the situation regarding natural persons, beneath which one can find the domicile–nationality dichotomy. The debates surrounding these two notions, which have been traditionally used as connecting factors in conflict of laws rules relating to personal matters, played a relevant role in the historical development of private international law in Latin America.[42] This could explain to some extent the contradictions currently found in the Colombian legal system, which contains rules that are not coordinated with each other.[43] Chapter "Natural Persons in Colombian Private International Law" offers a coherent interpretative approach and discusses *de lege lata* and *de lege ferenda* solutions. In Chap. "Marriage and Marital Unions in Colombian Private International Law", García Matamoros further analyzes the rules that exist in Colombia regarding cross-border legal relationships linked to family, i.e., celebration, effects, and dissolution of marriage and marital union. In both Chaps. "Natural Persons in Colombian Private International Law" and "Marriage and Marital Unions in Colombian Private International Law", García Matamoros takes into consideration the relevant rules of the IADIP Draft, as well as the Draft Civil Code of Colombia prepared by the Universidad Nacional de Colombia in 2023. In Chap. "International Family Law in Colombia", Gloria Rivera Ocampo offers an overview of Colombian international family law, presenting the main agreements that are part of the Colombian legal system, in particular, to safeguard the interests of children. In addition, she points out that other subject matters, such as surrogacy and post-mortem insemination, remain unregulated in the country.

The last part of the book, which is Part VI (Chaps. "International Family Law in Colombia", "Private International Law and Colombian Business Associations Law", and "A New Beginning for Negotiable Instruments"), focuses on private international law concerning commercial matters. Thus, Juan Antonio Gaviria analyzes in Chap. "Private International Law and Colombian Business Associations Law" the substantive rules on business associations currently in force in Colombia and how they relate to private international law. To that end, he focuses on for-profit entities and their shareholders or partners. He observes such entities from a twofold perspective, i.e., as juridical persons and as international contracts. Gaviria further analyzes how the relevant rules distinguish between domestic and foreign companies. Through the chapter, the author considers the relevant provisions contained in the IADIP Draft. In Chap. "A New Beginning for Negotiable Instruments", Daniel Rojas-Tamayo offers a critical approach to Colombian private international law on negotiable instruments. It first calls his attention that just a few rules have been adopted in recent times, while the regulation on this subject matter in the previous

---

42 Ochoa Jiménez (2021, pp. 92–93).

43 cfr. Samtleben (1983), Ochoa Jiménez and Zapata Flórez (2022).

regional codifications is more extensive. He also observes the scarcity of rulings by the Colombian Supreme Court. Based on such considerations, he sustains that the IADIP Draft proposes an appropriate regulation that would modernize Colombian law on this subject matter. Chapter "The Lex Mercatoria Method: Addressing International Private Cases Beyond Conflict of Laws", written by Néstor Raúl Londoño Sepúlveda, closes this volume. The chapter aims at providing an analysis of the development, origins, and use in practice of the *lex mercatoria*. Londoño Sepúlveda argues that the *lex mercatoria* acts as an alternative to conflict of laws solutions. The author takes into account that the *lex mercatoria* has a non-state character, so it governs commercial transactions outside the conflict of legal system. Furthermore, he stresses its flexibility and usefulness in filling gaps and extending the scope of application of both national and international laws.

3 *Quo Vadis*, Colombian Private International Law?

The fact that Colombia does not have a systematically organized regulatory system on private international law, and that the subject is still little explored scientifically in the country, is a golden opportunity to (re)think how a special legislation on the subject can be better adjusted to the reality of the country. It is a great occasion for approaching Colombian private international law from theoretical and praxis-based viewpoints. Further studies from comparative law and from perspectives opened by the history, anthropology, or sociology of private international law will enormously contribute to this. While carrying out such a work, a better understanding of private international law can be acquired, in which it can be clearly seen that private international law is a legal and ethical field that provides us with "a technique that helps us conceptualize and address some of the most pressing issues of our time."[44] Failure to take this into account may lead to a considerable reduction in the use of the discipline's methodological and technical potential.[45]

The above refers not only to the fact, emphasized at times by academics and practitioners alike, that foreign companies or other commercial actors operate in the country, or domestic ones do so abroad, which is relevant to the country's economy. As can be seen from the various contributions to this book, private international law has a basic and cross-cutting nature that makes its use crucial also in the lives of people from all backgrounds, including disadvantaged and excluded groups. The role that private international law is called upon to play in this framework may be rightly described through the idea that it involves an "ethic of responsiveness",[46] which may help understand the role of the discipline from a global perspective. The issues involved are certainly relevant worldwide, particularly in a country like

[44] Michaels (2019, p. 11).

[45] Ruiz Abou-Nigm (2019, p. 383).

[46] See Michaels (2019).

Colombia, where approximately thirty-six percent of the total population—i.e., over 18 million people—live in poverty,[47] and there are increasing amounts of immigrants, many of whom have been forcibly displaced from other countries of the Global South. And, despite Úrsula's discontent, the noise they make is deafening.

References

Castaño Zuluaga LO (2002) Fernando Vélez: una vida consagrada al estudio del derecho. Estudios de Derecho LX(17):27

Champeau E, Uribe AJ (1899) Tratado de Derecho Civil Colombiano, vol 1. Librairie de la Société du Recueil Général de Lois et des Arrêts, Paris

DANE (2024) Pobreza y desiguldad. https://www.dane.gov.co/index.php/estadisticas-por-tema/pobreza-y-condiciones-de-vida/pobreza-y-desigualdad. Accessed 26 June 2024

Delage M (1937) La Teoría de Cock ante el derecho internacional privado. Revista del Colegio Mayor de Nuestra Señora del Rosario 32(313):333–346

Delic A (2017) The birth of modern private international law: the Montevideo Treaties (1889, amended 1940). http://opil.ouplaw.com/page/Treaties-Montevideo. Accessed 20 July 2024

Guerra Hernández VH (2016) Conflictos de jurisdicción y competencia en derecho internacional privado. In: García Matamoros L, Aljure Salame A (eds) Teoría general del derecho internacional privado. Universidad del Rosario and Legis, Bogota

Hernández-Bretón E (2009) Personajes para una Biografía del Derecho Internacional Privado Latinoamericano. Revista de la Facultad de Ciencias Jurídicas y Políticas, Universidad Central de Venezuela 133:279

Mantilla Rey R (1982) Apuntes de derecho internacional privado. Temis, Bogota

Marín Fuentes J (2014) Derecho internacional privado. Universidad de Medellín, Medellin

Michaels R (2019) Private international law as an ethic of responsivity. In: Ruiz Abou-Nigm V, Noodt Taquela MB (eds) Diversity and integration in private international law. Edinburgh University Press, Edinburgh, pp 11–27

Monroy Cabra MG (1983) Tratado de derecho internacional privado, 3rd edn. Temis, Bogota

Ochoa Jiménez MJ (2019) Normas de derecho internacional privado en materia de bienes: la regla lex rei sitae en América Latina y Colombia. Revista de Derecho Privado 37:153–183

Ochoa Jiménez MJ (2021) Exploring a minefield: private international law in Latin America, its neocolonial character, and its potentialities. Crit Anal Law 8(2):87–107

Ochoa Jiménez MJ, Zapata Flórez J (2022) Private international law rules regarding personal status in Colombia: a system in need of an overhaul. Anuario Mexicano de Derecho Internacional XXII:549–574

Oviedo Albán J (2012a) La ley aplicable a los contratos internacionales. International Law Revista Colombiana de Derecho Internacional 21:117–157

Oviedo Albán J (2012b) Los Principios UNIDROIT sobre los Contratos Comerciales Internacionales 2010. In: Oviedo Albán J (ed) Principios UNIDROIT sobre los Contratos Comerciales Internacionales 2010 "Black Letter Rules". Bogota, Ibañez, pp 12–54

Parra Aranguren G (1996) La primera etapa de los tratados sobre derecho internacional privado en América (1826-1940). http://www.ulpiano.org.ve/revistas/bases/artic/texto/RDUCV/98/rucv_1996_98_59-128.pdf. Accessed on 15 June 2024

Restrepo Hernández J (1914) Derecho Internacional Privado. Imprenta de la Luz, Bogota

Restrepo Hernández J (1917) Lecciones de Antropología. Revista del Colegio del Rosario 1917:424–429

[47] DANE (2024).

Review Commission (1984) Civil Code Draft. http://www.derecho.unal.edu.co/fileadmin/Codigo_Civil/Proyecto_Codigo_Civil_Prof_Valencia_Zea.pdf. Accessed 20 June 2024

Ruiz Abou-Nigm V (2019) Bridging and balancing: diversity and integration in private international law. In: Ruiz Abou-Nigm V, Noodt Taquela MB (eds) Diversity and integration in private international law. Edinburgh University Press, Edinburgh, pp 362–388

Salvadori M, Boutin Icaza G (eds) (2024) Colombian draft project on private international law. Quaderni Del Dipartimento Di Giurisprudenza Dell'Università Di Torino 34/2024

Samtleben J (1983) Derecho internacional privado en América Latina. Teoría y práctica del Código Bustamante. Depalma, Buenos Aires

Samtleben J (2023) Internationales Privat- und Prozessrecht in Lateinamerika. Tradition und Reform. Shaker Verlag, Duren

Uribe AJ (1900) Introducción. Introducción. Jurisprudencia colombiana extractada y concordada. Imprenta Nacional, Bogota

Vélez F (1891) Principios Generales del Derecho Internacional Privado. Imprenta del Departamento, Medellin

Yepes JM (1930). La contribution de l'Amérique latine au développement du droit international public et privé (Volume 32). In The Hague Academy Collected Courses Online / Recueil des cours de l'Académie de La Haye en ligne. Brill Nijhoff. https://doi.org/10.1163/1875-8096_pplrdc_A9789028606920_05

Zapata Giraldo A (2017) Colombia. In: Basedow J, Rühl G, Ferrari F, Miguel Asensio P (eds) Encyclopedia of private international law. Edward Elgar, Cheltenham

Zuleta E, Rincón R (2017) Interpretation and application of the New York convention in Colombia. Springer, Cham

María Julia Ochoa Jiménez . Dr. iur. and LLM from the University of Göttingen; lawyer and specialist in Intellectual Property from the Universidad de Los Andes; LLM, Universidad de Navarra; research fellow, University of Bonn, Alexander von Humboldt Foundation; visiting researcher, Max Planck Institute for Comparative and International Private Law; professor, Universidad de Antioquia (2016–2022); professor of Private International Law, Universidad Loyola.

Introductory Notions

Colombian Private International Law: Three Dimensions, One Perspective

María Julia Ochoa Jiménez

Abstract This and the next chapters address, in an introductory manner, two fundamental questions that lie at the root of private international law and serve to understand its broad conceptual scope. Both questions are approached from the Colombian perspective, considering the current situation of the discipline in the country. The first question, which is dealt with here, is quite wide and refers to the role that private international law plays in today's world. Thus, this chapter outlines what lies behind the national, international, and global dimensions of private international law, and also the relevance it has when it is particularly considered from the global perspective. The second question, on which the next chapter focuses, is not less vast and concerns the interactions between comparative law and private international law.

1 Introduction

The development of private international law in Colombia, as in the rest of Latin America, has gone hand in hand with its codification.[1] The first codifications of private international law adopted in the region by means of regional treaties are considered to mark the beginning of such efforts worldwide in modern times.[2] The conception of international private international law treaties in Latin America dates back to the beginning of the nineteenth century, being already foreseen during the formation of the new republics, in the *Tratado de Unión, Liga i Confederación*

[1] Samtleben (1983, pp. 3–51).

[2] See Delic (2017).

M. J. Ochoa Jiménez (✉)
Loyola University, Sevilla, Andalucía, Spain
e-mail: mjochoa@uloyola.es

M. J. Ochoa Jiménez, C. Madrid Martínez (eds.), *A Private International Law for Colombia*, Springer Textbooks in Law,
https://doi.org/10.1007/978-3-032-04106-7_2

Perpetua of 1826.[3] This led to the regional codification processes initiated with the Treaty of Lima of 1878, which was followed by the well-known Montevideo Treaties of 1888–1889, as well as by a whole array of international treaties adopted in the following centuries.

Yet, states often rely on their national experience in drafting international legal instruments. So, in Latin America, the adoption of private international law codifications at the international level has been intertwined with the specific approaches adopted by the different states in their own national systems.[4] These differed from each other, though it has been pointed out that the international codifications in the region "were achieved without the trouble of having to debate between intrinsically different approaches".[5]

In this context, it is worth noting that it is considered that the circumstances giving rise to the need for private international law rules occur first and foremost in the domestic sphere or are somehow related to it. Therefore, based on its sovereignty, each state establishes in its legal system how its domestic courts would resolve cases brought before them, including cases with foreign elements. This Westphalian idea of sovereignty underlies another: that law is the exclusive creation of states, i.e., that law is always state law.[6] Some call this methodological nationalism,[7] i.e., "conceiving of law exclusively within a state paradigm."[8]

Such methodological nationalism has historically been at the basis of national and international approaches to private international law. From a global perspective, things look different, as the idea that states have the monopoly of law production and law application is put into question. Philip Jessup's words about the misleading character of the term *international law*, and his preference for the use of the term *transnational law*, are relevant in this context still today. According to him, a special emphasis has historically been placed on the national state, but "we have not yet reached the stage of a world state"[9] and, even when it must be taken into account, he said, "the state, in whatever form, is not the only group with which we are concerned".[10]

The following is an attempt to introduce, considering the Colombian standpoint, some of the main issues involved in the aforementioned ideas.

---

[3] Samtleben (2023, p. 103).

[4] Samtleben (1983, p. 4).

[5] Delic (2019, p. 207).

[6] For discussions around this idea, see, e.g., Jansen and Michaels (2008), and Raz (2017).

[7] Duve (2020, p. 8), Michaels (2019, p. 629).

[8] Michaels (2019, p. 629).

[9] Jessup (1956, p. 1).

[10] ibid.

2 Private International Law as National law

Colombia introduced private international law in its national legal system in the nineteenth century. Since then, private international law has undergone various transformations in the country, while some of its main features have been maintained. The focus here is not on the contents of private international law provisions existing in the country, which will be dealt with in other contributions to this volume. Instead, in what follows, it will be addressed, in an approximative manner, the question of why private international law is *national* law and what are some of the main consequences that derive from this.

Private international law is national because each state decides how to regulate the acts, relations, or businesses that take place in its territory, as well as the persons and property therein. It does not matter whether such acts, relations, or businesses entail elements that are foreign to the state's own legal system. This has become unquestionable through the notion of state sovereignty, the use and acceptance of which have been consolidated over centuries. The national laws of each state, which must be applied by its domestic courts, are not supposed to be dictated by foreign states. Thus, a case with foreign elements being decided according to the law of another state —i.e., foreign law—is only possible if it is so established by the law of the state where the case is being decided, that is, the *lex fori*. This means that each state can primarily do so following its own internal or domestic rules, through any of the legal instruments that make up its national legal system. Thus, rules of private international law can be found in the constitution, codes on civil and commercial matters, special laws, etc., as well as in the decisions issued by the national authorities. There is thus an essential link between the power that the state has over its territory and the exercise of that power through law, including private international law.

Although judges may have room for discretion, the possibility of applying or not applying foreign law is legally established, through any domestically accepted means. Private international law calls "bilateral conflict rules"[11] those that allow the application of foreign law. Whereas "unilateral conflict rules"[12] are those rules that do not allow the application of foreign law and only accept the application of the *lex fori*, which means the national law or the law of the own territory. Therefore, the preference for applying national law is referred to in private international law as "unilateralism" or "territorialism".

In Colombia, the tendency toward territorialism has been quite pronounced. The territoriality-centered tradition in Colombia, the origins of which go back to the first national codifications, has remained strong to this day. A frequently cited rule in this respect is Article 18 of the Colombian Civil Code, which is identical to Article 14 of the Chilean Civil Code. According to this rule, Colombian law is binding both for

[11] Among the rules of private international law currently in force in Colombia, Article 1012 of the Colombian Civil Code can be considered one of the few examples in this regard.

[12] See, e.g., Article 20 of the Colombian Civil Code.

Colombians and foreigners. Rules such as Article 20 of the Civil Code, which governs property rights, and Article 869 of the Commercial Code, which applies to contracts, can be mentioned as examples of how such a territorial approach manifests itself in the realm of conflicts of laws. Just to mention another example, it can be noted that, although the divorce of marriages celebrated abroad is subject to the law of the conjugal domicile (Article 163 of the Civil Code), for marriages celebrated in Colombia the Colombian law is mandatory, to which the divorce produced abroad is also subjected (Article 164 of the Civil Code).[13]

The territorial approach adopted in Colombia is at the basis of the need for a comprehensive review of the private international law rules existing in the country. Territorialism, it may be said, is an expression of nationalism. It can also be said, of course, that territorialism in private international law exists because the state has the sovereignty to legislate in its territory. However, the notion of territorialism is not identical to that of state sovereignty: in the exercise of its sovereignty, the state may also legislate bilaterally, and it in fact does so, i.e., allowing the application of foreign law.

It is undisputed that the fact that private international law is national law implies that each state decides on the possibility of applying foreign law. Applying foreign law—or the legal possibility of doing so— is in line with the current realities of the world, since no state can, in fact, live in complete isolation. Additionally, it is now generally accepted that there is an intimate relationship between private international law and human rights.[14] The possibility of applying foreign law may imply a greater commitment on the part of states to respect human rights and guarantee them on an equality basis: "In private international law, equality meant … [that everybody] is equally governed by their own law and that each situation is governed by the law with which it is connected the most closely."[15] In the same sense, only when it is possible to have access to foreign courts and when there is the possibility that foreign judgments can be recognized and enforced in the national territory, can it be said that the right of access to justice beyond the borders of each state is being guaranteed.[16]

It can also be argued that the commitment of private international law to the protection of human rights may even manifest itself—albeit exceptionally—through the refusal to apply foreign law or to recognize a foreign judgment. This is done by the *forum* state when, in whatever form or extent, it has higher standards of protection than the state of origin of the law or judgment, in relation to the subject dealt with in the specific case. To this end, if the *forum* state includes fundamental rights as part of the basic principles and values protected by the public policy exception, then the law that is contrary to them should not be applied nor the judgment that

---

[13] Samtleben (2023, p. 62).

[14] Michaels (2024, p. 142).

[15] ibid., p. 144.

[16] See, e.g., ASADIP Principles on Transnational Access to Justice. https://www.asadip.org/v2/wp-content/uploads/2018/08/ASADIP-TRANSJUS-EN-FINAL18.pdf Accessed on 16 June 2024.

violates them be recognized. In Colombia, this is not included in any codified rules, but there is an emergent judicial practice in this direction.[17]

In sum, from a national perspective, private international law is observed within the boundaries of the national state. This does not exclude a kind of internationalization of domestic legal systems when rules of international origin—e.g., human rights—are absorbed at the domestic level and thus put into practice through national mechanisms. This happens in private international law, as well as in other legal fields.

3 Private International Law as International Law

Private international law has not only a national dimension, as described above, but also an international one. Internationality alludes here to the field of *public* international law. In simple terms, this refers to the processes in which states engage in dialogue, negotiate, and potentially legislate on a certain subject. Thus, when one considers that private international law is not only domestically determined but also internationally, then the focus is on the creation and eventual adoption of international treaties concerning issues in this field. Treaties stand out among the different sources of public international law established by Article 38 of the Statute of the International Court of Justice, but the rest of the sources included in this rule—i.e., custom, general principles, judicial decisions, and doctrine[18]—are of course relevant as well. In this vein, it is worth noting that public international law mechanisms also embrace international standards regarding private international law issues emanating from international organizations, being of particular interest to those included in, e.g., principles or model laws or provisions.[19]

---

[17] The Colombian Supreme Court has considered fundamental rights in cases on recognition of foreign judgments in, e.g., Supreme Court of Justice, Civil Chamber, Judgment of July 27, 2011, No. 11001-0203-000-2007-01956-00, and Supreme Court of Justice, Civil Chamber, Judgment of February 24, 2020, No. 11001-02-03-000-2019-02995-00.

[18] Statute of the International Court of Justice, Article 38: "1. The Court, whose function is to decide in accordance with international law such disputes as are submitted to it, shall apply:

(a) international conventions, whether general or particular, establishing rules expressly recognized by the contesting states;
(b) international custom, as evidence of a general practice accepted as law;
(c) the general principles of law recognized by civilized nations;
(d) subject to the provisions of Article 59, judicial decisions, and the teachings of the most highly qualified publicists of the various nations, as subsidiary means for the determination of rules of law. …"

[19] See, for example, the Principles on the choice of law in international commercial contracts of the Hague Conference on Private International Law (2015) or the UNCITRAL Model Laws on subject matters such as electronic commerce (1996), international commercial arbitration (amended in 2006), the use and cross-border recognition of identity management and trust services (2022). The UNIDROIT Model Clauses for the use of the UNIDROIT Principles of international commercial contracts is also an example in this regard.

The reason why private international law is international, in the sense noted above, is linked to the fact that all states share the need to decide how to deal with cases with multijurisdictional elements, which is easily explained by the interconnectedness of today's world. States may be thus interested in finding collective solutions by resorting to any of the mechanisms conceived by the sources of public international law mentioned above. Indeed, states undertake harmonization or unification processes by means of international treaties or instruments of other kinds, which can be very diverse in terms of their binding force. There are, in fact, continued discussions and negotiations that potentially lead to the adoption of such rules in the field of private international law. Colombia has done so, for example, by ratifying or acceding to an array of conventions of the Hague Conference on Private International Law (although it is not a member-state yet), by being a member of the International Institute for the Unification of Private Law (UNIDROIT) and having ratified several of the treaties adopted there or by being eligible for membership in United Nations Commission on International Trade Law (UNCITRAL), and also adopting its normative instruments.[20] It has also become a party of Conventions of the Organization of American States (OAS),[21] to which it is a member, and is subject to rules adopted by the Commission of the Andean Community of Nations, which are directly applicable in its territory.[22]

The above represents only part of what it means for states to make use of the mechanisms of public international law in the areas of conflict of laws and international procedural law. Certainly, states can adopt such rules as their own and absorb

[20] See, for example, the following Conventions of the Hague Conference of Private International Law to which Colombia is a party: Convention abolishing the requirement of legalization of foreign public documents, of 1961 (Approving Law No. 455 of 1998); Convention on the service abroad of judicial and extrajudicial documents in civil or commercial matters, of 1965 (Approving Law No. 1073 of 2006); Convention on the taking of evidence abroad in civil or commercial matters, of 1970 (Approving Law No. 1282 of 2009); Convention on the civil aspects of the international abduction of minors, of 1980 (Approving Law No. 173 of 1994); Convention on the taking of evidence abroad in civil or commercial matters, 1970 (Approving Act No. 1282 of 2009); Convention on the civil aspects of international child abduction, 1980 (Approving Act No. 173 of 1994); and Convention on the protection of children and cooperation in respect of intercountry adoption, 1993 (Approving Act No. 265 of 1996).

Other contributions to this book will describe the instruments adopted in each of the organizations of which Colombia is a member.

[21] See Inter-American Conventions on general rules of private international law, 1979 (Approving Act No. 21 of 1981); extraterritorial effectiveness of foreign judgments and arbitral awards, 1979 (Approving Act No. 16 of 1981); letters rogatory, 1975 (Approving Act No. 27 of 1988); evidence and information on foreign law, 1979 (Approving Act No. 49 of 1982); taking of evidence abroad, 1975 (Approving Act No. 31 of 1987); enforcement of interim measures, 1979 (Approving Act 42 of 1986); international commercial arbitration, 1975 (Approving Act No. 44 of 1986); conflicts of laws concerning the adoption of minors, 1984 (Approving Act No. 47 of 1987); maintenance obligations of 1989 (Approving Act No. 449 of 1998); international traffic of minors of 1994 (Approving Act No. 470 of 1998); and international return of minors of 1989 (Approving Act No. 880 of 2004).

[22] See, e.g., Decision No. 398 of the Commission of the Andean Community on international passenger transportation by road (January 27, 1997).

them into their domestic legal systems. In doing the latter, they may even be obliged to consider international treaties as binding within their respective systems with a higher status than national laws enacted by their legislative organs. This happens in the field of private international law in Article 2 of the Inter-American Convention on General Rules of Private International Law, which has been ratified by Colombia,[23] and states as follows:

> Choice of the applicable rule of law governing facts connected with foreign law shall be subject to the provisions of this Convention and other bilateral or multilateral conventions that have been signed or may be signed in the future by the States Parties.
>
> In the absence of an international rule, the States Parties shall apply the conflict rules of their domestic law.

However, the picture is not entirely complete if we limit ourselves to considering that states are just formally bound by such public international law instruments. Accepting and applying international mechanisms involves the interpretation of the rules they contain. A step in this direction occurs in Colombia when the Constitutional Court evaluates international treaties[24] in the process of their adoption and their final ratification by the executive.

The application by national courts of international standards that are not included in treaties is also part of this process. Various forms of application of the UNIDROIT Principles of International Commercial Contracts[25] have been identified: as an applicable law, as *lex mercatoria*, as a legislative and contractual model, and as a tool for interpretation and completion of national and international rules.[26] Among these various forms, the last two have been clearly accepted in the Colombian legal system.[27] The judicial practice based on the UNIDROIT Principles that has taken place in Colombia is an example in this regard.

In a critical vein, as an object of public international law, private international law would be reached by the complexities pointed out by some academics, e.g., the Third World approaches to international law (TWAIL), which see the discipline considering "actors and communities within the Third World other than states, the traditional unit of analysis".[28]

Now, in practice, also from an international perspective, it can be briefly said that private international law continues to be considered basically through a state-centered prism. International legal instruments on matters that fall within the scope of private international law are created directly by states, by subjects that emerge from states, e.g., international organizations, or by subjects that are recognized by

[23] Approving Act No. 21 of 1981.

[24] See, e.g., Judgment No. C-125/11 of the Constitutional Court of Colombia, regarding the 1995 UNIDROIT Convention on Stolen or Illegally Exported Cultural Objects.

[25] The UNIDROIT Principles of International Commercial Contracts and accompanying documents are available at https://www.unidroit.org/instruments/commercial-contracts/

[26] Oviedo Albán (2012, pp. 12–54).

[27] Supreme Court of Justice, Civil Chamber, Judgment of February 21, 2012, No. 11001-3103-040-2006-00537-01; Oviedo Albán (2012, p. 7).

[28] Angie (2023, p. 89).

them, e.g., chambers of commerce, different kinds of associations, arbitrators, or even the parties to a specific private agreement.

4 Private International Law in Global Perspective

In addition to the national and international dimensions, private international law has a global dimension as well. Global law can be understood in a wide variety of forms. Its manifestations are to be found in "regulations and agreements emerging within international organizations, international non-binding declarations, memoranda of understanding, general comments, guidelines, public and private codes of conduct, transnational company agreements, standards, terms of service, rankings, and reports".[29] As can be observed, rules of private international law may exist in any of these manifestations of global law. Global manifestations of private international law may actually interact with national or international sources,[30] such as the various instruments generated in international organizations, for instance, the UNIDROIT, or those arising from direct bilateral or multilateral interaction or negotiation between states.

Thus, whether expressed in rules that establish the applicable law, in rules on international jurisdiction or the recognition of foreign judgments, or even in substantive or direct rules—i.e., those that directly resolve the factual circumstances to which they refer[31]—private international law may be part of the global law.

Private international law is also considered to be part of the transnational law if one considers, for example, Jessup's classical definition of transnational law, according to which translational law includes "all law which regulates actions or events that transcend national frontiers. Both public and private international law are included, as are other rules which do not wholly fit into such standard categories".[32]

Furthermore, the global conception of law goes beyond a transborder idea of law, and even beyond the fact that it can be produced by a diversity of processes and subjects. What is decisive is that global law seeks to address problems that exist in various spheres on a global scale, independently of any pre-established legal–political divisions, and that concern humanity as a whole.

Addressing the above entails numerous complexities. However, what will be briefly discussed in this section is the consideration of private international law from a global perspective.[33] Viewing private international law from a global perspective

[29] See Golia (2024, p. 300).

[30] ibid.

[31] Goldschmidt (1990, pp. 7–8).

[32] Jessup (1956, p. 2).

[33] This idea is also used, though in a different sense, to refer to a way of situating "national legal histories". See Duve (2020 pp. 88).

does not mean failing to see it in its national or international (or even global) dimensions. In the way it is understood here, considering the global perspective does not mean overlooking the fact that in order to resolve cases with foreign elements, the applicable law may be any legal system created by states. Rather, it implies seeing the legal systems created by states "as one of the various legal formations"[34] that coexist in circumstances that interconnect the world or, as Raz puts it, make the world "smaller".[35]

This points to the consideration of the existence of a plurality of normative systems on a global scale. In other words, this leads to the idea of global legal pluralism, which poses a "descriptive and normative framework for understanding a world of overlapping jurisdictional assertions, both state and nonstate."[36] Global legal pluralism approaches have received increasing attention in recent years.[37] In this context, it has been suggested that, among all the techniques that have been proposed to resolve conflicts arising from this plurality of normative systems, the methodological approach offered by private international law would be the most appropriate.[38] This is due, it is argued, to the fact that, by allowing the application of foreign law, private international law has an attitude toward such normative plurality that is "not merely one of restraint but one of embrace".[39] Allowing the application of foreign law would represent a method that "operationalizes the entanglement and continues it through the institutions of one law applying the rules of another law".[40] This attitude of *embracing* is compatible with the idea of private international law as a law of tolerance which, based on its recognition of the extraterritoriality of foreign law, has been sustained by Werner Goldschmidt.[41]

Understanding private international law in such a way implies going beyond seeing it as part of global law or transnational law, in the sense noted above. Viewing private international law from such a global perspective means that—rather than being one more normative order among a diversity of normative orders, or a part or fragment within a broader normative order—it is a field that offers a receptive and tolerant analytical and methodological approach to the resolution to conflicts between the various normative orders existing at the global level.

A (re)configuration of private international law through a global prism allows this field to transcend the epistemological limits to which we may be confronted if we limit ourselves to the use of the idea of the nation-state. Looking at private international law from a global perspective involves reinforcing its *basic* nature and its

34 Raz (2017, p. 136).

35 Raz (2017, p. 151).

36 Berman (2020, p. 4).

37 See, e.g., Berman (2020).

38 Michaels (2019, p. 636).

39 ibid., p. 637.

40 ibid., p. 637.

41 Goldschmidt (1990, p. XXI).

cross-cutting implications: it implies taking into account the different thematic, conceptual, and technical complexities with which private international law deals.

This poses important challenges in the Colombian context. The reason for this is that the state-centered paradigm still prevails in the country through the prevalence of the doctrine of territorial private international law. It may be observed that non-state-centric approaches to commercial law, e.g., resorting to the (new) *lex mercatoria*, are certainly, increasingly recognized through the consideration of international standards such as the UNIDROIT Principles of International Commercial Contracts mentioned above. However, placing private international law in a global perspective goes far beyond that, since it reveals the great potential of this field to address pressing global challenges in diverse spheres.

When private international law is viewed from this perspective, the relevant role it can play in terms of, for instance, interculturality can be better appreciated. Interculturality appeals here to "a relational conception of the discipline devoted to converting its technical indifference into a technical (pluralist) commitment to normative societal changes".[42] The relevance of private international law in terms of interculturality may be understood, as Verónica Ruiz Abou-Nigm does, referring to the "potential that its methodologies and techniques have in contributing to the necessary accommodation of different legal cultures, and therefore for the difficult task of bridging, *inter alia*, traditions; parties' and states' interests; capitalist pressures and social and ethnographic cultural differences".[43] Of course, some sort of intercultural feature may be identified also within the field itself, since it can be said, as Eugenio Hernández-Bretón's rightly argues, that *mestizaje* characterizes Latin American private international law.[44]

An example of how methodologies and techniques of private international law can adopt an intercultural approach can be found in the rule on the international restitution of Indigenous cultural property which is contained in Article 68 of the Draft General Act on Private International Law for Colombia prepared by the *Instituto Antioqueño de Derecho Internacional Privado* (IADIP).[45] The content of such a rule is dealt with in another chapter of this volume.[46]

Such potential of private international law also reflects on the role, "still relatively new and not yet fully appreciated",[47] that it can play on different challenges related to sustainable development.[48] The United Nations 2030 Agenda for Sustainable Development indeed targets such challenges, e.g., inequality, extreme poverty, or the need for orderly, safe, regular, and responsible migration. These are

---

[42] Michaels and Ruiz Abou-Nigm (2023, p. 16).

[43] Ruiz Abou-Nigm (2019, p. 362).

[44] See Hernández-Bretón (2007).

[45] See Ochoa Jiménez (2019, 2024), Michaels and Ruiz Abou-Nigm (2023, p. 17).

[46] More about this in Chap. "Property Rights in Colombian Private International Law" of this volume.

[47] Tramhel (2024, p. 113).

[48] Michaels and Ruiz Abou-Nigm (2023), Tramhel (2024).

embedded in the four broad dimensions of sustainable development that have been recognized: economy, environment, social sustainability, and culture.[49] The appropriateness of mechanisms in the field of human rights law is widely accepted to address current global challenges of this nature. However, the realization of human rights across the borders of states requires the assistance of private international law to protect their "private side", as Ralf Michaels sustains.[50]

Some movements in this direction can be identified in certain decisions of the Colombian Supreme Court of Justice. As fundamental rights and their underlying principle of human dignity are part of the public policy clause, several decisions by the Supreme Court that dealt with the recognition of foreign judgments have shown how useful private international law can be in ensuring the protection of the dignity of traditionally excluded groups, i.e., persons with disabilities.[51] Thus, by preventing the recognition of judgments that threaten fundamental rights through recourse to the public policy clause, private international law proves to be equipped to protect the rights of disadvantaged peoples. In such a context, the exceptionality of the public policy clause actually reinforces that the above-mentioned receptivity and tolerance toward foreign law and foreign judgments are the general rule.

5 Final Remarks: Three Dimensions, One Perspective

Private international law has national, international, and global dimensions. The different normative sources that are part of Colombian private international law confirm this. Recognizing the threefold dimension of this legal field is important to fully understand its conceptual scope. However, each of these dimensions implies not only considering its various normative sources, which may originate from state and non-state actors. In addition, from each of these dimensions, it is possible to access different methodological and theoretical tools, as well as a vast repertoire of techniques for the processes of legal practice and decision-making.

In turn, the observation of private international law from a global perspective leads us to see that the conflict methodology developed for centuries by private international law can facilitate the harmonious coexistence on a global scale of the plurality of normative orders, which occurs mainly by allowing the cross-border application of foreign law. Thus, private international law is also equipped to deal with the protection of human rights beyond national borders.

---

[49] Tramhel (2024, p. 109).

[50] Michaels (2024, p. 131).

[51] Supreme Court of Justice, Civil Chamber, Judgment of February 24, 2020, No. 11001-02-03-000-2019-02995-00; Supreme Court of Justice, Civil Chamber, Judgment of October 10, 2022, No. 11001-02-03-000-2022-03107-00; Supreme Court of Justice, Civil Chamber, Judgment of October 1, 2021, No. 11001-02-03-000-2020-03024-00. See Ochoa Jiménez and Dávila (2024).

The above task, which implies a great commitment of the field, seems to have been assumed, at least partly, by the Colombian Supreme Court of Justice, as reflected in some of its decisions. However, this is still not sufficient. It is necessary to go deeper into what can be done to implement in the country the theoretical and technical potential of private international law. This should be understood as one of the main aims of the IADIP's proposal, to which the different chapters of this book refer.

References

Angie A (2023) Rethinking international law: a TWAIL retrospective. EJIL 34(1):7–122
Berman PS (2020) Understanding legal pluralism: from local to global, from descriptive to normative. In: Berman PS (ed) Oxford handbook on legal pluralism. Oxford University Press, Oxford, pp 1–36
Delic A (2017) The birth of modern private international law: the Montevideo Treaties (1889, amended 1940). http://opil.ouplaw.com/page/Treaties-Montevideo. Accessed 20 July 2024
Delic A (2019) The role of comparative law in the development of modern private international law (1750–1914). In: Van Hule I, Lesaffer R (eds) International law in the long nineteenth century (1776–1914). Brill Nijhoff, Leiden, pp 186–213
Duve T (2020) What is global legal history? Comp Leg Hist 8(2):73–115
Goldschmidt W (1990) Derecho internacional privado. Derecho de la tolerancia. Basado en la teoría trialista del mundo jurídico, 7th edn. Depalma, Buenos Aires
Golia A (2024) Global law and the individual. In: Sparks T, Peters A (eds) The individual in international law. Oxford University Press, Oxford, pp 295–319
Hernández-Bretón E (2007) Mestizaje cultural en el derecho internacional privado de los países de la América Latina. Academia de Ciencias Políticas y Sociales, Caracas
Jansen N, Michaels R (eds) (2008) Law beyond the state. Rethinking private law. Mohr Siebeck, Tubingen
Jessup P (1956) Transnationla law. Yale University Press, New Haven
Michaels R (2019) Global legal pluralism and private international law. In: Berman PS (ed) Oxford handbook on legal pluralism. Oxford University Press, Oxford, pp 629–648
Michaels R (2024) The right to have private rights. UTLJ 74(1):131–150
Michaels R, Ruiz Abou-Nigm V (2023) Towards private international law for everyone. Max Planck Institute for Comparative and International Private Law Research Paper Series No. 23/14
Ochoa Jiménez MJ (2019) Conflict of laws and the return of indigenous peoples' cultural property: a Latin American perspective. Int J Cult Prop 26(4):437–456. https://doi.org/10.1017/S0940739119000341
Ochoa Jiménez MJ (2024) Rights of Indigenous peoples and communities. In: Salvadori M, Boutin Icaza G (eds) Colombian draft project on private international law. Quaderni Del Dipartimento Di Giurisprudenza Dell'Università Di Torino 34/2024
Ochoa Jiménez MJ, Dávila JA (2024) Private international law and human dignity in Colombia (forthcoming)
Oviedo Albán J (2012) Los Principios UNIDROIT sobre los Contratos Comerciales Internacionales 2010. In: Oviedo Albán J (ed) Principios UNIDROIT sobre los Contratos Comerciales Internacionales 2010 "Black Letter Rules". Ibañez, Bogota, pp 12–54
Raz J (2017) Why the state? In: Roughan N, Halpin A (eds) In pursuit of pluralist jurisprudence. University Press, Cambridge, pp 136–162

Ruiz Abou-Nigm V (2019) Bridging and balancing: diversity and integration in private international law. In: Ruiz Abou-Nigm V, Noodt Taquela MB (eds) Diversity and integration in private international law. Edinburgh University Press, Edinburgh, pp 362–388
Samtleben J (1983) Derecho internacional privado en América Latina. Teoría y práctica del Código Bustamante. Depalma, Buenos Aires
Samtleben J (2023) Internationales Privat- und Prozessrecht in Lateinamerika. Tradition und reform. Shaker Verlag, Duren
Tramhel J (2024) Contribution of UNIDROIT to sustainable development. In: Köhler B, Gulati R, John T (eds) The Elgar companion to UNIDROIT. Edward Elgar, Cheltenham, pp 96–113

María Julia Ochoa Jiménez . Dr. iur. and LLM from the University of Göttingen; lawyer and specialist in Intellectual Property from the Universidad de Los Andes; LLM, Universidad de Navarra; research fellow, University of Bonn, Alexander von Humboldt Foundation; visiting researcher, Max Planck Institute for Comparative and International Private Law; professor, Universidad de Antioquia (2016–2022); professor of Private International Law, Universidad Loyola.

Private International Law and Comparative Law: A Colombian Approach

María Julia Ochoa Jiménez

Abstract This chapter, and the previous one, address, in an introductory manner and from the Colombian perspective, two fundamental questions that lie at the root of private international law and serve to understand its broad conceptual scope. The first question, which is dealt with in the previous chapter, refers to the national, international, and global dimensions of private international law, and the relevance it has when it is particularly considered in the latter perspective. Here, the focus is on the second question, which is not less vast and concerns the interactions between comparative law and private international law. In this regard, this chapter explores how some forms that the former adopts can be identified in the different ways in which the latter is practiced in Colombia.

1 Introduction

It has been stated that there is an intimate relationship between private international law and comparative law.[1] This relationship has attracted the attention of many authors and has given rise to an abundance of literature.[2] It has been even suggested that private international law itself must be understood in disciplinary terms as a comparative law, and based on such an assertion, it has been even proposed a new comparative method, i.e., "the conflict-of-law-comparative method".[3]

[1] Reimann (2019, p. 1340).

[2] See, e.g., Rabel (1945), Martinek (1994), Reimann (2019), Graziadei (2003), Michaels (2017, 2022), Delic (2019).

[3] Michaels (2022, pp. 175).

M. J. Ochoa Jiménez (✉)
Loyola University, Sevilla, Andalucía, Spain
e-mail: mjochoa@uloyola.es

M. J. Ochoa Jiménez, C. Madrid Martínez (eds.), *A Private International Law for Colombia*, Springer Textbooks in Law,
https://doi.org/10.1007/978-3-032-04106-7_3

The interconnection between private international law and comparative law is linked, in general terms, to the fact that both deal with the "diversity and plurality of legal systems".[4] They thus analyze *the other* or *the different*.[5] This more specifically points to *foreign* legal systems. Considering that private international law can be defined as "the body of law that determines what law should regulate a dispute that has multi-jurisdictional elements",[6] one may easily state that, starting with issues of characterization,[7] carrying out a legal comparison process is needed in order to make such a determination. At first glance, this seems not only self-evident but sufficient to explain why and how private international law and comparative law are interconnected. This way of looking at the relationship between private international law and comparative law may actually lead us to think that a legal comparison will always and necessarily be made in private international law. However, things are quite more complex.

Complexities are in part related to the fact that the concept of comparative law is not undisputed.[8] It is stated that it is at least threefold, as it embraces the comparison of legal rules and institutions of different legal systems, the analysis of mutual interactions and influences between legal orders (including the so-called legal transplants), and the development of a general understanding of law and legal theory on the basis of individual legal phenomena.[9]

In spite of such conceptual broadness, comparative law actually takes place in practice. In Latin America, this is made on a constant basis by scholars and legislators, as well as practitioners and judges.[10] In these different spheres, comparative law has interacted with private international law, as it was already identified at the first comparative law conference at the beginning of the twentieth century:

> Firstly, comparative private international law was a scholarly endeavor and, secondly, this scholarship was an important source for the drafting of legislation. Thirdly, comparative private law was used by lawyers in defending clients and judges when interpreting, applying, and enforcing foreign law.[11]

Now, legal systems emerged on the national or international level—and also in a pluralistic global perspective that transcends the state[12]—can be both the outcome (by means of a variety of interactions with other legal systems, e.g., mixing, hybridization) as well as the object of legal comparison. In the first sense, it is said that

---

[4] Michaels (2017, p. 417).

[5] Grosswald Curran (1998, p. 657).

[6] Riles (2005, p. 976).

[7] Graziadei (2003, p. 104).

[8] Michaels (2023, p. 13).

[9] Michaels (2017, p. 417).

[10] Bonilla Maldonado (2023, p. 11). On how comparative law is conducted by tribunals around the world, see, e.g., Andenas and Fairgrieve (2015).

[11] Delic (2019, pp. 186–187).

[12] Muir Watt (2019, p. 9) talks about "Contemporary contextualist approaches to comparison [that] tend to reject both the assimilation between law and rules, and law and state."

comparative legal methods were applied for example during the drafting of the 1888–1889 Montevideo treaties: "discussions were punctuated with references to the rich heritage of the continental European and common law traditions of conflict of laws and the growing array of positive law dealing with private international law in continental Europe and Latin America".[13]

In the second sense, legal systems are compared and, thus, the process of comparing is stressed. It is in this latter sense that it has been argued that the traditional forms of interaction between private international law and comparative law are transformed by the existence of supranational or overlapping legal regimes at multiple levels,[14] on the production of which awareness was heightened after the First World War, a time "saturated with the idea that international exchange does not allow the isolation of national legislations"[15] and began to consolidate after the end of the Second World War. In the twentieth century, the unification or harmonization of law was actually considered a primary objective of comparative legal studies.[16]

Certainly, the efforts toward the unification or harmonization of private law on the multilateral—e.g., at The Hague Conference, UNIDROIT, and UNCITRAL—or regional—e.g., at the OAS—levels blur the lines between national legal systems. And the results of such efforts have reached in different degrees the Colombian legal system, as may be seen throughout this volume.

Yet, the existence of international instruments and supra-national legal regimes has not displaced—and probably will not do so for a long time—the abovementioned traditional forms of interaction between private international law and comparative law. This is particularly true in countries such as Colombia, that are not part of, let us say, "strong" integration processes.[17]

In order to observe how interactions between private international law and comparative law occur, consideration can be paid to three traditional approaches to comparative law that have been identified in the specialized literature, i.e., culturalism, formalism, and functionalism.[18] These approaches emerge and adopt different characteristics at different historical moments; they can be understood as paradigms that do not disappear but may change over time. In this way, they tend to coexist or even amalgamate.[19]

This section aims to explore the question of whether it is possible to identify in Colombian private international law the presence of (some) features of the

[13] Delic (2019, pp. 188, 207).

[14] Reimann (2019, p. 1340); see also Muir Watt (2019, pp. 622).

[15] Rabel (1931).

[16] Cotterell (2019, p. 730).

[17] Colombia is a member of the Andean Community (CAN) and an associated member of MERCOSUR. Even when some unified private international law rules have been created in the CAN (e.g., on transportation) and some degree of legal unification exists in MERCOSUR with regard to free trade, such integration processes are far from having a comprehensive supra-national legal system regarding private international law.

[18] See Bonilla Maldonado and Michaels (2023, pp. 11–26).

[19] Michaels (2023, p. 14).

aforementioned comparative law approaches, i.e., culturalism, formalism, and functionalism, in each of the aforementioned spaces in which private international law and comparative law interact, i.e., the academic, legislative, and judicial spheres. The focus is not on the results of the comparison (concepts, doctrines, statutes, rules, decisions) but on the comparison itself and on the way in which this is made by academics, judges, or law drafters. This may represent an attempt to see how this comparison is made on the basis of "implicit knowledge which, precisely because it is not expressed, is as significant as it is difficult to discover".[20]

2 Comparative Law Approaches

2.1 Culturalism

In comparative law, culturalism implies the understanding that the law of a specific society is the result of that society's culture: legal institutions are products and expressions of local cultures and values.[21] Having emerged and consolidated throughout the ninetieth century, this approach does not focus on codified law, which began to proliferate from the middle of that century, but on "culture and identity",[22] i.e., on a kind of "cultural essence" that can easily be influenced by stereotypes.[23] By emphasizing the idea that different cultures are *essentially* different, culturalist comparative law is said to contain certain racist features, and because there is a tendency to consider culture as something static, that is, averse to radical change, this approach is said to have a conservative character as well. Moreover, a stratified and evolutionary character is attached to this approach because underlying it is the idea of modernizing the laws which, compared to European law (especially *common law* in contrast to those of the still existing British colonies), appear inferior and less developed. In the twentieth century, the culturalist comparative law approach transformed, so that the essentialist consideration of diversity becomes less determinant, while legal cultures are recognized to have a dynamic nature. Furthermore, a participatory dimension is added, and the comparatist is now involved in the process of comparison, in which it becomes central to understanding law, i.e., to give it meaning.[24] As Roger Cotterell states, culture "appears fundamental—a kind of lens through which all aspects of law must be perceived, or a gateway of understanding through which every comparatist must pass so as to have any genuine access to the meaning of foreign law".[25]

[20] Duve (2022, p. 26).

[21] Michaels (2022, p. 168).

[22] ibid.

[23] ibid.

[24] Michaels (2023, p. 18).

[25] Cotterell (2019, p. 711).

2.2 *Formalism*

The formalist approach to comparative law is influenced by the sociological positivism of the nineteenth century, and it is thus mainly based on observation. The comparatist no longer has legal cultures but specific rules and institutions as the object of such observation. Law being understood as rules and institutions, the comparison of legal rules (micro-comparison) becomes more relevant. The comparison of specific legal rules makes it easier to see the differences that exist between the laws being compared. This is the reason why this method of legal comparison is the most widespread in academia, even though it would have a more limited use in law-making processes aimed at normative unification. A hierarchical character is linked here to the superiority assigned to written European law, in the *civil law* tradition, which can be compared basically with laws that preserve this tradition. Thus, for example, unwritten laws applied in the colonies are set aside. Although belonging to the European tradition, or perhaps because of it, what has happened with respect to Latin American law is that it has been largely neglected by traditional comparative law and has been "put in the box of 'French' or 'Romanistic' legal family … as lacking sufficient originality".[26] Another characteristic attributed to formalist comparative law is that "much of comparative legal theory has referred to private law"[27] and that a kind of autonomy is assigned to private law rules with respect to society. In general, from a formalist perspective, it is considered that looking at the emphasis on rules and doctrines as part of the practice of law is important because it allows comparing that practice (which implies a way of understanding law) with other traditions that may understand it differently.[28]

2.3 *Functionalism*

Functionalism entered comparative law in the second half of the twentieth century. From this comparative law approach, legal rules are the responses of society to specific problems. It is considered that "the legal system of every society faces essentially the same problems".[29] In functionalist terms,

---

[26] Kleinheisterkamp (2019, pp. 253–254). This has been a tendency amid European (René David) or American (John Henry Merryman) scholars. This approach also underlies comparative work by Latin American scholars themselves, whose attempts at comparative law have sometimes resulted in works in which the author's own jurisdiction may receive little attention, as noted by Kleinheisterkamp (2019, p. 283).

[27] Muir Watt (2019, p. 609).

[28] See Michaels (2023, pp. 18–21).

[29] Zweiger and Kötz cited by Graziadei (2003, p. 102).

> comparative law must address the concrete problem [so that] the question to which any comparative study is devoted must be put in purely functional terms and that the problem must be stated without any reference to the concepts of one's legal system.[30]

This methodological approach considers that the best way to observe law is through judicial decisions since the responses that societies give to similar situations through such decisions will be diverse though often with similar results. This implies that "the only things which are comparable are those fulfilling the same function".[31] The functionalist comparatist understands that the result of the comparison should be aimed at finding "the best law",[32] that is, the one that best fulfills its function of addressing specific social problems. In the instrumentalist strand of functionalism, comparing implies evaluating in order to reform (in other words, "social engineering"[33]). In its sociological strand, functionalist comparative law sees law as a subsystem within the broader social system. Law responds to social needs in an adaptative way, understanding that it is possible to solve the same problem through solutions that may be different but equivalent (functional equivalence).[34]

3 Interactions Between Private International Law and Comparative Law in Colombia

As noted above, it has traditionally been recognized that private international law and comparative law interact in three areas. First, in the academic field, where comparative law may primarily act as a method to study private international law. Second, in law-making processes, in which legislative practices that deal with cross-border situations or disputes with multijurisdictional elements may be assisted by comparative law. Third, in the judicial sphere, where comparative law may be used as an operative tool to resolve specific cases.[35]

It has been pointed out that the comparison of specific private international rules (special part) is distinguished from that of general rules and techniques (general part).[36] Rules that fall in the first group are "rules like many others and can be compared just like those of contract, tort, or family law".[37] While comparing them, the

[30] ibid.

[31] ibid.

[32] See Michaels (2023, pp. 21–26).

[33] ibid.

[34] ibid.

[35] See Reimann (2019, p. 1356).

[36] In this book, the "general part" of private international law is referred to as "general theory" (see Chap. "General Institutions in Colombian Private International Law"). It is worth noting that both terms are often used in a non-accurate way as interchangeable by Latin American private international law doctrine so that the latter term is used to designate the general rules and techniques of private international law.

[37] Reimann (2019, p. 1356).

comparatist applies “the usual techniques (identifying similarities and differences, and so on) and pursues [and has] essentially the usual goals (recognition of alternative solutions, better understanding of one’s own system, inspiration for law reform, and so on)”.[38] In contrast, it is said that there cannot be a comparison as such regarding general concepts, which result from the existence of an “international legal community”.[39] However, in any legal regime also general concepts may be contained in rules “like many others” and can so be compared.

3.1 Academia

As is generally the case, the Colombian academia of private international law tends to consider legal doctrine as the only possible legal science and, consequently, relegates history, sociology, or anthropology to the margins of the science of private international law.[40] Thus, inside the framework of legal doctrine, comparative law has been used in the Colombian academia to study private international law at least in relation to the definition of private international law and the law of international contracts. With regard to the first area, it is important to emphasize the need for academic approaches to defining private international law to meet two main requirements: clarity and usefulness. Because of its cross-cutting nature, private international law must be accessible to specialists and non-specialists alike. That the discipline is clearly explained supports its implementation, in and out of courtrooms. However, the definition of the discipline seems to have been a rather difficult undertaking and such requirement have not always been met. It is not uncommon that, when it comes to explaining a legal concept, the authors seem to be faced with the choice of either relying on their own ideas or resorting to authoritative voices on the subject. The latter entails the risk of limiting themselves to stringing together unconnected ideas. When dealing with this, usually some kind of legal comparison is tried to be made.

Thus, for instance, when conceptualizing private international law in his book *Tratado de Derecho Internacional Privado*, Marco Gerardo Monroy Cabra, who has perhaps been the most influential private international law scholar in Colombia for a long time, resorts to several authors.[41] It seems interesting not only looking at the origin of the authors that he mentions there (who originate from Europe and Latin America) but also at the way of understanding private international law he brings. In this regard, he resorts to Spanish author José Ramón Orúe y Arregui, for example, to state that “the diversity [of private law systems] is an unequivocal

[38] See Reimann (2019, p. 1356).

[39] ibid.

[40] The comments that Correas (1995, p. 216) has made about legal theory in general embrace private international law.

[41] Reference is made to Monroy Cabra (1983); this volume has been followed by several editions and reprints until today.

symptom of progress, which favors the nations' desire for legal perfection and the development of their particularities".[42] Further on, however, he states that "if there is neither equal legal awareness nor equal state of civilization among peoples, it is logical that conflicts arise between individuals of different countries, which must be solved; and this is the reason or determining cause of private international law".[43] The author is certainly not making a comparison of the ways private international law is understood in Colombia and in other countries. However, behind the above quotations lies a culturalist approach to the way of comparing legal systems, which underlies the general notion of private international law, while clearly reproducing an essentialist, stratified, and evolutionary conception of law.

Let us take another example regarding a specific subject such as international contracts. In this regard, Colombian academia seems to be more interested in particular issues and in carrying out micro-comparison,[44] which implies a precise analysis based on the detailed observation of certain legal provisions. This is made, for example, by Jorge Oviedo Albán in his journal article *La Ley Aplicable a los Contratos Internacionales*.[45] There, he compares the rules containing conflictual and material solutions in the Inter-American Convention on the Law Applicable to International Contracts (1994 Mexico Convention), the Regulation (EC) 593/2008 of the European Parliament and of the Council of June 17, 2008 on the law applicable to contractual obligations (Rome I), and uniform commercial law instruments, in particular, the United Nations Convention on Contracts for the International Sale of Goods. The formalist approach is used by the author to compare these legal regimes with the Colombian rules on the subject (in particular, Articles 869 and 1328 of the Commercial Code), which are considered obsolete since they do not facilitate the resolution of cases involving cross-border business.[46] As is usual in functional comparison, the aim of the comparison he is making is to find the *best law* to propose a practical solution not based on legal reforms. He ends up stating that the *best law* is in the 1994 Mexico Convention, which was not ratified by Colombia. Therefore, he recommends applying the rules of this Convention by means of the Colombian Commercial Code (Article 7), which allows the subsidiary application of international commercial treaties not ratified by Colombia. Thus, formalism and functionalism overlap in such a comparative study.

---

[42] Monroy Cabra (1983, p. 3).

[43] ibid., p. 4.

[44] Samuel (2014).

[45] Oviedo Albán (2012).

[46] Ochoa Jiménez et al. (2019, p. 109).

3.2 Decision-Making

In Colombia, most judicial decisions of disputes with multijurisdictional elements concern the recognition and enforcement of foreign judgments. As regulated in the General Code of Procedure Law of 2012 (CGP), one of the main formal requirements to be met by requests for recognition of a foreign judgment is that "it is not contrary to Colombian laws or provisions of public order, with the exception of procedural rules" (Article 606 No. 2 CGP). Regarding this provision, the Supreme Court of Justice, which is the only court with jurisdiction on this matter (Article 605 CGP), has extensively interpreted the notion of public policy. To that end, it has made comparative law. Let us take a 2011 decision as an example,[47] which over time has become a reference for subsequent decisions on this subject matter. In this decision, the Colombian Supreme Court first takes a definition of public policy from a 1966 ruling of the Supreme Court of Spain that is cited in the Colombian literature,[48] which defines it as a set of legal, public and private, political, economic, moral, and even religious principles. To better support these ideas, in addition cites two Argentinian authors, Werner Goldschmidt and Osvaldo Marzorati, being the latter cited to make a reference to a decision by the Supreme Court of Switzerland on the distinction between mandatory provisions and public policy. Later on, the Colombian Supreme Court refers to common law countries and notes that they "follow the guidance from the United States of America" regarding the division of public policy into "domestic and international".[49] Based on a Spanish author, cited as Gonzalo Quiroga,[50] the Court states that such a doctrine is also followed in Spain, which has "a legal tradition that is similar to that of Colombia". Thus, it justifies the adoption of such ideas in Colombian law tracing a link to the United States of America through Spanish laws. It also seems to resort to the law of the United States of America because it recognizes some "authoritative" character in it. By emphasizing the similarities that Colombian law has with Spanish law (and not with the law of the United States of America), a comparison of law cultures is being made which is based on an essentialist conception of law, that is, such similarities are taken for granted, and there is no deeper consideration on the reasons behind such an assumption. There is also a certain stratified and evolutionary approach when such a comparison is made.

However, this has not impeded in the Colombian Supreme Court from being quite successful in giving concrete expression to the notion of public policy and thus

---

[47] Supreme Court of Justice, Civil Chamber, Judgment of July 27, 2011, file No. 11001-0203-000-2007-01956-00.

[48] See Álvarez Londoño and Galán Barrera (2001).

[49] It illustrates this with the case cited as Parsons & Whiltemore Overseas Co. Inc. v. Societe Generale de L'Industrie du Papier (RAKTA) 508 F2 d 696 (1974).

[50] The cited text corresponds to a doctoral thesis presented in 2004 at the Universidad Complutense in Madrid by Marta Gonzalo Quiroga, which is cited in the 2011 decision by the Colombian Court of Justice as Gonzalo Quiroga (2005).

developing its own theoretical and dogmatic approach to it. The above decision actually served to that end by recalling one of the Court's decisions from 1996,[51] according to which such notion should be limited to its fair proportions, so as not to banish, with generalizing and absolute criteria, the application of foreign judgments in the national territory. In that vein, the Supreme Court has included in a sort of catalog the principles that public policy usually involves, e.g., the prohibition of abusive exercise of rights, good faith, and due process. The kind of interaction it has had with the decisions of the Colombian Constitutional Court has helped in such a process.[52]

3.3 *Law-Making*

Colombian national legislation in the field of private international law is not comprehensive, even though several international treaties have been ratified and special national laws have been adopted in part following law models developed at the international level.[53] However, the main domestic legal instrument that contains conflict provisions is still the Civil Code of 1887.[54] This code entails the same provisions of the Civil Code of the *Estado Soberano de Santander* from 1858, which is said to be a copy of the Chilean Civil Code drafted by Andrés Bello.[55] The Santander Civil Code was adopted as the Civil Code of the United States of Colombia in 1873 and as the Civil Code of the Republic of Colombia in 1887.[56]

On April 20, 1980, the Colombian President created a Review Commission of the Colombian Civil Code.[57] The review had to be conducted within one year,[58] but this deadline was extended twice.[59] Finally, the Review Commission submitted a Draft to the Minister of Justice in 1984. The Statement of Reasons described the provisions that were then—and are still today—in force as follows:

> … as a whole, they represent an unintelligible and "monstrous" system … they are far from organizing a complete system of Colombia's private law relations with the rest of the states; they do not even indicate a general orientation.[60]

---

[51] Supreme Court of Justice, Judgment of November 5, 1996, No. 6130.

[52] This is suggested by Madrid Martínez (2021).

[53] For example, in 1999 Colombia adopted the UNCITRAL Model Law on electronic commerce of 1996 (Act No. 527 of 1999).

[54] Monroy Cabra (1983, p. 27).

[55] Mantilla Rey (1982, p. 26).

[56] ibid., p. 27.

[57] The members of this commission were prominent Colombian jurists: Arturo Valencia Zea, José Gabino Pinzón Martínez, José Alejandro Bonivento Fernández, Luis Manrique Naranjo, Pedro Lafont Pianetta, and Gilberto Peña Castrillón.

[58] Decree No. 959, April 28, 1980.

[59] In 1980 (Decree No. 1319, May 25, 1981) and 1984 (Decree No. 0098, January 18, 1984).

[60] Review Commission (1984, p. 13).

For the Review Commission, "the only intelligible principle is that of Article 18, according to which the law binds both nationals and foreigners who are residents in Colombia. This means that it is established the absolute territoriality of the law".[61] It however criticizes this absolute territoriality by stating that "it is at odds with modern doctrines on the subject. If all states were to adopt this system, international trade would become impossible".[62]

The Review Commission did not explicitly make any comparison to foreign legal systems to propose the private international law provisions included in the 1984 Draft. Nevertheless, it made some general comments that may be related to the way in which they conceived the comparative law that underlies private international law.

According to the members of the Commission, society must be taken into account to interpret conflictual rules. They rejected in this vein the exegetical method of legal interpretation. Instead, consideration must be given to the need to ensure the evolution and progress of law: the new private international law must be governed by "fundamental legal principles, unanimously accepted by *civilized nations* and binding on all persons, whether national or foreign".[63] Thus, according to the 1984 Draft, not only should attention be paid to law as an evolutionary phenomenon, but, since not all nations are equally civilized (and certainly not all non-European nations), the *degree of civilization* of the nation from which the legal principles originate must be taken into account. The 1984 Draft then sought to replace rules, that were more than a century old and certainly in need of revision, based on a nineteenth-century culturalist approach to comparative law, although at the same time, it advocated overcoming the exegesis characteristic of formalist comparative law.

The 1984 Draft was not passed. Until very recently, this was the only official proposal to reform the private international law provisions included in the Civil Code, the first version of which, as mentioned above, dates back to 1858. In 2021, a new proposal to review the Civil Code was prepared by the National University of Colombia, with the support of the Ministry for Justice, on the basis of the aforementioned 1984 Draft. A new version was published in 2023. This was not well received either and apparently for good reasons. The following is just an example of the way in which private international law is considered there: The reference made in the 2021 Draft to the violation of fundamental rights as grounds for rejecting the application of foreign law to have effects in Colombia (Article 21) was excluded, although it has been extensively regarded by the Supreme Court of Justice and the Constitutional Court in relation to the recognition of foreign judicial judgments and arbitral awards.

---

[61] ibid.

[62] ibid.

[63] ibid., p. 14 (Italics have been added).

4 Final Remarks: Originality in Colombian Private International Law

It has been said that Latin American law lacks originality.[64] Because the law of the region is considered European law,[65] it seems not to be attractive to legal comparatists. Such an idea has been traditionally attached to all normative systems of the different countries in the region. It also encompasses the different forms of normativity that have existed throughout its history, before, during, and after the colonial period. This has been called a "fiction" by Esquirol. According to him, behind the idea that Latin American law is European law is the fact that "In the name of liberal democracy, Latin American particularity is substituted, even by its defenders, for the aspiration to European society".[66]

There may be additional explanations for the assumption that Latin American law lacks originality, but it may basically be dismissed as simplistic. No normative system is pure but the result of processes of mixing, hybridization, and mutual translations.[67] In this sense, understanding law implies knowing the specific circumstances in which it emerges and exists, which can be related to the idea, that has been stressed by Eugenio Hernández-Bretón, that "law is necessarily relative".[68] In spite of this relativity, or perhaps because of it, it is reasonable to think that Colombian private international law has original features. Some of such features are undoubtedly shared with the Latin American region as a whole, where the history of this legal field is marked by a fruitful tradition that goes centuries back.

However, the aforementioned perception has prevented a more accurate approach to the study of the historical complexities that are at the core of the law of the region, including private international law. In this chapter, I have just sketched an approximation to the diverse imbrications existing between private international law and comparative law considering the Colombian context. Much remains to be studied about the originality that underlies the diverse and complex ways in which Colombian private international law has related, relates, and will relate in the future with other systems of private international law. Further studies could make it possible to observe, in addition to the instrumental relationship between comparative law and private international law that underlies their interactions mentioned above, the foundational relationships between the two fields, i.e., to what extent diverse legal ideas (may have) contributed to the development of private international law in the country.[69]

---

[64] Kleinheisterkamp (2019, pp. 253–254).

[65] See Esquirol (1997) citing René David.

[66] Esquirol (1997, p. 427).

[67] This is an idea on which Duve (2020, 2022) insists in relation to Latin American law, paying special attention to its historical developments. See also López Medina (2009). López Medina's work is particularly relevant regarding influences received by Colombian law.

[68] Hernández-Bretón (2015, p. 7).

[69] Delic (2019, p. 187).

References

Álvarez Londoño LF, Galán Barrera DR (2001) Derecho internacional privado, Colección estudios de derecho internacional, vol 3. Pontificia Universidad Javeriana, Bogota
Andenas M, Fairgrieve D (eds) (2015) Courts and comparative law. Oxford University Press, Oxford
Berman PS (2020) Understanding legal pluralism: from local to global, from descriptive to normative. In: Berman PS (ed) Oxford handbook on legal pluralism. Oxford University Press, Oxford, pp 1–36
Bonilla Maldonado D (2023) Introducción. Un mapa de los problemas centrales de la disciplina. In: Bonilla Maldonado D, Michaels R (eds) Derecho comparado. Materiales modernos y posmodernos. Uniandes, Bogota, pp 9–52
Correas O (1995) Pluralismo jurídico y teoría general del derecho, derechos y libertades. Revista del Instituto Bartolomé de las Casas 1995:215–240
Cotterell R (2019) Comparative law and legal culture. In: Reimann M, Zimmermann R (eds) The Oxford handbook of comparative law. Oxford University Press, Oxford, pp 710–733
Delic A (2019) The role of comparative law in the development of modern private international law (1750–1914). In: Van Hule I, Lesaffer R (eds) International law in the long nineteenth century (1776–1914). Brill Nijhoff, Leiden, pp 186–213
Duve T (2020) What is global legal history? Comp Leg Hist 8(2):73–115
Duve T (2022) Historia del derecho como historia del saber normativo. Revista de Historia del Derecho 63:1–60
Esquirol J (1997) The fictions of Latin American law (part I). Utah Law Rev 1997:425–470
Gonzalo Quiroga M (2005) Las normas imperativas y el orden público en el arbitraje privado internacional. Universidad Complutense de Madrid. ebrary.com
Graziadei M (2003) The functionalist heritage. In: Legrand P, Munday R (eds) Comparative legal studies: traditions and transitions. Cambridge University Press, Cambridge, pp 100–127
Grosswald Curran V (1998) Dealing in difference: comparative law's potential for broadening legal perspectives. Am J Comp Law 46(4):657–668
Hernández-Bretón E (2015) Prólogo. In: Morles Hernández A (ed) Historia del derecho mercantil venezolano. Universidad Monteávila and Universidad Católica Andrés Bello, Caracas
Kleinheisterkamp J (2019) Comparative law in Latin America. In: Reimann M, Zimmermann R (eds) The Oxford handbook of comparative law. Oxford University Press, Oxford, pp 253–254
López Medina D (2009) Teoría impura del derecho: la transformación de la cultura jurídica latinoamericana. Universidad de los Andes, Bogota
Madrid Martínez C (2021) Eficacia extraterritorial de sentencias: una mirada desde los sistemas venezolano y colombiano. Anuario de la Maestría de Derecho Internacional Privado y Comparado 3:417–439
Mantilla Rey R (1982) Apuntes de derecho internacional privado. Temis, Bogota
Martinek M (1994) Wissenschaftsgeschichte der Rechtsvergleichung un des internationalen Privatrecht in der Bundesrepublik Deutschland. In: Dieter S (ed) Rechtswissenschaft in der Bonner Republik. Suhrkamp, Frankfurt, pp 539–541
Michaels R (2017) Comparative law and private international law. In: Basedow J (ed) Elgar encyclopedia of private international law. Elgar Edward, Cheltenham
Michaels R (2022) Internationales Privatrecht als Rechtsvergleichung. Die kollisionsrechtlich-vergleichende Methode, Max Planck Institute for Comparative and International Private Law Research Paper Series, No. 22/19
Michaels R (2023) Introducción. Un mapa de los problemas centrales de la disciplina. In: Bonilla Maldonado D, Michaels R (eds) Derecho comparado. Materiales modernos y posmodernos. Uniandes, Bogota, pp 9–52
Monroy Cabra MG (1983) Tratado de derecho internacional privado, 3rd edn. Temis, Bogota
Muir Watt H (2019) Globalisation and comparative law. In: Reimann M, Zimmermann R (eds) The Oxford handbook of comparative law. Oxford University Press, Oxford, pp 599–624

Ochoa Jiménez MJ, Zapata Flórez J, Carrillo Gamboa P (2019) La elección del derecho aplicable en el derecho internacional privado en Colombia. Estudios Socio-Jurídicos, 21(1):91–120
Oviedo Albán J (2012) La ley aplicable a los contratos internacionales. International Law Revista Colombiana de Derecho Internacional 21:117–157
Rabel E (1931) El fomento internacional del derecho privado. In: Rabel E (ed) Gesamelte Aufsätz. J. C. B. Mohr, Tubingen, pp 35–72. 1967
Rabel E (1945) The conflict of laws: a comparative study. University of Michigan Press, Ann Arbor
Reimann M (2019) Comparative law and private international law. In: Reimann M, Zimmermann R (eds) The Oxford handbook of comparative law. Oxford University Press, Oxford, pp 1339–1370
Review Commission (1984) Civil Code Draft. http://www.derecho.unal.edu.co/fileadmin/Codigo_Civil/Proyecto_Codigo_Civil_Prof_Valencia_Zea.pdf. Accessed on 20 June 2024
Riles A (2005) A new agenda for the cultural study of law: taking on the technicalities. Buff L Rev 53:973–1033
Samuel G (2014) An introduction to comparative law theory and method. Hart Publishing. Oxford and Portland

María Julia Ochoa Jiménez . Dr. iur. and LLM from the University of Göttingen; Lawyer and specialist in Intellectual Property from the Universidad de Los Andes; LLM, Universidad de Navarra; research fellow, University of Bonn, Alexander von Humboldt Foundation; visiting researcher, Max Planck Institute for Comparative and International Private Law; professor, Universidad de Antioquia (2016–2022); professor of Private International Law, Universidad Loyola.

An Introduction to the Private International Law of the Latin American Countries Today

Eugenio Hernández-Bretón

Abstract This chapter provides a comprehensive overview of the evolving landscape of private international law in Latin America. It highlights how Latin American countries have historically followed a territorialist approach but have increasingly modernized their legal frameworks over the past twenty-five years. Countries such as Venezuela, Uruguay, and Panama have enacted new Acts, while others like Cuba and Mexico have introduced reforms focusing on specific areas like international family law and civil procedure. Despite this modernization, traditional instruments like the Bustamante Code and Montevideo Treaties continue to coexist with these new legal developments. The chapter emphasizes the importance of continued academic and judicial engagement to assess the effectiveness of these evolving legal frameworks in practice.

> We become what we see of ourselves in the eyes of others.
> VS Naipaul, The Mimic Men (1967)

1 Scope

It is the general view of commentators that the best word to describe the approach of Latin American countries—in theory, and in practice—toward private international law well up into the doorstep of the twenty-first century is "territorialism".[1] But this is not an essay to make a new presentation on why or how the private

[1] Herrera Mendoza (1960), Valladão (1952), Trigueros (1980), Fernández-Arroyo (1994), Pereznieto (1985), Samtleben (2010a, b).

E. Hernández-Bretón (✉)
Facultad de Ciencias Jurídicas y Políticas, Universidad Central de Venezuela, Caracas, Venezuela
e-mail: eugenio.hernandez-breton@bakermckenzie.com

M. J. Ochoa Jiménez, C. Madrid Martínez (eds.), *A Private International Law for Colombia*, Springer Textbooks in Law,
https://doi.org/10.1007/978-3-032-04106-7_4

international law of the Latin American countries transited from its early Spanish, French, or Portuguese origins up to where it stood at the end of the twentieth century,[2] when certainly "territorialism" was the name of the game. Regardless of their venerable status, this chapter will not go over again to highlight what an important role the Bustamante Code (to which The Bahamas—as of January 23, 2017—adhered with the express reservation to Articles 1 to 273, inclusive and to Articles 295 to 437, inclusive[3]), the Montevideo Treaties, the Mercosur Treaties, or the Inter-American Conventions have played (and, as we will see, continue to play) in the development of private international law of the region,[4] but rather it aims to provide an introductory overview of the current status of the several national and autonomous conflict of law rules in force today in the Latin American countries, from Argentina and Chile, close to the South Pole, through the vast territories of South and Central America, up to Mexico bordering the United States America, with a touch of the views of the Spanish- and French-speaking countries of the Caribbean Sea. We aim to provide the reader with enough information that would allow him or her to dig for more information if interested in how the private international law of Latin America looks today (or perhaps how it will look tomorrow!). This is the challenging (and ever-changing) scenery we are about to unveil.

2 Overview

The stable ground of private international law in Latin American countries was shaken by several successive local legal (earth)quakes that have given a new face to this discipline in the region.

During the past twenty-five years, Latin American countries have been very active in modernizing their legislation on private international law. The legislative efforts, however, have a different reach and do not follow a common pattern. A group of countries starting with Venezuela (1998)[5] and followed by the Dominican Republic (2014),[6] Panama (2015),[7] and more recently Uruguay (2020)[8] have enacted new comprehensive special laws on private international law, whereas Paraguay

---

[2] Parra-Aranguren (1982, 1998).

[3] See current status in: https://www.oas.org/en/sla/dil/inter_american_treaties_a-31_bustamente_code_signatories.asp

[4] See Parra-Aranguren (1979), Maekelt (1982, 2005), Samtleben (1983).

[5] Ley de Derecho Internacional Privado of August 6, 1998, Gaceta Oficial Nr. 36511 of August 6, 1998. See generally, Monleón N (2008); Samtleben (2023j).

[6] Ley de Derecho Internacional Privado, Ley Nr. 544 of December 5, 2014, Gaceta Oficial of December 18, 2014. See generally, Tomás Ortiz de la Torre (2018); Samtleben (2023e).

[7] Código de Derecho Internacional Privado, Ley Nr. 61 of October 7, 2015, Gaceta Oficial Digital Nr. 27885-A of October 8, 2015. See generally, Samtleben (2023g); Boutin G et al. (2019).

[8] Ley General de Derecho Internacional Privado, Ley Nr. 19920 of November 27, 2020, Diario Oficial of December 16, 2020. See generally, Samtleben (2023i).

(2015)[9] issued legislation specifically dealing with international contracts, and Cuba updated its private international law system in a significant manner through a special law on Economic Contracts (2012),[10] and amendment to its Code of Procedures (2021),[11] and most importantly, through a new Code of Families (yes, note that it is not a Code of Family but a Code of Families) (2022).[12]

The major changes in Costa Rica have been on international family law matters, regarding both conflict of laws and civil procedure issues. These changes are included in the Family Code (2019),[13] which came into effect on October 1, 2024, and in the Family Procedural Code (2016).[14] In El Salvador, the most significant changes are in respect of international civil procedure law matters as reflected in the Code of Civil and Commercial Procedures (2008 as amended 2010)[15] and in the Special Act on Adoptions (2016).[16] Guatemala has kept the rules on private international law (including some international civil procedure rules) in the Judicial Branch Act (1989),[17] and regulated international adoption in the Adoptions Act (2007)[18] following the 1993 Hague Convention on Protection of Children and Co-operation in Respect of Intercountry Adoption. Changes in the conflict rules of Honduras can be particularly seen in the Family Code (2013)[19] regarding international adoptions, and in the Labor Code (2003),[20] whereas amendments to the international civil procedure rules are contained in the Civil Procedure Code (2007).[21] In Nicaragua, the most significant developments are found in the Family Code (2014)[22] and in the

[9] Ley sobre el Derecho Aplicable a los Contratos Internacionales, Ley Nr. 5393 of January 14, 2015, Gaceta Oficial of January 20, 2015. See Samtleben (2023k).

[10] Ley de la Contratación Económica, Decreto-Ley Nr. 304 of November 1, 2012, Gaceta Oficial Nr. 62 of December 27, 2012.

[11] Código de Procesos, Ley Nr. 141 of October 28, 2021, Gaceta Oficial of December 7, 2021.

[12] Código de las Familias, Ley Nr. 156 of July 22, 2022, Gaceta Oficial Nr. 87 of August 17, 2022.

[13] Código de Familia, as amended by Ley Nr. 9747 of October 23, 2019, La Gaceta of February 12, 2020, Alcance Nr. 19.

[14] Código Procesal de Familia, Ley Nr. 9747 of October 23, 2019, La Gaceta of February 12, 2020, Alcance Nr. 19.

[15] Código Procesal Civil y Mercantil, Decreto Legislativo Nr. 712 of November 14, 2008, Diario Oficial of November 27, 2008, as amended by Decreto Legislativo Nr. 319 of May 26, 2010, Diario Oficial of May 31, 2010.

[16] Ley Especial de Adopciones, Decreto Legislativo Nr. 282 of February 17, 2016, Diario Oficial of November 4, 2016.

[17] Ley del Organismo Judicial, decreto Nr. 2-89 of March 28, 1989, Diario de Centroamérica of April 3, 1989.

[18] Ley de Adopciones, Decreto Nr. 77-2007 of December 20, 2007, Diario de Centro América of December 21, 2007.

[19] Código de Familia, as amended by Decreto Nr. 35-2013 of September 5, 2013, La Gaceta of September 6, 2013.

[20] Código del Trabajo, as amended by Decree Nr. 32-2003 of March 3, 2003, La Gaceta of April 16, 2003.

[21] Código Procesal Civil, Decreto Nr. 211-2006 of February 20, 2007, La Gaceta of May 26, 2007.

[22] Código de Familia, Ley Nr. 870 of August 26, 2014, La Gaceta of October 8, 2014.

Code of Civil Procedure (2015).[23] However, conflict of law issues, e.g., regarding the connecting factor for family matters of foreigners, remain unclear, while Nicaraguan nationals are subject to Nicaraguan law regardless of their place of residence.[24] Despite the recent changes in the domestic laws of the Central American countries, especially in Panama, there is a proposal for a Model Act of Private International Law for those countries[25] still under consideration.

Argentina enacted a new Civil and Commercial Code (2014)[26] which includes rules on private international law and included rules on jurisdiction of courts and on international cooperation but refrained from regulating the recognition of foreign judgments (apparently because of constitutional law grounds), while Puerto Rico did pass a new Civil Code (2020)[27] covering conflict of law rules. Although Brazil has not recently issued significant rules on conflict of laws, it enacted a Code of Civil Procedure (2015)[28] improving, to some extent, pre-existing international procedural rules. The recent amendments to the Lei de Introdução ao Código Civil Brasileiro,[29] where the most significant Brazilian conflict of law rules are, did not change the substance of the old rules.[30] The Brazilian Statute on Children and Adolescents (2009)[31] deals with international adoptions. Despite Chile's faithful adherence to the 1855 Civil Code of Andrés Bello[32] and to its territorial approach to conflict of law problems, the national legislature enacted statutes dealing with

[23] Código Procesal Civil, Ley Nr. 902 of August 5, 2015, La Gaceta of October 9, 2015.

[24] Samtleben (2023b, pp. 707–709).

[25] Villalta Vizcarra (2016, pp. 836) et passim.

[26] Código Civil y Comercial de la Nación, Ley Nr. 26994 of October 7, 2014, Boletín Oficial of November 8, 2014, particularly Articles 2594-2671. See generally, Scotti L (2020); Samtleben (2023e).

[27] Código Civil, Ley Nr. 55 of June 1st, 2020 as amended by Ley Nr. 19 of August 2, 2021, and by Ley Nr. 150 of August 12, 2024, Laws of Puerto Rico Annotated (LPRA), Title 31, Articles 30-66. Apparently, the new Civil Code has not been officially translated (Muñiz-Argüelles 2023, p. 401 note 10). Unless there is a provision to the contrary, in case of discrepancies between the Spanish and the English versions of a law the Spanish text will prevail (Article 26). See also, Tomás Ortiz de la Torre (2020).

[28] Código de Processo Civil, Lei Nr. 10406 of March 16, 2015, Diário Oficial da União of March 17, 2015. See Samtleben (2023d).

[29] Lei Nr. 12376 of December 30, 2010, Diário Oficial da União of December 31, 2010 Lei Nr. 12874 of October 29, 2013, Diário Oficial da União of October 30, 2013.

[30] In a nutshell, the major modification was to change the name of the old law to Lei de Introdução às Normas do Direito Brasileiro. See Samtleben (2023a, p. 73–74).

[31] Estatuto da Criança e do Adolescente, Lei Nr. 8069 of July 13, 1990, Diário Oficial da União of July 16, 1990 as amended by Lei Nr. 12010 of August 3, 2009, Diário Oficial da União of August 4, 2009, Articles 51-52-D.

[32] Código Civil of 1855, Decreto con Fuerza de Ley Nr. 1 of May 16, 2000, Diario Oficial of May 30, 2000, as amended by Ley Nr. 19947 of May 7, 2004, Diario Oficial of May 17, 2004 and Ley Nr. 21400 of December 9, 2021, Diario Oficial of December 10, 2021.

specific issues of conflict of laws and international civil procedure related to marriage and divorce,[33] common law marriage,[34] and international adoption.[35]

The recent legislation enacted in Ecuador includes amendments to the Civil Code (2005/2015),[36] the Commercial Code (2019),[37] the Organic General Code of Procedures (2009),[38] and some other special laws,[39] which in the aggregate have not brought major changes in respect of the pre-existing legislation but do incorporate rules embodied in international treaties such as the 1961 Hague Convention on the Apostille.[40] Similarly, Haiti incorporated the relevant provisions of the 1993 Hague Convention on Protection of Children and Co-operation in Respect of Intercountry Adoption in its Adoption Reform Act (2013).[41]

Mexico is a federal republic composed of thirty-two states each with its own conflict of law rules. Accordingly, the references made in this chapter are limited to the federal codes and laws and to those in force in the City of Mexico. The Federal Civil Code of 2000[42] followed the Civil Code of the Federal District of 1987 establishing domicile as the main connecting factor for capacity and other family law matters and abandoning the strict territorialism of the Civil Code of 1928. However, the Civil Code of the Federal District (now Civil Code of Ciudad de Mexico) of 2000[43] went back to territorialism.[44] The new rules on international civil procedure

---

[33] Ley de Matrimonio Civil, Ley Nr. 19947 of May 7, 2004, as amended by Ley Nr. 21400 of December 9, 2021, Diario Oficial of December 10, 2021.

[34] Ley de Acuerdo de Unión Civil, Ley Nr. 20830 of May 13, 2015, Diario Oficial of April 21, 2015, as amended by Ley Nr. 21400 of December 9, 2021, Diario Oficial of December 10, 2021.

[35] Ley sobre Adopción de Menores, Ley Nr. 19620 of July 26, 1999, Diario Oficial of August 5, 1999.

[36] Código Civil as recodified on May 10, 2005, Registro Oficial of June 24, 2005, Suplemento, and as amended by Ley of June 16, 2015, Registro Oficial of June 19, 2015, Segundo Suplemento.

[37] Código de Comercio, Ley of May 9, 2019, Registro Oficial of May 29, 2019, Suplemento.

[38] Código Orgánico General de Procesos, Ley of May 12, 2005, Registro Oficial of May 22, 2015, Suplemento, as amended by Ley of August 7, 2018, Registro Oficial of August 21, 2018, Suplemento. Also, Código Orgánico de la Función Judicial, Ley of March 3, 2009, Registro Oficial of March 9, 2009, Suplemento.

[39] Código de la Niñez y de la Adolescencia, Ley Nr. 100 of December 17, 2002; Ley de Compañías as amended by Ley of May 6, 2009, Registro Oficial of My 15, 2009, by Ley of April 29, 2014, Registro Oficial of May 20, 2014, Suplemento, by Ley of December 27, 2017, Registro Oficial of December 29, 2017, Segundo Suplemento and by Ley of December 1, 2020, Registro Oficial of December 10, 2020, Tercer Suplemento.

[40] Código de la Niñez y de la Adolescencia, Ley Nr. 100 of December 17, 2002, Articles 180–189.

[41] Loi réformant l'adoption, Loi of October 29, 2013, Le Moniteur of November 15, 2013, numéro extraordinaire.

[42] Código Civil Federal, Decreto of May 23, 2000, Diario Oficial de la Federación of May 29, 2000.

[43] Código Civil para el Distrito Federal, Decreto of May 22, 2000, Gaceta Oficial del Distrito Federal of May 22, 2000, as amended by Decreto May 27, 2004, Gaceta Oficial del Distrito Federal of June 9, 2004, Decreto of July 21, 2010, Gaceta Oficial de la Ciudad de México, July 29, 2010 and by Decreto of July 20, 2012, Gaceta Oficial de la Ciudad de México of Juy 23, 2012.

[44] Samtleben (2023a, p. 75).

contained in the National Code of Civil and Family Procedures (2023),[45] including rules on evidence, jurisdiction of courts, international cooperation, children restitution, videoconferencing in international cases, information on foreign law, recognition and enforcement of foreign judgments and awards, shall be gradually put into effect in the entire country, both at the federal and state level, by no later than April 1, 2027.[46]

Draft comprehensive legislation on private international law is being prepared and/or discussed in Chile, Colombia, Mexico, and Bolivia (particularly concerning international contracts).[47] Peru prepares an amendment[48] of the private international law rules embodied in Book 10 of its Civil Code (1984).[49]

A group of countries have enacted domestic legislation under the influence of the Model Inter-American Law on Secured Transactions[50] that include a few conflicts of law rules (Colombia,[51] El Salvador,[52] Guatemala,[53] Honduras,[54] Nicaragua[55]). The doctrine of *forum non conveniens* has also—in one way or another—been the subject of keen interest in the region. Some countries accept it as an exception to the exercise of international jurisdiction by national courts (most notably for maritime cases Panama[56] and Venezuela,[57] and in general terms, the Dominican Republic[58]). Some other countries have enacted blocking legislation vis-à-vis *forum non*

---

[45] Código Nacional de Procedimientos Civiles y Familiares, Decreto of June 6, 2023, Diario Oficial de la Federación of June 7, 2023.

[46] Código Nacional de Procedimientos Civiles y Familiares, Second Transitory Article.

[47] Hernández-Bretón (2022).

[48] Hernández-Bretón (2022).

[49] Código Civil, Decreto Legislativo Nr. 295 of July 24, 1984, El Peruano of Juy 25, 1984, as amended by Ley Nr. 26572 of January 3, 1996, El Peruano of January 5, 1996, and by Decreto Legislativo Nr. 1071 of June 27, 2008, El Peruano June 28, 2008, Articles 2046-2111. See generally, Samtleben (2023h).

[50] Ley Modelo InterAmericana sobre Garantías Mobiliarias of 2002, CIDIP VI/Res.5.02.

[51] Ley de Garantías Mobiliarias, Ley Nr. 1676 of August 20, 2013, Diario Oficial of August 20, 2013.

[52] Ley de Garantías Mobiliarias, Decreto Legislativo Nr. 488 of October 4, 2013, Diario Oficial of October 14, 2013.

[53] Ley de Garantías Mobiliarias, Decreto Nr. 51-2007 of November 8, 2007, Diario de Centro América of November 16, 2007.

[54] Ley de Garantías Mobiliarias, Decreto Nr. 182-2009 of September 22, 2009, La Gaceta of January 28, 2010.

[55] Ley de Garantías Mobiliarias, Ley No. 936 of October 14, 2016, La Gaceta of October 25, 2016

[56] Ley de Procedimiento Marítimo, in the version of Ley of June 30, 2009, Gaceta Oficial Digital Nr. 26322 of July 13, 2009, Article 22.

[57] Ley de Comercio Marítimo, as amended by Ley of January 4, 2006, Gaceta Oficial January 5, 2006, Article 333.

[58] Ley de Derecho Internacional Privado, Article 23).

conveniens declared by foreign courts (Ecuador,[59] Guatemala,[60] and Nicaragua[61]), which are of questionable constitutionality.[62]

One aspect worth noting is that, in the understanding of Latin American countries, private international law is a broad subject matter not limited to the rules of choice of law but includes the rules of international civil procedural law. Nonetheless, this introduction does not deal with the related subject of international commercial arbitration. As can be confirmed by the references made in the preceding paragraphs to recent legal enactments throughout the region, another aspect to be highlighted is that Latin American domestic codifications are not contained in one single legal instrument but in a series of different bodies of law; their aggregate compose the relevant and individual national legal system together with the applicable international treaties in force. The recent developments in the region also show a trend of siding with domicile rather than nationality as the "personal law" or main connecting factor for choice of law rules on personal, family, and inheritance matters. As notable exceptions to this trend are worth mentioning, the laws of Panama[63] and Cuba,[64] although with different reach. In Honduras, Honduran law is the personal law for Honduran nationals[65] and strict territorialism still appears to be favored concerning foreigners.[66]

The principle of party autonomy and the *lex mercatoria* as applicable law for international contracts have made important inroads in Venezuela, Argentina, Panama, Dominican Republic, Paraguay, and Uruguay mostly because of the generous impact of the Inter-American Convention on the Law Applicable to International Contracts (CIDIP V, Mexico City 1994).[67] Similarly, the general rules of private international law adopted in the domestic laws of the Latin American countries received to a significant extent the influence of the Inter-American Convention on General Rules of Private International Law (CIDIP II, Montevideo 1984).

---

[59] Ley Nr. 55 of January 27, 1998, Registro Oficial of January 30, 1998,

[60] Ley de Defensa de los Derechos Procesales de Nacionales y Residentes, Decreto Nr. 34-97 of May 7, 1997, Diario de Centro América of June 12, 1997.

[61] Ley Especial para la Tramitación de Juicios promovidos por las Personas afectadas por el Uso de Pesticidas fabricados a base de DBCP, Ley Nr. 364 of November 23, 2000, La Gaceta of January 17, 2001.

[62] Garro (2005, pp. 187–189).

[63] Código de Derecho Internacional Privado, Article 23.

[64] Código Civil, Ley Nr. 59 of July 16, 1987, Gaceta Oficial Extraordinaria Nr. 9 of October 15, 1987, which has been amended for family law matters by the Código de las Familias, Article 458. However, under Article 462 of the Código de las Familias marital status matters are governed by the law of the nationality of the spouses, and in the absence thereof (perhaps in the absence of a common nationality of the spouses) by the law of their (common) domicile.

[65] Código Civil of 1906, Decreto Nr. 76-06 of January 19, 1906, Article 13, https://www.oas.org/dil/esp/codigo_civil_honduras.pdf

[66] Samtleben (2023a, pp. 66–67).

[67] Madrid Martínez (2021), Hernández-Bretón (2020), Posenato (2010).

3 Conclusion

The end of the twentieth century and the first two decades of the twenty-first century have witnessed an extraordinary number of significant developments in the private international law of the Latin American countries that have changed the image of the entire region vis-à-vis the rules of this elusive subject. This is not to say that the sacrosanct Bustamante Code, the Montevideo Treaties, or the Inter-American Conventions are gone, but that they must coexist with the new national legislative developments. The new rules will need to be tested in practice; in turn, commentators—to a greater or lesser extent—have produced well-reasoned literature that should help in the correct understanding and application of the new rules. But to put it in the words of Ernst Rabel, the father of comparative private international law, the practical usefulness of all the newly enacted set of rules in the Latin American countries "has yet to be tried in the fire of litigation".[68] Only time will tell!

References

Boutin G et al. (2019) Código de Derecho Internacional Privado de la República de Panamá. Ley Nr. 61 (de 7 de octubre de 2015). Jurídica Pujol, S.A.
de Maekelt T (1982) General rules of private international law in the Americas. New approach. Recueil des Cours de l'Academie de Droit International 177:193–379
de Maekelt T (2005) La codificación interamericana desde la perspectiva de la codificación estatal de derecho internacional privado. In: Fernández Arroyo DP, Mastrángelo F (eds) El futuro de la codificación del derecho internacional privado en América. De la CIDIP VI a la CIDIP VII. Alveroni Ediciones, Córboba, pp 27–51
Fernández-Arroyo D (1994) La codificación del derecho internacional privado en América Latina. Eurolex, Madrid
Garro AM (2005) Forum non conveniens: disponibilidad y adecuación en los foros latinoamericanos desde una perspectiva comparada. DeCita 04(2005):174–206
Hernández-Bretón E (2020) Tesoros de derecho internacional privado y comparado en América Latina. Universidad Monteávila-Baker McKenzie, Caracas
Hernández-Bretón E (2022) De la evolución reciente del derecho comercial internacional en Latinoamérica. Revista Chilena de Derecho Internacional Privado 8(1):103–114
Herrera Mendoza L (1960) La Escuela Estatutaria en Venezuela y su evolución hacia la territorialidad. In: Estudios sobre Derecho Internacional Privado y Temas Conexos. Empresa El Cojo, Caracas, pp 121–236
Madrid Martínez C (2021) La contratación internacional en el derecho internacional privado Colombiano. Perspectiva comparada. Ediciones UNAULA, Tirant Lo Blanch, Bogota
Muñiz-Argüelles L (2023) The 2020 revision of the Puerto Rican civil code: a brief explanation of major changes. J Civil Law Stud 15(1):393–428
Parra-Aranguren G (1979) Recent developments of conflict of Laws conventions in Latin America. Recueil des Cours de l'Academie de Droit International 164:55–170
Parra-Aranguren G (1982) Codificación del Derecho Internacional Privado en América. Universidad Central de Venezuela, Caracas

[68] Rabel (1958, p. 46).

Parra-Aranguren G (1998) Codificación del Derecho Internacional Privado en América, vol II. Universidad Central de Venezuela, Caracas
Pereznieto Castro L (1985) La tradition territorialiste en droit international privé dans les pays d'Amerique Latine. Recueil des Cours de l'Academie de Droit International 190:271–400
Posenato N (2010) Autonomia della volontà e scelta della legge applicabile ai contratti nei sistema giuridici latino-americani. CEDAM, Milan
Rabel E (1958) The conflict of laws a comparative study. Vol I. Introduction: family law, 2nd edn. University of Michigan Law School, Ann Arbor
Samtleben J (1983) Derecho internacional privado en América Latina. Teoría y práctica del Código Bustamante. Volumen I Parte General. Depalma, Buenos Aires
Samtleben J (2010a) Territorialität der Gesetze. In: Rechtspraxis und Rechtskultur in Brasilien und Lateinamerika. Beiträge aus internationaler und regionaler Perspektive. Schriften der Deutsch-Brasilianischen Juristenvereinigung, vol 40. Shaker Verlag, Aachen, pp 344–369
Samtleben J (2010b) El principio de la territorialidad en América Latina. In: Rechtspraxis und Rechtskultur in Brasilien und Lateinamerika. Beiträge aus internationaler und regionaler Perspektive. Schriften der Deutsch-Brasilianischen Juristenvereinigung, vol 40. Shaker Verlag, Aachen, pp 370–403
Samtleben J (2023a) El derecho internacional privado en América Latina (2017). In: Internationales Privat- und Prozessrecht in Lateinamerika. Tradition und Reform. Band I: Rechtsordnungen. Schriften der Deutsch-Brasilianischen Juristenvereinigung, vol 56. Shaker Verlag, Düren, pp 59–76
Samtleben J (2023b) Nicaragua. In: Internationales Privat- und Prozessrecht in Lateinamerika. Tradition und Reform. Band I: Rechtsordnungen. Schriften der Deutsch-Brasilianischen Juristenvereinigung, vol 56. Shaker Verlag, Düren, pp 705–724
Trigueros Saravia E (1980) La evolución de nuestro derecho internacional privado. In: Estudios de Derecho Internacional Privado. Universidad Nacional Autónoma de México, México, pp 133–150
Valladão H (1952) Le droit internationale privé des états américains. Recueil des Cours de l'Academie de Droit International 81:1–116
Villalta Vizcarra AE (2016) La conveniencia de una Ley Modelo de Derecho Internacional Privado para Centroamérica. Anuario Español de Derecho Internacional Privado XVI:835–856

Additional Readings

Monleón N (2008) Das neue internationale Privatrecht von Venezuela. Mohr Siebeck, Tübingen
Samtleben J (2023d) Länderbericht Brasilien (2023). In: Internationales Privat- und Prozessrecht in Lateinamerika. Tradition und Reform. Band I: Rechtsordnungen. Schriften der Deutsch-Brasilianischen Juristenvereinigung, vol 56. Shaker Verlag, Düren, pp 155–213
Samtleben J (2023e) Argentinien. In: Internationales Privat- und Prozessrecht in Lateinamerika. Tradition und Reform. Band I: Rechtsordnungen. Schriften der Deutsch-Brasilianischen Juristenvereinigung, vol 56. Shaker Verlag, Düren, pp 327–350
Samtleben J (2023g) Panama. In: Internationales Privat- und Prozessrecht in Lateinamerika. Tradition und Reform. Band I: Rechtsordnungen. Schriften der Deutsch-Brasilianischen Juristenvereinigung, vol 56. Shaker Verlag, Düren, pp 419–485
Samtleben J (2023h) Peru. In: Internationales Privat- und Prozessrecht in Lateinamerika. Tradition und Reform. Band I: Rechtsordnungen. Schriften der Deutsch-Brasilianischen Juristenvereinigung, vol 56. Shaker Verlag, Düren, pp 487–523
Samtleben J (2023i) Uruguay. In: Internationales Privat- und Prozessrecht in Lateinamerika. Tradition und Reform. Band I: Rechtsordnungen. Schriften der Deutsch-Brasilianischen Juristenvereinigung, vol 56. Shaker Verlag, Düren, pp 527–563

Samtleben J (2023j) Venezuela. In: Internationales Privat- und Prozessrecht in Lateinamerika. Tradition und Reform. Band I: Rechtsordnungen. Schriften der Deutsch-Brasilianischen Juristenvereinigung, vol 56. Shaker Verlag, Düren, pp 587–593

Samtleben J (2023k) Paraguay. In: Internationales Privat- und Prozessrecht in Lateinamerika. Tradition und Reform. Band I: Rechtsordnungen. Schriften der Deutsch-Brasilianischen Juristenvereinigung, vol 56. Shaker Verlag, Düren, pp 729–745

Scotti L (2020) Manual de derecho internacional Privado, 2nd edn. Thomson Reuters La Ley, Buenos Aires

Tomás Ortiz de la Torre JA (2018) El nuevo derecho internacional privado de la República Dominicana. Anales de la Real Academia de Doctores de España 3(2):250–277

Tomás Ortiz de la Torre JA (2020) El nuevo derecho internacional privado de Puerto Rico: breve nota acerca del sistema conflictual del Título Preliminar del Código Civil 1 de junio de 2020. Anales de la Real Academia de Doctores de España 5(2):261–278

Eugenio Hernández-Bretón, Professor of Private International Law, International Civil Procedure Law and Comparative Law at Universidad Central de Venezuela and Universidad Monteávila in Caracas; Former President of the Academy of Political and Social Sciences of Venezuela; Honorary Member of the American Association of Private International Law (ASADIP); Doctor of Laws (Heidelberg), LL.M. (Tübingen), LL.M. (Columbia U.), Abogado (Universidad Católica Andrés Bello, Caracas).

International Procedural Law

International Jurisdiction in Colombia

Claudia Madrid Martínez

Abstract This chapter explores the rules on international jurisdiction in Colombia. It examines the criteria used to determine which courts have jurisdiction over private international law cases, which is the initial step in resolving such cases. It takes account of Colombian current law and the rules included in the Draft General Act on Private International Law for Colombia prepared by IADIP.

1 Introduction

Faced with a private relationship of an international nature, the first thing the judge must do, once this internationality has been ascertained, is to determine whether he or she can hear the case. This refers to the so-called international jurisdiction or international judicial competence, i.e., the power to hear and decide private international law cases. This, together with international cooperation and the extraterritorial effectiveness of judgments, make up international procedural law, which is a discipline that, in most legal systems, is part of private international law.[1]

Like in a domestic case, in an international dispute, the determination of the competent court is the first issue to be decided. And its examination—in particular, regarding the criteria for the jurisdiction attribution—depends on the private international law of each state. In Colombia, the judge will have to resort to the criteria

This text is a result of the project "General Theory of Private International Law", code 2024-68470, Universidad de Antioquia, July 2024.

[1] This is despite the alleged emancipation of international procedural law from private international law. See Pfeiffer (1995, pp. 9–10).

C. Madrid Martínez (✉)
University of Antioquia, Medellín, Antioquia, Colombia

M. J. Ochoa Jiménez, C. Madrid Martínez (eds.), *A Private International Law for Colombia*, Springer Textbooks in Law,
https://doi.org/10.1007/978-3-032-04106-7_5

contained, in the first place, in the international treaties and, failing that, to those established in the state legislation.

In this chapter, before entering into the analysis of the jurisdiction criteria of Colombian private international law in force and contrasting them with those proposed in the Draft General Act on Private International Law for Colombia that was prepared by the *Instituto Antioqueño de Derecho Internacional Privado* (IADIP) (hereinafter, "IADIP Draft"), some general notions regarding the so-called jurisdiction or international judicial competence need to be clarified.

2 General Notions

As a general rule, each state determines the cases in which its courts may hear and decide situations of private international law. This power is called jurisdiction in some systems[2] and international judicial competence[3] in others. In the case of Colombia, although some authors indeed use the term "conflict of jurisdictions"[4] to refer to the necessary determination of the competent judge in cases of private international law, the doctrine usually prefers the expression international judicial competence.[5] The latter is the expression used by the IADIP Draft (Section Two of Chapter Four). In this chapter, the term international jurisdiction is used due to its widespread acceptance in the English language.

From the procedural point of view, Rojas Gómez admits that the expression "lack of jurisdiction", used by Article 100, first paragraph of the General Code of Procedure,[6] refers to cases in which the power to hear and decide the case is in the hands of a foreign judge, an arbitral tribunal, or an administrative authority. Thus, although in his opinion it is an "exotic" hypothesis that a judge lacks jurisdiction, it is evident that the author gives the expression jurisdiction a connotation different

---

[2] This is what occurs in the Venezuelan Act on Private International Law. See Hernández-Bretón (2004, pp. 57–58). In Germany, the expression "*internationale Zuständigkeit*" is used, which could be translated as international jurisdiction. See Pfeiffer (1995, pp. 18–20), Schack (2002, pp. 64–66).

[3] For example, Regulation (EU) No. 1215/2012 of the European Parliament and of the Council of 12 December 2012 on jurisdiction and the recognition and enforcement of judgments in civil and commercial matters (Brussels I Bis), refers to "court jurisdiction" (*competencia judicial* in Spanish). In the case of the Spanish system, although neither the Organic Act of the Judiciary (BOE, No. 157, July 2, 1985) nor the Act on Civil Procedure (BOE, No. 7, January 8, 2000) expressly refers to judicial international compentence, this is the expression used by scholars. See Espinar (1988, pp. 9–13); Esplugues (2002, pp. 8–11).

[4] Zuleta (2010, p. 13).

[5] Marín Fuentes (2016a, pp. 15–17).

[6] Act No. 1564 of 2012 (July 12).

from that which identifies it with power, authority, or faculty of the state, with a "public function", in the sense of Article 228 of the Political Constitution of Colombia.[7] When referring to the "lack of competence", Rojas Gómez considers that this occurs within the same jurisdiction.[8] The General Code of Procedure, however, does not seem to establish differences between one and the other, when establishing the procedure for its procedural treatment.

In any case, because the notion of sovereignty usually surrounds any discussion of jurisdiction, the task of its determination is generally left to the state legislator.[9] Goldschmidt, resorting to Scelle's "*dédoublement fonctionnel*" thesis,[10] understands that, although the natural legislator for the regulation of these matters is the supranational legislator, this often fails to perform its functions and leaves them in the hands of state legislators, who are responsible for establishing the cases in which their courts may hear cases of private international law.[11]

To carry out this task, state legislators usually take two paths: first, to establish, using special rules, the attributive criteria that will determine the cases in which their courts may hear and decide cases of private international law, as occurs in the Argentinian,[12] Dominican,[13] Panamanian,[14] or Venezuelan[15] systems, among others; or, second, to admit the application, in the absence of express rules, of the provisions on domestic territorial jurisdiction. This would be, in principle, the case of Colombian private international law.

Indeed, in Colombia, it has been accepted, with certain nuances, the application of Articles 15 to 33 of the General Code of Procedure, which are rules that regulate domestic territorial jurisdiction, to cases of determination of international jurisdiction,[16] "with undesirable results, especially concerning certain matters (such as contractual matters)".[17]

But let us bear in mind from now on that leaving international jurisdiction in the hands of rules of domestic jurisdiction is inconvenient, largely because of the effects

---

[7] Constitutional Gazette No. 116, July 20, 1991.

[8] Rojas (2013, pp. 228–229).

[9] "After all, the jurisdiction of judges is a domestic matter originating in constitutional rules that in no way take into account the rules of other States on the jurisdiction of their judges". See Zuleta (2010, p. 13), Zapata Giraldo (2017, p. 1984).

[10] Scelle (1932/1934).

[11] Goldschmidt (1954, p. 71).

[12] The Civil and Commercial Code regulates "international jurisdiction" between Articles 2601 and 2612.

[13] Between Articles 8 and 28, the Dominican Act on Private International Law regulates "Dominican jurisdiction".

[14] The Panamanian Act, which refers to "international judicial competence", regulates it in Articles 10 to 17.

[15] The Venezuelan Act establishes the criteria for the attribution of jurisdiction between Articles 39 and 42.

[16] Zapata Giraldo (2017, p. 1984).

[17] Orejudo (2013, p. 682).

produced by the determination of international jurisdiction, effects that reach even to the substance of the procedure.[18] Thus, in addition to its immediate effect, which is precisely the determination of international jurisdiction, this process also produces mediate effects. In the first place, it must be considered that the determination of international jurisdiction also determines the applicable private international law rules; so that, when the international jurisdiction of the Colombian courts is affirmed, its private international law will be responsible for determining the law applicable to both the form of the proceeding and the merits of the dispute.

Second, the rules on international jurisdiction determine the so-called "cost of procedural internationality", referring to the costs of international service of process, the taking of evidence abroad, and even the possibility of enforcing the judgment in a state other than the one whose courts rendered it. These costs will of course have to be assessed mainly by the plaintiff. Finally, mention is made of the "risks of jurisdictional internationality", associated with the fact of having to resort to a foreign forum to enforce the subjective rights in dispute, which is what happens with recourse to the tools of international cooperation.

However, this inclination toward state regulation of international jurisdiction does not necessarily translate into the absence of rules of conventional origin. Indeed, in most systems, conventional rules coexist with state rules, as is the case even in Colombian Private International Law, in which the Montevideo Treaties on International Civil Law (Articles 56 to 67) and on International Commercial Law,[19] the bilateral treaty with Ecuador (Articles XXIV–XXVI)[20] and the Inter-American Conventions on international return of children (Article 8),[21] on support obligations (Articles 8 and 9)[22] and on adoption of minors (Articles 15 to 17)[23] share application with the General Code of Procedure.

This duality of sources makes it necessary to consider that the conventional or state origin of the rules conferring international jurisdiction is important due to the function they perform. Indeed, as noted above, on other occasions,[24] that the rule on international jurisdiction contained in an international treaty distributes jurisdiction among the state's parties; so that if, once the treaty in force is applied, the international jurisdiction falls on another of the state's parties to it and not on Colombia, the judge must be satisfied with declaring the lack of international jurisdiction. On the other hand, if the rule is of the state of origin, its function is limited to the attribution of international jurisdiction to Colombian courts, without being able to rule on the jurisdiction of foreign courts. In the latter case, it is a unilateral regulation.

---

[18] I will follow on this point: Virgós and Garcimartín (2000, pp. 40–41).

[19] Act No. 33 of 1992 (December 30).

[20] Act No. 13 of 1905 (April 8).

[21] Act No. 620 of 2000 (October 25) and Act 880 of 2004 (January 19).

[22] Act No. 449 of 1998 (August 4).

[23] Act No. 47 of 1987 (December 3).

[24] Madrid (2010, pp. 99).

This is the understanding of Virgós Soriano and Garcimartín Alférez, for whom each state freely decides on its jurisdiction, with the only limits imposed by Public International Law, and each state has, therefore, its own system of international jurisdiction. This explains the unilateral formulation of the rules and the lack of communication between the various state systems. The cited authors add—rightly—that insofar as there is no supranational court, the positive and negative conflicts of international jurisdiction that arise due to the unilateral nature of the rules must also be resolved unilaterally.[25] In any case, this concurrence, according to the ASADIP Principles on Transnational Access to Justice,[26] "shall be informed by the principle of judicial cooperation, which seeks to achieve effective justice" (Article 3.1).

The unilaterality in the regulation of international jurisdiction gives rise to cases of concurrence or positive conflict of jurisdiction, i.e., it is possible that, in the application of its own criteria, more than one state establishes the international jurisdiction of its own courts to hear the same private international law relation, in which case, the initial decision will remain in the hands of the plaintiff. In the case of parallel litigation, i.e., if the process is attempted simultaneously in more than one state, the solution to avoid duplication of efforts and the possible obtaining of contradictory judgments for common law countries comes from the *forum non conveniens*, while in civil law states, the matter is resolved using *lis pendens* or pending litigation.[27] The latter would be the case in Colombia.

Indeed, in current Colombian private international law, the only reference to pending litigation is made by the General Code of Procedure, when regulating preliminary questions. I am referring to Article 100.8, a rule that seems to be limited to the pendency of the same case before two local courts when the requirements regarding the identity of the subjects, the object, and the cause are verified.[28] For such reason, considering the specificities of international litigation, the IADIP Draft included in Article 34 a solution that, based on Article 3.7 of the ASADIP Principles, provides:

> Colombian courts shall suspend the exercise of their jurisdiction when the same cause, with the same object and between the same parties, has been previously initiated in the court of a State that is reasonably related to the matter or the parties unless it is evident that in that forum the process will not be resolved in a fair, effective and diligent manner.
>
> The suspension based on *lis pendens* may be extended until the decision in the foreign State acquires the force of *res judicata*, provided that such a decision is rendered within a reasonable period and may be effective in Colombia.

The approach of this rule seeks to promote respect for foreign jurisdiction while protecting the rights of the parties to a fair and efficient trial. In addition, the rule allows the stay for pending litigation to be maintained until the foreign decision

---

[25] Virgós and Garcimartín (2000, pp. 39–40).

[26] Approved by the Assembly of the American Association of Private International Law, ASADIP, at its meeting held in Buenos Aires, on November 12, 2016. See http://www.asadip.org/v2/wp-content/uploads/2018/08/ASADIP-TRANSJUS-ES-FINAL18.pdf

[27] Brand (2013, pp. 1005–1011).

[28] Rojas (2013, pp. 234–235).

acquires the force of *res judicata*, provided that such a decision is rendered within a reasonable period and is enforceable in Colombia. This mechanism promotes legal certainty and consistency in the resolution of international disputes, avoiding duplication of processes and enhancing the effectiveness of decisions in transnational litigation.

Well, unilateralism in the regulation of international jurisdiction may also lead, although less frequently, to a negative conflict, i.e., none of the states involved agrees to hear the case. In this case, in accordance with the principle of transnational access to justice,[29] the state before which the dispute is brought could assume jurisdiction to avoid incurring in denial of justice. In this case, and in others in which the right of transnational access to justice may be affected, the IADIP Draft—inspired by Article 3.10 of the ASADIP Principles—provides that "Colombian courts may assume jurisdiction, although this Act does not formally attribute it to them when the performance of a judicial proceeding abroad appears to be impossible. In this case, the Colombian court of the place having the closest links with the object of the litigation shall have jurisdiction" (Article 19).[30]

Let us now examine the criteria for international jurisdiction established by Colombian private international law.

3 Criteria for International Jurisdiction in Colombian Private International Law

3.1 A Necessary Preliminary Note

As it is explained in the Chap. "General Institutions in Colombian Private International Law", Colombian private international law does not have rules for the characterization of the elements of the conflict rules. This also applies to the rules on international jurisdiction. Thus, the subsumption of a specific case in the factual situation of a rule on international jurisdiction and the interpretation of the attributive criteria contained in the chosen rule depends on an *ex lege fori* characterization, unless a particular treaty proves otherwise by means of an autonomous characterization. The latter is the case of the Montevideo Treaty on International Civil Law which, in Title II, provides autonomous characterizations for domicile.

Outside the scope of application of the Treaty, it must be considered, for example, that the reference of a rule to domicile will lead to understand this criterion in

[29] Madrid and Ochoa (2015, pp. 281 ff).

[30] Similarly, Article 3136 of the Civil Code of Québec provides: "Even if an authority in Québec does not have jurisdiction to hear a dispute, it may, however, if an action abroad proves impossible or if it cannot be required to be brought there, hear the dispute if it has a sufficient connection with Québec".

the terms of Articles 76 to 86 of the Colombian Civil Code.[31] Thus, in the case of natural persons, the domicile will be in the place where they have their "residence accompanied, actually or presumptively, by the intention to remain there" (Article 76). Similarly, if the rule establishes as a criterion of international jurisdiction the place of performance of an obligation, this place will be understood as that "designated by convention" (Article 1645 Civil Code) and, in the absence of an election, in the case of a certain good, it will be the place where it was located at the time of the birth of the obligation and, in other cases, the domicile of the debtor (Article 1646 Civil Code). The same would occur with the place of performance of a contract, understood as the place of residence of the offeror (Article 864 Code of Commerce[32]).

3.2 *International Jurisdiction in International Treaties*

3.2.1 Bilateral Treaty with Ecuador

In a title entitled "Competence of the national courts over legal acts performed outside the Republic, and over those celebrated by foreigners who do not reside in the Republic", the bilateral treaty with Ecuador provides some criteria of international jurisdiction designed essentially for contractual relationships. First, the general forum of the defendant's domicile is recognized for contracts entered abroad. Indeed, Article XXIV of the Treaty provides that "[t]hose who have a domicile established in the Republic, whether nationals or foreigners and whether present or absent, may be sued before the territorial courts for the performance of contracts entered into in the other country". Thus, in the case of a contract executed in Ecuador, the Colombian courts may hear the case if the defendant is domiciled in Colombia.

If the defendant is domiciled abroad, Article XXV provides that the Colombian courts shall have international jurisdiction if the contract was entered into with a Colombian national or with a foreigner domiciled in Colombia. Furthermore, according to Article XXVI, foreigners, "even if they are absent", may be sued in Colombia, to comply with obligations contracted or to be performed in Colombia; when real action is brought against them concerning property located in Colombia; and, finally, "[i]f it has been stipulated that the Tribunals of the Republic shall decide disputes relating to obligations contracted in the other country". This last expression seems to include the choice of forum agreements.[33] Thus, if the parties have decided to submit the dispute to the Colombian courts, even if the contracts were entered into abroad, the Colombian courts will have international jurisdiction to hear the matter.

---

[31] Act No. 84 of 1873 (May 26).

[32] Decree No. 410 of 1971 (March 27).

[33] This has been admitted by: Zapata de Arbeláez (2010, p. 50).

3.2.2 Treaties of Montevideo

Title XIV of the Treaty of Montevideo on International Civil Law contains criteria conferring "jurisdiction" for the various relationships regulated by this treaty. In the first place, concerning the so-called "personal actions", that is, actions that protect obligations, and that can only be brought against the obligor and his/her heirs, Article 56 provides that they must be brought "before the judges of the place to whose law the act that is the subject matter of the suit is subject".

Article 56 thus refers to the so-called principle of parallelism, also known as the Asser criterion,[34] since this author is recognized as the first to refer to this rule, which implies an inversion of the logical order of operation of private international law, by making international jurisdiction dependent on the determination of the applicable law.[35] Asser based this principle on convenience since the judge of the state whose law is competent is the best judge to hear the case. In no way is this principle formulated as one of exclusive jurisdiction since this would deny the extraterritoriality of the law.[36] However, it should be borne in mind that this principle does not work properly if the applicable law is not known at the beginning of the proceeding nor does it achieve its purpose in cases where several laws are to be applied since international jurisdiction can only reside in one law.[37]

This criterion was strongly challenged by von Bar, in whose opinion the principle of parallelism destroys the foundations of private international law, and rather the court whose law has given decisive form to the act should be considered. Thus, although it may seem that the first step is the determination of the applicable law, as in the case of parallelism, in fact, the starting point is the determination of jurisdiction and, on this basis, its private international law will determine the substantive law that will give decisive form to the act. The contract, for example, receives its decisive form from the law of the place of its conclusion or performance, depending on what is indicated by the conflict rule of the judge.[38]

The other criterion enshrined in Article 56 is the defendant's domicile. With respect to this criterion, the doctrine has held that it works as a "concurrent forum" in favor of both parties. Indeed, from the defendant's point of view, this forum gives him the facility to litigate before the courts of his/her own domicile, avoiding the inconvenience of appearing before a foreign court. For the plaintiff, this criterion is beneficial since the debtor's domicile usually coincides with the place where the assets on which it may eventually enforce its claim are located.[39]

After this general rule, the Treaty of Montevideo on International Civil Law establishes solutions for particular cases, some of which are due to the time of the

---

[34] See Vescovi (2000, p. 42).

[35] See Hernández-Bretón (2004, p. 83).

[36] Asser (1893, p. 176).

[37] Goldschmidt (1954, pp. 74–75).

[38] von Bar (1889, pp. 427 ff.).

[39] Dreyzin et al. (2003, pp. 169–170).

treaty and which, rather than providing realistic answers to cases of private international law, generate some problems.

In this regard, for matters related to the status and capacity of persons, the treaty declares the courts of the last domicile of the alleged absentee to be competent for all matters relating to the declaration of absence (Article 57). Concerning the capacity or incapacity of persons for the exercise of civil rights, the judges of the domicile of the person shall have international jurisdiction (Article 58). For actions relating to the personal aspects of parental authority and guardianship and curatorship over minors and incapable persons, the courts of the domicile of the parents, guardians, or curators shall have international jurisdiction (Article 59). On the other hand, for matters relating to the assets of the incapable, the courts of the place where such assets are located shall have international jurisdiction (Article 60). Finally, the rendering of accounts of guardians and curators will be made before the judge of the place in which the position was granted (Article 61).

Concerning the personal effects of the marriage and its termination by nullity, divorce, or dissolution, the judges of the conjugal domicile will have international jurisdiction (Article 62). Actions in respect of marital property, on the other hand, must be brought in the courts of the place where the property is located (Article 63). This last solution can generate multiple inconveniences when the marital property is composed of assets located in more than one state, since this criterion, territorialist, can lead to a concurrence of competent courts, with the problems referred to above.

The same can be said of the solution adopted by the Treaty in matters of succession, since in such a case, Article 66 provides that the courts "of the places where the inherited property is situated" shall have jurisdiction. The Treaty assumes that in matters of succession, the real element—the form of transfer of ownership—is more important than the personal element—continuity of the legal personality of the *de cuius*—which leads, with the usual problems, to a splitting of jurisdiction and the concurrence of several courts having jurisdiction to hear the same case, which may give contradictory judgments.

The regulation of successions—disregarding the fact that it deals with entire estates (*universitas iuris*)—in no way differs from the solution adopted for the assets individually considered. Indeed, following Article 67, actions *in rem* and mixed actions shall be heard by the courts of the place of location of the property and, in the case of an action relating to several properties located in different places, the court of the place of each of the properties may hear the case.

Now, regarding the persons and the family, Article 64 of the Montevideo Treaty establishes a kind of *forum necessitatis*, by admitting the competence of the courts of the residence of the persons to dictate urgent measures relating to personal relations between spouses and to the exercise of parental authority and guardianship. Through the *forum necessitatis* it is "recognized that the judge may accept international jurisdiction, even if in principle he does not have it, with the aim of avoiding the denial of justice".[40] With this idea in mind and inspired by Article 43 of the Venezuelan Act on Private International Law, the IADIP Draft provides in Article 33 that "Colombian courts may order protective measures for persons who are in Colombia, even if they lack jurisdiction to hear the merits of the dispute".

Finally, the Montevideo Treaty on International Civil Law establishes a special solution for cases in which the existence or dissolution of civil companies is disputed. In such cases, the courts of the domicile of the corporation will have jurisdiction (Article 67).

The Montevideo Treaty on International Commercial Law, on the other hand, contains rules that establish international jurisdiction criteria for particular matters, without there being a general rule for commercial relations. Thus, concerning commercial companies in general, Article 7 provides that "if a company domiciled in one State carries out operations in another which give rise to legal disputes, it may be sued in the courts of the latter State". In the case of a branch, its operations shall be subject to the courts of its domicile, this being understood as the place in which it operates (Article 6).

In the case of insurance, claims against insurers must be brought in the courts of their domicile (Article 10). For actions related to collisions, the courts of the state in whose waters these events take place shall have international jurisdiction (Article 11) and, in the case of collisions in international waters, the courts of the place where the vessel first arrives after the event shall have international jurisdiction (Article 12). A similar solution is established for cases of shipwreck, with the particularity that if the shipwreck occurs in waters not subject to the jurisdiction of any state, the courts of the flag of the ship or of the domicile of the defendant will have jurisdiction, at the option of the plaintiff (Article 13).

In the case of a contract of affreightment, "the courts of the country in which the shipping agency with which the charterer has contracted shall have jurisdiction" (Article 14), but if the agency does not exist at the time of the commencement of the litigation, the court of the domicile of any of the parties or representatives of the company shall have international jurisdiction. If the charterer acts as plaintiff, he/she may apply to the courts of the charterer's domicile (Article 15).

The courts of the place of location of the goods on which a loan has been made shall have international jurisdiction to hear actions brought between the giver and the payer. If the loan cannot be enforced on such goods, the courts of the place where the contract was made or of the domicile of the defendant may be seized (Article 18). The courts of the port in which the voyage terminates shall be competent to hear cases of particular damage (Article 23); whereas the general average shall be heard by the courts of the state in which the cargo is delivered (Article 24), but if the voyage is revoked before departure or the vessel is forced to return to the port of loading, the courts of that port shall be competent to hear the case (Article 25).

Finally, while lawsuits arising from securities will be brought before the courts of the domicile of the defendant (Article 34), bankruptcy cases will be heard before

[40] Bardel and Merino (2023, p. 178).

the judges of the domicile of the bankrupt (Article 35) and, if the latter has more than one domicile, the courts of those domiciles will have international jurisdiction (Article 35), a solution with which the Treaty addresses the aforementioned problem of fragmenting the relationship between different jurisdictions.

3.2.3 Inter-American Conventions

Within the codification promoted by the Organization of American States, three conventions are of interest to this topic. The first is the Inter-American Convention on the International Return of Children, Article 6 of which provides that "[j]udicial or administrative authorities of the State Party in which the child habitually resided immediately before the removal or retention shall have jurisdiction to consider a petition for the child's return".

The first thing to note is that the cited rule refers to judicial or administrative authorities of the place of the child's habitual residence. This inclusion of the administrative authorities is because in some states the return proceedings—as well as others in family matters, as will be noted below—do not give rise to a judicial process but to an administrative action. In addition, it is stated that it is the place where the child was habitually resident at the time "immediately before the removal or retention"; this is intended to avoid possible misunderstandings at the time of determining jurisdiction.

The Convention also establishes a kind of *forum necessitatis* for urgent cases, which allows the plaintiff to choose between the authorities of the state party where the child was wrongfully removed or retained or the state party where the wrongful act or fact giving rise to the claim occurred. This alternativity seems to be motivated by the need to ensure the possibility of return, since the merits of the dispute fall within the international jurisdiction of the judge of the child's habitual residence.

The second instrument of interest is the Inter-American Convention on Support Obligations, which devotes Articles 8 and 9 to the regulation of "Jurisdiction". Thus, as a general rule, Article 8 allows the plaintiff to choose between the "judge or authority" —this is another situation that has been de-judicialized—of the creditor's domicile or habitual residence; the "judge or authority" of the debtor's domicile or habitual residence; or the judge or authority "of the State to which the debtor is connected by personal links such as possessing property, receiving income or obtaining financial benefits", the latter to ensure the enforcement of a possible judgment. The same rule admits the jurisdiction of any other state, provided that the defendant has entered an appearance without challenging the jurisdiction of the court.

If what is sought is an increase in the amount of support, the international jurisdiction will correspond to the judges and authorities referred to above, but the action for the termination or reduction of support must be brought before the same judge or authority that fixed it (Article 9).

Third, the Inter-American Convention on Conflicts of Laws concerning the Adoption of Minors begins by admitting the jurisdiction of the authorities of the adoptee's habitual residence to decree the adoption (Article 15), and then provides that the annulment or revocation of the adoption shall be within the jurisdiction of the courts of the place of the adoptee's habitual residence (Article 16.1). In addition, "the conversion, where it is permitted, of simple adoption into full adoption, adoptive legitimation, or similar institutions" may be brought, at the option of the plaintiff, before "the authorities of the State of habitual residence of the adoptee at the time of the adoption; those of the State of domicile of the adopter (or adopters); or those of the State of domicile of the adoptee, if he has a domicile of his own at the time the conversion is requested" (Article 16.2).

Finally, "[t]he judges of the State of the domicile of the adopter (or adopters) shall be competent to rule on matters concerning the relations between the adoptee and the adopter (or adopters) and the family thereof until the adoptee has a domicile of his own", but "[a]s soon as the adoptee has his own domicile, the judge of the domicile of the adoptee or that of the adopter (or adopters) shall, at the option of the petitioner, have jurisdiction" (Article 17).

3.3 *Domestic Regulation*

As said earlier, there are no rules on international jurisdiction in Colombian Private International Law from a state source, so "[o]nly by resorting to the rules of jurisdiction of each judge would it be possible to know whether the matter can be heard by the Colombian courts".[41] Therefore, recourse must be had to the rules on territorial jurisdiction laid down by the General Code of Procedure, and these rules, according to Orejudo Prieto de los Mozos, constitute a monist model, in the sense that "a Colombian judge will be competent in international litigious situations if the rules on territorial jurisdiction grant him/her jurisdiction".[42]

When it comes to the application of rules on territorial jurisdiction to the determination of international jurisdiction, it is necessary to read them from an international perspective.[43] Indeed, although this situation has not historically been rare to Private International Law, having special rules for international jurisdiction, distinct from the rules of domestic jurisdiction, provides clarity to the extent that each regulation serves its own interests, which do not always coincide.[44] However, the fact remains that, although only from a proceduralist conception could be admitted the transposition of rules of internal territorial jurisdiction to the regulation of

[41] Zuleta (2010).

[42] Orejudo (2013, p. 687).

[43] Marín Fuentes affirms that international judicial competence "ends up being absorbed by merely domestic jurisdictional competence". See Marín Fuentes (2016b, p. 206).

[44] Kropholler (2001, p. 568).

international jurisdiction,[45] in France even today, the determination of international jurisdiction depends on the rules of internal territorial jurisdiction.[46]

Article 28.1 of the General Code of Procedure begins by establishing, for "contentious proceedings", that if the defendant is domiciled in Colombia, the Colombian courts may hear the case. However, this criterion operates, as the rule itself admits, "unless otherwise provided by law", which implies its residual nature. Thus, the other special criteria established in Article 28 of the General Code of Procedure will be applied in preference to the criterion of the defendant's domicile. As stated briefly below, in some cases, the domicile of the defendant is excluded—granting "privative" jurisdiction to a different forum—and in other cases, it constitutes an alternative to the special criterion—for which the Code uses the expression "shall also have jurisdiction".

In contrast to this rule, the IADIP Project admits the criterion of the defendant's domicile as a general rule. Indeed, according to Article 18, "Colombian courts shall have jurisdiction to hear all types of civil and commercial cases when the defendant, regardless of his/her nationality, is domiciled in Colombia". If the defendant is domiciled outside Colombia, the jurisdiction of the Colombian courts will be determined in accordance with the special criteria established in Articles 21 to 33 (Article 20), to which I will refer below.

In any case, it is worth mentioning that the Draft devotes its third chapter to establishing autonomous characterizations for domicile, which are applicable, as recognized in Article 16, to cases of determination of the competent court. Thus, in the case of natural persons, domicile is "in the territory of the state where he/she has his/her habitual residence with the intention of exercising his/her rights there" (Article 11). For legal entities, the domicile "is in the State where the principal place of business or professional activities of the legal entity is located" (Article 15).

Well, before taking a look at the main special criteria, it is necessary to consider that Article 28.1 also provides that, in case of a plurality of defendants with different domiciles, the plaintiff may choose among them, so that, in a private international law case, if at least one of the defendants is domiciled in Colombia, the Colombian courts will have international jurisdiction to hear the case, if the plaintiff so chooses.

Next, the legislator in Article 28.1 establishes the rule closest to a regulation of Private International Law, by providing that if the defendant is not domiciled in Colombia, the judge of his/her residence will have jurisdiction, provided that it is in Colombia. If the defendant does not have a residence in Colombia either, its courts will have jurisdiction if the plaintiff has his/her domicile here. This solution, however, could violate the right of access to justice of the defendant who is not domiciled in Colombia and may make the process more expensive by requiring service abroad.

---

[45] Although Guerra Hernández recognizes it as inconvenient "to extrapolate the rules on domestic jurisdiction by territory to PIL cases", he ends up admitting that there seems to be no other way to avoid a possible denial of justice. See Guerra Hernández (2016, pp. 356–358 and 367).

[46] Bureau and Muir Watt (2010, pp. 146, 148).

In family law matters, Article 28.2 distinguishes between two cases. In the first place, proceedings relating to support obligation, annulment of civil marriage and divorce, cessation of civil effects, separation of bodies and property, declaration of existence of de facto marital union, liquidation of conjugal or patrimonial partnership, and in the precautionary measures on persons or property linked to such proceedings or to the annulment of catholic marriage, in which case, "the court of the previous common domicile will also have jurisdiction"—which suggests alternativity with the domicile of the defendant—provided that the plaintiff keeps it.

The second case refers to "proceedings for support obligation, loss or suspension of parental authority, investigation or challenge of paternity or maternity, custody, personal care and regulation of visits, permission to leave the country, precautionary measures on persons or property related to such proceedings, in which the child or adolescent is plaintiff or defendant". In this case, "the jurisdiction corresponds exclusively to the judge of the domicile or residence of the child or adolescent". Unlike the previous assumption, with the expression I have highlighted, in this case, the jurisdiction of the defendant's domicile does not seem to operate.

In family law, the IADIP Draft contains three rules that provide for jurisdiction in matters of marriage, filiation, and adoption. Thus, Article 21 recognizes, with respect to marriage, the right of foreign citizens to marry in Colombia before competent Colombian authorities.[47] It also provides that "Colombian courts are competent to hear any lawsuit concerning the validity of the marriage and its effects when one of the spouses is domiciled in Colombia".

According to Article 22 of the Draft, filiation and other relations between parents and children may be litigated in Colombia if, at the time of the lawsuit, the person whose filiation is involved or the person whose paternity or maternity is invoked or contested, is domiciled in Colombia; or if both have Colombian nationality. For adoption, as provided in Article 23, Colombian courts will have international jurisdiction if the person whose adoption is involved is domiciled in Colombia at the time of the adoption.

To hear actions relating to contracts, Article 28.3 of the General Code of Procedure provides that "the judge of the place of performance of any of the obligations is also competent", which means that the plaintiff may sue in Colombia whether the contract is to be performed in Colombia or whether the defendant is domiciled in Colombia. However, the most problematic aspect of this rule is that its final part provides that "[t]he stipulation of contractual domicile for judicial purposes shall be deemed not to be written", which seems to exclude the possibility of agreeing on choice of forum clauses, which means leaving aside the main criterion recognized in different national systems for international contracts.

---

[47] Under the current system, Colombian authorities may only witness a marriage between Colombians, or between a foreigner and a Colombian. If both parties are foreigners, the marriage must be celebrated before diplomatic or consular authorities of the foreign country. This is provided for in Article 1 of Act No. 266 of 1938 (December 21).

Assuming a solution similar to the one accepted by the French scholars[48] and case law,[49] interpreting the similar solution in Article 48 of the Code of Civil Procedure of 1975, Zapata de Arbeláez argues that the limitation established in Article 28.3 of the General Code of Procedure, "is only applicable in the domestic issues and should not be interpreted in the sense of preventing the principle of free will to operate in international contracts", therefore, the author considers "as valid the clauses that modify the rules of territorial jurisdiction".[50]

Colombian case law, on the other hand, seems to go in the opposite direction by rejecting the possibility of agreeing on the choice of court agreements. Although analyses have been made when assessing the derogatory effect of these agreements on the jurisdiction of Colombian courts, it certainly contrasts the favorable attitude towards the choice of law clauses while proscribing the possibility of choosing the court, on the understanding that contractual autonomy would be limited to the choice of an arbitral tribunal and the choice of the applicable law, excluding any possibility of modifying the rules on jurisdiction.[51] It is unclear, however, the effect of a choice of court agreement extending jurisdiction to Colombian courts, i.e., when there is no other element conferring jurisdiction other than the will of the parties.

In any event, this shortcoming of the system—which reinforces the need for a reform of Colombian private international law—contrasts with the broad admission of the derogatory effects of arbitration, both domestic and international, in Act No. 1563 of 2012 (July 12). Indeed, in matters of arbitration, it is recognized that before an arbitration agreement, the "judicial authority to which a dispute is submitted on a matter that is the subject of an arbitration agreement shall refer the parties to arbitration if so requested by any of them, at the latest, in the opportunity for the answer to the claim" (Article 70).

In contractual matters, the IADIP Draft clearly distinguishes between the positive and negative effects of choice of court agreements. The negative or derogatory effect of choice of court agreements is admitted by Article 27 of the Draft, by providing that "[w]hen the parties in their agreement validly choose a foreign court, the Colombian court must decline jurisdiction, unless it is a case of exclusive jurisdiction of the Colombian courts".

Regarding the positive effect, that is, the possibility of choosing a Colombian court, it is admitted both for freely negotiated contracts—"those in which the parties

---

[48] Bureau and Muir Watt (2007, pp. 266–267).

[49] Cass. civ. 19 février 1930, *Mardelé v. Muller*, in: *Revue Critique de Droit International Privé*, 1931, pp. 514 ff. Cass. civ. 17 décembre 1985, *Cie. De Signaux et d'Entreprise Électriques v. Société Sorelex*, in: https://www.legifrance.gouv.fr/affichJuriJudi.do?oldAction=rechExpJuriJudi&idTexte=JURITEXT000007015807&fastReqId=525994944&fastPos=1

[50] Zapata de Arbeláez (2003, p. 378).

[51] Supreme Court of Justice, Civil Cassation Chamber, judgment of April 18, 2002, file T-1100122030002002-0109-01. Superior Court of the Judicial District of Bogotá, Civil Chamber, judgment of March 27, 2009, File 242001429 01, April 30, 2002, *Ace Seguros, S.A. v. Gecolsa, S.A.* et al.

have equal bargaining power" (Article 24.3)—and for asymmetric contracts—"those in which one of the parties does not have equal or equivalent bargaining power"—but in the latter case the choice of the court must take place "after the dispute has been initiated". This is a limitation that constitutes a kind of protection for the weaker party (Article 25.3).

In both cases, the election may be express or tacit. The expression "the express choice of the Colombian courts must be established in writing" is to be interpreted in the light of the principle of functional equivalence contained in Article 6 of Act 527 of 1999 (August 18), to admit that the choice is contained in an exchange of data messages. The tacit choice—derived from the conduct of the parties—"will derive from the conduct of the plaintiff when filing the lawsuit and on the part of the defendant when performing any action at trial other than opposing the lack of jurisdiction" (Article 26).

For cases in which the parties do not agree on a choice of forum agreement, in the case of freely negotiated contracts, Colombian courts will have international jurisdiction when the contract has been concluded in Colombia; or when the disputed obligation has been or must be performed in Colombia (Article 24.1 and 2). If the contract is asymmetric, jurisdiction will be attributed to the Colombian courts if the party with less bargaining power is domiciled in Colombia, even when acting as plaintiff; or when the disputed obligation has been or must be performed in Colombia (Article 25.1 and 2).

Now, back to Article 28 of the General Code of Procedure, I must refer that, according to paragraph 6, in cases of actions relating to tort liability, the judge of the place where the act occurred shall also have jurisdiction. The solution contained in Article 28 of the Draft IADIP contains in this matter alternative forums that overcome the problematic characterization of the place where the wrongful act occurred, as an expression of the principle of *forum delicti commissi*. Thus, Article 28 allows the plaintiff to file its claim before the Colombian courts in cases where the event giving rise to the obligation has occurred in Colombia; or when the harmful effect has occurred or threatens to occur, in whole or in part, in Colombia. As a particular fact, it should be noted that the parties may decide to expressly or tacitly submit to the Colombian courts, provided that such submission occurs after the occurrence of the event.

For actions *in rem*—exercise of rights in rem, division proceedings, demarcation, expropriation, easements, possessory proceedings of any nature, restitution of tenancy, declaration of ownership and of vacant and unclaimed property—"the judge of the place where the property is located shall have exclusive jurisdiction" (Article 28.7). Thus, if the property is in Colombia, the Colombian courts will have international jurisdiction. In this matter, the IADIP Project does not contain any criterion of jurisdiction, however, it recognizes as having exclusive jurisdiction the cases in which "rights in immovable property located in Colombia" are discussed (Article 32). In any case, this case of exclusive jurisdiction is characterized by the Draft as exceptional, so it "must be interpreted restrictively, and cannot be extended to other issues that may arise concerning the same matter" (Article 32).

In the case of entire estates, the General Code of Procedure expressly refers to two cases. The first refers to bankruptcy proceedings, for which "the judge of the domicile of the debtor shall have exclusive jurisdiction" (Article 28.8). This solution suggests that if any of the assets that form part of the insolvent party patrimony are located in Colombia, the Colombian courts will have jurisdiction to hear the case. It should also be noted that for acts of international cooperation requested by foreign authorities in cross-border insolvency proceedings, the Superintendence of Corporations and the courts of the debtor's principal domicile will have jurisdiction. This is in accordance with Article 89 of Act No. 1116 of 2006 (December 27), which establishes the corporate insolvency regime in the Republic of Colombia.

The second case of entire estates regulated by the General Code of Procedure is related to successions. Thus, Article 28.12, provides that "[i]n succession proceedings, the judge of the last domicile of the deceased in the national territory shall have jurisdiction, and in the event that at his death he had several, the one corresponding to the main seat of his business". This solution, unlike the one established in the Montevideo Treaty on International Civil Law, tends to the unitary treatment of succession.

The IADIP Draft, on the other hand, does not distinguish between the different cases of entire estates and establishes, in general, that for actions related to them, Colombian courts will have international jurisdiction if the domicile of the debtor or assets that form an integral part of the entire estate are in Colombia (Article 30).

However, both the General Code of Procedure and the IADIP Draft establish special criteria for the case of actions for the protection of intellectual property. Thus, Article 28.11 of the procedural rule provides for the jurisdiction of the court of "the place where the right was violated or the act was performed, or where it takes effect if it was performed abroad, or the place where the company or establishment operates or where the defendant exercises the activity when the violation or the act is linked to these places". This same criterion applies to cases of unfair competition. Article 29 of the IADIP Draft, on the other hand, admits the international jurisdiction of Colombian courts when the defendant is domiciled in Colombia or, failing that, when the protection of the right is invoked before a Colombian court.

With respect to legal entities, the General Code of Procedure refers to two cases, the first one relating to cases of nullity, dissolution and liquidation of companies, disputes between partners in relation to the company, for which the court of the main domicile of the company shall have jurisdiction (Article 28.4); and the second one, referring to proceedings against the legal entity, which may be brought before the courts of its main domicile (Article 28.4); and the second, referring to proceedings against the legal entity, which may be brought before the courts of its main domicile; and, "in the case of matters related to a branch or agency, the judge of the branch or agency and the judge of the agency shall have jurisdiction, on a preventive basis" (Article 28.5). The IADIP Draft is silent in this respect.

Finally, in cases of voluntary jurisdiction, Article 28.13 of the General Code of Procedure distinguishes between cases of guardianship of children or adolescents, and guardianship of persons with disabilities, for which the court of the residence of the incapacitated person will have jurisdiction; cases of declaration of absence or death due to disappearance of a person, for which the court of the last domicile of the absent or disappeared person will have jurisdiction; and "other cases", which will be heard by the court of the domicile of the person promoting the voluntary jurisdiction proceeding. The IADIP Draft simplifies the solution, indicating the competence of the Colombian courts "to hear acts of voluntary jurisdiction when the person who motivates them has or has had his/her domicile in Colombia" (Article 31).

4 Conclusion

International jurisdiction is a fundamental pillar in the structure of private international law. It defines the capacity of the courts of a state to hear and decide disputes involving foreign elements. The determination of such jurisdiction not only influences the forum in which the dispute will be resolved but also impacts the legal system applicable to the merits of the case, thus affecting the rights and obligations of the parties involved. In this context, it is crucial that states develop clear and precise regulations governing international jurisdiction, thus promoting the protection of transnational access to justice and legal certainty at the international level.

In Colombia, the current regulatory framework presents an obsolete approach by continuing to resort to the rules on domestic territorial jurisdiction, which can result in complex situations that can undermine the effectiveness of the judicial system and transnational access to justice. Therefore, the need for a system of private international law for Colombia that includes an effective regulation designed from access to justice for the determination of the international jurisdiction of Colombian courts is highlighted.

References

Asser TMC (1893) Derecho internacional privado. Completada por A. Rivier (translated by Fernández Prida J). La España Moderna, Madrid

Bardel D, Merino Calle I (2023) El foro de necesidad y el acceso internacional a la justicia ante la vulneración de derecho humanos por partes de sujetos económicos privados. Cuadernos de Derecho Transnacional 15(2):167

Brand RA (2013) Challenges to forum non conveniens. N Y Univ J Int Law Polit 45:1003

Bureau D, Muir Watt H (2007) Droit international privé 2. Partie spéciale. Presses Universitaires de France, Paris

Bureau D, Muir Watt H (2010) Droit international privé 1. Partie general. Presses Universitaires de France, Paris

Dreyzin de Klor A, Uriondo de Martinoli A, Noodt Taquela MB (2003) Dimensiones convencional e institucional de los sistemas de jurisdicción internacional de los Estados mercosureños. In: Fernández Arroyo D (ed) Derecho internacional privado de los Estados del MERCOSUR. Zavalia, Buenos Aires, p 169

Espinar Vicente JM (1988) Derecho procesal civil internacional. La Ley, Madrid

Esplugues Mota C (2002) Aspectos de derecho internacional privado de la nueva Ley de Enjuiciamiento. Revista de Derecho, Universitat de València 2002:1
Goldschmidt W (1954) Sistema y filosofía del derecho internacional privado, vol III, 2nd edn. Ediciones Jurídicas Europa América, Buenos Aires
Guerra Hernández VH (2016) Conflictos de jurisdicción y competencia en el derecho internacional privado. In: García Matamoros L, Aljure Salame A (eds) Teoría general del derecho internacional privado. Legis and Universidad del Rosario, Bogota, p 349
Hernández-Bretón E (2004) Problemas contemporáneos de derecho procesal civil internacional venezolano. Editorial Sherwood, Caracas
Kropholler J (2001) Internationales Privatrecht: einschließlich der Grundbegriffe des Internationalen Zivilverfahrensrechts, 4th edn. Mohr Siebeck, Tubingen
Madrid Martínez C (2010) Criterios atributivos de jurisdicción en el sistema venezolano de derecho internacional privado. In: Derecho procesal civil internacional. Academia de Ciencias Políticas y Sociales, Universidad Central de Venezuela, Caracas
Madrid Martínez C, Ochoa Muñoz J (2015) Problemas de acceso trasnacional a la justicia en el Derecho internacional privado. Perspectiva latinoamericana. In: Secretaría General de la OEA, XLI Curso de Derecho Internacional, Washington, p 281
Marín Fuentes JL (2016a) Derecho procesal civil internacional. Universidad de Medellín, Medellín
Marín Fuentes JL (2016b) La competencia judicial en Colombia, una mirada desde el derecho internacional privado. Revista de Derecho Privado 9:195
Orejudo Prieto de los Mozos P (2013) El derecho internacional privado colombiano ante la Ley Modelo OHADAC de Derecho Internacional Privado. Anuario Español de Derecho internacional privado XIII:681
Pfeiffer T (1995) Internationales Zuständigkeit und prozessuale Gerechtigkeit. Die internationale Zuständigkeit im Zivilprozess zwischen effektivem Rechtsschutz und nationaler Zuständigkeitspolitik. Vittorio Klostermann, Frankfurt am Main
Rojas Gómez ME (2013) Lecciones de derecho procesal, 5th edn. ESAJU, Bogota
Scelle G (1932) Précis de droit des gen, vol 1. Sirey, Paris
Schack H (2002) Internationales Zivilverfahrensrecht: ein Studienbuch, 3th edn. Beck, Munich
Vescovi E (2000) Derecho procesal civil internacional, Uruguay, el Mercosur y América. Ediciones Idea, Montevideo
Virgós Soriano M, Garcimartín Alférez F (2000) Derecho procesal civil internacional. Litigación internacional. Civitas, Madrid
Von Bar CL (1889) Theorie und praxis des internationalen Privatrechts, vol II, 2nd edn. Hahn, Hannover
Zapata de Arbeláez A (2003) Validez de las cláusulas atributivas de jurisdicción en la contratación internacional. Perspectiva de derecho colombiano. In: Zapata de Arbeláez A (ed) Derecho internacional de los negocios. Alcances, vol III. Universidad Externado de Colombia, Bogota, p 357
Zapata de Arbeláez A (2010) El régimen jurídico de los contratos internacionales en Colombia. In: Zapata de Arbeláez A (ed) Derecho internacional de los negocios. Alcances, vol III. Universidad Externado de Colombia, Bogota, p 13
Zapata Giraldo A (2017) Colombia. In: Basedow J, Rühl G, Ferrari F, Miguel Asensio P (eds) Encyclopedia of private international law. Edward Elgar, Cheltenham, p 1981
Zuleta Londoño A (2010) Las cláusulas de selección de foro y selección de ley en la contratación internacional: una visión desde el derecho internacional privado colombiano. Revista de Derecho Privado 44:1

Claudia Madrid Martínez PhD in Law, *Magister Scientiarum* in Private International Law and Comparative Law, and lawyer from the Universidad Central de Venezuela (UCV); postdoctoral researcher, University of Cologne, Alexander von Humboldt Foundation (2012–2014); tenured professor, Universidad Central de Venezuela; associate professor, Universidad de Antioquia; member, Research Group Knowledge, Power, and Law, Universidad de Antioquia.

International Judicial Cooperation in Colombia

Luis Alfredo Pinilla

Abstract This chapter provides an introduction to the Colombian regulation on international cooperation in civil and commercial matters. It describes the international treaties to which the country is a party, as well as the national legal framework on the subject. To this end, the chapter briefly presents the essential aspects of the most relevant treaties for Colombia. In doing so, it addresses in particular the 1965 Hague Service Convention and the 1970 Hague Evidence Convention. Furthermore, the chapter describes how letters rogatory and *exhortos* are regulated in domestic legislation. It also comments briefly on the proposal for international legal cooperation contained in the IADIP Draft General Act.

1 Introduction

As stated in the *Guide to International Judicial Cooperation* prepared by the Ministry of Foreign Affairs of Colombia, international judicial cooperation is the collaboration or mutual assistance between states to perform the procedures required for service of process, taking of evidence, and other activities related to proceedings that are carried out outside the territory of the requesting state.[1] This kind of international cooperation is thus performed by diverse acts. Apart from the service of process and evidence gathering mentioned above, the authorities also carry out the taking of testimony and statements, interrogations, or inquiries.[2]

International judicial cooperation is based on the recognition and enforcement of decisions by a foreign judicial—or even extrajudicial—authority. The main parties

[1] Ministry of Foreign Affairs of Colombia (2009, p. 9).

[2] ibid., p. 17.

L. A. Pinilla (✉)
Facultad de Jurisprudencia, Universidad del Rosario, Bogotá, Colombia
e-mail: apinilla@pinillalegal.com

M. J. Ochoa Jiménez, C. Madrid Martínez (eds.), *A Private International Law for Colombia*, Springer Textbooks in Law,
https://doi.org/10.1007/978-3-032-04106-7_6

in such a cooperative relationship are the states—one of them is the requesting state and the other one is the requested state—that act through their competent authorities in each case.[3] Behind the legal regime created to govern international judicial cooperation lies the legal impossibility of exercising coercive powers outside the borders of a state.

In order to implement international judicial cooperation, states rely primarily on bilateral or multilateral international agreements and customary law. In their absence, the domestic law of the requested state applies. Under international treaties, each state shall designate a central authority. In this way, both the requesting and the requested state can have authorities in charge of carrying out judicial cooperation in a centralized manner. These authorities issue and receive requests for judicial cooperation.

Colombia follows the continental or civil law system. Therefore, assistance is provided even in the absence of valid international cooperation agreements or treaties. This practice is based on the goodwill of the state issuing the letter of request, which is a matter of discretionary cooperation,[4] and may consider the principle of reciprocity.[5]

Now, the main international cooperation mechanisms are the letters rogatory and the *Exhorto* or *Despacho Comisorio*. The latter terms are translated into English as "letter of request" or "letter rogatory". In this regard, it is worth noting that the Inter-American Conventions refer to letters rogatory, while the Hague Conventions refer to letters of request. But, in general, international treaties may consider *exhortos* and letters rogatory as equivalent. However, under Colombian procedural law, they differ from each other.

A letter rogatory[6] is an international cooperation mechanism whereby a judicial authority in one country requests a judicial authority in another country to perform a specific judicial procedure, such as service of process, taking of evidence, or obtaining information. Letters rogatory are regulated in international treaties as well as in Colombian domestic legislation.

The *exhorto*—or *despacho comisorio*—is referred to in the Colombian Code of Civil Procedure (CGP Article 609), according to which this is requested by a judicial or administrative authority in Colombia to a Colombian consular agent to perform a specific procedure for a legal process or investigation.

Here, both terms may be considered synonymous. In what follows, a distinction will be necessary just when referring to Colombian laws and regulations.

The chapter presents the international and national framework of international judicial cooperation currently existing in Colombia and how this matter is envisaged in a legislative proposal. Section I briefly presents the essential aspects of the most relevant treaties for Colombia. In doing so, it addresses in particular two

---

[3] ibid., p. 13.

[4] Bermann et al. (2021, p. 297).

[5] ibid., p. 12.

[6] "Letters of request" may usually be known as "letters rogatory".

treaties, i.e., the Convention on the Service Abroad of Judicial and Extrajudicial Documents in Civil or Commercial Matters, adopted at The Hague on November 15, 1965 (Hague Service Convention), and the Convention on the Taking of Evidence Abroad in Civil or Commercial Matters, adopted at The Hague on March 18, 1970 (Hague Evidence Convention). Furthermore, Section II presents a short description of how letters rogatory and *exhortos* are regulated in domestic legislation. Finally, Section III comments briefly on the proposal on this subject contained in the Draft General Act on Private International Law for Colombia prepared by the *Instituto Antioqueño de Derecho Internacional Privado* (IADIP).

2 International Treaties

The following treaties deal with international cooperation in civil and commercial matters and are currently in force in Colombia: Montevideo Treaty on International Procedural Law, signed on January 11, 1889;[7] Inter-American Convention on Letters Rogatory signed in Panama on January 30, 1975;[8] Additional Protocol to the Inter-American Convention on Letters Rogatory signed in Montevideo on May 8, 1979;[9] Inter-American Convention on the Taking of Evidence Abroad in Civil or Commercial Matters signed in Panama on January 30, 1975;[10] Additional Protocol to the Inter-American Convention on the Taking of Evidence Abroad signed in La Paz on May 24, 1984;[11] Convention on the Service Abroad of Judicial and Extrajudicial Documents in Civil or Commercial Matters, signed in The Hague on November 15, 1965;[12] Convention on the Obtaining of Evidence Abroad in Civil or Commercial Matters, signed in The Hague on March 18, 1970.[13]

The following subsections describe these international instruments. The last two conventions—the Hague Service Convention and the Hague Evidence Convention—are discussed in more detail due to their global applicability, whereas the Inter-American Convention applies to the Americas and Spain. Additionally, while the Inter-American Convention is thoroughly explained and addressed in the Colombian Guide to International Judicial Cooperation, there is currently no official publication available regarding the Hague Conventions.

[7] Approval Act No. 68 of 1920.

[8] Approval Act No. 27 of 1988.

[9] Approval Act No. 27 of 1988.

[10] Approval Act No. 31 of 1987.

[11] Approval Act No. 31 of 1987.

[12] Approval Act No. 1073 of 2006.

[13] Approval Act No. 1282 of 2009.

2.1 Treaty of Montevideo on International Procedural Law (1889)

This treaty was adopted by Argentina, Bolivia, Paraguay, Peru, Uruguay, and Colombia. Its objective is to establish rules regarding the procedure by which the participating states must perform certain procedural acts[14] for the purpose of materializing international cooperation.

Within the framework of this treaty, letters rogatory may refer to garnishments, appraisals, inventories, or preventive proceedings.[15] It is worth noting that, unlike other international instruments, the Montevideo Treaty on International Procedural Law of 1889 does allow for garnishments.

2.2 Inter-American Convention on Letters Rogatory (1975)

The Inter-American Convention on Letters Rogatory (Inter-American Service Convention) was adopted at the First Specialized Inter-American Conference on Private International Law and was signed by countries of Central and South America, as well as Mexico, the United States of America, and Spain. It simplifies and standardizes the communication system between judicial authorities of different countries to obtain cooperation in procedural acts of a merely formal nature, particularly in the matter of service or process. For the purposes of this Convention, the terms "*exhortos*" or "*cartas rogatorias*" are considered synonyms in the Spanish text.[16]

This Convention applies to the letters rogatory issued in civil or commercial proceedings by the judicial bodies of a state party, which aim to: perform procedural acts of a merely formal nature, such as service of process, summonses, or subpoenas abroad, and the taking of evidence abroad, unless any reservations are expressly made in this regard.[17] However, in the interest of avoiding controversy, the Convention expressly declares "acts involving coercive enforcement" to be outside its scope of application.[18]

The Convention establishes that letters rogatory may be transmitted to the requested authority by the interested parties through judicial channels, through consular officials or diplomatic agents, or the Central Authority of the requesting or requested state, as the case may be.

Each state party must inform the General Secretariat of the Organization of American States about the competent Central Authority to receive and distribute

---

[14] Articles 1 and 2.

[15] Article 10.

[16] While the Convention equates letters rogatory with "*exhortos*", Colombian domestic legislation identifies them as separate terms (Art. 1, Convention).

[17] Article 2.

[18] Article 3. See also Parra-Aranguren (1982, p. 335).

requests or letters rogatory. In Colombia, the Central Authority is the Division of Migratory and Consular Affairs and Citizen Services of the Ministry of Foreign Affairs.

The essential formal requirements of letters rogatory are established in Article 5, which requires their translation into the official language of the requested state (b) and their proper legalization (a). The latter is not required when transmitted through consular or diplomatic channels or the central authority.[19] Letters rogatory must be accompanied by the documents that will be delivered to the required party and may include authenticated copies of the lawsuit and its annexes, as well as any texts or resolutions that serve as the basis for the requested action, to deliver them to the served or summoned party.

Letters rogatory are processed following the laws and procedural norms of the requested state (*lex fori*).[20] However, the requesting judicial body may execute the letter rogatory through a special procedure or accept the observance of additional formalities in the execution of the requested action, provided that they are not contrary to the laws of the requested state.

The costs and other expenses incurred during the processing are borne by the parties involved, but the requested state may perform the proceedings even if the letter rogatory does not indicate the person responsible for the expenses.[21]

Consular officials or diplomatic agents of the state parties may perform proceedings in the state where they are accredited, provided that they do not contradict its laws. In the execution of such proceedings, they may not employ acts involving measures of compulsion.[22] This rule limits the activity of consular officials to acts of a merely formal nature or the taking of evidence and obtaining of information abroad, as the execution of seizure measures would imply coercive action, which is prohibited in this article.

The requested state may refuse to comply with a letter rogatory when it is manifestly contrary to public order (*ordre public*).[23]

2.3 *Additional Protocol to the Inter-American Convention on Letters Rogatory (1979)*

The main purpose of the Additional Protocol to the Inter-American Service Convention is to facilitate and ensure the effective application of the Convention, in the area of official notifications and communications abroad, through the transmission of letters rogatory from the central authority of a requesting state to the central

---

[19] Article 6. See also Parra-Aranguren (1982, p. 336).

[20] Article 10.

[21] Article 12.

[22] Article 13.

[23] Article 17.

authority of a requested state.[24] This Protocol does not apply to the taking of evidence and obtaining of information abroad.

This Protocol establishes three forms that contain the formal requirements that must be fulfilled: Annex "A", which consists of the letter rogatory, Annex "B", which contains the reports to be delivered to the defendant, and Annex "C", which aims at verifying the completion of the required proceedings.

To avoid excessive costs, the Protocol only requires the translation of the copy of the summons of the request that initiates the respective procedure. All other accompanying documents and actions must be in the original language and do not require any additional legalization if they bear the seal of the requesting authority.[25]

In Colombia, this Protocol was adopted through the same law that approved the Inter-American Convention on Letters Rogatory and is currently in force. It is also in force in Chile, Ecuador, the United States, Mexico, Panama, and Uruguay.

2.4 *Inter-American Convention on the Taking of Evidence Abroad (1975)*

The purpose of the Inter-American Convention on the Taking of Evidence Abroad is to simplify and standardize the system of communication between the judicial authorities of different countries to obtain cooperation in obtaining evidence abroad.[26] It is limited to regulating the procedural aspects of obtaining or receiving evidence abroad through letters rogatory issued in judicial proceedings by judicial authorities, in civil or commercial matters.[27]

The convention is similar to the Inter-American Service Convention. It establishes the same requirements as those for processing letters rogatory. It also stipulates that the execution of the letter rogatory requires that the interested party make available to the requested judicial body the measures necessary to comply with the request.

The Convention requires that the requested action is not contrary to any legal provision of the requested state that expressly prohibits it. Compliance with a letter rogatory may also be refused if it seeks to obtain evidence prior to judicial proceedings, or when it concerns the procedure known in common law countries as pretrial discovery of documents.[28]

Article 12 considers the scenario of a refusal by the person called to testify. It expressly acknowledges the validity of invoking impediment, exception, or duty to

[24] Parra-Aranguren (1982, p. 555).

[25] Article 4. Parra-Aranguren (1982, p. 406).

[26] Preamble of the Treaty.

[27] Article 2.

[28] Article 9.

refuse testimony under the law of the requested state, or under the law of the requesting state, if specified in the request itself or confirmed by the requesting authority.

The judicial assistance provided does not imply any commitment to recognize the jurisdiction of the requesting judicial body or allow the future extraterritorial effectiveness of the final decision. Similarly, the Convention does not address the admissibility or evaluation of evidence, nor does it determine who bears the burden of proof.[29]

The procedure is the same as that outlined in the Inter-American Service Convention. One particularity of this Convention, however, is that it emphasizes the competence of *lex fori* concerning the means of coercion that may be used.

The Convention provides a detailed list of the information that must be annexed to the request for assistance. Article 4 thus requires:

1. A clear and precise statement of the purpose of the evidence requested.
2. Copies of the documents and decisions that serve as the basis and justification of the letters rogatory as well as such interrogatories and documents as may be needed for its execution.
3. The names and addresses of the parties to the proceeding, as well as of the witnesses, expert witnesses, and other persons involved, and any information needed for the taking of evidence.
4. A summary report of the proceeding and the facts giving rise to it, if needed for the taking of evidence.
5. A clear and precise statement of such special requirements or procedures as may be requested by the authority of the state of origin for the taking of evidence.

2.5 *Additional Protocol to the Inter-American Convention on the Taking of Evidence Abroad (1984)*

This Protocol was approved with the aim of strengthening and facilitating international cooperation in judicial proceedings as provided for in the Inter-American Convention on the Taking of Evidence Abroad. It was adopted in Colombian legislation by the same law that approved the Inter-American Convention on the Taking of Evidence Abroad.

According to this Protocol, each state party shall designate a central authority to perform the functions outlined in the Convention and communicate this designation to the General Secretariat of the Organization of American States.[30]

The Convention sets out two forms containing the formal requirements that must be fulfilled: Annex "A", which consists of the letter rogatory, and Annex "B", which

[29] Article 9. Parra-Aranguren (1982, p. 338).

[30] Article 1.

contains a certificate of compliance with the letter rogatory to request the taking of evidence.[31]

When the competent authority of the requested state receives the letter rogatory through judicial or diplomatic channels, it will transmit the letter to the judicial body for processing, in accordance with domestic law.[32] In turn, the requested judicial body will apply the appropriate coercive measures provided for in its legislation.[33]

The processing of letters rogatory will be free of charge. However, each state may request the requester of the evidence to pay for the processing, in accordance with its internal legislation.[34] Based on reciprocity criteria, states may specify that they will not charge for proceedings in certain matters or will only charge a fixed amount.[35]

2.6 Convention on the Service Abroad of Judicial and Extrajudicial Documents in Civil or Commercial Matters (1965)

This convention, which was signed in The Hague on November 15, 1965, and is in force in more than forty-four countries, applies in civil or commercial matters to cases in which a judicial or extrajudicial document must be sent abroad for service or delivery between two countries that are members of the Convention.

The purposes of the Convention are to ensure that judicial and extrajudicial documents requiring service of process or delivery are brought to the notice of their recipients with sufficient time, and to improve international cooperation and simplify and expedite the service process.[36]

The Convention does not define "civil or commercial matters". This has led to different interpretations among legal systems. For example, litigants from the United States have attempted to serve defendants in European countries for antitrust practices or for the collection of punitive damages, which in some countries has resulted in a refusal to proceed with these services of process as they involve public order laws or sanctions considered criminal, such as punitive damages.

[31] Article 3.

[32] Article 3.

[33] Article 4.

[34] Article 6.

[35] Article 8.

[36] Some countries were concerned about the use of a notification system known as "*notification au parquet*", whereby notification is carried out by depositing the documents with a government official of the requesting state. This Convention eliminates the possibility of such a notification mechanism operating; the idea is that the notification must inform the recipient with sufficient time to participate in the process. See Born and Rutledge (2007, p. 859).

The Convention expressly provides that its rules shall not apply when the address of the recipient of the document is unknown.[37]

According to the Convention, each state shall designate a central authority[38] to receive requests for services or transmissions from another contracting state and to proceed accordingly. Concurrently, the Convention also provides for alternative methods of service, provided they are not objected to through a reservation by the requested states.[39]

The competent authority or official, in conformity with the laws of the state of origin, shall address to the central authority of the requested state a request in accordance with the model form annexed to the Convention, without any legalization or other formality being required.[40] In Colombia, the central authority is the Division of Migratory and Consular Affairs and Citizen Services of the Ministry of Foreign Affairs.[41]

If the document is to be served, the central authority may request that the document be written in or translated into the official language—or one of the official languages—of the country. The central authority shall issue a certificate in accordance with the form annexed to the Convention. Such certificate shall describe the execution of the request, indicate the form, place, and date of execution, as well as the person to whom the document was delivered or specify the event that prevented execution.

Each contracting state is empowered to proceed directly, through its diplomatic or consular agents, to the service of judicial documents on persons abroad, without coercion. Unless the state of destination objects, the Convention does not preclude the possibility of sending judicial documents directly by post to persons in the requested state.[42] This last provision of the Convention may have a considerable impact on Colombia since the country did not make any reservation on the possibility of service by post.

Only if the requested state considers that such compliance would infringe on its sovereignty or security may it refuse to comply with a request for service under the provisions of the Convention.

---

[37] Article 1.

[38] Article 2.

[39] Colombia ratified the Convention without reservations.

[40] Article 3. It is important to remember that, in the United States of America, any lawyer authorized to practice in a US court is considered a judicial officer, and, therefore, could directly transmit their request to the central authority of the requested country. See Kurtz (2009, p. 206).

[41] http://www.hcch.net/index_es.php?act=authorities.details&aid=953

[42] Or in Colombia (Art. 10).

2.6.1 Methods of Service

The Convention provides for three methods of service reflected in three forms, two of which must be completed by the party requiring service through the central authority. These forms must be completed in English or French. However, the central authority of each country may require that the documents to be served be translated into its official language.

1. The first form contains the "Request for service abroad of a judicial or extrajudicial document", which requires service by one of three methods:
   (a) Article 5(a): by a method prescribed by its internal laws for service of documents in domestic actions concerning persons who are within its territory;
   (b) Article 5(b): by a particular method requested by the applicant, unless such method is incompatible with the law of the state addressed; or.
   (c) Article 5, second paragraph: the document may always be served by delivery to an addressee who accepts voluntarily.
2. The second form refers to the "Essential Elements of the Document". This form requires the applicant to provide a concise description of the action and to state the name and address of the requesting authority, the identity of the parties to the action, the nature and purpose of the document, and the nature and purpose of the proceedings and amount in dispute, if any.
3. The third form is the "Certification". The central authority shall transmit a certificate of service to the applicant or his attorney. The Central Authority shall certify whether the document was served; if so, the date, time, and place of service; the method by which service was performed; the identity of the individual to whom the documents were delivered; and, if the documents were not served, a note of that fact, as well as the explanatory facts.

2.6.2 Characteristics of the Methods of Service

Service in Accordance with Article 5(a)

As noted above, this consists of using a method for notification in domestic cases. In these cases, the central authorities have insisted that the application be translated into the official language, which is not required for the application itself. The central authorities of some countries, e.g., Germany and Japan, have even requested that the annexes be translated into the official language.[43]

Service in Accordance with Article 5(b)

This subparagraph allows the requesting party to ask the central authority to effect service in a particular manner. The requested state is not required to accept a form of service incompatible with its domestic law.

---

[43] Born and Rutledge (2007, p. 861).

Similarly, Article 5(b) does not require service to be accomplished in the official language, if it is accomplished in accordance with the method of service required by the requesting state. However, justice and common sense would lead us to believe that the summons should, at a minimum, be translated into the official language.

Service following Article 5, Second Paragraph

This method allows the defendant to voluntarily accept service, provided that it is consistent with local law, also known in continental civil law as simple delivery. Countries such as France, Belgium, The Netherlands, and Sweden are familiar with this type of service: Documents are left at a local police station where the defendant can voluntarily go to collect them.[44] The request is usually accompanied by a statement that the defendant is free to not accept the documents.

Additionally, the Convention does not require that service in this form must include a translation into the official language; however, the central authority may refuse to effect voluntary service of a document that is not in the official language.

2.6.3 What Happens When a Country Is a Party to Both the Inter-American Letters Rogatory Convention and the Hague Service Convention?

In general terms, when the Hague Service Convention and the Inter-American Convention on Letters Rogatory are both in force in a country, the latter shall prevail. In other words, the procedure to be followed is one regarding the letter rogatory. This was the conclusion reached by the Supreme Court of the United States of America when comparing the mandatory language of the Inter-American Convention with the permissive language of the Hague Convention.[45]

In Colombia, the Supreme Court has not issued any judgment regarding which of both conventions would prevail. It thus appears that both conventions may be used at the same time. However, it should be noted that the Hague Service Convention cannot be used if the defendant's address is unknown.

2.7 *Convention on the Taking of Evidence Abroad in Civil or Commercial Matters (1970)*

According to this Convention, which is currently in force in Colombia and in sixty-five other countries around the world,[46] in civil or commercial matters, the judicial authority of a contracting state may, in accordance with the provisions of its law, request the competent authority of another state, through letters of request, to obtain

[44] Born and Rutledge (2007, p. 862).

[45] Koh (2008, p. 185).

[46] https://www.hcch.net/en/instruments/conventions/status-table/?cid=82

evidence and perform other judicial acts. Subject to certain limitations, the authority receiving the request shall execute the letters of request it has received. The central authority then forwards the request to its local authority for execution, including coercive mechanisms, and the evidence obtained shall be returned to the requesting court.

The purpose of the Convention is to facilitate the transmission and execution of requests for evidence, as well as to improve the effectiveness of judicial cooperation in civil and commercial matters.

However, this Convention is subject to significant limitations. First, it only applies to obtaining evidence in civil and commercial matters. The Convention was drafted in the same manner as the Hague Service Convention. Likewise, the Convention does not define civil or commercial and a review of the negotiations does not reveal what the states meant these terms to encompass. For example, in the United States of America and the United Kingdom, civil or commercial issues exclude criminal matters, but include tax, administrative, or public law (antitrust law) issues.[47] The second limitation is that the Convention is limited to requests for assistance from judicial authorities, excluding agencies and bodies of the executive branch. Finally, the Convention is limited to the taking of evidence or the performance of other judicial acts. These acts are not defined in the Convention itself, but it is clear from the preparatory works that they include taking testimony, obtaining documents, and inspecting property.

The international cooperation mechanism provided for in the Convention is the letter of request.[48] The Convention provides that each contracting state shall designate a central authority responsible for receiving letters of request issued by a judicial authority of another contracting state and forwarding them to the competent authority for execution.

The central authority shall be organized according to the modalities prescribed by the requested state. Letters of request shall be forwarded to the central authority of the requested state without the intervention of another authority of that state. In Colombia, the central authority is the Division of Migratory and Consular Affairs and Citizen Services of the Ministry of Foreign Affairs.[49]

The obligation to execute letters of request has two important conditions. First, contracting states must obtain the evidence and apply appropriate coercive measures in accordance with domestic law. Second, Article 9 states that the letter of request must be executed expeditiously.

Article 12 of the Convention allows the recipient state to refuse to comply with non-judicial taking of evidence or to execute letters of request that the state considers would affect its sovereignty or security.

Pursuant to Article 23, the contracting states have the option of declaring that they will not execute letters rogatory issued for the purpose of obtaining the

[47] Born and Rutledge (2007, p. 964).

[48] Article 2.

[49] http://www.hcch.net/index_es.php?act=authorities.details&aid=944

production of documents prior to trial, as this procedure is known in common law countries.

Diplomatic officials or consular agents are authorized by Article 15 to take statements from nationals of the requesting nation. This option is nevertheless subject to several limitations: First, consuls may not use coercion to obtain the evidence. Second, a state may declare that consular agents may take evidence only after obtaining authorization from the local authority. And third, consular agents may take evidence for ongoing processes, as opposed to processes that are being studied or contemplated.

In turn, Article 16 authorizes consular agents to take the evidence of nationals of the nation where they are stationed, subject to conditions similar to those mentioned in Article 15. Article 17 authorizes commissioners[50] to take evidence in the receiving state. Although the conditions of Articles 16 and 17 are similar, in this particular case, the commissioner must be appointed by a judicial authority of the requesting state.

A letter of request shall specify the following information: the requesting authority and, if possible, the requested authority; the identity and address of the parties and, if applicable, their representatives; the nature and subject matter of the request, as well as a summary of the facts; the evidence to be obtained or any judicial proceedings to be executed. Where appropriate, the letter of request shall also state the names and addresses of the persons to be heard; the questions to be put to the persons to be examined or the subject matter about which they are to be heard; the documents or other objects to be examined; and any requirement that the statement be given under oath or by solemn affirmation, without oath.[51]

A letter of request must be written in the language of the requested authority or be accompanied by a translation into that language.

A contracting state may declare that members of the judicial personnel of the requesting authority of another contracting state may be present at the execution of a letter of request, prior authorization of the declaring state.[52]

The judicial authority executing a letter of request shall apply the laws of its own country regarding the form of execution. However, the requesting authority's request for the application of a special procedure shall be granted, unless this procedure is incompatible with the law of the requested state, or its application is impossible because of the judicial practice of the requested state or because of practical difficulties.[53]

When executing a letter of request, the requested authority shall apply the appropriate means of compulsion provided for under its domestic law in the cases and to the same extent as it would be obliged to apply to the execution of a letter rogatory from the authorities of its own state.

---

[50] Persons specifically appointed for this purpose by a court of the requesting state.

[51] Article 3.

[52] Article 8.

[53] Article 9.

A letter of request shall not be executed when the person designated therein invokes a privilege to refuse or an impediment to give evidence that has been established by the laws of either the requested or requesting state.

3 Domestic Legislation

In Colombian domestic legislation, there is a clear difference between an *exhorto* and a letter of request. An *exhorto* is a request issued by a Colombian authority, either judicial or administrative, directed to the Colombian Consul to perform certain proceedings within the context of a judicial process or administrative procedure. A letter of request is a request issued primarily by a Colombian or foreign judicial authority within the framework of a judicial process. It must be addressed to the counterpart authority in another country or in Colombia, respectively, requesting the execution of a specific judicial proceeding, taking of evidence, or that information be provided.

In this context, it is worth mentioning the regulations introduced by Act No. 2213 of 2022. During the Covid-19 pandemic, Colombia approved new regulations authorizing the service of process by email. This Act authorizes service or process by e-mail but does not differentiate between service of process in Colombia and service of process abroad.

Many appellate courts and administrative bodies have argued that, according to the principles of territoriality of Colombian laws, service of process by e-mail is valid only on Colombian territory.[54] Some administrative bodies have accepted service of process abroad by e-mail.[55]

---

[54] In the case No. 76001-31-03-009-2021-00280-01 Cervecería del Valle v. Distribuidora González Restrepo the Appelate Tibunal of Cali, decided that service by email as authorized by regulation issued during the Covid 19 pandemic was only valid if service is to be made in "Colombian territory."

[55] In Auto No. 67601, on June 26, 2023, the Ministry of Commerce, Industry and Tourism, Superintendency of Industry and Commerce stated the following: "In this scenario, the service of process of a foreign company can be carried out in two ways: through the in-person regime or by following the special provisions established for digital procedures. If the first option is chosen, the Convention signed between the states must be applied, which in this specific case would be the Inter-American Convention on Letters Rogatory, to which both Peru and Colombia are parties. This agreement was formalized in Law 27 of 1988, which outlines the procedure to be followed and even includes the forms that must be completed for the intended purposes.

Alternatively, the newly enacted Law 2213 of 2022 can be used, which introduced a special form of service via digital channels. In Article 8, it allows for the possibility of serving process to the defendant through such means. In this sense, as it is a special law that governs electronic service of process and applies the principles of speed and procedural economy, it can be applied to this type of matter, as long as the electronic address of the party to be served is known."

In the case STC7677-2021 the Colombian Supreme Court of Justice when deciding a constitutional claim (*acción de tutela*) confirmed that a company based in Israel must be served using the

The Supreme Court has not yet issued any jurisprudence or judgment on whether the notification of procedural acts by e-mail is valid.

As can be seen from the content of the treaties set forth above, such international instruments have not even considered the use of e-mail for the purpose of notification of procedural acts. In this context, it is finally worth noting that any treaty in force in Colombia must be applied by virtue of the *pacta sunt servanda* principle, given the superiority of treaties over domestic law.

4 International Legal Cooperation in the IADIP Draft General Act

The *Instituto Antioqueño de Derecho Internacional Privado* (Institute of Private International Law of Antioquia, IADIP) has prepared the Draft General Act on Private International Law for Colombia prepared by the (hereinafter, "IADIP Draft General Act").[56] This proposal is important because it is the first initiative of this kind in a long time to update the scarce and confusing regulations on private international law in Colombia.

The IADIP Draft General Act includes the regulation on judicial cooperation in Section Five (On International Legal Cooperation), specifically in Article 35 (International Legal Cooperation). According to this rule, Colombian courts may address any competent foreign authority, through letters rogatory and requests for judicial assistance, for the purpose of conducting citations, obtaining evidence, or any other judicial act necessary for the proper implementation of the process. Similarly, they shall promptly process letters rogatory and requests for judicial assistance from foreign courts that comply with the applicable principles of International Law.

Article 35 of the IADIP Draft General Act clearly reflects in written law, the commitment to international cooperation between judicial authorities, both by the judicial authority issuing the letter rogatory (active cooperation) and by the receiving state (passive cooperation), in accordance with the principles of International Law. As proposed in the IADIP Draft, Colombian courts should promptly process letters rogatory.

Hague International Convention and not by email as authorized by regulation issued during Covid 19 pandemic.

[56] Instituto Antioqueño de Derecho Internacional Privado (IADIP) (2021) Draft Bill on Private International Law for Colombia, Medellin.

5 Concluding Remarks

In conclusion, Colombia's framework for international judicial cooperation is rooted in two international systems, which are based on the Inter-American Conventions on Letters Rogatory and on the Taking of Evidence, with a regional scope, and the Hague Conventions on Service Abroad and on the Obtaining of Evidence, with a global scope.

Overall, Colombia's legal framework for international judicial cooperation seeks to balance adherence to international norms with the flexibility needed for evolving global legal practices. Nevertheless, the growing relevance of electronic communication, as exemplified by Act No. 2213, highlights new challenges that may require further clarification in future legislation or case law.

The regulation proposed by the IADIP Draft reflects, in such a context, an important step in modernizing and streamlining the legal framework, aiming to clarify procedures and enhance cooperation between judicial authorities across borders. The process of sending and receiving letters rogatory is an essential mechanism in this cooperation, and the proposed regulation emphasizes both active and passive cooperation.

References

Bermann G, William D, Childress DE (eds) (2021) Transnational litigation in a nutshell, 2nd edn. West Academic Publishing, Saint Paul

Born GB, Rutledge PB (2007) International civil litigation in the United States. Aspen Publishers, New York

Koh HH (2008) Transnational litigation in United States courts. Foundation Press, New York

Kurtz B (2009) First fundamentals of international practice. Cross-border litigation and dispute resolution. New York State Bar Association, New York

Ministry of Foreign Affairs of Colombia (2009) Guide to international judicial cooperation, Bogota

Parra-Aranguren G (1982) Codificación del derecho internacional privado en América. Universidad Central de Venezuela, Facultad de Ciencias Jurídicas y Políticas, Caracas

Luis Alfredo Pinilla Lawyer, Rosario University School of Law; specialist in Commercial Law, Andes University of Colombia; Master of Laws in General Legal Studies, New York University School of Law; Master of Laws in Corporate Law; Member of the New York State Bar.

Extraterritorial Effect of Judgments in Colombian Private International Law

María Julia Ochoa Jiménez and José Luis Marín Fuentes

Abstract This chapter deals with how the Colombian legal system addresses the recognition and enforcement of foreign judgments and arbitral awards. In order to do this, it presents the relevant rules of the General Code of Procedure Law of 2012 and Act No. 1563 of 2012. Attention is also paid to the ways in which these rules have been applied in practice by the Civil Chamber of the Supreme Court of Justice. Such a practical approach allows us to introduce the novelties included in the IADIP Draft General Act on Private International Law for Colombia.

1 Introduction

A Colombian woman and a Peruvian man married in Japan and divorced after five years in the latter country. One year later, the woman returns to Colombia and claims that her status as a divorced woman be recognized in Colombian territory.[1] A Colombian company signed an agreement in Moscow with a company from the United States, one of the clauses of which states that any dispute related to that agreement will be resolved by arbitration in New York. Once a dispute between both companies has been resolved in accordance with such clause, the winning party demands that the arbitration award be recognized in Colombia.[2] Are the

[1] Supreme Court of Justice, Civil Chamber, Judgment of February 22, 2017, No. SC2228-2017.

[2] Supreme Court of Justice, Civil Chamber, Judgment of July 27, 2011, No. 11001-0203-000-2007-01956-00.

M. J. Ochoa Jiménez (✉)
Loyola University, Sevilla, Andalucía, Spain
e-mail: mjochoa@uloyola.es

J. L. Marín Fuentes
Facultad de Derecho, Universidad de Medellín, Medellín, Colombia
e-mail: jlmarin@udemedellin.edu.co

M. J. Ochoa Jiménez, C. Madrid Martínez (eds.), *A Private International Law for Colombia*, Springer Textbooks in Law,
https://doi.org/10.1007/978-3-032-04106-7_7

divorced Colombian woman and the company with an arbitration award in its favor entitled to get what they want?

The situations above exemplify the increasing presence of cross-border migration and international trade[3] in Colombia. Such situations are relevant to Colombian private international law. They are, in effect, governed by private law and contain one element—or several elements—that link them to at least one foreign legal system, the application of which may lead to a different solution from the one that could be found under Colombian law. To resolve a private international law situation, it must be decided if Colombian courts have jurisdiction to decide and, if so, which legal system they must apply. In cases like the ones mentioned above, however, a quite different question arises, i.e., that of the recognition and enforcement in Colombia of a judgment pronounced by a foreign court or of an arbitral award rendered in an arbitration proceeding that took place abroad. As Marín Fuentes points out, this is one of the most important aspects of international procedural law.[4]

Based on the principle of territoriality, a judicial judgment is an act of a sovereign state and, therefore, it has legal effects only in its state of origin.[5] In this vein, doubts may arise about whether—and, if yes, under which circumstances—judicial decisions or arbitral awards issued in a foreign country can be recognized, and consequently become *res judicata*, in another country's territory.[6] If that is possible, not only contradictions can be dodged but also costs: The costs of conducting a new proceeding are not only for the parties but also for the states, which must assume all the costs involved in putting in motion their judicial machinery.[7] And, perhaps more importantly, violations of the fundamental right to effective judicial protection can be avoided.[8]

---

[3] This is linked to the fact that, in recent years, Colombia has entered into a number of international trade agreements that are currently in force with several states or groups of states, namely the Andean Community, Venezuela, Mexico, the Common Market of the South (MERCOSUR), Chile, the Northern Triangle, which includes Guatemala, El Salvador, and Honduras, as well as Canada, the European Free Trade Association (EFTA), the United States, the European Union, South Korea, Costa Rica, and the Pacific Alliance, of which Chile, Colombia, Mexico, and Peru are members. These treaties contain rules that directly govern specific subjects to promote international trade between the parties, mostly concerning tariff and non-tariff preferences. This means that they have not been conceived from a conflict of law perspective, even though they are embraced by private international law *lato* sensu. In practice, however, they are of relevance also from a conflictual perspective, as the international business transactions they promote give rise to cross-border situations that may indeed raise issues of conflict of jurisdiction or conflict of laws in, for example, contractual or related matters.

[4] Marín Fuentes (2021, p. 254).

[5] Wurmnest (2012). The same explanation for the relevance of the international recognition of foreign judgments is stressed by, e.g., Calvo Caravaca and Carrascosa González (2002).

[6] Marín Fuentes (2021, p. 254). See also Supreme Court of Justice, Civil Chamber, Judgment of July 12, 2017, No. SC9909-2017.

[7] No solo las partes incurren más costos si se realizara un nuevo proceso, también los Estados, pues estos asumen todos los costos que implica la puesta en funcionamiento de su maquinaria procesal.

[8] This is generally accepted in contemporary private international law. See, e.g., Marín Fuentes (2021), Calvo Caravaca and Carrascosa González (2002); ASADIP Principles on Transnational

Contradictions can emerge from the fact that each jurisdiction issues a particular pronouncement according to its own law, and it is very likely that the procedural and substantive law of a foreign country differs from the *lex fori*. This derives from the sovereignty principle, as it has been stated by the Colombian Supreme Court of Justice:

> to require that … all the laws of the states in question should coincide exactly, or, in other words, that the rules of law should not only be inspired by the same principles but be literally the same … is contrary to the sovereignty and self-determination of the states to create their own legislation.[9]

This chapter deals with how the Colombian legal system responds to the question of the recognition and enforcement of foreign judgments or arbitral awards, which is one of the main areas with which private international law is concerned. Regarding the terminology, it is worth noting that the following three notions are different and must therefore be distinguished from each other:[10] (i) the recognition, and the conditions under which it can take place, (ii) the so-called exequatur, i.e., the procedure of the declaration of enforceability of the foreign judgment by an institution of the state in which enforcement is sought, and (iii) the subsequent enforcement of the judgment in the other country, which occurs according to enforcement mechanisms existing in this latter country.

The chapter focuses in the second and third sections on the relevant rules of the General Code of Procedure Law of 2012 and Act No. 1563 of 2012 on national and international arbitration. Of course, international treaties in force to Colombia are also relevant,[11] even though here they are not dealt with in detail. Such treaties are, regarding foreign judicial decisions, the Treaty on the Execution of Foreign Acts,[12] the Treaty on Procedural Law of the South American National Congress of Montevideo,[13] the Treaty on Private International Law[14] and the Convention on the Execution of Civil Judgments,[15] and, in relation to foreign arbitral awards, the United Nations Convention on the Recognition and Enforcement of Foreign Arbitral Awards,[16] and the Inter-American Convention on the Validity of Foreign Judgments and Arbitral Awards.[17]

The different ways in which Colombian law regulates the recognition of foreign judgments, on the one hand, and foreign arbitral awards, on the other, have

Access to Justice (TRANSJUS). https://www.asadip.org/v2/wp-content/uploads/2018/08/ASADIP-TRANSJUS-EN-FINAL18.pdf. Accessed 16 June 2024.

[9] Supreme Court of Justice, Civil Chamber, Judgment of June 1, 2016, No. SC10089-2016.

[10] See Wurmnest (2012), Madrid Martínez (2021).

[11] Marín Fuentes (2021, p. 255).

[12] Approval Act No. 16 of 1913.

[13] Approval Act No. 68 of 1920.

[14] Approval Act No. 13 of 1905.

[15] Approval Act No. 6 of 1908.

[16] Approval Act No. 39 of 1990.

[17] Approval Act No. 16 of 1981.

consequences in practice. As will be seen in the fourth section, the obsolete regulation on this matter that is contained in the General Code of Procedure Law of 2012 leads national judges to approach the former in a manner that threatens the circulation of judicial decisions across national borders and, in that way, the international access to justice. This makes evident the need to revise such regulations.

In this context, the fifth and last section of the chapter provides a description of the improvements made in this regard by Draft General Act on Private International Law for Colombia that was prepared by the *Instituto Antioqueño de Derecho Internacional Privado* (IADIP) (hereinafter, "IADIP Draft"), which include a set of significantly innovative rules.

2 Recognition and Enforcement of Foreign Judicial Judgments

The recognition and enforcement of foreign judgments is regulated by Articles 605 to 607 of the Colombian General Code of Procedure Law, the *Código General del Proceso* (CGP), approved by Act No. 1564 of July 12, 2012, which replaced the Civil Procedure Code of 1970, the *Código de Procedimiento Civil*. However, the CGP does not substantially modify the previous regulations.

Article 605 CGP establishes two general requirements. First, the document whose recognition is sought must be a judgment or an equivalent decision, which has been adopted by a foreign court in a contentious or voluntary jurisdiction proceeding. By interpreting this rule, the Colombian Supreme Court of Justice has excluded administrative decisions.[18] One of the main innovations of the IADIP Draft is the consideration of the extraterritorial effect of decisions of the latter sort, as will be pointed out below in the last section.

Another requirement contained in Article 605 CGP is reciprocity, which means that "a foreign judgment will only be recognized and enforced in Colombia if a Colombian judgment would also be recognized and enforced in the foreign country concerned".[19] Two kinds of reciprocity can be identified in Article 605 CGP. The first one is the so-called diplomatic reciprocity (*reciprocidad diplomática*), which presupposes the existence of an international treaty between Colombia and the state of origin, according to which both parties are obliged to mutually recognize the judgments of their respective national courts.

In application of this rule, the bilateral treaties signed by Colombia with Ecuador (1905)[20] and with Spain (1908)[21] are usually mentioned when the recognition regarding judgments coming from any of these two countries is claimed. According

[18] Supreme Court of Justice, Civil Chamber, Judgment of March 8, 2016, No. AC1309-2016.

[19] Stöber (2021, p. 217).

[20] Approving Act No. 13 of 1905.

[21] Approving Act No. 07 of 1908.

to Calvo Caravaca and Carrascosa González, the main goal of the latter treaty was actually to overcome the rigidity of internal reciprocity requirements and their conditions to operate.[22]

There are also multilateral treaties on this subject. Among them, two regional treaties stand out, namely, the 1889 Montevideo Treaty on International Procedural Law (Articles 5 to 7)[23] and the 1979 Inter-American Convention on the Validity of Foreign Judgments and Arbitral Awards.[24] Colombia is not a party to the Convention of the Hague Conference on the Recognition and Enforcement of Foreign Judgements in Civil and Commercial Matters of 1971.

The other kind of reciprocity contained in Article 605 CGP is the so-called internal or legal reciprocity (*reciprocidad legal*), which operates in absence of an international treaty. According to it, foreign judgments and similar judicial orders will have in Colombia "the force recognized in the source country for those issued in Colombia". Article 605 CGP, thus requires that the legal system of the state of origin allows the recognition of Colombian judgments. This means, in other words, that such a system also contains legal reciprocity as a general rule,[25] as was noted by Echandía[26] in relation to Article 556 of the Law on Judicial Organization and Civil Procedure,[27] which was replaced by the abovementioned Civil Procedure Code of 1970 and also required legal reciprocity for the recognition of judgments issued in a foreign country.

Reciprocity is one of the features of the Colombian regulation on the recognition of foreign judgments that make this process quite restrictive, though there are other requirements that have such effect, as explained below. Not surprisingly, the reciprocity required by Article 605 CGP has been widely criticized as outdated.[28]

From the standpoint of fundamental rights, this restriction threatens the exercise of the rights of access to justice and due process. This is clearly stated in Article 7 No. 1 of the Principles on Transnational Access to Justice that were adopted by the American Association of Private International Law (ASADIP) in 2016. There, the extraterritorial effectiveness of the judgments themselves is recognized as a fundamental right, which, however, is not considered violated if the adoption of the

[22] Calvo Caravaca and Carrascosa González (2002, p. 589).

[23] Approving Act No. 68 of 1920. This treaty was signed by Argentina, Bolivia, Colombia, Paraguay, Peru and Uruguay. The 1940 Treaty of Montevideo also refers to this subject in comparable terms, but Colombia is not a party to this latter instrument. More on this subject in Marín Fuentes (2021).

[24] Approving Act No. 32 of 1992. The parties to this convention are Argentina, Bolivia, Brazil, Colombia, Ecuador, Mexico, Paraguay, Peru, Uruguay and Venezuela.

[25] This had been already noted by Echandía (1963, p. 341) in relation to Article 556 of the Law on Judicial Organization and Civil Procedure (Act No. 105 of October 17, 1931, replaced by the abovementioned Civil Procedure Code of 1970), which required legal reciprocity for the recognition of judgments issued in a foreign country.

[26] Echandía (1963, p. 341).

[27] Act No. 105 of October 17, 1931.

[28] See Orejudo (2013).

judgment, or its recognition or enforcement, would in turn entail a violation of fundamental rights (Article 7 No. 2). Accordingly, these principles also consider that reciprocity is contrary to the right of access to justice (Article 7 No. 6).

The ASADIP Principles on Transnational Access to Justice are certainly progressive and represent a step forward in the development of international procedural law in the legal systems of the region. However, it should be kept in mind that, by their nature, they are not mandatory, i.e., national courts are not obliged to apply them. They nevertheless play an outstanding role, while establishing minimum standards to guarantee access to justice, in accordance with international human rights law and the principles enshrined in most modern constitutions. Thus, they might be applied if the parties have agreed that the procedural aspects of their legal relationship are governed by them unless such an agreement is expressly prohibited by the legal system of the forum.[29] They can also serve as a model in law-making processes at the international and national levels, and this is the role they have played in the work carried out by IADIP in the preparation of the Draft, the relevant rules of which are presented below.

Apart from the aforementioned reciprocity requirement, an additional hurdle that applicants encounter is that pursuant to Article 30 No. 4 CGP the only national authority with competence on this subject is the Civil Appeals Chamber of the Colombian Supreme Court of Justice. There is just one exception in this regard, namely, when a different judicial authority has jurisdiction by virtue of an international treaty. This difficulty is also addressed in the IADIP Draft by introducing more flexibility and bringing the competent authorities closer to the interested party.

Pursuant to Article 606 CGP, the Colombian Supreme Court of Justice must thus examine whether the foreign judgment fulfills the following requirements:

1. It does not relate to rights *in rem* constituted in assets that were in Colombian territory at the time of the initiation of the process in which it was issued.
2. It is not contrary to the laws or Colombian provisions of public policy (*orden público*), except for procedural rules.
3. It is enforceable under the law of the state of origin and a presented in a certified copy.
4. The matter on which it is based is not within the exclusive jurisdiction of Colombian courts.
5. There is no trial or enforceable judgment by a Colombia court with the same cause.
6. If it has been issued in a contentious proceeding, that the requirement of due summons and contradiction of the defendant has been complied with, in accordance with the law of the state of origin, which is presumed by the enforceability of the judgment.
7. The exequatur requirement must be fulfilled.

[29] See ASADIP Principles on Transnational Access to Justice (TRANSJUS).

A few words might be said in connection with some of these requirements. As for the requirement contained in Article 606 No. 1 CGP, one can easily ascertain that the *forum rei sitae* rule is behind it. It should be noted that this is the only place in the Colombian domestic legal system where one may identify a reference to the *forum rei sitae* rule in its international dimension, i.e., regarding cases with a foreign element. However, this is a rather indirect reference, and the scope of application of this rule is limited to the recognition of foreign judgments.

Article 606 No. 2 addresses the public policy requirement. In general terms, as Martiny points out, the notion of public policy is in private international law equivalent to *ordre public*.[30] Now, this has been the requirement to be met by a foreign judgment that the Colombian Supreme Court of Justice has dealt with most extensively. Following the court, the concept of public policy that has been adopted by Colombian private international law has at least three characteristics.[31] The first one is that it refers to the foundations on which the domestic legal system is based, i.e., fundamental rules and principles of Colombian law.[32] It additionally entails a certain degree of malleability or adaptability to the social and political reality of the state of the *forum*,[33] also described as a changing character.[34] For that reason, when resorting to the public policy clause, the judge must interpret it dynamically. In this regard, the court has said that public policy involves

> a problem of justice that requires us to take into account the evolution of this concept in space and time, an examination that must always be based on legal criteria currently in force and not on a literal consultation of the provisions of the law … [this is] the dynamic, tolerant, and constructive public policy demanded by the international community in the contemporary world.[35]

Finally, it is worth noting that the Colombian Supreme Court has held that the public policy clause is of an exceptional nature. This has also been highlighted by Colombian legal literature, according to which the public policy clause is "an exception to the normal application of foreign laws or foreign judgments or awards rendered abroad".[36] An outstanding consequence of the exceptional nature of the public policy clause is that it must be interpreted in a restrictive manner. This latter characteristic certainly stresses the idea pointed out by Martiny that public policy is increasingly being viewed as a negative concept, that is, as a defense instrument, whereas its positive role as a means aimed at the enforcement of domestic

---

30 Martiny (2012).

31 Supreme Court of Justice, Civil Chamber, Judgment of July 27, 2011, No. 11001–0203–000-2007-01956-00.

32 Burgos (2023), Roldán Pardo (2010).

33 See Roldán Pardo (2010).

34 Kramberger Škerl (2011).

35 Supreme Court of Justice, Civil Chamber, Judgment of July 27, 2011, No. 11001–0203–000-2007-01956-00.

36 Holguín Holguín cited by Roldán Pardo (2010, p. 7).

(mandatory) law finds less prominence.[37] However, the exceptionality of the public policy clause clearly reinforces in this context the fact that recognition of foreign judgments should be the general rule.

Behind the requirement referred to in Article 606 CGP is the fact that in the state of origin, as well as in the requested state, the attribution of jurisdiction over the subject matter of the decision may fall into one of the following three situations. First, the courts of both states have concurrent jurisdiction. Second, the courts of none of the states has jurisdiction. Third, the courts of the requested state have exclusive jurisdiction. In principle, recognition of the foreign judgment is not possible in the third scenario but only in the first and second scenarios. It may be noted that the second scenario gives rise to a situation in which the legal establishment of the *forum necessitates*, which is addressed in another contribution to this book,[38] becomes relevant in order to avoid the denial of justice.

Regarding Article 606 No. 7 CGP, in order to fulfill the exequatur requirement, the procedure of Article 607 CGP must be completed. As will be seen, the way in which this latter rule regulates such procedure seems questionable if we take a serious view—and we certainly should—of the recognition of the extraterritorial effectiveness of judgments as a fundamental right, as stated in the aforementioned ASADIP Principles. These establish, for example, the incidental recognition of the foreign judgment, if its effectiveness is invoked in the course of a proceeding and without affecting the conduct of the respective exequatur procedure (Article 7 No. 10). It does not seem feasible to include such a possibility in the framework set forth in Article 606 No. 7 of the aforementioned CGP.

In accordance with Article 607 CGP, the exequatur procedure starts with the submission of the application made by the claimant with the aim to give legal effect to a foreign judgment in Colombia. Article 607 CGP provides that the request must be filed before the Civil Appeals Chamber of the Colombian Supreme Court of Justice, to which the party affected by the judgment must be summoned if the foreign judgment has been issued in contentious proceedings. If the foreign judgment or any other document is not in Spanish, a certified translation must be submitted together with a copy of the originals.

Article 607 CGP further provides the following five specific rules which govern the exequatur procedure. Pursuant to the first rule, the application must contain the evidence deemed relevant. The second rule reinforces the mandatory character of the requirements of Article 606 No. 1 to 4 CGP, the absence of which must lead to the rejection of the application. The third rule, which implies the need to respect the right to due process, states that the application must be delivered to the affected party together with the judgment, and to the counsel engaged with the representation on grounds of the specific nature of the matter (see Article 91 CGP) within a period of five days. According to the fourth rule, an order must be issued after notification of the application, in order to take evidence and set a date for the taking of

[37] Martiny (2012).

[38] Chapter "International Jurisdiction in Colombia" of this volume.

evidence, the hearing of the parties, and the delivery of the judgment. Finally, if the exequatur is granted and the foreign judgment needs enforcement, the competent court decides on enforcement, following the procedural general rules.

3 Recognition and Enforcement of Foreign Arbitration Awards

Article 30 No. 4 CGP provides that the Civil Appeals Chamber of the Colombian Supreme Court of Justice has competence for the recognition of foreign arbitral awards. Nevertheless, the exequatur of these decisions does not fall under the CGP regulations mentioned above. Article 605 CGP states that the exequatur of arbitral awards is subject to the legal rules that regulate this area. Remission is thus made to Act No. 1563 of 2012 on national and international arbitration, also known as the *Estatuto de Arbitraje Nacional e Internacional*.[39] This regulation explicitly excludes the application of rules set forth in the CGP on reasons, requirements, and formalities for refusal of recognition of foreign judgments in cases regarding the recognition and enforcement of foreign arbitral awards.[40]

The Second Section of the Act No. 1563 of 2012 establishes the rules on international arbitration. In this section, Chapter IX is devoted to the recognition and enforcement of arbitral awards that have been adopted abroad, for example, if it has been rendered by the International Chamber of Commerce or an arbitration center in a foreign country, which are generally run by the Chambers of Commerce. Chapter IX includes the requirements to be satisfied (Article 111), the grounds for rejection (Article 112), the functional competence (Art. 113), the applicable law (Article 114), and the procedure to be followed (Article 115).

According to Article 111 No. 2, awards rendered in international arbitrations whose seat is Colombia are considered national, and therefore they are not subject to the recognition procedure that Act No. 1563 of 2012 contains in its Second Section. They are so directly enforceable without the need for recognition, except when the appeal for annulment has been waived, in which case recognition shall be required. Decisions on recognition of the arbitral awards conducted in accordance with Act No. 1563 of 2012 are processed in sole instance and no appeal proceeds against it (Article 113).[41]

Now, according to Article 114 of Act No. 1563 of 2012, not only the rules contained there are applicable to the recognition and enforcement of arbitral awards in Colombia but also international treaties, when signed and ratified by Colombia. In

[39] This regulation on international arbitration is based on the UNCITRAL Model Law of 1985 amended in 2006, as well as on different regulations, among which the UNCITRAL Arbitration Rules and those established by the International Chamber of Commerce stand out.

[40] Article 114 of the Act No. 1563 of 2012.

[41] See Burgos (2023).

this regard, the United Nations Convention on the Recognition and Enforcement of Foreign Arbitral Awards (New York Convention) of 1958, to which 172 states are parties,[42] and the Inter-American Convention on the Validity of Foreign Judgments and Arbitral Awards (Inter-American Convention) of 1979,[43] with ten states parties, are also relevant.

The general rules regarding the recognition and enforcement of arbitral awards rendered abroad are set forth in Article 111 of Act No. 1563 of 2012:

1. The arbitral award shall be enforceable before the competent judicial authority, at the request of the interested party, irrespective of the country in which it was rendered.
2. The party relying on an award or applying for its enforcement shall produce the original award or a copy thereof. If the award is not in Spanish, the competent judicial authority may request the party to submit a translation of the award into Spanish.
3. Awards rendered in international arbitrations whose seat is Colombia and considered national awards, as noted earlier. They are thus directly enforceable without previous recognition, except when the appeal for annulment has been waived, in which case recognition shall be required.
4. For the enforcement of awards rendered by an arbitral tribunal whose seat is outside Colombia, prior recognition by the competent judicial authority shall be required.

The above-mentioned documents must accompany the request for the recognition presented by the interested party before the competent judicial authority (Article 115). If such documentation is duly presented, the competent judicial authority shall admit the request and transfer it to the other party or parties. Once the award is recognized in whole or in part, its enforcement shall be heard by the competent judicial authority (Article 116).

Apart from the advantage linked to the fact that these regulations can be applied to awards rendered in any country of the world, they also embrace a higher degree of legal certainty. Thus, Article 112 provides the cases in which the recognition of an arbitral award, irrespective of the country in which it was rendered, can be denied. These are substantially identical to the legal grounds for setting aside an international arbitral award issued in Colombia and are also aligned to Article V of the 1958 New York Convention.[44]

The recognition of an arbitral award may be refused, regardless of the country in which it was rendered, in the cases and on the grounds specified in Article 112. At the request of the party, if the party proves any of the following facts. First, the incapacity of this person at the time of the arbitration agreement or the invalidity of the agreement. Second, she or he was not duly notified of the appointment of an

[42] Approving Act No. 39 of November 20, 1990.

[43] Approving Act No. 16 of January 22, 1981.

[44] Garcés-Díaz (2024).

arbitrator or of the commencement of the arbitral proceedings. Third, the award deals with a dispute not provided for in the agreement. But if the decisions contained in the award exceed the terms of the agreement, the provisions of the award that relate to matters submitted to arbitration may be recognized and enforced when they can be separated from those that are not. Fourth, the composition of the tribunal or the procedure has not been in accordance with the agreement or the law of the country where the arbitration was held or conducted. And fifth, that the award is not yet binding or has been annulled or suspended by a judicial authority of the country where the arbitration was held. The same rule allows the judge to proceed ex officio when the subject matter of the dispute is not arbitrable under Colombian law or the recognition or enforcement of the award would be contrary to the international public policy of Colombia.

The Colombian Supreme Court of Justice has the aforementioned regulations. By so doing, when ruling on the recognition of an award by the International Chamber of Commerce,[45] it has be stated that the concept of public policy must be interpreted according to the principle that recognition and enforcement should be favored, which the court inferred from Article III of the 1958 New York Convention and Article 4 of the 1979 Inter-American Convention. Such reasoning is compatible with the idea, which has been stressed by the Court, that the collaboration between states facilitates the movement of people and capital, which is inherent to the globalized character of today's society. The continuity of legal relations in space has been considered the most important mission attributed to modern private international law.[46]

The Supreme Court has furthermore stated that the recognition of foreign arbitral awards is governed by some general guiding principles that serve as a reference and source of interpretation and, to some extent, limit the action of the competent courts.[47] According to the first of such principles (pro-international interpretation), the institutions governing international arbitration must be analyzed in a self-referential manner, in accordance with the most widely accepted exegetics in the world. The objective is to favor homogenization in the application of such institutions. More specifically, the Court clarifies that recourse to local rules to disentangle the content of transnational rules or to complement them should be excluded.

The Court also points out that preference should be given to granting binding force to the award, even in case of doubt, unless it should be rejected as a ground for refusal. This principle is of pro-recognition and pro-enforcement interpretation. Thus, for example, if the same provision admits multiple interpretations, this must be resolved in favor of the interpretation that makes the least stringent requirements for recognition.

---

[45] Supreme Court of Justice, Civil Chamber, Judgment of July 12, 2017, No. SC9909-2017.

[46] See Madrid Martínez (2021).

[47] Supreme Court of Justice, Civil Chamber, Judgment of July 12, 2017, No. SC9909-2017. See Cano Valencia (2020, p. 146).

The restrictive character of the grounds for refusal is another principle. Thus, the list of seven grounds for refusal mentioned above, five of which are applicable at the request of a party and two that may be applied ex officio by the judge, which are also entailed in the 1958 New York Convention, constitutes a *numerus clausus* list.

In addition, the court before which the exequatur is sought shall confine its examination to the verification of the formal requirements established in the regulations for granting it, without examining the substantial legal arguments. On the basis of this is the principle of the non-substantial nature of the examination. Behind it is the fact that the recognition proceeding is not an additional instance, nor an appeal for review.

Finally, the principle of double control refers to the control that takes place first in the country where the award was rendered, under the law of that country and taking effect only in that jurisdiction, and the control thereafter in the country where its recognition is sought, which involves a review based on the public policy of that country.

4 Some Figures on the Recognition of Foreign Judgements and Arbitral Awards in Practice

In 2016 and 2017, the majority of cases on recognition of foreign judgments that the Colombian Supreme Court of Justice examined[48] referred to judgments from the United States and Spain (approximately 40% each), as a preliminary research study has shown. In that study, it was found that, apart from two cases regarding the recognition of foreign arbitration awards, practically all requests were on family matters.[49]

In general, the results of this research revealed that in practice, the rejection of the recognition of foreign judgments is the rule in Colombia. In 2016, about 79% of a total of 111 applications were rejected and the situation was quite similar the following year, when rejection reached about 74% of a total of 123 applications.[50] As for the rejection causes, in 2016, for example, most of the applications were rejected because the claimant did not prove that the judgment was enforceable (48%), or that the interested parties had been notified (11%), or because a legal translation of the document was not provided (11%). Reciprocity was used as a reason for rejection in five cases (6%) and public policy in four (5%). The fact the claimant used the incorrect procedure, the lack of legalization, and the existence of rights *in rem* in assets located in Colombia were reasons for rejection in three cases (4%) each. And

[48] These findings were part of a presentation made by María Julia Ochoa Jiménez at the Kieler Woche organized by the University of Kiel, Germany, in June 2018.

[49] Ochoa Jiménez (2018).

[50] Decisions are available at: http://consultajurisprudencial.ramajudicial.gov.co:8080/WebRelatoria/csj/index.xhtml

that the document was not of a judicial nature, but contained an administrative act, was mentioned in two cases (3%).[51]

Although the Covid-19 pandemic is likely to have affected these figures, it might be expected that the whole picture is still quite similar today. These figures point to the need to review the criteria legally required by the regulation in force, and how they may be threatening the fulfillment of the right of access to justice.

Though deeper studies are needed, in general, the results of the above preliminary research study revealed that the rejection of the recognition of foreign judgments is the rule in Colombia. Certainly, as shown above, the country has updated its legal system regarding the recognition and enforcement of foreign arbitral awards in accordance with generally accepted international standards. But the situation appears particularly critical with respect to foreign decisions other than arbitral awards.

Given this, the *Instituto Antioqueño de Derecho Internacional Privado* (IADIP) has been considering how to improve this latter regulation. These efforts have resulted in the proposal of the regulation presented below.

5 The Effectiveness of Foreign Decisions in the IADIP Draft

The proposed regulation on the effectiveness of foreign decisions is in the Fifth Chapter (Articles 36 to 39) of the IADIP Draft. It refers not only to foreign judicial judgments but also include administrative decisions. Pursuant to Article 36, foreign judicial judgments and administrative decisions can produce effects in Colombia through a summary proceeding, without substantive review. However, this rule sets forth six requirements that foreign judgments and decisions must comply with: (1) that the authorities of the state in which the decision was rendered are competent according to reasonable criteria; (2) that the decision is not subject to any appeal and is final according to the law of the state in which it was rendered; (3) that the due process rights of the parties have been respected; (4) that the subject matter of the dispute does not fall within the exclusive jurisdiction of the Colombian authorities; (5) that Colombian courts have not ruled on the dispute in a decision not subject to appeal through ordinary channels between the same parties, on the same subject matter and for the same cause of action; or a foreign decision that has ruled on the case has not been previously recognized in Colombia; and (6) that the decision is not contrary to Colombian public policy, for which purpose the criteria established in Article 6 of this Act shall be considered.

One of the main changes that the IADIP Draft introduces can be found in Article 37. It eliminates the exclusive competence of the Civil Chamber of the Supreme Court of Justice. According to the new rule, the application for recognition of the probatory and *res judicata* effects of a foreign judgment may be filed with the

[51] Ochoa Jiménez (2018).

authority before which such effects are sought. The Civil Appeal Chamber of the Supreme Court of Justice remains competent only with respect to the request for recognition regarding judgments with enforcement in the Special District of Bogotá. For enforcement in other departments, the respective Superior Civil District Courts shall have jurisdiction. As Marín Fuentes points out, this change introduced by the IADIP Draft will benefit the claimant.[52]

Formal requirements are set forth in Article 38, according to which the application for recognition must be submitted in writing and be accompanied by: (1) the complete text, legalized and, if applicable, translated, of the foreign administrative or judicial decision; (2) a certificate proving that the decision is not subject to ordinary appeals, that it is final, and that it has the force of res judicata when these requirements cannot be deduced from the decision itself; and (3) in case of a judgment or decision by default, an official document stating that the convicted person was lawfully summoned and did not take advantage of the opportunity to assert his/her rights.

The IADIP Draft proposes a quite simplified procedure. As stated in Article 36, and in harmony with the ASADIP Principles on Transnational Access to Justice, the IADIP Draft provides a summary proceeding. Thus, after clarifying that the application for recognition must be accompanied by the formal requirements established in Article 38, Article 39 states that the competent authority shall reject the application if any of such formal requirements are missing, and that the application shall also be accompanied by proof of the requirements established in Article 36.

The party against whom the foreign judgment is to be enforced shall be notified of the application and shall have fifteen days to oppose the recognition, to provide evidence of such refusal, and to assert its rights. Upon expiration of this period, the competent authority shall issue the decision. No appeal shall lie against a decision on the recognition of a foreign administrative or judicial decision. And, once the recognition has been granted, if the party so requests, it shall be enforced immediately, by the procedure established in the corresponding regulations.

6 Final Remarks

In Colombia, the cross-border circulation of arbitral awards is being facilitated. The legal certainty that the regulation of Act No. 1563 of 2012 embodies is noteworthy. When applying this regulation, the Colombian Supreme Court of Justice has additionally gone further significantly, e.g., through the consideration of principles according to which the recognition must be favored, and the international dimension of these decisions must be taken into account. Thus, with a high degree of probability, the question of the recognition of a foreign arbitral award posed in the introduction to this chapter can be answered in the affirmative.

---

[52] Marín Fuentes (2024, p. 113).

However, things can be different with regard to the recognition and enforcement of foreign judgments, as illustrated in the introduction to this chapter through the case concerning the Colombian woman divorced in Japan. As has been discussed above, the rules contained in the *Código General del Proceso* are significantly restrictive. Such restrictiveness threatens the exercise of fundamental rights, such as the rights of access to justice and due process, as included in the ASADIP Principles on Transnational Access to Justice. They appropriately establish that judges and other state authorities shall always endeavor to favor the effectiveness of foreign decisions when interpreting and applying the requirements that such decisions must meet.

In this vein, the IADIP Draft represents a step forward in the development of a special legal framework for Colombian private international law in general. This is particularly true with regard to the recognition and enforcement of foreign judicial decisions, which is aligned with contemporary trends, linked as they are to the norms and standards that are part of international human rights law.

References

Burgos MA (2023) Colombia's Supreme Court of Justice: recent decisions on recognition and enforcement of foreign awards, Kluwer Arbitration Blog. https://arbitrationblog.kluwerarbitration.com/2023/04/17/colombias-supreme-court-of-justice-recent-decisions-on-recognition-and-enforcement-of-foreign-awards/. Accessed on 3 June 2024

Calvo Caravaca AL, Carrascosa González J (2002) Exequátur entre España y países iberoamericanos. In: Kleinheisterkamp A, Lorenzo Idiarte GA (eds) Avances del derecho internacional privado en América Latina. Liber Amicorum Jurgen Samtleben, Fundación de Cultura Universitaria, Montevideo, pp 575–596

Cano Valencia JC (2020) El reconocimiento y la anulación de laudos arbitrales extranjeros en Colombia: un análisis de la jurisprudencia de la Corte Suprema de Justicia. Anuario de Derecho Privado 2:141–165. https://doi.org/10.15425/2017.353

Echandía D (1963) Tratado de derecho procesal civil, vol III. Temis, Bogota

Garcés-Díaz LR (2024) Reviewing Colombian supreme court judgments on international arbitral awards. The American Review of International Arbitration, Blog. https://aria.law.columbia.edu/reviewing-colombian-supreme-court-judgments-on-international-arbitral-awards/. Accessed on 4 June 2024

Kramberger Škerl J (2011) European public policy (with an emphasis on exequatur proceedings). J Priv Int Law 7(3):461–490. https://doi.org/10.5235/jpil.v7n3.461

Madrid Martínez C (2021) Eficacia extraterritorial de sentencias: una mirada desde los sistemas venezolano y colombiano. Anuario de la Maestría de Derecho Internacional Privado y Comparado 3:417–439

Marín Fuentes JL (2021) Derecho internacional privado: síntesis y análisis evolutivo. Grupo Editorial Ibáñez, Bogota

Marín Fuentes JL (2024) The recognition of international judicial decisions in the draft act on private international law for Colombia. In: Salvadori M, Boutin Icaza G (eds) Colombian draft project on private international law. Quaderni Del Dipartimento Di Giurisprudenza Dell'Università Di Torino 34/2024

Martiny D (2012) Public policy. Max Planck Encyclopedia of European Private Law. https://maxeup2012.mpipriv.de/index.php/Public_Policy. Accessed 24 August 2023

Ochoa Jiménez MJ (2018) Der aktuelle Stand des internationalen Privatrechts in Kolumbien. Presentation at the Kieler Woche, Kiel. Unpublished manuscript
Orejudo P (2013) El derecho internacional privado colombiano ante la Ley Modelo OHADAC. Anuario Español de Derecho Internacional Privado XIII:681–697
Roldán Pardo JF (2010) El estado del arte del concepto de orden público internacional en el ámbito del derecho internacional privado y el arbitraje internacional. Revista de Derecho Privado 44:1-30
Stöber M (2021) Recognition and enforcement of foreign court decisions in Colombia. In: Trunk A, Hatzimihail N (eds) EU civil procedure law and third countries. Which way forward? Nomos, Baden-Baden, pp 213–202
Wurmnest W (2012) Recognition and enforcement of foreign judgments. Max Planck Encyclopedia of European Private Law. https://max-eup2012.mpipriv.de/index.php/Public_Policy. Accessed 3 June 2024

María Julia Ochoa Jiménez Dr. iur. and LLM from the University of Göttingen; Lawyer and specialist in Intellectual Property from the Universidad de Los Andes; LLM, Universidad de Navarra; research fellow, University of Bonn, Alexander von Humboldt Foundation; visiting researcher, Max Planck Institute for Comparative and International Private Law; professor, Universidad de Antioquia (2016–2022); professor of Private International Law, Universidad Loyola.

José Luis Marín Fuentes PhD in law, Universidad de Buenos Aires; LLM in Private International Law, Panthéon-Assas Université; LLB, University of Antioquia; Member, American Association of Private International Law; professor of Private Law and International Contracts, Universidad de Medellín.

Applicable Law: Cross-Cutting Questions

Sources and Methodological Plurality of Private International Law in Colombia

Claudia Madrid Martínez

Abstract This chapter deals with two issues concerning the general theory of private international law considering the Colombian context: the sources of private international law and its methodological plurality. It addresses the complex interplay of sources in Colombian private international law and how it is rooted in a combination of international treaties and domestic laws that challenges the identification of a hierarchical order between them. The chapter also examines how the methodological plurality of Colombian private international law involves the application of internationally mandatory rules, special substantive rules, and conflict rules, highlighting its diverse and layered approach.

1 Introduction

First of all, it is worth noting that to denote the *general part* of private international law, the term *general theory* is widely used among Latin American scholars, and so it is in this chapter. The existence of codified rules on the general theory of private international law has long been the subject of intense debate in specialized circles. This may be explained by referring to the complexity that lies behind the idea of a private international law general theory itself, as well as to the complexity of the object of this discipline, e.g., cross-border legal relations. Some understand that codified rules on this subject ratify the autonomy of the field and contribute to the construction of a scaffolding on which it can function. As Goldschmidt noted, "a

This text is a result of the project "General Theory of Private International Law", code 2024-68470, Universidad de Antioquia, July 2024.

C. Madrid Martínez (✉)
University of Antioquia, Medellín, Antioquia, Colombia

M. J. Ochoa Jiménez, C. Madrid Martínez (eds.), *A Private International Law for Colombia*, Springer Textbooks in Law,
https://doi.org/10.1007/978-3-032-04106-7_8

science without a general part is like a person without a head".[1] Others, such as Juenger, think that the general theory of private international law reveals the tensions that the lack of uniform rules of applicable law causes in the multilateral system.[2]

Now, despite some skepticism, a general theory of private international law does exist. It deals with its fundamental problems from philosophical, methodological, and technical perspectives.[3] And it allows us to think about the problems of private international law in terms of private international law itself,[4] considering "its own arsenal of concepts, institutions and methods".[5]

Even among those who recognize the importance of the general theory of private international law, there has been no agreement as to its content. Aguilar Navarro, for example, linked it directly to all the problems derived from the work of the conflict rule.[6] However, when it is understood that the purpose of private international law is to provide a solution to international private relations, in addition to the issues of determining the applicable law, which is considered through the so-called methodological plurality of private international law,[7] the general theory should include provisions relating to international procedural law (international jurisdiction,[8] international legal cooperation, and extraterritorial effectiveness of judgments) and an introduction referring to the fundamental notions (purpose, content, sources, history).[9]

In Colombia, the general part of Mantilla Rey's *Apuntes de Derecho Internacional Privado* includes aspects relating to the determination of the applicable law, including references to some of the general institutions—characterization, *renvoi*, recognition of validly created legal situations, *fraus legis* and public policy—and the determination of the competent authority and the extraterritorial effectiveness of judgments.[10] Something similar can be found in Monroy Cabra's work, the fourth part of which is devoted to conflicts of laws and examines the conflict rule and some of the general institutions, as well as a reference to the extraterritorial effectiveness of judgments.[11]

Although a realistic view of the general theory should certainly be extended in the second of the above-mentioned senses, from a historical perspective or "purely

---

[1] Goldschmidt (1995, p. 18).

[2] See Juenger (2006, p. 77).

[3] Maury (1936, pp. 330–332 and 416).

[4] Madrid (2012, p. 156).

[5] Calvo Caravaca and Carrascosa González (2022, p. 99).

[6] Aguilar (1982) (Vol I), p. 94.

[7] Madrid (2004, pp. 28–32).

[8] Kegel and Schurig refer to the existence of a certain parallelism between the general part of private international law and the so-called "international jurisdiction". Kegel and Schurig (2004, p. 51).

[9] Fernández Arroyo (1998, pp. 42–43).

[10] Mantilla Rey (1982).

[11] Monroy Cabra (2016, pp. 211–312).

conflictualist", in Fernández Arroyo's words,[12] it has been devoted to the study of the problems arising from the application of the conflict rule and foreign law. This is the viewpoint that has prevailed in the Inter-American sphere.[13] The Inter-American Convention on General Rules of Private International Law[14] has been described as "the most transcendent document" of the codification promoted by the Organization of American States.[15] For Goldschmidt, this treaty is the "adjectivized generality", referring to the general problems of private international law focused on the conflict rule.[16]

The general theory, linked to the functioning of the conflict rule, is part of what Marín Fuentes calls the "essential core" of private international law, the part of this discipline in charge of responding to the so-called conflict of laws, that is, the determination of the law applicable to international legal relations.[17]

In any case, the importance of the general theory has been recognized by European scholars, who have even put into question the need for its regulation. Jayme, for example, argued that such a regulation facilitates the application of private international law and avoids contradictions that arise in practice since it makes no sense for the same private international law institutions to receive different regulations depending on the system to which they belong.[18]

However, although Latin America has the Inter-American Convention on General Rules, ratified by ten states including Colombia, at the level of domestic codification, progress has been more modest. At this time, only four states have special legislations on private international law in which the general theory is regulated in some detail—Venezuela (1998), Dominican Republic (2014), Panama (2014), and Uruguay (2020)— and in very few cases, Civil Codes contain rules of private international law that include the general theory, namely, Peru (1984), Mexico (1985), and Argentina (2014). In most countries, including Colombia, unilateral conflict rules are still in force. Directly or indirectly, such rules are based on Article 3 of the French Civil Code of 1804. Being unilateral, they require an enormous effort from the judge to integrate the numerous—and foreseeable—gaps that they raise, and, in addition, these rules are devoid of the general guidelines that the general theory would provide them with.

In the particular case of Colombia, scholars have been in favor of a necessary reform of the private international law,[19] to provide it with rules adapted to the reality of today's world, to detach it from unilateralist conceptions and gaps that often

[12] Fernández Arroyo (1998, p. 40).

[13] Goldschmidt (1979, p. 150).

[14] Ratified by Colombia through Act No. 21 of 1981 (January 2022), Official Gazette 35.711, February 27, 1981.

[15] Maekelt (2010, p. 128).

[16] Goldschmidt (1979, p. 142).

[17] Marín Fuentes (2021, p. 48).

[18] Jayme (2013, pp. 35–36).

[19] Zapata Giraldo (2017, p. 1981).

lead the judge to ignore the internationality of relations and to apply, without further explanation, Colombian law, or based, in some cases, on a principle of territoriality that has been superseded by most of the systems in the region, including Chile, whose Civil Code has inspired the Colombian legislator.[20]

In 1984, Valencia Zea recognized in the explanatory memorandum of his Draft Civil Code for Colombia this need and emphasized that the only principle common to the rules of Colombian private international law was the principle of absolute territoriality of the law, described by the author as reflecting an "antiquated conception ... at odds with modern doctrines on the subject. If all states were to adopt such a system, international trade would become impossible".[21]

Today, when the Political Constitution of Colombia[22] recognizes the duty of the state to promote "the internationalization of political, economic, social and ecological relations on the basis of equity, reciprocity, and national convenience" (Article 226), it is necessary to rethink Colombian private international law from its roots, including the necessary scaffolding found in the general theory.

Thus, considering the current situation of Colombian private international law and the solutions proposed by the *Instituto Antioqueño de Derecho Internacional Privado* (IADIP) in the Draft General Act on Private International Law for Colombia (hereinafter, "IADIP Draft"), this chapter intends to offer some contribution in the search for solutions to private international law cases through which material justice is possible.[23] To such end, this chapter addresses, from a Colombian perspective, two issues that are traditionally part of the general theory of private international law: the system of sources of private international law and its methodological plurality.

2 Sources of Colombian Private International Law

One of the most complex issues of private international law is the fact of working with rules from sources of different hierarchy. Indeed, private international law draws its solutions from both international treaties and domestic rules, and this has even been recognized by the International Court of Justice.[24] In any case, this coexistence of rules obliges the judge to decide, before undertaking the solution of a case of private international law, whether to apply a treaty or to apply the domestic rules.

[20] Vial (2013, p. 895).

[21] Superintendencia de Notariado y Registro (1984, p. 13).

[22] *Constitutional Gazette* No. 116, July 20, 1991.

[23] See Juenger (2006).

[24] This was recognized by the International Court of Justice in its judgment of 12 July 1929 (PCIJ Series A. No. 20), in the Serbian loans case, available at: https://jusmundi.com/fr/document/decision/fr-emprunts-serbes-arret-friday-12th-july-1929 This was reiterated in a judgment of the same date (PCIJ Series A. No. 21), in the case of the Brazilian loans. Available at: https://jusmundi.com/fr/document/decision/en-brazilian-loans-judgment-friday-12th-july-1929

Moreover, in case of gaps, it is necessary to determine what tools are available for their integration.

Colombian private international law has only one rule, in an international treaty, which refers to the sources. I am referring to Article 1 of the Inter-American Convention on General Rules of Private International Law, which recognizes the preferential application of international treaties over domestic rules. In accordance with this rule, the second paragraph of Article 1 of the IADIP Draft provides that "International treaties signed and ratified by Colombia and in force in the Colombian legal system shall have a preferential application to the provisions of this Act".

Legal doctrine has added other sources that would be directly applied or would serve to fill the gaps in the positive rules. Thus, some scholars refer to the important role that custom would play, as well as analogy *legis* and analogy *iuris.*[25]

In general terms, however, the constitutional text plays a prominent role. The Political Constitution of Colombia refers to itself as the "rule of rules" (Article 4). as "the first and most important source of law",[26] which, in addition to establishing the criteria for the interpretation and application of Colombian private international law, establishes some solutions to be considered in international relations: filiation and capacity (Article 42); protection of human rights (Article 89); nationality (Article 96); and the legal status of foreigners (Article 100).[27]

Below the Constitution, there are international treaties, within which a distinction is made between those "that recognize human rights and prohibit their limitation in states of exception" (Article 93 Constitution), and the others. The former, which "prevail in the internal order" (Article 93 Constitution), are part of the so-called block of constitutionality, i.e., they are positive rules that, without having been expressly included in the Constitution in a strict sense, are integrated into it due to an express referral of the constitutional text itself.[28]

As the Constitutional Court has stated,

> [n]ot all international treaties and conventions are part of the block of constitutionality, since, as the case law of this Court has stated on several occasions, "international treaties, by the mere fact of being so, do not form part of the block of constitutionality and, therefore, do not have a normative hierarchy superior to that of ordinary acts". In effect, the Court has indicated that, unless expressly referred to in higher rules, only those international treaties and conventions that recognize human rights (i) and that prohibit their limitation in states of exception (ii) constitute parameters of constitutional control. For this reason, treaties of international humanitarian law, such as the Geneva Conventions, Protocols I and II and certain rules of the Pact of San José, Costa Rica, among others, form part of the constitutional block.[29]

With respect to treaties that are not part of the block of constitutionality, it has been understood that they have the rank of law. In particular, the Constitutional Court has

[25] Ochoa and Carrillo (2020, pp. 22–23).

[26] Monroy Cabra (2016, p. 39).

[27] Marín Fuentes (2021, p. 71).

[28] Fuentes (2010), p. 28.

[29] Constitutional Court, Judgment C-582, August 11, 1999.

referred to treaties on economic and regional integration matters, which despite not being part of the block of constitutionality, are also binding for Colombia because of the principle *pacta sunt servanda*.[30] This reasoning is applicable to treaties regulating economic, fiscal, customs, monetary, technical aspects[31] and, it can be added, private international law. According to the Constitutional Court, these treaties "have been incorporated into domestic law and become part of the set of provisions validly applicable in the national territory—as laws of the Republic—their compliance is equally unavoidable by the competent authorities".[32]

Although in these cases, authors such as Fuentes Contreras refer to the adoption of the dualist thesis, due to the need for a ratification process and prior controls by Congress (Articles 150.16 and 224 Constitution) and the Constitutional Court itself (Article 241.10 Constitution),[33] the Colombian law seems to be closer to the so-called moderate monism as set forth by Verdross, for whom both legal systems—domestic and international—are in a relationship of coordination under the supremacy of natural law.[34]

In any case, the legal status of treaties that are not part of the block of constitutionality does not prevent the scholars from recognizing the supremacy of treaties over domestic legislation.[35] Indeed, "although the international system does not pronounce on monism or dualism, that is, it does not affirm the unity or division of systems, nor does it refer to the validity of domestic rules when they conflict with international rules, it does make it clear that, in the international scenario, international law must prevail over domestic law".[36]

Given the supremacy of the treaty, it is necessary to recognize that, in matters of private international law, Colombia has a significant number of treaties from important codification forums such as the United Nations,[37] the Organization of American

---

30 Constitutional Court, Judgment C-400, August 10, 1998; Constitutional Court, Judgment C-155, March 7, 2007.

31 Constitutional Court, Judgment C-1118, November 1, 2005.

32 Constitutional Court, Judgment C-155, March 7, 2007.

33 Fuentes (2010, p. 36).

34 Verdross (1982, pp. 94–104).

35 Caicedo Castilla (1967, p. 9).

36 Acosta (2016, p. 20).

37 Convention on the Recovery Abroad of Maintenance, (Act No. 471 of 1998); Convention on Contracts for the International Sale of Goods, (Act No. 518 of 1999); Convention on the Recognition and Enforcement of Foreign Arbitral Awards, (Act No. 39 of 1990); Convention on the Rights of the Child, (Act No. 12 of 1991).

States,[38] and the Hague Conference on Private International Law.[39] Colombia also has treaties from the end of the nineteenth century—the Montevideo treaties of 1889[40]—and the beginning of the twentieth century— the bilateral treaty with Ecuador[41]—that contribute nothing to the modernization of the system. However, these treaties are still in force and, strictly speaking, if the concrete case involves legal systems of states party to them, the judge must apply them, as mentioned above, in preference to domestic rules.

As stated above, in the absence of treaties, either because there is no treaty in force for Colombia that regulates the matter under discussion, or because even if there is a treaty, it is not applicable because it is not in force in the other states whose laws are involved, domestic legislation must be applied and in that case—except in international arbitration that has modern rules based on the UNCITRAL Model Law on international commercial arbitration, contained in the National and International Arbitration Statute (Act No. 1563 of 2012)[42]—the situation does not improve.

Indeed, the Colombian domestic private international law is of a statutory nature. The main provisions are found in the Civil Code, in force since 1873, whose Articles 19, 20, 21, and 22 regulate the personal, real, and mixed statutes, with a notable predominance of the unilateral method. In addition to these rules, other rules scattered in the Civil Code itself regulate aspects such as the celebration of marriage (Article 127.9), divorce of marriage celebrated abroad (Article 163), and divorce decreed abroad of marriage celebrated in Colombia (Article 164), the patrimonial regime of marriage celebrated abroad (Article 180), successions (Articles 1.012; 1.053; 1.054; 1.068,10; 1.084; 1.085; and 1.086), and mortgages (art. 2.436). In addition to these provisions, there are some isolated rules contained in the Commercial Code (Articles 869 and 1328) and in other special acts.

---

[38] Inter-American Conventions on General Rules of Private International Law (Act No. 21 of 1981); Conflicts of Laws Concerning the Adoption of Minors (Act No. 47 of 1987); Support Obligations (Act No. 449 of 1998); International Traffic in Minors (Act No. 470 of 1998); International Return of Children (Acts No. 620 of 2000 and Act No. 880 of 2004); Extraterritorial Validity of Foreign Judgments and Arbitral Awards (Act No. 16 of 1981); Proof on and Information on Foreign Law (Act No. 49 of 1982); Execution of Preventive Measures (Act No. 42 of 1986); Legal Regime of Powers of Attorney to be used Abroad (Act No. 80 of 1986); Taking Evidence Abroad and its Additional Protocol (Act No. 31 of 1987); Letters Rogatory and its Additional Protocol (Act No. 27 of 1988); International Commercial Arbitration (Act No. 44 of 1986).

[39] Conventions on the Civil Aspects of International Child Abduction, (Act No. 173 of 1994); Protection of Children and Cooperation in Respect of Intercountry Adoption, (Act No. 265 of 1996); Abolishing the Requirement of Legalization for Foreign Public Documents, (Act No. 455 of 1998); Service Abroad of Judicial or Extrajudicial Documents in Civil or Commercial Matters, (Act No. 1073 of 2006); Taking of Evidence Abroad in Civil or Commercial Matters, (Act No. 1282 of 2009).

[40] Treaty on International Procedural Law (Act No. 68 of 1920) and Treaty on International Civil Law and Treaty on International Commercial Law (Act No. 33 of 1992).

[41] Treaty on Private International Law between the Republic of Colombia and Ecuador (Act No. 13 of 1905).

[42] *Act No. 1563 of 2012*, Official Gazette No. 48,489, July 12, 2012.

With this scenario, it is not difficult to foresee that multiple gaps may arise and in such cases, the judge will have to resort to the general solutions that Colombian law provides for these cases, so that it will apply, in the first place, the rules that "regulate similar cases or matters, and in their absence, the constitutional doctrine and the general rules of law" (Article 8 Act No. 153 of 1887). The general principles of law, scholar opinions, and case law accompany the process of interpretation of the law (Article 4 Act No. 153 of 1887).

Finally, I must refer to custom, whose value has been recognized both in civil matters—although "in no case shall it have force against the law" (Article 8 Civil Code)—and in commercial matters, where it "shall have the same authority as Commercial Law, provided that it does not manifestly or tacitly contradict it and that the facts constituting it are public, uniform and reiterated in the place where the services are to be rendered or the relations to be regulated by it have arisen" (Article 3 Commercial Code).

Case law has even admitted international custom as a source, based on Article 38 of the Statute of the International Court of Justice. In this regard, the Labor Chamber of the Supreme Court of Justice admitted the value of this source of law to decide a case of immunity from jurisdiction, arguing that,

> The fact that Colombia has not approved the United Nations Convention on Jurisdictional Immunities of States and their Property of 2004, which in Article 11 allows judges to take cognizance of conflicts related to labor contracts, does not mean that there is a gap or absence of regulation.
>
> On the contrary, there is a general and uniform practice of a significant number of countries around the world that recognizes and accepts the existence of an international custom according to which the judges of the receiving State may hear lawsuits related to employment contracts with embassies or consulates of foreign countries.[43]

Well, with respect to the gaps that may arise in an international commercial relationship, it is worth referring, albeit briefly, to Article 7 of the Commercial Code, a rule according to which "International trade treaties or conventions not ratified by Colombia, international trade customs that meet the conditions of Article 3, as well as the general principles of Commercial Law, may be applied to commercial issues that cannot be resolved according to the preceding rules".[44]

With reference to unratified treaties and general principles of Commercial Law, the application of *lex mercatoria*, a fundamental source for modern private international law[45] which has already been recognized by Colombian case law[46] and

[43] Supreme Court of Justice, Labor Chamber, Judgment AL2343-2016, April 20, 2016.

[44] See analysis of this rule in Madrid (2021, pp. 223–228).

[45] Madrid (2013, pp. 333 ff.).

[46] Supreme Court of Justice, Civil Chamber, Judgment July 1, 2008, Exp. No. 2001-00803-01; Supreme Court of Justice, Civil Chamber, Judgment August 1, 2011, Exp. No. 11001-3103-026-2000-04366-01; Supreme Court of Justice, Civil Chamber, Judgment August 30, 2011, Exp. No. 11001-3103-012-1999-01957-01; Supreme Court of Justice, Civil Chamber, Judgment February 21, 2012, Exp. No. 11001-3103-040-2006-00537-01.

scholars,[47] is admitted. Commenting on a 2012 decision in which the Supreme Court applied the UNIDROIT Principles on International Commercial Contracts,[48] Oviedo Albán stated that the Supreme Court employs a broad conception of law, that is, not identified with law in a formal sense, but rather including other forms of regulation not necessarily dependent on the state, as is the case, precisely, of the referred Principles.[49] Due to the importance of this source for international contracting, it will be dealt with *infra* in the corresponding section.

3 Methodological Plurality in Colombian Private International Law

Being international relationships the object of private international law, this discipline cannot be limited to the use of the conflict rule. This broad understanding of the object of private international law is the reason why it has been accepted that private international law is not only concerned—as the statutory schools stated—with indicating the scope of application of its own law, but that its task is to determine the applicable law.[50] To that end, in addition to the conflict rule, private international law makes use of substantive rules, in particular internationally mandatory rules—*lois de police*—and special substantive rules.[51] Thus, "conflict rule" is not the same as "rule of private international law".[52] This is what is meant by the expression "methodological plurality".[53]

The above categories of rules are based on the order of application. Thus, in order for the judge to resort to special substantive rules, he/she must first rule out the existence of internationally mandatory rules and, in turn, to apply the conflict rules, he/she must determine the non-existence of substantive rules since it is at that moment when a real conflict of laws arises.[54]

As discussed below, the attitude of Colombian private international law toward each of the three types of rules is very different.

---

[47] León (2019, pp. 185–193).

[48] At the time of the commentary, the 2010 version of the Principles was applicable. The latest version is from 2016, https://www.unidroit.org/instruments/commercial-contracts/unidroit-principles-2016/

[49] Oviedo (2013, pp. 16–18).

[50] See Francescakis (1958, p. 10).

[51] Batiffol (1973, pp. 75 ff.).

[52] See Madrid (2004).

[53] Meeusen proposes a more complex enumeration. Meeusen (2012, p. 42).

[54] See Carrillo Salcedo (1976).

3.1 *Internationally Mandatory Rules* (lois de police)

International mandatory rules, also known as *lois de police*, seem to be absent from scholarship[55] and case law analysis in Colombia. However, under the appearance of a rather positivist conception of public policy in private international law, there is some reminiscence of these kinds of rules.[56]

From the viewpoint of public policy, internationally mandatory rules "are considered to be so important and sensitive … that they are intended to be applied, always or at least when the situation is closely connected with the forum country",[57] and this happens "regardless of whether the issue as such is governed by foreign law and regardless of the contents of that foreign law".[58] These are "rules that must be applied 'inexorably' to legally internationalized factual situations, irrespective of the provisions of the conflict rules of the forum".[59] Its future regulation in Colombian private international law could be a "healthy" way to redirect the pernicious principle of territoriality of law, regulating and limiting its operation.

With this idea in mind, and inspired by Article 11 of the Inter-American Convention on the Law Applicable to International Contracts[60] and Article 9 of Regulation (EC) No. 593/2008 of the European Parliament and of the Council of 17 June 2008 on the law applicable to contractual obligations (Rome I),[61] Article 4 of the IADIP Draft states:

> Notwithstanding the provisions of this law, the judge shall apply the overriding mandatory rules of Colombian law which, according to this Act, must prevail even when a foreign law is competent.
>
> The judge may take into account the overriding mandatory rules of other States closely connected with the case, considering the consequences of their application or non-application.

This rule imposes the application of the Colombian internationally mandatory rules and leaves the judge free to assess their application when they belong to a law closely related to the case. Regarding the first assumption, despite being criticized by some authors, because it would encourage the states to unilaterally establish this kind of rules, this case does not seem to pose many problems in practice, because it is natural that each state protects, through these rules, certain principles of its own system, which it considers essential.

The greatest problems arise, on the other hand, when the mandatory rules belong to the law of a state with which the relationship is closely connected, as referred to in the second paragraph of Article 4 of the IADIP Draft. For this reason, regarding

[55] Rojas Tamayo (2018, pp. 124–125).

[56] Basedow (2013, pp. 432–437).

[57] Bogdan (2011, p. 182).

[58] ibid.

[59] Hernández-Bretón (2007, p. 93).

[60] https://www.oas.org/juridico/spanish/tratados/b-56.html

[61] https://eur-lex.europa.eu/legal-content/ES/TXT/PDF/?uri=CELEX:32008R0593&from=EN

these, it is not usual to speak of mandatory application, but rather of a consideration or taking into account which, in any case, is an option to the judge. Although the application of foreign mandatory rules is not peacefully accepted, since the role of the "forum in the protection of general interests based on economic-social reasons expressed in rules issued by third states"[62] is not clear, the reality of specific cases may impose its consideration, as occurred in the emblematic case of *Regazzoni v. Sethia, Ltd*, in which an English court considered, in its decision, a rule of Indian law—the law of the place of performance of the contract—characterized as mandatory, even though the contract was subject to English law.[63]

3.2 Special Substantive Rules

Once the judge ascertains that there are no internationally mandatory rules to regulate the case, the second step is the application of the so-called special substantive rules, which directly regulate—substantive—situations of an international character—special.[64] Thus, these rules, which in Lalive's opinion constitute "*à côté du régime normal, une sorte de régime parallèle prenant en considération les éléments d'extranéité de la* donnée",[65] are mainly found in international treaties, since it is through these instruments that true unification or, at least, harmonization—which is fundamental for international trade—can be more easily achieved.[66]

This method then makes it possible to apply rules of international origin to relations of an international nature, which certainly looks more coherent and highlights the inconvenience of applying domestic rules to international situations,[67] which—in Bucher's words—could prove in some cases impossible or inappropriate. Bucher concludes that these rules respond better to the specificities of international relations.[68]

In Colombian law, special substantive rules have found a clearer acceptance, although they have not necessarily been understood as part of private international law. In this sense, the statement of Rodríguez Fernández is illustrative, who seems to remain attached to the conception of private international law as exclusively devoted to resolving the conflict of laws by means of conflict rules. According to him,

> The purpose of private international law rules is to indicate to the judge or arbitrator which domestic rule should be applied to the merits of the dispute or contract, which is why it is

---

[62] See Hernández-Bretón (2007, p. 93).

[63] (1956) 2 Q.B. 490; (1956) 2 All E.R. 487; (1956) I Lloyd's Rep. 435; 100 Sol. Jo. 417, C.A.; on appeal; (1958) A.C. 301; (1957) 3 All E.R. 286; (1957) 3 W.L.R. 752; 101 Sol. Jo. 848 H.L.

[64] Loquin (2006, pp. 24–26).

[65] Lalive (1977, p. 91).

[66] See van Hecke (1969, p. 465).

[67] See Alfonsín (1982, pp. 173–175).

[68] Bucher (2009, p. 28).

> pointed out that the techniques of private international law are insufficient and inadequate to handle the complex issues arising in the field of international trade. The attempt to localize a private situation in a legal system is a solution based on a metaphysical theory, which served its creators to support a historical phenomenon but has no place in today's legal world.[69]

In any case, one of the best known and most representative instruments of this substantive method is the 1980 Vienna Convention on Contracts for the International Sale of Goods.[70] Although its application by the Colombian courts is still scarce, scholars unequivocally admit its practical importance.[71] With a few exceptions,[72] the various components of the so-called *lex mercatoria* tend to use this method, as can be seen, for example, in the UNIDROIT Principles or in the Incoterms of the International Chamber of Commerce.[73]

3.3 Conflict Rules

In the absence of substantive rules—internationally mandatory or special substantive rules—the judge must determine the law applicable to the dispute, in other words, the judge must resolve the conflict of laws, and, for this purpose, he/she must resort to the conflict rule, whose mission is precisely to indicate the competent law, without giving an answer to the merits of the case. Its structure and operation have made it the target of multiple criticisms by scholars. But from the practical point of view, its importance is undeniable, mainly due to the fact that the material regulation has not managed to cover all areas of private life, not even for contractual obligations, an area that would be thought to be more prone to unification than, e.g., family law.

In any case, the domestic regulation—as well as some of the international treaties to which Colombia is a party—uses the classic conflict method, i.e., it works based on rules that, rather than directly resolving the issues raised, indicate the law according to which the solution must be found.[74] The application of the conflict rules, according to some scholars, is mandatory for judges who, based on the principle *iura novit curia*, must know and apply them as part of Colombian law.[75]

---

[69] Rodríguez Fernández (2016, p. 95).

[70] Act No. 518 of 1999 (August 4), in: *Diario Oficial* No. 43,656, August 5, 1999.

[71] As Oviedo Albán recognizes, the Vienna Convention represents an important contribution to the solution of "real problems arising from the differences between the different regimes". See Oviedo (2008, p. 76).

[72] This is particularly the case of the Hague Principles on the Choice of Law in International Commercial Contracts (https://assets.hcch.net/docs/21356f80-f371-4769-af20-a5e70646554b.pdf), which contain conflict of law rules.

[73] https://iccwbo.org/business-solutions/incoterms-rules/incoterms-2020/

[74] García (2016, pp. 33 ff.).

[75] Sánchez (2016, p. 104).

However, when the Colombian judge must apply the domestic conflict rules, he/she encounters several problems along the way, since these rules, as I have stated before, have a unilateral nature, inherited from the statutory influence that was exerted, since the 1804 French Civil Code, on the state codification in America and from which Andrés Bello did not escape. These rules indicate the scope of application of Colombian law and view reality in a very fragmented manner. Because of that, it is necessary for the judge to bilateralize them,[76] using analogy or general principles of law.

Finally, it is worth to hold in mind that conflict rules, due to their structure, can only produce two effects: to order the application of the domestic law—with which the judge should not have any problem—or to order the application of a foreign law, a case in which interesting considerations and, it is fair to say, some complications arise.

References

Acosta Alvarado PA (2016) Zombis vs. Frankenstein: Sobre las relaciones entre el Derecho internacional y el Derecho interno. Estudios Constitucionales 14(1):15

Aguilar Navarro M (1982) Derecho internacional privado, 4th edn. Universidad Complutense, Madrid

Alfonsín Q (1982) Teoría del derecho privado internacional. Ediciones Idea, Montevideo

Basedow J (2013) The law of open societies: private ordering and public regulation of international relations: general course on private international law. Recueil des Cours de l'Académie de Droit International de La Haye 360:9

Batiffol H (1973) Le pluralisme des méthodes du droit international privé. Recueil des Cours de l'Académie de Droit International de La Haye 139(2):75

Bogdan M (2011) Private international law as a component of the law of the forum: general course on private international law. Recueil des Cours de l'Académie de Droit International 348:9

Bucher A (2009) La dimension sociale du Droit international privé: cours général. Recueil des Cours de l'Académie de Droit International de La Haye 341:9

Caicedo Castilla JJ (1967) Derecho internacional privado, 6th edn. Temis, Bogota

Calvo Caravaca AL, Carrascosa González J (2022) Tratado de Derecho internacional privado, 2nd edn. Tirant Lo Blanch, Valencia

Carrillo Salcedo JA (1976) Derecho internacional privado, 2nd edn. Tecnos, Madrid

Fernández Arroyo D (1998) Derecho internacional privado. Advocatus, Cordoba

Francescakis P (1958) Le théorie du renvoi et les conflits des systèmes en droit international privé. Sirey, Paris

Fuentes Contreras ÉH (2010) Papel jurisdiccional en la aplicación de las normas internacionales. Fundación Universidad de Bogotá Jorge Tadeo Lozano, Bogota

García Matamoros LV (2016) Conflicto de leyes y reglas de colisión. In García Matamoros L, Aljure Salame A (eds) Teoría general del Derecho internacional privado. Universidad del Rosario, Legis, Bogota, pp 33 ff.

Goldschmidt W (1979) Normas generales de la CIDIP-II: hacia una teoría general del Derecho internacional privado interamericano. Anuario Jurídico Interamericano 1979:141

Goldschmidt W (1995) Derecho internacional privado. Depalma, Buenos Aires

[76] Wolff (1958, p. 93).

Hernández-Bretón E (2007) Mestizaje cultural en el Derecho internacional privado de los países de la América Latina. Academia de Ciencias Políticas y Sociales, Caracas
Jayme E (2013) Kodifikation und Allgemeiner Teil im IPR. In: Leible S, Unberath H (eds) Brauchen wir eine Rom 0-Verordnung? Jenaer Wissenschaftliche Verlagsgesellschaft, Jena, p 33
Juenger FK (2006) Derecho internacional privado y justicia material (translated by Fernández D, Fresnedo C). Universidad Iberoamericana, Mexico, Porrúa
Kegel G, Schurig K (2004) Internationales Privatrecht, 9th edn. C.H. Beck, Munich
Lalive P (1977) Tendances et méthodes en Droit international privé: cours général. Recueil des Cours de l'Académie internationale de La Haye 155:3
León Robayo EI (2019) La nueva Lex mercatoria en el Derecho latinoamericano de contratos. Bogotá: Universidad del Rosario; Tirant Lo Blanch
Loquin E (2006) Les règles matérielles internationales. Recueil des Cours de l'Académie Internationale de La Haye 322:9
Madrid Martínez C (2004) La norma de derecho internacional privado. Universidad Central de Venezuela, Caracas
Madrid Martínez C (2012) Instituciones generales de derecho internacional privado: más allá del problema conflictual. In: Guerra VH, Madrid Martínez C, Pérez Y (eds) Estudios de Derecho internacional privado, Homenaje a Tatiana Maekelt. Universidad Católica Andrés Bello, Caracas, p 155
Madrid Martínez C (2013) Notas sobre la lex mercatoria: entre el silencio del legislador europeo y el silencio de los Estados americanos. In: Moreno Rodríguez J, Fernández Arroyo D (eds) Libro Homenaje a Roberto Díaz Labrano. CEDEP, ASADIP, Asunción, p 333
Madrid Martínez C (2021) La contratación internacional en el Derecho internacional privado colombiano. Perspectiva comparada. Tirant lo Blanch, Ediciones UNAULA, Bogota
Maekelt T (2010) Teoría general de Derecho internacional privado. 2ª ed. actualizada y ampliada. Serie Estudios No. 87. Academia de Ciencias Políticas y Sociales, Caracas
Mantilla Rey R (1982) Apuntes de Derecho internacional privado. Parte general. 2ª ed. corregida y aumentada. Editorial Temis, Bogota
Marín Fuentes JL (2021) Derecho internacional privado. Síntesis y análisis evolutivo. Grupo Editorial Ibáñez, Bogota
Maury J (1936) Règles générales des conflits de lois. Recueil des Cours de l'Académie de Droit. International 57:329
Meeusen J (2012) Le Droit international privé et le principe de non discrimination. Recueil des Cours de l'Académie de Droit International de La Haye 353:9
Monroy Cabra MG (2016) Derecho internacional privado, 7th edn. Temis, Bogota
Ochoa Jiménez MJ, Carrillo Gamboa P (2020) Elementos conceptuales y prácticos esenciales para la solución de casos de Derecho Internacional Privado en Colombia. Documentos de Trabajo. Facultad de Derecho y Ciencias Políticas, Universidad de Antioquia, Medellin
Oviedo Albán J (2008) Regulación del contrato de compraventa internacional. Antecedentes, estructura y fuentes. Ibáñez, Bogota
Oviedo Albán J (2013) Los Principios UNIDROIT como reglas aplicables al contrato internacional. A propósito de la sentencia de la Corte Suprema de Justicia colombiana de 21 de febrero de 2012. Universidad Sergio Arboleda 3:7
Rodríguez Fernández M (2016) Introducción al Derecho comercial internacional, 2nd edn. Universidad Externado de Colombia, Bogota
Rojas Tamayo D (2018) El Derecho aplicable al contrato. Estudio comparado, crítico y prospectivo en Derecho internacional privado colombiano. Universidad Externado de Colombia, Bogota
Sánchez Sánchez H (2016) La aplicación y prueba del derecho extranjero. In: García Matamoros L, Aljure Salame A (eds) Teoría general del Derecho internacional privado. Universidad del Rosario, Legis, Bogota, pp 95 ff.
Superintendencia de Notariado y Registro (1984) Proyecto de Código Civil. Bogotá.
van Hecke G (1969) Principes et méthodes de solution des conflits de lois. Recueil des Cours de l'Académie de Droit International de La Haye 126:419

Verdross A (1982) Derecho internacional público, 6th edn. Biblioteca Jurídica Aguilar, Madrid
Vial Undurraga MI (2013) La autonomía de la voluntad en la legislación chilena de Derecho internacional privado. Revista Chilena de Derecho 40(3):891
Wolff M (1958) Derecho internacional privado (translated by Marín López A). Bosch, Barcelona.
Zapata Giraldo A (2017) Colombia. In: Basedow J, Rühl G, Ferrari F, de Miguel AP (eds) Encyclopedia of private international law. Edward Elgar, Cheltenham, p 1981

Claudia Madrid Martínez PhD in law, *Magister Scientiarum* in Private International Law and Comparative Law, and lawyer from the Universidad Central de Venezuela (UCV); postdoctoral researcher, University of Cologne, Alexander von Humboldt Foundation (2012–2014); tenured professor, Universidad Central de Venezuela; associate professor, Universidad de Antioquia; member, Research Group Knowledge, Power, and Law, Universidad de Antioquia.

Application of Foreign Law in Colombia

Claudia Madrid Martínez

Abstract The application of foreign law is one of the most intricate aspects of private international law. This issue entails both procedural and substantive complexities. In many cases, judges opt to apply their domestic law due to the challenges of understanding foreign legal systems. This chapter delves into procedural implications, distinguishing when foreign law is treated as law or as a fact. Moreover, it outlines the Colombian legal framework, emphasizing the "mixed system" that makes both judges and parties responsible for knowing foreign law and that must be balanced by some flexible guidelines that have been provided by the Constitutional Court.

1 Introduction

One of the most complex issues of private international law relates to the application of foreign law.[1] Although it is a rule generally accepted that national judges must investigate and apply foreign law ex officio, in practice it is common that they avoid doing so, and instead apply their own law. This can happen due to lack of knowledge or to the complexity of the problems involved. Certainly, it is not an easy task to know foreign law sufficiently and to apply it. Therefore, legal systems must have clear rules to guide judges on the way forward.

This text is a result of the project "General Theory of Private International Law", code 2024-68470, Universidad de Antioquia, July 2024.

[1] This was, in fact, the first problem posed by the postglossators when they wondered about the extraterritorial application of the law.

C. Madrid Martínez (✉)
University of Antioquia, Medellín, Antioquia, Colombia

M. J. Ochoa Jiménez, C. Madrid Martínez (eds.), *A Private International Law for Colombia*, Springer Textbooks in Law,
https://doi.org/10.1007/978-3-032-04106-7_9

Before examining what Colombian private international law currently states on this subject matter and the proposals for reviewing it, I will briefly examine in this chapter the theories that have been raised around the issue of the application of foreign law. This is, to a large extent, the core of the general part of private international law.

2 General Considerations

It is precisely the conflict rules that led to another major problem addressed by the general theory of private international law: the application of foreign law.[2] The substantive and procedural implications of the application of a foreign legal system, much discussed by the scholars,[3] make this discipline more complex and, therefore, it is even more necessary to have clear rules.

It is worth noting that applying foreign law has two dimensions, i.e., substantive and procedural, and that both depend on the way in which the ideas of *law* and *foreign* are understood, as well as their opposites *fact* and *own*. The procedural dimension depends on whether the foreign law is considered as *law* or as a *fact*, and the substantive dimension depends on whether it is considered foreign or own.

Regarding the procedural dimension, considering foreign law as law implies that the judge must apply it ex officio, so that the parties do not have any burden with respect to its allegation and proof. This does not imply recognizing that foreign law responds to the principle *iura novit curia*—the judge does not have to know all the laws of the world—but rather it translates into an obligation for the judge to investigate the content, meaning, and validity of foreign law. Additionally, being so, there are no time limits regarding its arrival to the process, so foreign law can be incorporated at any stage of the process. Finally, the control of cassation with respect to the lack of application, false application, or erroneous interpretation is applicable to the infringement of the foreign rule.

When foreign law is, on the contrary, considered as a fact, the procedural consequences are the opposite of those mentioned above. In this sense, being a fact, the foreign law must be alleged and proven by the parties, and the judge is not obliged to apply it ex officio; it must be brought to the proceeding at the time provided for the arrival of the facts; and, finally, no recourse in cassation shall be available for infringement in the application of the foreign law.

The substantive consequences depend on whether the foreign law is considered foreign or own. If it is considered foreign, the determination of whether the rule is

[2] See Sánchez Sánchez (2016, pp. 95 ff.).

[3] Alfonsín (1982, pp. 493–521).

in force, both in time and in space—in the case of states in which more than one law coexists—the validity, the sources and the interpretation depend on the foreign law. This panorama changes radically when foreign law is considered as its own and, for this purpose, it is necessary either to incorporate the foreign rule as a kind of legal consequence of the conflict rule[4] or to recreate it in the own law.[5] In any case, what is recreated or incorporated is a rule in force, so characterized by that foreign law. The other aspects—validity, interpretation, sources—will now depend on the judge's law.

An important point that separates both perspectives is related to the thesis of maximum and minimum remission. Thus, if the thesis of foreign law as foreign law is assumed, the maximum remission would be accepted, so that foreign law would be applied as an indivisible whole, which implies the consideration of the foreign conflict rule and the possible *renvoi* that could occur. The application of the foreign law as own law, on the other hand, implies the acceptance of the minimum remission, so that what is incorporated or recreated is the substantive rule in force in the foreign law, excluding the conflict rules and, consequently, the *renvoi*.

3 Colombian Private International Law

3.1 Current Rules

Colombian private international law currently in force has two rules regarding the application of foreign law. The first rule is Article 2 of the Inter-American Convention on General Rules, which provides as follows:

> Judges and authorities of the States Parties shall enforce the foreign law in the same way as it would be enforced by the judges of the State whose law is applicable, without prejudice to the parties' being able to plead and prove the existence and content of the foreign law invoked.

This rule—according to Werner Goldschmidt—enshrines, first, "the principle of the officiality of the application of foreign law", since the task falls in the hands of the judge who must, ex officio, investigate and apply foreign law; and, second, "the theory of legal usage[6] and the principle of tolerance by proclaiming that applying foreign law means applying it 'as it would be enforced by the judges of the state whose law is applicable'".[7] Without accepting Goldschmidt's legal usage thesis, Parra-Aranguren has stated that this rule accepts the principle according to which

[4] Ago (1932, pp. 66–68).

[5] Lorenzen (1924, pp. 736 ff.).

[6] See Goldschmidt (1995, p. 223).

[7] Goldschmidt (1979, p. 151).

"foreign law must be applied in the same way as it is applied in its country of origin".[8]

Colombian case law has shown that Article 2 of the Convention "assimilates the foreign rule to a question of law and, therefore, places the primary responsibility for its application on the judges. However, it does not rule out the possibility that the parties interested in the proceedings may participate in the proof of the content of the foreign provision".[9] Indeed, it is the judge who is responsible for investigating and applying the foreign law ex officio, without prejudice to a possible collaboration of the parties, which would not constitute, in any case, a procedural burden in the strict sense.[10]

This reasoning, within the framework of the Convention, would be reinforced by the provisions of Article 4 of the same treaty, a rule according to which "All the appeals provided for in the procedural law of the place where the proceedings are held shall also be admissible for cases in which the law of any of the other States Parties is applicable", which implies that the errors of the Colombian judge in the application of foreign law, once the other requirements contemplated by Colombian procedural law have been met, would be subject to control through the extraordinary remedy of cassation.

However, Colombian domestic law provides a procedural solution regarding the "proof" of foreign law, which has led case law to refer to the so-called "mixed system" of proof of foreign law. I refer to Article 177 of the General Procedural Code:[11]

> The text of legal norms that do not have national scope and that of foreign laws shall be adduced in copy to the process, *ex officio* or at the request of a party.
>
> The total or partial copy of the foreign law must be issued by the competent authority of the respective country, by the consul of that country in Colombia or requested to the Colombian consul in that country.
>
> An expert opinion rendered by a person or institution expert by reason of his knowledge or experience as to the law of a country or territory outside Colombia may also be attached, regardless of whether he/she is qualified to act as an attorney there.
>
> In the case of unwritten foreign law, it may be proved by the testimony of two or more lawyers of the country of origin or by means of an expert opinion under the terms of the preceding paragraph.
>
> These rules shall apply to resolutions, circulars and concepts of the administrative authorities. However, their presentation will not be necessary when they are published on the web page of the corresponding public entity.
>
> Paragraph. When necessary, proof of its validity shall be requested.

Based on this rule, the Constitutional Court has stated that

---

[8] Parra-Aranguren (1998, p. 102).

[9] Constitutional Court, judgment SU 768, October 16, 2014.

[10] This is to be understood without prejudice to the fact that Colombian procedural law requires, as a requirement of the claim, that the grounds of law be stated (art. 82.8 General Code of Process), since, in fact, "in accordance with the principle *iura novit curia*, it corresponds to the judge to apply the law regardless of the law invoked by the parties, since it is the duty of the judge to correctly determine the law". See Montaño Bedoya (2020, p. 31).

[11] *Act No. 1564 of 2012*, Official Gazette No. 48,489, July 12, 2012.

> foreign law is not approached as a simple factual question, since the judicial authorities are expressly responsible for its enforcement, but neither is it a matter of pure law since the Colombian legal system recognizes that its content, scope, and validity may also be alleged, proven and discussed by the interested parties.[12]

In order to reconcile the powers of the judge to apply foreign law ex officio and the diligence of the parties in informing about foreign law, the Constitutional Court recognized that the determination of when this activity is a burden of the parties and when it is an obligation of the judge depends on the specific case, so it developed a guide with three criteria to be considered by the judge: relevance, quality of the parties, and availability of the rule.

The criterion of relevance involves an analysis to determine whether or not the foreign law is an accessory element within the litigation so that if it is an accessory matter, the burden would fall primarily on the parties, but if, on the contrary, "it constitutes a central aspect within the judicial review on which the effective enjoyment of rights depends, the impulse of the judge must be greater". The second criterion has to do with the quality of the parties, thus, ensuring a fair solution:

> When the party interested in the proof of foreign law is a physical or legal person with easy access to the foreign rule (e.g. because it is a multinational with headquarters and representation in the other country), the duty of the judge is reduced. On the contrary, in the presence of a person of special constitutional protection, with limited financial and professional resources, the intervention of the judge in obtaining the foreign law … becomes stronger.

Finally, the availability of the rule has to do with whether the applicable rule is easily accessible to the parties. If it is, they can bring it to the process and, if it is not, "the judge must be more active in the search for foreign law, making use of diplomatic channels through the Foreign Ministry, especially with those countries with which a cooperation agreement on the matter has been agreed". These and other means are referred to in the Inter-American Convention on Proof of and Information on Foreign Law,[13] a treaty in force for Colombia the purpose of which "is to establish rules governing international cooperation between the States Parties for obtaining elements of proof of and information on the laws of each of them" (art. 1).

In sum, according to the Constitutional Court, the task of bringing foreign law into the process is incumbent upon both the parties and the judge, and the weight between the tasks of one and the other will depend on the circumstances of the specific case. Although it is fair to recognize that this position has sometimes been ignored by the case law. The reason—I do not rule it out—may be the absence of clear rules. Thus, in 2021, the Supreme Court of Justice heard and denied the exequatur to a Venezuelan judgment whose *res judicata* nature was established in the Venezuelan law, because the plaintiff did not prove either the executory nature of the judgment or the Venezuelan rule that established such nature.[14]

---

[12] Constitutional Court, Judgment SU 768, October 16, 2014.

[13] Act 49 of 1982 (December 16).

[14] Supreme Court of Justice, Civil Chamber, Judgment AC238-2021, February 8, 2021.

Regarding the means of evidence, it should be taken into consideration that the Inter-American Convention on Proof of and Information on Foreign Law provides in Article 3 that "the suitable means of proof contemplated in both the law of the State of origin and the law of the State of destination" may be used. The same rule considers a suitable means, among others,

a. Documentary proof consisting of certified copies of legal texts together with an indication of their validity, or judicial precedents;
b. Expert testimony, consisting of opinions of attorneys or experts on the matter; and.
c. The reports of the State of destination on the text, validity, meaning, and scope of its law on specific points.

Based on the distinction contained in Article 177 of the General Procedural Code, Manrique-García considers that written rules may be accredited "by means of a document that has been submitted to the respective diplomatic formalities" and, in the case of unwritten rules, these may be accredited "by means of the testimony of lawyers of the country of origin of the foreign law to be proved (expert witnesses), but the only means of proof of foreign commercial custom is the certificate issued by the diplomatic agent, prior certification of the foreign entity that performs the functions of chamber of commerce. If such a certificate does not exist, it will have to be supplemented with two lawyers specialized in Commercial Law. It ends with the idea that the international custom, that which does not belong to any state or nation, has no defined evidentiary regulation".[15]

What stands out in Colombian private international law is a certain silence with respect to the possibility of resorting to technology to obtain information on foreign law. Indeed, Article 177 limits itself to timidly recognizing the importance of information obtained by electronic means, with respect to "resolutions, circulars and concepts of the administrative authorities", in cases where these "are published on the web page of the corresponding public entity".

In other legal systems, it has been recognized that

> To ascertain foreign law, the most accessible and useful resources for the judge are documents and Internet sources from the relevant jurisdiction. These include foreign statutes, commentaries, textbooks, and other publications. In different countries, the government, the courts, or other institutions provide information on their own legal system on the Internet for foreign stakeholders. The EU has developed, in cooperation with the notariat and academia, several Internet databases on specific areas of private law, in particular marriage and succession.[16]

Considering the veracity of the information, I see no obstacles for the judge or the parties to resort to the Internet to prove the content, meaning, and validity of the foreign law.

[15] Manrique-García (2012, pp. 67–68).

[16] Nishitani (2017, p. 23).

3.2 De Lege Ferenda

The proposal to review the Civil Code that was prepared by the National University of Colombia does not contain any provisions in this regard. Draft General Act on Private International Law for Colombia that was prepared by the *Instituto Antioqueño de Derecho Internacional Privado* (IADIP) contains for its part two rules referring to foreign law. In Article 2, the IADIP Draft provides for the ex officio application of foreign law, without ruling out the collaboration of the parties who, without having a procedural burden as such, may collaborate by bringing foreign law to the process. In addition, this rule admits the procedural remedies in case of infringements to the application of such foreign law and establishes a solution for the cases in which a law within which different legal systems coexist is declared competent. "The conflict of laws arising between those systems shall be resolved in accordance with the principles in force in the corresponding foreign law". Article 3 provides in turn that "The interpretation of the competent foreign law shall be made in accordance with the foreign law itself".

References

Ago R (1932) Nuovi indirizzi del Diritto internazionale privato. Cedam Casa Editrice, Padua

Alfonsín Q (1982) Teoría del Derecho privado internacional. Ediciones Idea, Montevideo

Goldschmidt W (1979) Normas generales de la CIDIP-II: hacia una teoría general del Derecho internacional privado interamericano. Anu Jur Interam 1979:141–155

Goldschmidt W (1995) Derecho internacional privado. Depalma, Buenos Aires

Lorenzen E (1924) Territoriality, public policy and the conflict of laws. Yale Law Journal, 33, 736ff.

Manrique-García J (2012) La prueba de la ley extranjera en Colombia: análisis comparado. International Law, Revista Colombiana de Derecho Internacional 20:51

Montaño Bedoya JV (2020) Manual de teoría general del proceso. Tirant lo Blanch, Ediciones UNAULA, Bogota

Nishitani Y (2017) Treatment of foreign law: dynamics towards convergence? - general report. In: Nishitani Y (ed) Treatment of foreign law - dynamics towards convergence? Ius Comparatum, global studies in comparative law, vol 26. Springer, Cham, p 3

Parra-Aranguren G (1998) Curso general de Derecho internacional privado. Problemas selectos y otros estudios, 3rd edn. Facultad de Ciencias Jurídicas y Políticas, Universidad Central de Venezuela, Caracas

Sánchez Sánchez H (2016) La aplicación y prueba del derecho extranjero. In: García Matamoros L, Aljure Salame A (eds) Teoría general del Derecho internacional privado. Universidad del Rosario, Legis, Bogota, p 95

Claudia Madrid Martínez PhD in law, *Magister Scientiarum* in Private International Law and Comparative Law, and lawyer from the Universidad Central de Venezuela (UCV); postdoctoral researcher, University of Cologne, Alexander von Humboldt Foundation (2012–2014); tenured professor, Universidad Central de Venezuela; associate professor, Universidad de Antioquia; member, Research Group Knowledge, Power, and Law, Universidad de Antioquia.

General Institutions in Colombian Private International Law

Claudia Madrid Martínez

Abstract This chapter focuses on the general rules and concepts of private international law that address the challenge of determining applicable law in cross-border cases. It discusses how Colombian private international law lacks codified rules on these institutions, as well as the way in which the IADIP Draft addresses them, in particular following the Inter-American Convention on General Rules of Private International Law.

1 Introduction

The application of conflict rules and, consequently, of foreign law is based on the so-called general institutions of private international law. These are general cross-cutting concepts that are largely accepted as fundamental to private international law and as being at the core of this field.[1] Characterization, incidental question, juridical relationships validly established (vested rights), adaptation, *renvoi*, evasion of law (*fraus legis*), unknown institution, and public policy (*ordre public*) are among such concepts. They seek to respond to problems that emerge from the foreignness of private international law situations and the need to determine the law that governs

This text is a result of the project "General Theory of Private International Law", code 2024–68470, Universidad de Antioquia, July 2024.
This chapter, which deals with a subject that has been part of my research for over twenty years, is based on a previous work carried out in the framework of a project directed by Marguerita Salvadori (University of Turin).

[1] Neuhaus (1976, pp. 41–46).

C. Madrid Martínez (✉)
University of Antioquia, Medellín, Antioquia, Colombia

M. J. Ochoa Jiménez, C. Madrid Martínez (eds.), *A Private International Law for Colombia*, Springer Textbooks in Law,
https://doi.org/10.1007/978-3-032-04106-7_10

them. These general institutions act as tools given to the judge to face the vicissitudes of dealing with these kinds of situations.

In Colombian private international law, apart from public policy, which has had an important case law development, and *renvoi*, which is rejected pursuant to Article 101 of Law No. 1563 of 2012, general institutions practically do not exist. In this regard, the Draft General Act on Private International Law for Colombia that was prepared by the *Instituto Antioqueño de Derecho Internacional Privado* (IADIP) (hereinafter, "IADIP Draft") makes an enormous contribution, as its second chapter extensively deals with the problems in the application of conflict of law rules. Two legal proposals drafted prior to the IADIP Draft, namely, the Draft Civil Code by Valencia Zea and the Draft Civil Code prepared by the National University of Colombia (UNAL), only refer to public policy and *fraus legis*.

In addition to the general institutions, i.e., public policy, *fraus legis*, *renvoi*, juridical relationships validly established and adaptation, the IADIP Draft regulates matters relating to internationally mandatory rules and the application and interpretation of foreign law, which refers to one of the processes included in characterization and the unknown institution. In general, these solutions are close to those of the Inter-American Convention on General Rules of Private International Law. However, any reference to previous, preliminary, or incidental issues is omitted, considering their limited practical application.

These general institutions can be divided into two groups. The first group includes institutions that make possible to apply foreign law, i.e., characterization, unknown institution, *renvoi*, juridical relationships validly established and adaptation. The second group embrace those that, on the contrary, reject the application of foreign law, i.e., public policy and *fraus legis*.

2 Institutions that Facilitate the Application of Foreign Law

2.1 Characterization

Characterization is one of the most intricate problems of private international law. Its complexity derives from the fact that it involves three fully distinct but interconnected processes, the confusion of which does nothing to clarify the scenario.[2] These three processes, which I do not discuss in detail here, are related to the three elements of the conflict rule: the factual situation, the connecting factor, and the legal consequence.

[2] Hernández-Bretón (2007, pp. 228–229).

First, the term characterization is used to refer to the process by which the judge determines the nature of the concrete case to be analyzed, to subsume it within the factual situation of a specific conflict rule or rule on international jurisdiction.[3] Second, characterization is also often used to refer to what should more appropriately be called "interpretation" of the connecting factors,[4] and even of the criteria of international jurisdiction. Third, this term may designate the process by which, once the applicable law has been determined, the judge will have to consider the criteria of that law to interpret its provisions. This third process does seem to be exclusively connected with the conflict rules and their main consequence: the application of foreign law.

Of these three processes, the third one is commonly regulated since it is closely linked to the application of foreign law. The interpretation of foreign law is in fact a systematic consequence of its application.[5] Thus, Article 2 of the Inter-American Convention on General Rules mandates to interpret foreign law in accordance with the criteria in force in the foreign law itself: foreign law shall be applied "in the same way as it would be enforced by the judges of the State whose law is applicable".

As said above, the IADIP Draft is aligned with the Convention and assumes the thesis of application of foreign law as foreign law: "The interpretation of the competent foreign law shall be made in accordance with the foreign law itself" (Article 3, first paragraph).

Traditionally, three solutions have been proposed to deal with the problems linked to the process of characterization, which relates to the determination of the law that will provide the interpretation of the rules involved in the specific case. In this regard, Kahn[6] and Bartin[7] proposed the characterization *ex lege fori*. According to it, the criteria contained in the substantive law of the judge must be considered. This is the solution accepted by some scholars, as well as by legislation[8] and case law. However, exceptions are admitted in relation to, e.g., goods, contracts, the form of the wills, and the unknown institution.

In favor of this thesis, it is argued that when the national legislator elaborates the conflict rule—or jurisdiction rule—they consider the concepts of their system. Moreover, the application of foreign law constitutes a diminution of the sovereignty of the forum and the least that the state can reserve for itself is the extent of that diminution. Finally, it is argued that characterization under foreign law is difficult. Furthermore, *ex lege fori* characterization would be closed and chauvinistic, which fails with regard to unknown institutions.[9]

---

[3] Magalhães (1964, p. 215).

[4] Betti (1975, pp. 95 and 102).

[5] Alfonsín (1982, pp. 496 and 498).

[6] Kahn (1891, pp. 1 ff.).

[7] Bartin (1897, pp. 25 ff), Bartin (1930, pp. 561 ff.).

[8] Arts. 12.1 Spanish Civil Code; 3.1 Hungarian Act on Private International Law; 3078 Quebec Civil Code Quebec.

[9] Maekelt (2010, pp. 325–326).

Despite criticisms, a logical interpretation of Private International Law leads to the understanding that the first approach to the nature of the concrete relationship, with which the competent rule is determined, must necessarily be carried out by the material criteria of the *lex fori*.[10] There is no other way of arriving at the applicable—or presumably applicable—law that provides elements of characterization of the legal relationship. Moreover, there is no other possible way to proceed, when the judge is looking for the rule that will determine whether they have jurisdiction.

The second theory proposed is the so-called *ex lege causae* characterization. Despagnet,[11] to whom this thesis is attributed, proposed that the characterization is made according to the criteria of the substantive law presumably applicable to the relationship. This thesis is somewhat complicated since it is not possible to characterize a specific relationship based on the law competent to regulate it, for a simple reason that before the characterization it is not yet known which is the applicable law, it is not even known which is the rule that will lead to that law, since the characterization is the process to follow to individualize the conflict rule to be used.[12]

In practice, the rules through which the *ex lege causae* characterization is enshrined do not assume the consideration of the substantive law applicable to the relationship, but rather, those that order to consider a law other than the *lex fori* are considered as such.[13] Despite this nuance, the thesis of the *ex lege causae* characterization has not succeeded in imposing itself. Its disadvantages have motivated Italian scholars to propose double characterization, according to which a primary characterization of the terms of the judge's conflict rule would be carried out, according to the judge's law, after which a secondary characterization of the terms of foreign law would be carried out according to the material rule of that foreign law. The secondary would not influence the primary characterization.[14]

These solutions, however, have the disadvantage of having to resort to the internal substantive law of the states to interpret the private international law rules. For this reason, Rabel proposed the thesis of autonomous characterization.[15] In Rabel's opinion, if the rule of private international law is autonomous from domestic law, it is different in its structure, nature, and function, therefore it cannot obey the same characterization criteria of domestic law. Thus, through the comparative method, it is possible to obtain unitary and universal characterizations that would be used by the judge in private international law cases.

According to Rabel, when the German Civil Code regulates guardianship by the national law of the person concerned, the concept of guardianship must not depend either on the substantive law of the forum or on the foreign substantive law but must be obtained by a logical operation of abstraction based on the notions provided by

[10] Magalhães (1964, pp. 211–212) and Betti (1967, p. 679).

[11] Despagnet (1898, pp. 253 ff.).

[12] On the difficulties of this solution, see Alfonsín (1982, p. 327).

[13] Brazilian Civil Code (arts. 8 and 9); Peruvian Civil Code (art. 2055).

[14] Ago (1936, pp. 323–324).

[15] Rabel (1931, pp. 241 ff.).

comparative law. Thus, guardianship is to be understood as what the civilized world generally understands: an institution of law whose purpose is the representation or protection of persons who do not have full capacity and who are not subject to the power of their parents.[16]

This relative abundance of theoretical solutions contrasts with the absence of regulation. Hernández-Bretón considers that the lack of agreement on theoretical solutions and the conceptual and practical deficiencies in juridical decisions have generated a negative attitude and a state of despair concerning the impossibility of a legislatively formulated solution. He cites, e.g., discussions regarding the Inter-American Convention on General Rules and the lack of consensus among national scholars and case law, which led to the absence of an explicit solution.[17] Perhaps it is better not to solve a problem than to solve it poorly.[18]

Colombian private international law has some rules establishing autonomous characterization. In this line can be included the treaties that regulate issues related to children and adolescents, which generally begin by defining these persons, or in matters of arbitration, which contain rules defining the arbitration agreement. Also in domestic law, Article 21 of the Civil Code defines what is to be understood by the "form" and "authenticity" of documents for the application of the *locus regit actum* rule. But, in addition to these rules, there is no solution to the problem of characterizations.

The Inter-American Convention on General Rules, as said above, does not give general guidelines to the judge to solve this problem, beyond the solution in the matter of interpretation of foreign law. Now, the IADIP Draft limits itself to referring to the case of interpretation of foreign law and preferred not to bind the judge to characterize exclusively with the material criteria of the *lex fori*, nor according to the criteria prevailing in the law presumably applicable to the relationship, with the difficulties that both solutions entail.

2.2 Unknown Institution

Applying foreign law as foreign law is not easy when this law enshrines institutions unknown to the *lex fori*, so the effect of implementing this institution is the rejection of foreign law. In his *System des heutigen römischen Rechts*, Savigny already raised two exceptions to the application of foreign law within the international legal community. The first one refers to those rules strictly imperative in nature—today overriding mandatory rules or *lois de police*—and the second refers to the unknown institution.[19]

[16] Rabel (1931, pp. 256–257).
[17] Hernández-Bretón (2007, p. 229).
[18] Goldschmidt (1979, p. 150).
[19] Savigny (1879, pp. 138 ff.).

It is certainly difficult to differentiate these two exceptions to the application of foreign law formulated by Savigny since he exemplified the unknown institution through slavery and polygamy, cases that are closer to prohibited institutions, which can for that reason fall within the overriding mandatory rules. This has led the doctrine to think that if there are foreign institutions that are inapplicable for reasons other than the incompatibility of ethical criteria, Savigny's system lacked the precision to serve as a guide for the legislator or the judge.[20]

Today, unknown institution has been progressively eliminated as an easy mechanism to reject the application of foreign law and its new conception requires a review of the judge's law to determine if there are no analogous institutions, which favors its consideration as an institution directly related to values.[21]

In this regard, Article 3 of the Inter-American Convention on General Rules provides as follows:

> Whenever the law of a State Party has institutions or procedures essential for its proper application that is not provided for in the law of another State Party, this State Party may refuse to apply such a law if it does not have any like institutions or procedures.

This rule is quite broad, as it refers not only to "institutions" but also to "procedures". On the other hand, however, it enshrines the unknown institution in a restrictive manner since foreign law can only be excluded if there are no analogous institutions or procedures in the *lex fori*.

In these cases, the so-called "functional characterization" is very valuable, i.e., in the absence of a certain institution in the *lex fori*, the only solution is to determine its social function, to find the institution that in the *lex fori* performs the social or economic function closest to the foreign institution.[22]

Some scholars argue that the unknown institution is nowadays in disuse. Nevertheless, from the wording of the Convention's rule, it can be inferred that what it seeks is to prevent the judges from excluding foreign law out of ignorance, before having to rule out the existence of an analogous institution in their law. It is worth so emphasizing that with the term "may", its application is enshrined not as an obligation for the judge, but as a power that the judge may exercise only after examining each specific case to determine whether the exclusion of foreign law is justified.

In any case, determining the lack of knowledge of an institution will depend on the characterization. However, characterization can only be carried out through foreign law. In fact, some legislations regulate the unknown institution in rules regarding characterization and they do so in a positive manner, that is, not as a mechanism to reject foreign law, but rather to tend to its application, since it is stated that, in the cases of unknown institutions, characterization must be made under foreign law.[23] In this sense, I think that applying the unknown institution should be oriented toward making the rejection of foreign law a last resort.

---

[20] Garde Castillo (1947, pp. 90–91).

[21] Maekelt (1998, p. 25).

[22] Fernandez and Sanchez (2004, p. 131).

[23] Arts. 3.2 Hungarian Decree-Act on Private International Law and 3078 Quebec Civil Code.

This reasoning is followed by Article 3 of the IADIP Draft. The second paragraph of this rule refers to the interpretation of foreign law in the following terms:

> When the competent foreign law has institutions or procedures essential for its proper application that are not provided for in Colombian law, the application of such foreign law may be refused, provided that Colombian law does not have any analogous institutions or procedures.

The fact that this rule, which is inspired by the Inter-American Convention on General Rules, is contained in the article relating to the application of foreign law, contributes to understanding the unknown institution, not as a tool to discard foreign law, but as an instrument that tends to its application, making use of the functional characterization.

2.3 Renvoi

The *renvoi* arises when the conflict rule of the forum refers to foreign law, and—accepting the maximum referral—the conflict rule of this latter law refers, in turn, to the law of the forum or to the law of a third state. Such a situation is considered to be a negative conflict of laws because both the *lex fori* and the law the application of which in stated by the conflict rule of the forum refrain from regulating the legal relationship.[24]

For this negative conflict to occur, three conditions must be met. First, the connecting factors used by the conflict rules involved must be different. Such diversity may derive from the literalness of the connecting factor (e.g., nationality or domicile) or its interpretation (e.g., domicile in fact or domicile in law). Second, the *lex fori* must admit the application of the foreign conflict rule. In other words, the *lex fori* must consider the foreign law in its entirety, both its material and conflict rules (maximum referral). Finally, the foreign conflict rule must refer to the application of another law.

When the foreign conflict rule refers to the law of the forum, it is a "first-degree" *renvoi*. If reference is made to the law of a third state, it is a "second-degree" *renvoi*. It may also happen that the law of that third state, in turn, refers to the law of the forum in a "circular" *renvoi*, or to another state in a "subsequent" *renvoi*.

Traditionally, scholars have been divided between those in favor of *renvoi* and those who deny its usefulness.[25] Regardless of this, the problem of overcoming the legal loophole resulting from the impracticability of the conflict rule of the forum

---

[24] Aguilar Navarro therefore suggests the presence of an apparent gap. Aguilar (1982, p. 150).

[25] First jurisprudential recognition in *Collier* vs. *Rivaz* case (England, 1841) and the *Forgo* case (France, 1878).

cannot be ignored, in cases where the foreign law to be applied cannot be applied to a specific case.[26]

The argument according to which, the *renvoi* facilitates the uniform solution of conflicts of laws is widely known. However, this is not entirely true since the solutions vary depending on the forum in which the dispute arises. To achieve international harmony of solutions, the foreign law must not accept the *renvoi*, because if it accepts it, the solutions that the foreign courts would give to the case would be contrary to those given by the courts of the forum.[27] Thus, only a second-degree *renvoi*, under certain conditions, could be useful to achieve this international harmony of solutions.[28]

Respect for the indivisibility of foreign law is also an argument in favor of the institution, since, through *renvoi*, a substantive rule of the foreign legal system could not be applied if its application is not admitted by the corresponding conflict rule of this legal system. Thus, if the principle according to which foreign law must be applied as foreign law is considered, a substantive rule cannot be applied when the legislator that issued it does not want it to be applied. Moreover, the theory of *renvoi* is justified because it discourages deliberate choice of forum by promoting uniform results.[29]

On the other hand, opponents of *renvoi* argue that the *lex fori* is also indivisible, and its mandate is disobeyed when a law other than that indicated by the conflict rule is applied. According to Bartin, when the legislators make a conflict rule and choose a connecting factor, they think that the substantive law indicated is the best law to regulate the relationship, be it the law of nationality or the law of domicile, or the law of the place where the goods are located or the law of the place where the act is performed.[30] So, to apply a different law is to disobey their mandate.

Some have considered *renvoi* as a *circulus vitiosus* (Kahn) or an international tennis game (Buzatti). Such conceptions are intended to highlight the underlying legal uncertainty: determining the applicable law depends on the law the application of which is contained in the foreign conflict rule.[31]

As can be seen, disagreement revolves around *renvoi* among scholars, case law, and private international law rules.[32] However, there are certain issues on which a certain uniformity in the solutions is beginning to be perceived. For example, it is

---

[26] Niboyet and Quadri see in the disinterest in foreign law a suppression of the international character of the relationship. See Aguilar (1982, pp. 170–171).

[27] Lewald (1929, p. 526).

[28] Calvo and Carrascosa (2022, p. 254).

[29] Maekelt (2010, p. 348).

[30] Bartin (1931, p. 1260), Pillet (1913, p. 10).

[31] Calvo and Carrascosa (2022, p. 254).

[32] Arts. 3 Italian Act on Private International Law; 14 Swiss Act on Private International Law; 5 Austrian Federal Act on Private International Law; 4 Hungarian Decree-Act on Private International Law; and 12.2 Spanish Civil Code accept *renvoi*. There is rejection in arts. 2048 Peruvian Civil Code; 27 Egyptian Civil Code; 32 Greek Civil Code; 16 Brazilian Civil Code; and Sec. 7 and 8 *Restatement second.*

common to exclude *renvoi* in contract matters when the parties can choose the applicable law. Some systems extend this rejection to all cases where conflictual autonomy is allowed, as is the case with Article 4.2 of the Introduction Act to the German Civil Code.

Renvoi is also usually excluded when the matter falls within the scope of an international treaty. The purpose of the treaty's conflict rules is to replace the conflict rules of the contracting states. For this reason, it does not seem reasonable that when the conflict rule of the treaty designates the law applicable to a relationship, the reference should include the conflict rules of that law.[33]

This is probably the reason for the silence that the Inter-American Convention on General Rules maintains regarding *renvoi*. Indeed, although the draft of this Convention explicitly rejected *renvoi*, in the final text, the matter was silenced at the suggestion of Valladão, for whom *renvoi*, together with characterization, is a "very controversial matter, not yet settled".[34] Goldschmidt, however, considered that, despite its absence, *renvoi* is "sociologized" in the theory assumed by the Convention with regard to the application of foreign law.[35]

In any case, the only rule in force in Colombia regarding the *renvoi* is the first paragraph of Article 101 of the Statute on National and International Arbitration, and what it does is exclude it. Indeed, after admitting that the parties may choose the law applicable to the merits of the arbitration dispute, the rule provides that "The indication of the law of a State shall be understood to refer, unless otherwise expressed, to the substantive law of that State and not to its conflict of laws rules". The exclusion of *renvoi* in this matter is justified by the play of conflictual autonomy and the need to respect the application of the law chosen by the parties. However, the rule itself allows the parties to express the contrary, i.e., to choose a conflict rule, so that in such a case there would be *renvoi*.

Concerning *renvoi*, the IADIP Draft establishes a general rule that accepts it up to the second degree and rejects the other types. Article 8 of the IADIP Draft provides:

> When foreign law declares Colombian law applicable, Colombian substantive rules shall apply.
>
> When the competent foreign law declares applicable the law of a third State, which in turn declares itself applicable, the substantive law of that State shall apply.
>
> In all other cases, the substantive law designated by the Colombian conflict rule shall apply.
>
> When an international treaty applies to the disputed relationship, the provisions of the treaty itself shall apply regarding *renvoi*.

The inclusion of this rule—inspired by Article 4 of the Venezuelan Act on Private International Law—provides legal certainty by clearly establishing the rules of the game. Thus, in cases other than first- and second-degree *renvoi*, the law to which the

[33] Lewald (1929, p. 578).

[34] Reported in: Parra-Aranguren (1979, p. 165).

[35] Goldschmidt (1979, p. 153).

Colombian conflict rule refers shall be applied, avoiding one of the criticisms made of this figure and its infinite game of remissions.

In addition to this general rule, the IADIP Draft admits the exclusion of *renvoi* in two areas. The first refers to cases in which an international treaty applies, in which case "the provisions of the treaty itself shall apply regarding to *renvoi*". As stated above, although this is beginning to change,[36] in these cases, *renvoi* is usually rejected because it may undermine the harmonization or standardization sought by treaties .[37]

The second case refers to international contracts. Here, it is influenced by the Inter-American Convention on the Law Applicable to International Contracts and the Hague Principles on the Choice of Law in International Commercial Contracts. Article 80 of the IADIP Draft provides that "For the purposes of the application of this section, 'law' means the law in force in a State, excluding its conflict rules". Thus, by excluding the possibility of applying foreign conflict rules, *renvoi* in international contracts is excluded, whether the parties have chosen the law applicable to the contract or whether it has been determined by the judge.

2.4 Vested Rights

One of the main obstacles encountered by the conflict rule is the possible disregard of a legal situation created under the protection of a given legal system, due to the application of the law indicated by it. For this reason, it has been necessary to establish an exception to the conflict rule of the forum, and this has been found in the vested rights or, as they are known today, juridical relationships validly established.

This institution was historically considered as the foundation of private international law, a tradition originating from the Dutch school of the seventeenth century, and later developed by the Anglo-Americans. However, today it is conceived as an exception to the normal functioning of the conflict rule according to which the judge must ascertain that a given legal situation has been validly created both in form and in substance under a legal system different from their own, and then recognize it under their law.[38]

In Savigny's opinion, to determine whether rights are duly acquired, it is necessary to know beforehand according to which legislation this acquisition must be decided. This question was answered in different ways by different authors. For Pillet, for example, a right can only be considered validly acquired when its acquisition took place according to the law declared applicable by the conflict rule of the forum, consequently these acquired rights lack effectiveness *ex proprio vigore.*[39]

---

[36] Davì (2012, pp. 254 ff.).

[37] Derruppé (1993, pp. 3 ff.).

[38] Parra-Aranguren (1998, pp. 193 ff.).

[39] Pillet (1923, (Vol I), pp. 33–39).

This solution was adopted by the Peruvian Civil Code (Article 2050) and by the Bustamante Code (Article 8).

For Meijers, on the other hand, the conflict rules of the forum should not apply when all the laws connected with the legal relationship, at the time of its creation or extinction, agree in declaring only one of them as competent, an agreement that must be recognized everywhere.[40] This theory is reflected in the Inter-American Convention on General Rules, whose Article 7—referring to "juridical relationships" instead of "vested rights"[41]—mandates that such juridical relationships must have been constituted by "all the laws" with which the relationship had contact at the time of its creation.

Understanding the difficulty of this solution, Makarov proposed that the law designated not by "all the laws", but by the "preponderant majority" of the laws connected with the factual assumption should be considered. Later, Makarov supplemented his ideas with the recommendation to investigate whether the parties, at the time of concluding the act, could have foreseen the court that could decide any eventual dispute between them.[42]

Now, in the current Colombian system, in addition to the general rule of Article 5 of the Inter-American Convention, there are a couple of rules in the Montevideo Treaty on Civil Law, that include solutions in matters of movable conflicts based on vested rights. Article 2 thus provides that "The change of domicile does not alter the acquired capacity", while Article 30 states that "The change of location of movable property does not affect the rights acquired under the law of the place where they exist at the time of their acquisition".

In Colombian domestic law, there is no rule regulating this institution, hence the importance of the IADIP Draft. This Draft has a general rule and a couple of special solutions that are close to the rules of the Montevideo Treaty. Regarding the general rule, Article 9 of the IADIP Draft provides:

> A juridical relationship validly created in a foreign State, according to the law of that State, shall be recognized in Colombia, provided that at the time of its creation, it had a sufficient connection with that State and is not manifestly contrary to the essential principles of Colombian public policy.

It is a rule modeled on Article 9 of the Uruguayan Act on Private International Law and seeks to simplify the work of the institution, which translates into a guarantee of recognition of juridical situations validly created according to foreign law.

In addition to the principle of recognition, both Article 5 of the Inter-American Convention and Article 9 of the IADIP Draft establish the manifest contradiction to the essential principles of public policy as an exception to the recognition of these relationships.

Regarding public policy, Niboyet stated that its operation will vary in its intensity depending on whether it is the creation or recognition of rights, and, in the case of

---

[40] Meijers (1938, 225–226).

[41] See Parra-Aranguren (1998, pp. 207–208).

[42] Makarov (1955, pp. 445–446).

recognition, it only produces a negative effect, never a positive one.[43] Indeed, it is possible that an act, that is contrary to the local public policy, may only be sanctioned regarding the consequences which, in themselves, are not compatible with the essential principles of the state hearing case.[44] Francescakis does not agree with this thesis because he understands that the difference between rights and their effects cannot be established with enough precision. Legal issues that are presented as effects of a previous situation can also be considered independent rights.[45]

In addition to this general rule, the IADIP Draft, as already mentioned, establishes two rules that reflect this principle: Article 42, according to which "The change of domicile does not restrict the capacity acquired under the law of the previous domicile", and Article 67, which orders to respect the legal situations validly created in case of displacement of movable property, so that the change of location does not affect the rights acquired under the law of the previous location.

2.5 *Adaptation or Harmonic Application*

The operation of the conflict of law rule can lead to the fragmentation of the applicable law in a legal relationship. This may happen either because it is a complex relationship in itself, as is the case with contracts governed by different laws depending on their various elements (capacity, substance, form, etc.), or because it involves several situations that arise from the same legal event, and therefore, they are closely linked, as occurs in the case of the succession rights of the surviving spouse. In these cases, it is necessary to adapt the different applicable laws to obtain a harmonious and fair solution. Thus, the adaptation is only one case among others, where the inadequacy of the conflict technique is clearly shown.

Despite being recognized as one of the central figures of current private international law,[46] adaptation has been at the center of complex debates on its requirements, its scope of action, and the determination of its solutions.[47] Adaptation, in short, can be defined as a figure that responds strictly to the problems of incompatibility of laws simultaneously applicable to the same legal situation, and whose operation transfers to the judge special powers to disregard and modify the rules at stake, to achieve material justice.[48]

As a result of this definition, it must be understood that adaptation needs two requirements. First, the fragmentation of the applicable law to a relationship,[49]

[43] Niboyet (1928, pp. 562–568).

[44] Pillet (1923, (vol II), pp. 359–360).

[45] Francescakis (1969, p. 503).

[46] Maekelt (2010, p. 332).

[47] Ochoa (2005, p. 271).

[48] Ochoa (2005, p. 272).

[49] Wolff (1958, p. 160).

which derives from the application of the conflict rule.[50] Second, there must be an incompatibility between the various applicable laws, so that if there are several and there is no contradiction between them, but they can be applied harmoniously, there is still no need to adapt. According to Ochoa Muñoz, incompatibility derives from the local character of the material laws, in the sense that these laws have been issued to regulate domestic legal relations, and therefore, their normative groups complement and integrate each other forming harmonic systems.[51] However, it is important to add that the state legislator is not obliged to adapt to the regulations of foreign laws.

In short, the judge must use adaptation when there is a contradiction between two or more simultaneously competent substantive laws.[52] Such a process will imply a modification, either of the conflict rule or of the simultaneously or successively applicable substantive rules, so that a harmonious and coherent regulation of the international case can take place.[53]

Following Kegel and Schurig, there is a private international law solution and a private substantive law solution. According to the conflictual solution, the legal fragmentation of the relationship will be attacked by the selection of a single conflict rule. This is a special characterization for the special purpose of avoiding the contradiction of rules. It is a preventive solution. The material solution, on the other hand, involves the manipulation of one of the applicable material laws, to attack the incompatibility. It is a curative solution.[54] Both solutions generate certain problems, and neither is satisfactory. Concerning the conflict solution, the first problem to be faced will be determining the conflict rule that will be disapplied. Starting from the ideas of Kegel and Schurig, who do not give a special answer to this problem but propose in a general way the weighing of interests in each case,[55] Ochoa Muñoz proposes sacrificing the less solid interests to protect those of greater importance, a task that is not easy.[56]

Commenting on the material solution, Alfonsín stated that it does not respect the content of the applicable rules, transforming the judge into a legislator, and authorizing them to regulate extra-national relations according to their ideas of justice.[57] Therefore, according to Ochoa Muñoz, this power transferred to the judge cannot be understood as absolute freedom of decision, which could lead to outrageous and arbitrary decisions without the possibility of control by higher instances. For him,

[50] Parra-Aranguren (1979, p. 184).

[51] Ochoa (2005, p. 274) and Bouza (1977, p. 30).

[52] Kegel und Schurig (2004, p. 360).

[53] Bouza (1977, pp. 12 and 29).

[54] Kegel und Schurig (2004, p. 361).

[55] Kegel und Schurig (2004, p. 362).

[56] Ochoa (2005, p. 279).

[57] Alfonsín (1982, p. 627).

the judge's freedom to decide by material justice is limited to the content of each of the conflicting laws and is therefore limited by its scope.[58]

Perhaps because of the difficulties presented by each of these solutions, Maekelt stated that in matters of adaptation, there are no definitive rules, and the solution must depend, in any case, on the characteristics of each situation and on the judge, whose task will be to find the most suitable solution. She emphasizes the value-based nature of this institution, which makes it possible to combat excessive formalism and achieve a functional result according to material justice. Echoing Neuhaus' ideas, Maekelt recommends considering adaptation as an exception, which will make it possible to avoid violating legal certainty.[59]

In Colombian private international law, only Article 9 of the Inter-American Convention on General Rules refers to adaptation, without leaning toward either of the two solutions mentioned above. The rule, instead, adopts two principles: first, the various aspects of the same relationship may be governed by different laws, configuring what the doctrine has called *dépeçage*; and second, mechanical conflictual criteria are abandoned in favor of a fundamental guiding criterion: equity in the specific case.[60] The solution chosen by this rule corresponds to Goldschmidt's idea of regulating the adaptation by giving just a broad guideline to judges so that they enjoy greater freedom to achieve the ends pursued by the laws involved.[61] But this cannot be interpreted as allowing any kind of arbitrariness by judges, who tend to apply the *lex fori* invoking difficulties in the application of the conflict rule as an excuse.[62]

Promoting the main role of the judge, who has first-hand knowledge of the specific case, the IADIP Draft assumes the solution of the Inter-American Convention, by providing in Article 10 as follows:

> The different laws that may be applicable to regulate various aspects of one and the same juridical relationship shall be applied harmoniously to attain the purposes pursued by each of such laws.
>
> Any difficulties that may be caused by their simultaneous application shall be resolved in light of the requirements of equity in each specific case.

Despite the advantages of this solution, several questions may arise, for example, at what point the judge should make use of the adaptation and in which cases the application of this method should be limited. Regarding the first question, it can be affirmed that adaptation inevitably appears in the last phase of application of the conflict rule, when applying the substantive rules designated by the conflict rules. Thus, the adaptation acts, not when the judge is selecting the applicable law, but

[58] Ochoa (2005, p. 227).

[59] Maekelt (2010, p. 335).

[60] See Articles 14.V Mexican Civil Code and 7 Venezuelan Act on Private International Law.

[61] Goldschmidt (1979, p. 153).

[62] Bouza (1977, p. 28).

when they are dealing with the harmonization of the various substantive laws that have been designated by the conflict rules.[63]

As to whether adaptation should be limited to cases of incompatibility between different laws applicable to the same legal situation, my answer must be in the affirmative. In this regard, it is convenient to differentiate between the cases that give rise to adaptation *stricto* sensu and those that require "substitution" or "transposition" of institutions,[64] both based on the theory of equivalence. Adaptation arises in any case in which there is a mismatch in the result because of several different laws applicable to the same case.[65]

3 Institutions that Reject the Application of Foreign Law

The institutions discussed in the previous section accompany the application of foreign law. Even the unknown institution, in the form in which it is regulated by the Inter-American Convention on General Rules and by the IADIP Draft, fulfills this authorizing function by leaving the judge with the power to disapply foreign law, only in cases in which the *lex fori* does not provide for an analogous institution (functional characterization).

On the other hand, the institutions discussed below have the function of causing the eviction of foreign law: public policy due to the manifest incompatibility of the application of foreign law with the essential principles of the *lex fori*, and *fraus legis* due to the conduct of the parties to fraudulently circumvent the application of foreign law to govern the legal relationship.

3.1 *Public Policy (***ordre public***)*

In private international law, public policy is a mechanism for the protection of the essential principles of a given legal system. Public policy in private international law differs from public policy in domestic law: the latter limits individual autonomy, while the former limits the application of foreign law.[66] Public policy in private international law acts in two areas: in the procedural sphere to prevent the recognition of foreign judgments[67] or arbitration awards,[68] for violation of substantive or procedural principles; and, in matters of applicable law, when the law to which the

[63] Fernández and Sánchez (2004, p. 376).

[64] See Bouza (1977, pp. 84–87).

[65] Fernández and Sánchez (2004, pp. 376–377).

[66] Fresnedo (2016, pp. 99–100).

[67] Madrid (2003, pp. 361 ff).

[68] Madrid (2006, pp. 79 ff).

conflict rule of the forum leads contains provisions whose application is manifestly incompatible with the fundamental principles of that legal system.[69] In this chapter, the main interest lies in the second function. This refers to the cases where foreign law does not apply.

As previously stated, Article 5 of the Inter-American Convention on General Rules establishes that "The law declared applicable by a convention on private international law may be refused the application in the territory of a State Party that considers it manifestly contrary to the principles of its public policy (*ordre public*)". Colombian case law has interpreted this concept similarly in cases referring to the recognition of foreign judgments and awards, which is somewhat paradoxical. In an exequatur decision released in 1994, the Civil Chamber of the Supreme Court of Justice recognized that there is a limit to the state's obligation to apply foreign law. This limit is determined by the specific circumstances of the case and the potential impact on essential principles that safeguard society's values.[70]

The principles safeguarded by public order are unique in each society. This has led scholars to use the term public policy in private international law instead of "international public policy". The latter phrase implies the existence of universally recognized principles, but such principles are specific to each state system: They can vary among countries.[71] Therefore, public policy does not have an international nature since it safeguards principles that are integral to the fundamental framework of the domestic law of every state.[72] This idea was adopted by the Civil Chamber of the Colombian Supreme Court of Justice in the exequatur decision of 1994 referred to above.[73] The Chamber acknowledged that public policy is crucial for safeguarding the society it serves, encompassing principles related to political, moral, religious, and economic interests.[74]

It is important to keep in mind that these principles can also change over time. Each state has its own unique principles that continuously evolve. Therefore, it is important to consider that they may vary over time.[75] In 1994, the Colombian Supreme Court, emphasizing the significance of public policy in judicial decision-making, stressed that judges must ensure that their decisions align with current principles of public policy, which are subject to changes like the so-called laws of public policy.[76]

Public policy is also a flexible concept that involves the judge's assessment of the values, considering the specific case and the harm caused by the foreign law in

---

[69] Both accepted by Colombian scholars. See Roldán (2010, p. 7).

[70] Supreme Court of Justice, Civil Chamber, Judgment of July 19, 1994, file 3894.

[71] Parra-Aranguren (1998, p. 129).

[72] See Fresnedo (2016, p. 100).

[73] Supreme Court of Justice, Civil Chamber, Judgment of July 19, 1994, file 3894.

[74] Supreme Court of Justice, Civil Chamber, Judgment February 29, 1996, file 3626.

[75] de Angulo (1972, pp. 369 ff.).

[76] Supreme Court of Justice, Civil Chamber, Judgment of July 19, 1994, file 3894. See also Supreme Court of Justice, Civil Chamber, Judgment of July 13, 1995.

forum.[77] Public policy is responsible for safeguarding outcomes rather than theoretical legal principles. Its role is to ensure that solutions are aligned with the core values of justice within each specific legal system.[78]

For public policy to intervene, certain requirements must be met. The first requirement is the implementation of the conflict rule. This ensures that if a dispute is resolved using an overriding mandatory rule, there will be no need for public policy intervention.[79] If the specific case is resolved by applying a specific international rule designed for cases that involve foreign elements, the judge's conflict rule and public policy may not apply. For example, this may be the case in a contract governed by the 1980 Vienna Convention on Contracts for the International Sale of Goods. Second, it is essential that the conflict rule results in the enforcement of foreign law. When the conflict rule of the forum declares its law as applicable, the judge is not dealing with a case of public policy. Instead, the competent law to govern the corresponding relationship is simply the *lex fori.*[80] Ironically, the public policy's intervention, which previously required the application of a conflict rule, now hinders its mission by excluding the law it had indicated. Third, it is essential to ensure that the foreign law being used does not contradict the fundamental principles of the *lex fori*. This assessment should not depend on the theoretical aspects of foreign law but rather on its practical application and the consequences it produces, as mentioned earlier.[81] For this reason, it seems possible that the same rule of foreign law may contradict the fundamental principles in certain cases while not doing so in others. Hence, it is not crucial to assess foreign law as a complete system, but rather focus on evaluating the effects it has on a particular case.

For public policy to operate, it does not matter if the foreign rule is different or even contradictory to the corresponding substantive rule of the forum, even if that rule is mandatory, what is important is that there is a clear violation of fundamental principles.[82] Allowing its intervention in minor discrepancies may be misinterpreted as a form of public policy in domestic law. This misinterpretation could devastate the content and principles of the conflictual system and should be avoided at all costs.[83]

In different legal systems, it is typical to require a "manifest incompatibility" between the outcome of applying a foreign rule and the fundamental principles of the forum. This phrase is commonly found in many documents from the Hague Conference,[84] where it was initially approved, as well as in many of the Inter-

[77] Supreme Court of Justice, Civil Chamber, Judgment of July 19, 1994, file 3894.

[78] See Madrid (2005, pp. 290–294).

[79] Parra-Aranguren (1998, p. 126).

[80] Sánchez-Covisa (1976, p. 446).

[81] Parra-Aranguren (1998, p. 127).

[82] Fresnedo (2016, p. 100).

[83] Sánchez-Covisa (1976, pp. 446–447).

[84] Within the Conventions to which Colombia is a party, the use of this expression in Article 24 of the Hague Convention on Adoption is noteworthy.

American Conventions that Colombia has ratified.[85] In some national private international law systems, the incompatibility must be obvious or manifest.[86] Whereas, others require simple incompatibility,[87] so that a mere difference between the *lex fori* and the foreign law is not seen as a violation of public policy.[88]

When discussing the phrase "manifestly incompatible", Diamond explained that something is only considered incompatible when it is clearly or manifestly incompatible. However, this may cause us to assume that there is a distinction between what is incompatible and what is manifestly incompatible. The purpose of this phrase is to favor foreign law by giving it the benefit of the doubt when a judge is uncertain about its incompatibility.[89]

In Colombian domestic private international law, there is no explicit rule concerning public policy. However, based on the Inter-American codification—especially the Inter-American Convention on General Rules—the Supreme Court in Civil Chamber has interpreted public policy as a reservation clause. This clause is designed to prevent the acceptance of a foreign law that, despite being characterized as the competent law to govern a certain matter, blatantly contradicts the fundamental principles on which the national legal system is based.[90]

The IADIP Draft also understands public order as a reservation clause and Article 6 establishes that "The dispositions of foreign law which must be applied in conformity with this Act shall be excluded only when their application will produce results manifestly incompatible with essential principles of Colombian public policy". This wording is similar to the one used by the Inter-American codification.

This rule intentionally departs from the second paragraph of Article 21 of the UNAL Draft Civil Code, which states that "For foreign laws to produce effects in Colombia, they must not be contrary to public policy, *bonnes moeurs*, or fundamental rights".[91] Although the concept of *bonnes moeurs* is usually omitted in private international law rules, the reference to fundamental rights is of great importance for public policy, and this has been recognized by case law.

Finally, the manifest incompatibility of the result of applying foreign law with the fundamental principles of the judge's legal system will only provoke the action of public policy if there is a sufficient connection with the forum, in a clear

[85] This expression can be found in the Inter-American Conventions on General Rules (art. 5); Letters Rogatory (art. 17); Taking of Evidence Abroad (art. 16); on Validity of Foreign Judgments and Arbitral Awards (art. 2.h); on the Execution of Preventive Measures (art. 12); International Return of Children (art. 25); and Maintenance Obligations (art. 22).

[86] Arts. 6 EGBGB; 3081 Quebec Civil Code; 8 Venezuelan Act on Private International Law; and 17.3 Paraguayan Act on international contracts.

[87] Art. 2600 Argentine Civil and Commercial Code.

[88] Arts. 86 Dominican Act on Private International Law and 5 Uruguayan Act on Private Internacional Law.

[89] See Diamond (1986, p. 292).

[90] Supreme Court of Justice, Civil Chamber, Judgment of November 5, 1996, file 6130.

[91] This rule, except for the reference to fundamental rights, reproduces the second paragraph of Article 16 of the Valencia Zea Draft.

reference to the doctrine known as *Inlandsbeziehung* or *Binnenbeziehung*.[92] This requirement, in addition to illustrating the relativity and national nature of public policy, is directly connected with the importance of the harm principle for forum.[93] Parra-Aranguren recognizes that this connection requirement can be very useful in avoiding abuses by judges.[94] Following this criterion, the second paragraph of Article 6 of the IADIP Draft expressly refers to the necessary intensity of the connection between Colombia and the relationship as an element to be considered by the judge in assessing incompatibility. In addition to this element, the judge must also take into consideration "the level of social harm and the gravity that the application of such foreign rule in Colombia would produce". This reinforces the exceptional nature of public policy.

However, this conception of public policy in private international law necessarily leads us to the thorny terrain of determining the fundamental principles of a legal system. The judge is faced with two essential problems. In the first place, the term "principle" directly implies that it is not a positive, expressed rule. Second, its characterization as "fundamental" or "essential", since not all principles can be considered as such. Those of an eminently technical nature, without teleological or ethical connotation, whose respect is not necessary to ensure the coherence of a given system, are ruled out.[95]

Among scholars, there have been attempts to solve the problem of determining the fundamental principles. The first is verified in the confusion of public policy with the territoriality principle that arises from Mancini's work.[96] However, after multiple failures in the attempt to delimit the principles, it is now understood that a list of matters considered to be of public policy or cases in which the judge's law would apply directly cannot be drawn up. The only instrument that echoed the aprioristic thesis of public policy, proposed by Mancini, was the Bustamante Code which has been widely criticized for it.[97]

In any case, it is not the legislator but the judge who determines the principles the violation of which would trigger public policy in each specific case, observing whether and to what extent a fundamental principle deserves to prevent the application of foreign law.[98] To avoid arbitrariness by judges, it is advisable that case law, which is an expression of the social conscience of the time,[99] performs such work, as recognized by the Colombian Supreme Court of Justice.[100]

---

[92] See Kahn (1891), Madrid (2005, p. 296), Bucher (1995, p. 192), Batiffol and Lagarde (1993, p. 576).

[93] Bucher (1995, pp. 189–191).

[94] Parra-Aranguren (1998, pp. 136–137).

[95] Bonomi (1998, pp. 201–202).

[96] Cock Arango stated that sovereignty constituted an insurmountable obstacle to the application of foreign law. Cock (1952, pp. 12–13).

[97] Goldschmidt (1979, p. 147).

[98] Kegel und Schurig (2004, pp. 530–536).

[99] Betti (1967, p. 292).

[100] Supreme Court of Justice, Civil Chamber, Judgment of July 19, 1994, file. 3894.

To guide the judge, Jayme proposed several steps to follow to determine in which cases, due to the intervention of public policy, foreign law should be excluded. Such "concretization criteria" are the determination of the meaning and purpose of the foreign law; the examination of the weakness of the legislative policy of the foreign rule; a comparative law study; consideration of the relevance of the domestic rule; and finally, the determination of the domestic connection. These approaches make it easier to ground cases in which public policy must act, but no single step is of value on its own.[101]

The IADIP Draft is close, in this sense to the aforementioned UNAL Draft Civil Code and understands the difficulties faced by the judge in the application of public policy. It so establishes in Article 6 that "A foreign rule that is manifestly incompatible with fundamental rights shall not be applied". Such a conception, as stated above, is linked to the treatment given to public policy by the Colombian Supreme Court of Justice.

Understanding that public policy in private international law is limited to the basic or fundamental principles of the institutions,[102] and that the violation of a mandatory rule is not enough,[103] the Supreme Court of Justice has included in a sort of catalog, the principles regarding which public policy is usually involved, e.g., the prohibition of abusive exercise of rights, good faith, the impartiality of the arbitral tribunal, and respect for due process,[104] equality, personal and national dignity,[105] and the grounds of divorce.[106]

In addition to these principles, the Court considers as the object of public policy protection, the standards that safeguard a minimum of morality in society.[107] In short, the Supreme Court has stated that international public policy refers to the most basic notions of morality and justice, which serve as a substrate for legal institutions, both substantive and procedural, viewed in a restrictive manner.[108] This way of looking at public policy in private international law has been reiterated by the Supreme Court itself in a recent decision of the Civil Chamber in which it compiles these criteria,[109] which have also been reiterated by the Constitutional Court.[110]

After excluding the foreign law whose application is intolerable in the forum, the judge has a new task, which is to determine the rule with which to fill the gap left by the foreign rule that has been unapplied. This task will depend on the function that

[101] Jayme (1991, pp. 215–270).

[102] Supreme Court of Justice, Civil Chamber, Judgment July 27, 2011, file 2007-01956-00.

[103] Supreme Court of Justice, Civil Chamber, Judgment May 12, 2017, file 2015-01074-00.

[104] Supreme Court of Justice, Civil Chamber, Judgment July 27, 2011, file 2007-01956-00; Supreme Court of Justice, Civil Chamber, Judgment April 18, 2017.

[105] Supreme Court of Justice, Civil Chamber, Judgment SC10089, July 25, 2016.

[106] Supreme Court of Justice, Civil Chamber, Judgment SC4683, November 5, 2019.

[107] Supreme Court of Justice, Civil Chamber, Judgment, September 7, 2016, file 2014-02737-00.

[108] Supreme Court of Justice, Civil Chamber, Judgment, July 12, 2017, file 2014-01927-00.

[109] Supreme Court of Justice, Civil Chamber, Judgment, January 15, 2019, file 2016-03020-00.

[110] Constitutional Court, Judgment T-354, August 6, 2019.

each law attributes to its own rules vis-à-vis the foreign law indicated by the conflict rules.

German scholars, for example, conceive public policy as a reservation clause, an exceptional provision which, as such, must be interpreted restrictively: only if the judge does not find a solution in the foreign law itself may they have recourse to the *lex fori*.[111] This is the solution adopted by the Portuguese Civil Code (Article 22.2). Although the Dominican Act on Private International Law (Article 86.II) and, paradoxically, the Italian Act (Article 16.2) admit the total eviction of the law initially indicated by the conflict rule, before ordering the application of the *lex fori*, they establish the application of the law indicated by other connecting factors provided by the same conflict rule, assuming the thesis of the subsidiary law, which would be truncated if the conflict rule has only one connecting factor. The classic Italian scholars, on the contrary, consider the public policy as a rule, so that the gap left by the eviction of foreign law must be filled with its rules.[112] The Peruvian Civil Code (Article 2049) and the Austrian Act (art. 6), which expressly order the application of the *lex fori*, are aligned with this thesis. On the contrary, some legal systems, including the Venezuelan Act (Article 8), the Paraguayan Act on international contracts (Article 17.3), the Argentine Civil and Commercial Code (Article 2600), as well as the Inter-American Conventions, are silent in this respect, which leads judges to normally apply their own national law.[113]

In Colombia, as can be inferred from the case law, the trend seems to point to the application of Colombian law in case of eviction of foreign law. Thus, the third paragraph of Article 6 of the IADIP Draft provides, particularly approaching the Peruvian rule, that "When a provision of the competent foreign law is not applicable due to such incompatibility, Colombian law shall apply".

3.2 *Evasion of Law (***fraus legis***)*

Certain connecting factors allow the parties to modify them in order to obtain the application of a rule more favorable to the realization of their wishes, thus circumventing the mandatory rules of the normally applicable law, which may be the *lex fori* or a foreign law.[114] Such situations constitute cases of fraud or evasion of law under private international law.

For fraud to occur, in addition to such material element, i.e., the change of the conflict rule's connecting factor through a technically regular procedure, a

[111] *Reichsgericht* of 19 December 1922, RGZ 106, 82, cited in: Kegel und Schurig (2005, p. 539).

[112] Ago (1936, pp. 296–298).

[113] Parra-Aranguren (1998, p. 141).

[114] Parra-Aranguren (1998, pp. 143–144 and 150).

psychological element is required, i.e., the intention to avoid the application of the normally applicable law.[115]

Thus, the essence of fraud is the combination of deceitful intent (*animus fraudulentus*) and action to obtain a result different from the one intended by the imperative rule evaded.[116] This is its main difference with the violation of the law, because while the conduct that embodies the violation directly opposes or confronts the text of the law, the act that constitutes the fraud injures its spirit and sense.[117]

This institution has been harshly criticized because of the difficulty of proving *animus fraudulentus*. It has also been argued that the same objectives could be achieved by other institutions. The most frequent confusion arises with public policy. Goldschmidt argued in this respect that fraud is a general negative characteristic of any legal rule, while public policy is the general negative characteristic of the legal consequence of the conflict rule since it is only through its intervention that the possibility of applying foreign law arises. He added, furthermore, that public policy is a value judgment on foreign law, while fraud on the law implies a value judgment on the attitude of the parties.[118]

In this sense, Kegel and Schurig argue that while public policy guarantees material justice, since it only intervenes when the content of the foreign law grossly violates the sense of justice of the forum, fraud against the law only censures how the connecting factor is created. This is therefore a mere question of conflictual justice, which is why public policy is inefficient in solving the problem of fraud.[119]

Despite the clear differences between public policy and fraud, the imperative nature of the rules protected through the *fraus legis* can certainly lead to applying public policy rather than fraud. Article 6 of the Inter-American Convention on General Rules does not help to clarify the picture. It provides:

> The law of a State Party shall not be applied as foreign law when the basic principles of the law of another State Party have been fraudulently evaded. The competent authorities of the receiving State shall determine the fraudulent intent of the interested parties.

The express reference in this rule to "the basic principles of the law of another State Party" is striking, since it has traditionally been understood that the evasion must affect the mandatory rules of the *lex fori*.[120] However, according to Maekelt, the reference to the "principles of another State party" broadens the scope of the fraud, although it also makes it more difficult to implement in practice.[121] Regarding the content of the basic principles, no further explanation has been given, perhaps the difference with those principles protected by public policy is given, not by their

[115] Maury (1952, pp. 161–162).
[116] See Verplaetse (1938, p. 26).
[117] Miaja (1976, p. 400).
[118] Goldschmidt (1952, pp. 289–292).
[119] Kegel und Schurig (2004, p. 494).
[120] Loussouarn and Bourel (1993, p. 288).
[121] Maekelt (1982, p. 320).

content, but by the intervention of the fraudulent animus in the change of the connecting factor.

Despite the concerns generated by the rule of the Inter-American Convention, the IADIP Draft favors its solution, and Article 7 refers to the artificial avoidance of the essential principles of the law designated by the conflict rule. Article 7 also refers to the conflictual effect of fraudulent evasion of the law, by providing for the eviction of the law whose application has been fraudulently sought, even if it is the *lex fori*. Although the rule does not indicate it, the gap that occurs should be filled with the rules of the evaded law.

Although Article 7 of the Uruguayan Act on Private International Law was also considered as a model, the IADIP Draft departed from that rule because it is limited to punish the evasion of Uruguayan law, and it is preferred to privilege the fact that if fraud punishes the attitude of the parties, this sanction should be imposed regardless of whether the evaded law is Colombian or foreign. For this reason, the content of the third paragraph of Article 16 of the Valencia Zea Draft and the third paragraph of Article 21 of the UNAL Draft Civil Code was not considered, since according to both rules "No one may take advantage of a legal situation created in applying foreign law in fraud of Colombian law".[122]

Finally, Article 7 of the IADIP Draft is silent regarding the material effects directly related to the application of the *fraus omnia currumpit* principle to annul acts concluded in fraud of the law. However, it must be admitted with Loussouarn and Bourel that if the act conforms to the law of the place where it was born, the forum cannot decide on its validity. The only thing in its power is to disregard its effects on its territory. Thus, rather than nullity, it is a question of unenforceability.[123]

4 Conclusions

At this point, I would like to stress the convenience of having a private international law that responds to the progress of the matter and to Colombia's reality. In the IADIP Draft, the traditional content of the general theory of private international law is guided by the need to provide the judge with tools to achieve material justice in each specific case.

The enshrinement of the principles of the general theory of private international law, currently absent in Colombian private international law, would represent a great advance for the subject and would undoubtedly contribute to its consolidation, not as just another branch of law with little practical application, but as what it really is: a fundamental tool to face challenges that globalization implies for every person's life.

[122] Although Ochoa states that the rule does not explicitly require the presence of the subjective element, in my opinion the use of the word "fraud" denotes itself the need for fraudulent intent, without which there would be no place to speak of fraud, neither in domestic law nor in private international law. See Ochoa (2021, p. 387).

[123] Loussouarn and Bourel (1993).

References

Ago R (1936) Règles générales des conflits de lois. Recueil des Cours de l'Académie de Droit International 58:243 ff

Aguilar Navarro M (1982) Derecho internacional privado (vol I), 4ª edn. Universidad Complutense, Madrid

Alfonsín Q (1982) Teoría del derecho privado internacional. Ediciones Idea, Montevideo

Bartin E (1897) De L'impossibilité d'arriver à une suppression définitive des conflits de lois. Journal de Droit International 1897:25 ff

Bartin E (1930) Le doctrine des qualifications et ses rapports avec le caractère national du conflit de lois. Recueil des Cours de l'Académie de Droit International 31(1):561 ff

Bartin E (1931) Encore le renvoi. Clunet 1931:1256 ff

Batiffol H, Lagarde P (1993) Droit international privé, 6th edn. Librairie Générale de Droit et de Jurisprudence, Paris

Betti E (1967) La interpretación de los conceptos calificadores en el derecho internacional privado (translated by Sansó B). Universidad Central de Venezuela, Caracas, pp 677 ff

Betti E (1975) Interpretación de la ley y de los actos jurídicos (translated by de los Mozos JL) Revista de Derecho Privado, Madrid

Bonomi A (1998) Le norme imperative nel Diritto internazionale privato. Considerazione sulla Convenzione europea sulla legge applicabile alle obbligazioni contrattuali del 19 giugno 1980 nonché sulle leggi italiana e svizzera di Diritto internazionale privato. Zürich: Schulthess Polygraphischer Verlag

Bouza Vidal N (1977) Problemas de adaptación en derecho internacional privado e interregional. Tecnos, Madrid

Bucher A (1995) Droit international privé suisse. Helbing & Lichtenhahn, Bâle

Calvo Caravaca AL, Carrascosa González J (2022) Tratado de derecho internacional privado, 2nd edn. Tirant Lo Blanch, Valencia

Cock Arango A (1952) Tratado de Derecho internacional privado. Universidad Nacional de Colombia, Bogota

Davì A (2012) Le renvoi en droit international privé contemporain. Recueil des Cours de l'Académie de Droit International 352:9 ff

de Angulo RM (1972) Du moment auquel il faut se placer pour apprécier l'ordre public international. Revue Critique de Droit International Privé 65:369 ff

Derruppé J (1993) Le renvoi dans les conventions internationales. Juris-Classeur. International 532-3(1):3 f

Despagnet F (1898) Des conflits de lois relatifs à la qualification des rapports juridiques. Journal de Droit International pp 253 ff

Diamond A (1986) Harmonization of Private International Law relating to contractual obligations. Recueil des Cours de l'Académie de Droit International, 199(4), 233 ff

Fernández Rozas JC, Sánchez Lorenzo S (2004) Derecho internacional privado (3.ª d.). Madrid: Thomson-Civitas

Francescakis P (1969) Ordre public. Encyclopédie Juridique Dalloz, Répertoire de Droit International, F-Z, 498 ff

Fresnedo de Aguirre C (2016) Public policy: common principles in the American states. Recueil des Cours de l'Académie de Droit International 379:73 ff

Garde Castillo J (1947) La "institución desconocida" en derecho internacional privado. Instituto Editorial Reus, Madrid

Goldschmidt W (1952) Sistema y filosofía del derecho internacional privado, 2ª edn. EJEA, Buenos Aires

Goldschmidt W (1979) Normas generales de la CIDIP-II: Hacia una teoría general del derecho internacional privado interamericano. Anuario Jurídico Interamericano 1979:141 ff

Hernández-Bretón E (2007) En materia de calificaciones, reenvío y otros asuntos de derecho internacional privado. Cuadernos Unimetanos 11:227 ff
Jayme E (1991) Métodos para la concretización del orden público en el derecho internacional privado (translated by Hernández E). Revista de la Facultad de Ciencias Jurídicas y Políticas 82:215 ff
Kahn F (1891) Gesetzeskollisionen, Ein Beitrag zur Lehre des Internationalen Privatrechts. Jherings-Jährbücher 1 ff
Kegel G, Schurig K (2004) Internationales Privatrecht, 9th edn. Verlag C.H. Beck, Munich
Lewald H (1929) La théorie du renvoi. Recueil des Cours de l'Académie de Droit International 29(4):487 ff
Loussouarn Y, Bourel P (1993) Droit international privé, 4th edn. Précis Dalloz, Paris
Madrid Martínez C (2003) Breves notas sobre el orden público y el reconocimiento de decisiones extranjeras en el sistema venezolano de derecho internacional privado. In: Parra Aranguren F (ed) Libro Homenaje a Juan María Rouvier. Tribunal Supremo de Justicia, Caracas, p 361 ff
Madrid Martínez C (2005) Artículo 8. Orden público. In: Maekelt T et al. (eds), Ley de Derecho Internacional Privado comentada(vol I). Universidad Central de Venezuela, Caracas, pp 289 ff
Madrid Martínez C (2006) El rol del orden público en arbitraje comercial internacional. Revista de la Facultad de Ciencias Jurídicas y Políticas 126:79 ff
Maekelt T (1982) General rules of private international law in the Americas. New approach. Recueil des Cours de l'Académie de Droit International 177:193 ff
Maekelt T (1998) Antecedentes y metodología del Proyecto. Parte general del Derecho internacional privado. Proyecto de Ley de Derecho Internacional Privado (1996). Biblioteca de la Academia de Ciencias Políticas y Sociales, Caracas, 15 ff
Maekelt T (2010) Teoría general de Derecho internacional privado, 2nd edn. Academia de Ciencias Políticas y Sociales, Caracas
Magalhães Collaço I (1964) Da qualificação em Direito internacional privado. Editorial Império, Lisboa
Makarov A (1955) Les cas d'application des règles de conflits étrangères. Revue critique de Droit international privé 44:431 ff
Maury J (1952) L'éviction de la Loi normalement compétente: L'ordre public et la fraude a la loi. Universidad de Valladolid, Valladolid
Meijers EM (1938) La question du renvoi. Bulletin de l'institut Juridique. International 38:191 ff
Miaja de la Muela A (1976) Derecho internacional privado, vol I, 7th edn. Atlas, Madrid
Neuhaus PH (1976) Die Grundbegriffe des Internationalen Privatrechts, 2nd edn. Paul Siebeck, Tubingen
Niboyet JP (1928) Manual de Droit international privé, 10th edn. Sirey, Paris
Ochoa Jiménez MJ (2021) Las normas de Derecho internacional privado: observaciones al Proyecto de Código Civil de la Universidad Nacional de Colombia. Revista de Derecho Privado 41:373 ff
Ochoa Muñoz J (2005) Artículo 7. Adaptación. In: Maekelt T et al (eds) Ley de Derecho Internacional Privado comentada, vol I. Universidad Central de Venezuela, Caracas, p 265 ff
Parra-Aranguren G (1979) Convención Interamericana sobre Normas Generales de Derecho internacional privado (Montevideo, 1979). Anuario Jurídico Interamericano 1979:157 ff
Parra-Aranguren G (1998) Curso general de Derecho internacional privado. Problemas selectos y otros estudios, 3th edn. Universidad Central de Venezuela, Caracas
Pillet A (1913) Contre la théorie du renvoi. Revue de Droit International Privé et de Droit Pénal International 1 ff
Pillet A (1923) Principios de Derecho internacional privado (translated by Rodríguez N, González C) Librería General de Victoriano Suárez, Madrid
Rabel E (1931) Das Problem der Qualifikation. RabelsZ 5:241 ff
Roldán Pardo JF (2010) El estado del arte del concepto de orden público internacional en el ámbito del Derecho internacional privado y el arbitraje internacional. Revista de Derecho Privado 44:2 ff

Sánchez-Covisa J (1976) Orden público internacional y divorcio vincular. In: Obra Jurídica de Joaquín Sánchez-Covisa. Ediciones de la Contraloría General de la República de Venezuela, Caracas, p 441 ff
Savigny FC (1879) Sistema de derecho romano actual (translated by Mesía J, Poley M), 2nd edn. Góngora y Cía, Madrid
Verplaetse J (1938) La fraude à la loi en Droit international privé. Paris
Wolff M (1958) Derecho internacional privado (translated by Marín López A). Bosch, Barcelona

Claudia Madrid Martínez PhD in Law, *Magister Scientiarum* in Private International Law and Comparative Law, and lawyer from the Universidad Central de Venezuela (UCV); postdoctoral researcher, University of Cologne, Alexander von Humboldt Foundation (2012–2014); tenured professor, Universidad Central de Venezuela; associate professor, Universidad de Antioquia; member, Research Group Knowledge, Power and Law, Universidad de Antioquia.

Property

Property Rights in Colombian Private International Law

María Julia Ochoa Jiménez

Abstract This chapter deals with how the *lex rei sitae* rule is introduced in Latin America in general and in Colombia in particular. It critically discusses its inclusion in the legal instruments currently in force in Colombia and takes into account how it is approached in the IADIP Draft. After briefly describing how this proposal refers to intellectual property, the chapter turns to the quite innovative regulation it contains regarding the international restitution of cultural property in general and of Indigenous cultural objects in particular. Finally, the chapter briefly refers to the IADIP Draft's rules on mobile conflicts and jurisdiction before concluding with some final remarks.

1 Introduction

If a person of any nationality is the owner of real estate located in Argentina, Peru, or Ecuador, the rights that such person has over such property are governed by the Argentinian, Peruvian, or Ecuadorian legal systems, respectively. Likewise, Colombian rules would apply if the property were located in the territory of Colombia. For most people, this may seem self-evident. But, in fact, it is so because, in the legal system of each of these countries, there is a legal rule—to be more precise, a private international law rule—according to which such rights are subject to

This text is partially based on a previous work carried out in the framework of a project directed by Marguerita Salvadori (University of Turin). See also Ochoa Jiménez (Revista de Derecho Privado 37:153–183, 2019; Int J Cult Prop 26(4):437–456, 2019).

M. J. Ochoa Jiménez (✉)
Loyola University, Sevilla, Andalucía, Spain
e-mail: mjochoa@uloyola.es

M. J. Ochoa Jiménez, C. Madrid Martínez (eds.), *A Private International Law for Colombia*, Springer Textbooks in Law,
https://doi.org/10.1007/978-3-032-04106-7_11

the legal system of the state in which the property is located. This private international law rule is called *lex rei sitae*.[1]

The wide acceptance of this rule, which has a strong territorial basis, is largely explained by the relevance that property rights have for the protection of the territorial sovereignty of the state of location,[2] which is evident in relation to real property.[3] Other reasons mentioned in support of the *lex rei sitae* rule are the legal certainty it provides,[4] its predictability[5] and its favorability with respect to the rights of third parties.[6]

In the case of immovable property, the application of this rule does not usually pose major difficulties. But the location of other types of property may not be that easy. Movable goods, for example, can in principle be moved from one country to another without great trouble. Thus, some national legal systems adopt, as will be seen in this chapter, rules other than the *lex rei sitae* for cases involving rights in property other than real estate. The need to revisit the *lex rei sitae* rule arises in connection with concerns regarding, e.g., intellectual property, cultural property, or movable assets subject to security rights.

Article 20 of the Colombian Civil Code contains the main conflictual rule on property rights in the Colombian legal system. Based on Article 16 of the Chilean Civil Code drafted by Andrés Bello in the mid-nineteenth century, it basically follows the trend marked by Friedrich Carl von Savigny, according to which the *lex rei sitae* rule applies to any type of property. It thus moves away from the regulation that distinguished between conflicts of laws in matters of real property—governed by the law of the place of location—and personal property—governed by the law of the domicile of the owner. The latter solution was in force for a short time in part of the Colombian territory, in Articles 12 and 13 of the Civil Code of the Antioquia Department of 1864.[7]

Article 20 of the Civil Code has several weaknesses. The use of obsolete terms and their confusing wording, together with a unilateral formulation, makes its revision necessary. As will be discussed in this chapter, although the rules of the Draft General Act on Private International Law for Colombia prepared by the *Instituto Antioqueño de Derecho Internacional Privado* (IADIP) (hereinafter, "IADIP Draft") maintains the *lex rei sitae* rule, it takes several steps forward by clarifying

---

[1] In English, the use of the term *lex situs* is often preferred.

[2] Bonnemaison (2013), p. 295.

[3] Junker (2017), p. 362.

[4] Herrán Medina (1959), p. 224; Niboyet (1951), p. 486; Symeonides (2016), p. 584.

[5] Symeonides (2016), p. 584.

[6] This can be seen in the German system, where Article 43.1 of the Introductory Act to the Civil Code provides for the *lex rei sitae* rule. The rule of Article 932 of the German Civil Code is also considered to be applicable in international situations: "…the acquirer becomes the owner even if the thing does not belong to the seller, unless the acquirer does not act in good faith at the time he acquires ownership …" See Schellerer (2016), p. 13.

[7] This codification is no longer in force.

the contents of the rule, while taking into consideration the developments that have occurred in relation to certain special types of property.

The chapter is structured as follows. First, I briefly present the historical development of the *lex rei sitae* rule and how it was introduced in Latin American legal systems. Subsequently, I critically discuss how this rule is established in the legal instruments currently in force in Colombia, particularly in the Civil Code. In the longest part of the chapter, I deal with the regulation proposed by the IADIP Draft, where a distinction is made between different types of property. The first group of rules is included in Article 66 and deals with property in transit, property subject to security rights, ships, aircraft, and other means of transport, and publicity of acts of creation, transfer, and extinction of property rights. After briefly describing the intellectual property rule, which is the focus of another contribution to this book, I turn to the cultural property regulation contained in the IADIP Draft, which deals with the international restitution of cultural property in general and of Indigenous cultural objects in particular. This latter aspect, which is one of the most outstanding innovations brought by the IADIP Draft, leads me to describe the rights of Indigenous peoples and communities, whose protection underlies such regulation and, more broadly, the relationship between Indigenous peoples and communities and private international law. Finally, the chapter refers to the rules of the IADIP Draft on mobile conflicts and jurisdiction. I conclude with some final remarks.

2 Why the *Lex Rei Sitae* Rule? A Historical Answer

The *lex rei sitae* rule generally applies to rights in movable and immovable property. However, this is not and has not always been the case. In the Kingdom of Prussia, the General Law for the Prussian States (*Allgemeines Landrecht für die Prussischen Staaten*) of 1794 contained the rule that movable property "followed the person."[8] Similarly, in the following century, the American Joseph Story argued in his Commentaries, first published in 1834, that such property should be governed by the legal system of the domicile of the owner (*lex domicilii*).[9] This solution reflects the distinction supported by statutist theories between the rules *mobilia sequuntur personam*—i.e., movable property follows the person—and *immobilia reguntur lege loci ubi cita*—i.e., immovable property is governed by the legal system of the place where it is located.[10] In Latin America, this solution was adopted in the Civil

[8] Junker (2017), p. 362.

[9] Story (1846), pp. 636–637.

[10] Bonnemaison (2013), p. 296; Larrea Holguín (1962), p. 182; Martiny (2012), p. 119; Tenorio (1955), p. 311.

Code of the Argentine Republic of 1869 and is largely maintained in its Civil and Commercial Code now in force.[11]

It is worth noting that the Civil Code of the State of Antioquia of 1864[12] established in Article 13 that the rights and obligations relating to movable property were governed by the laws of the country of domicile or residence of the owner. Whereas the *lex rei sitae* rule applied only to situations relating to rights over real estate (Article 12 of the Antioquian Civil Code). In German law, the rule *mobilia personam sequuntur* was replaced by the influence of Friedrich Carl von Savigny in the nineteenth century, to give way to the principle that subjects all kinds of property to the application of the legal system (Article 12 of the Antioquian Civil Code).

In German law, the rule *mobilia personam sequuntur* was replaced by the influence of Friedrich Carl von Savigny in the nineteenth century, to give way to the principle that subjects all kinds of property to the application of the legal system of the place of location.[13]

In Latin America, this principle was adopted by the Venezuelan Andrés Bello in his work *Principios Generales del Derecho Internacional* (General Principles of International Law), the first edition of which dates from 1832. At that time, the nations of our region, anxious to have their own bodies of law, saw the old Prussian rules as outdated and worthless.[14] During his years in England, Bello had been influenced by the Dutch school of the seventeenth century. The territorial approach was embodied in the idea of *comitas gentium*[15]—i.e., international comity—sustained by the Dutch school, since the recognition of foreign laws within the territory of a state was only justified by reasons of comity, i.e., from convenience and tacit

[11] Civil and Commercial Code of the Nation. Act No. 26.994, October 1, 2014.

[12] Civil Code of the Sovereign State of Antioquia. Issued by the Constituent Assembly. Official edition, 1864. According to the Colombian Constitution of 1858, each of the eight existing states could dictate its own Civil Code. Valencia Zea (2000), p. 32.

In the aspect I am dealing with here, the Antioquian Code differs from the Civil Code of Chile. However, the latter, drafted by Bello, was followed by the codes enacted by the states grouped under the *Confederación Granadina*, as well as by the code sanctioned in 1873, which has been in force for the entire Republic since 1887. As Mayorga notes, "at the time of the creation of the Federal State of Antioquia, Manuel Ancízar, who had become a close friend of Andrés Bello during his stay as a diplomat in Santiago, approached the latter to ask him to send him the Civil Code he had drafted for Chile because, given that the States that were being formed in Colombia had the power to dictate the Civil Code, had the attribution to dictate the civil and penal legislation that they believed convenient, it was his purpose to take advantage of the 'knowledge of other countries and to prefer, to any other, the legal doctrines professed in our South America' as a fundamental step towards 'the desired social unity' of the continent." See Mayorga (2017).

[13] Savigny accepts, only exceptionally, the application of the law of domicile in the case of movable property whose place of location is unclear. See Samtleben (2018), note 275. See also Junker (2017), p. 362; Larrea Holguín (1962), p. 182; Tenorio (1955), p. 311.

[14] Lira Urquieta (1981), p. xiv.

[15] Samtleben (2010a), p. 345.

consent of nations,[16] and not by the existence of an obligation or duty of a juridical nature.[17]

In Latin America, the reception of territorialism was marked by two circumstances that favored it. Its defense was based on the need to reaffirm, vis-à-vis Spain and the rest of the states, the national sovereignty of the republics that had just achieved their independence, of which Bello was a strong supporter.[18] In this context, Bello went as far as to affirm that "foreign law is not law among us."[19]

In addition, in Latin America, the historical roots of the principle of territoriality go back to Spanish law.[20] This principle had been used in the Iberian Peninsula to consolidate political power, first, in the seventh century to deal with a situation in which the norms of Roman law and those of the Germanic groups coexisted, and in the Middle Ages, it was used by *Alfonso El Sabio* to deal with the coexistence of numerous local jurisdictions.[21]

In Bello's doctrine, the application of the *lex rei sitae* rule was clearly a manifestation of his territorial position. According to him, from the empire and dominion—which are the two sovereignty forms[22]—emanates "the power to give laws on the acquisition, enjoyment, alienation, and transmission of the properties existing in the territory of the state."[23] Hence, the law "of the state in which the real estate is located is the one that determines what concerns them, even when they are possessed by

---

[16] Delic (2019), p. 188.

[17] In the second edition of Praelectionum Juris Civilis Tomi Tres, of whose title 3, part 2, book 1, the work *De Conflictu Legum Diversarum in Diversis Imperiis* forms part, Ulrich Huber puts forward the fundamental ideas of the Dutch school of the seventeenth century by these three famous maxims: (1) The laws of each state have force within the limits of that government and bind all those subject to it, but not beyond it. (2) All persons within the limits of a government, whether living there permanently or temporarily, are considered subject to it. (3) Sovereigns will thus act out of courtesy, rights acquired within the limits of a government retain their force everywhere insofar as they do not impair the power or rights of such government or of its subjects. Cf. Lorenzen (1919), pp. 199–242.

[18] Samtleben (1982), p. 168.

[19] Bello (1873), p. 64, note 3. The Chilean Constitution of 1812 also stated the following: "No decree, providence or order emanating from any authority or Court outside the territory of Chile shall have any effect; and those who attempt to give it value shall be punished as State offenders." See Samtleben (1982), p. 168.

[20] Samtleben (2010a), p. 345.

[21] Samtleben recalls how, in the history of private international law, there are numerous examples of this political use of the principle of territoriality, citing, in addition to Huber's ideas, within the Dutch doctrine of the seventeenth century, the ideas of D'Argentré, developed in France in the sixteenth century. Samtleben (2010b), pp. 371–372.

[22] Bello states: "Sovereignty, which insofar as it disposes of things is called dominion, insofar as it gives laws and orders to persons is properly called empire." See Bello (1873), p. 61.

This is the same rationale Fauchille finds for applying the law of the place of location to resolve conflicts of laws in matters of real rights. Fauchille, quoted by Tenorio (1955), pp. 310–311.

[23] Bello (1873), p. 63.

foreigners or by persons domiciled in a foreign country,"[24] while for movable property the same rule applies, being limited only in succession cases.[25]

Bello relied on these ideas while fulfilling the task of drafting the Civil Code, entrusted to him by the Chilean government. Thus, in Article 16 of this code, which was adopted in 1855, the application of the law of location[26] was included in a unilateral manner:[27]

> Property located in Chile is subject to Chilean law, even if its owners are foreigners and do not reside in Chile.
>
> This provision shall be understood without prejudice to the stipulations contained in contracts validly executed in a foreign country.
>
> But the effects of contracts executed in a foreign country to be performed in Chile shall be governed by Chilean law.

Through the Chilean Civil Code, the territorial principle came to exert a definitive influence on Latin American private international law that continues to this day.[28] Likewise, the use of the *lex rei sitae* rule has also been widespread[29] in most countries of the region for all kinds of property.

3 Territoriality in the Colombian Civil Code

The principle of territoriality is central to private law in Colombia.[30] Framed within this principle, Article 20 of the Colombian Civil Code contains the same regulation as its original version of 1887:[31]

> The goods located in the *territories*, and those found in the *states*, in whose property the Nation has an interest or right, are subject to the provisions of this Code, even when their owners are foreigners and reside outside of Colombia.
>
> This provision shall be without prejudice to the stipulations contained in contracts validly concluded in a foreign country.

---

[24] Bello (1873), p. 63.

[25] Ibid. p. 63.

[26] Article 3 of the French Civil Code refers to this point, mentioning only immovable property: "Immovable property, including that owned by foreigners, is governed by French law."

[27] The traditional unilateral formulation of the *lex rei sitae* rule in Latin American private international law is rooted in the Chilean Civil Code. See Samtleben (2018).

[28] Samtleben (1982), p. 167.

[29] Samtleben (2018), p. 101.

[30] See, e.g., Código Civil de Colombia, Article 18: "The law is mandatory for both nationals and foreigners residing in Colombia." Territorial conflict of rules can be found in the national legislations of other Latin American countries as well, e.g., Article 14 of the Chilean Civil Code. See Hernández-Bretón (2007), p. 25; Samtleben (2010c), p. 443.

[31] According to Mayorga, "... despite several drafts, the Civil Code adopted for the Republic in 1887 is the one that currently governs the country ..." See Mayorga (2017).

> But the effects of such contracts, to be fulfilled in any territory, or in cases that affect the rights and interests of the nation, shall be in accordance with this code and other civil laws of the *union*.

The use of the term "territories" and "states" in the first paragraph of this rule, and "union" in its last paragraph, may immediately catch the reader's attention. The reason is that they do not correspond to current legal and political terms and concepts.[32] This shows us, on the one hand, that, despite the numerous amendments made to the Civil Code since its adoption, Article 20 has not been revised and, on the other hand, that its content is not easy to understand and interpret. However, the presence of such words cannot be overlooked and must be read in the light of their current meaning.[33] Thus, "territories" should be read in the singular, as referring to the national territory, while "states" should be understood as synonymous with "departments"—i.e., the thirty-three administrative entities that form the country—and "union" as referring to the Republic of Colombia.

Article 20 of the Colombian Civil Code contains a unilateral conflict of laws rule, since, when referring to rights over property located in Colombia, it mandates the application of the Colombian legal system. This rule can be analyzed by dividing it into three parts.[34] First, it states in its first paragraph the *lex rei sitae* rule in broad terms without distinguishing between movable and immovable property.[35] Thus, all property located in Colombian territory is subject to the Colombian legal system, provided that "the Nation has an interest or right" in it. This last sentence covers, for example, property included in the cultural heritage, in respect of which the interest of the Colombian state is undeniable[36] and is evident in relation to archaeological objects (Articles 63 and 72 of the Political Constitution).[37]

Second, Article 20 refers to the application of the *lex rei sitae* rule to contracts entered into abroad. Thus, the existence and validity of such contracts that deal with property located in Colombia, over which the Colombian state has some right or interest, must be recognized within the Colombian territory. This rule does not refer to contracts on property located in the country, on which the Colombian state does not have any right or interest, nor to contracts on assets not located in the country.[38]

Third, considering that in Colombia only the existence and validity of contracts entered into abroad must be recognized, according to the third paragraph of Article

---

[32] For a synopsis of the history of the Colombian Civil Code, see Valencia Zea (2000), p. 31; Mayorga (2023).

[33] Act No. 57 of 1887, Article 2.

[34] Cfr. Zapata (2016), p. 194. A rule consisting of these three parts, but only with respect to immovables, is found in Article 12 of the Civil Code of the State of Antioquia (Act 20) of 1864.

[35] Cfr. Cock Arango (1952), p. 262.

[36] Cfr. Zapata (2016), p. 192.

[37] Political Constitution of Colombia, Article 63: "… the archaeological heritage of the Nation and other assets determined by law are inalienable, imprescriptible and unseizable," and Article 72: "… The archaeological heritage and other cultural assets that make up the national identity belong to the Nation and are inalienable, unseizable and imprescriptible …"

[38] Cfr. Zapata (2016), p. 194.

20, the national law governs the effects of contracts on property located in Colombia that have been entered into abroad, provided that such effects occur in the national territory or affect rights and interests of the Colombian state. In the latter case, it would be irrelevant, as Zapata argues, the place where such effects are produced.[39]

In Colombia, as in other countries, the *lex rei sitae* rule acts as the general rule, so that in specific cases, rules on special matters would prevail. It should be noted that, however, although according to Article 1012 of the Civil Code succession is governed by the law of the last domicile of the deceased, a judgment of the Supreme Court of Justice established in 2016 that the law of the place of location of the succession property is applicable if the deceased is domiciled in another country but has Colombian nationality.[40]

It is also worth noting that, at the regional level, the 1889 Treaty of Montevideo on International Civil Law includes the *lex rei sitae* rule in Article 26:[41] "Property, whatever its nature, is exclusively governed by the law of the place where it exists as to its quality, its possession, its absolute or relative alienability, and all the legal relations of a real nature to which it is susceptible." An antecedent of this rule is found in the Treaty of Private International Law, or Treaty of Lima, of 1878, which did not enter into force, but its text is largely the same as the Treaty that Colombia and Ecuador signed bilaterally in 1903.[42] The structure of Article 20 of the Civil Code coincides with the form of the *lex rei sitae* rule of the latter Treaty,[43] but here an exception is made regarding successions.

In the IADIP Draft, property rights are dealt with in Chapter Twelve. This chapter, which is made up of Articles 66–68, contains the rules relating to the law that must be applied by Colombian courts in cases regarding such matters. The regulation on jurisdiction, which will be mentioned in the last session of this chapter, is included in Chapter Four.

The general conflict of laws rules entailed in Chapter Twelve essentially maintain the legal tradition based on the *lex rei sitae* rule, which is followed in Article 20 of the Civil Code. However, the rules proposed in the IADIP Draft are more comprehensive and specialized. Above all, it is worth mentioning that the general rule of Article 66, first paragraph, contains the *lex rei sitae* rule in a bilateral manner: "Property and rights thereon are governed by the laws of the state in which they are

[39] Cfr. Zapata (2016), p. 196.

[40] Supreme Court of Justice of Colombia, Civil Cassation Chamber, Judgment of September 16, 2016, No. AC7803-2016, file No. 11001-02-03-000-2015-03168-00.

[41] This rule was later included in Article 32 of the Montevideo Treaty of 1940 on International Civil Law, to which Argentina and Paraguay are parties; cfr. Samtleben (2014), p. 580.

[42] Cfr. Samtleben (1982), p. 14.

[43] Treaty on Private International Law of June 18, 1903 (Colombia, Act 13 of 1905), Article 3: "The assets existing in the Republic shall be governed by the national laws, even if their owners are foreigners and do not reside therein, except as provided in the title of successions. This provision does not limit the power of the owner of such property to enter into contracts valid in the other country, but the effects of such contracts, when they are to be performed in the Republic, shall be governed by its laws."

located." National courts must thus apply Colombian law if the property is situated in Colombian territory, but foreign law if the property is located abroad. In similar terms, the *lex rei sitae rule* is included in the IADIP Draft (Article 95, first paragraph) regarding acquisitive prescription (usucapion): "Acquisitive prescription of movable or immovable property is governed by the law of the place where it is located." The bilateral form in which the *lex rei sitae* rule is conceived in the aforementioned articles goes beyond what is permitted by the marked territorial approach of the unilateral formulation of Article 20 of the Civil Code. Article 66 of the IADIP Draft also excludes any reference to obsolete terms regarding the political and territorial organization of the country. There are no confusing allusions to international contracts either. All this together makes Article 66 a rule that provides greater legal certainty.

However, nowadays, the *lex rei sitae* rule alone is doubtlessly insufficient to cover the whole spectrum of situations related to property rights. In this regard, as will be described below, Article 66 of the IADIP Draft also entails some special rules that consider the legal developments that have taken place in relation to certain types of property.

4 Property Rights in the IADIP Draft General Act on Private International Law for Colombia

4.1 Special Rights of Article 66

In Article 66 of the IADIP Draft, there are four special rules regarding property in transit, property subject to security rights, ships, aircraft, and other means of transport, and publicity of acts of creation, transfer, and extinction of property rights. The second paragraph of Article 66 states that: "The acquisition and loss, by legal acts, of rights over goods in transit are governed by the law of the state of destination." The application of the law of destination in this type of situation can be found in private international law codifications of different Latin American countries. In the Dominican Republic, for example, Article 77 of the Private International Law Act provides a similar rule. This has been adopted in other countries, such as Switzerland (Article 101, Swiss Federal Private International Law Act of December 18, 1987), Belgium (Article 88, Belgian Code of Private International Law of July 16, 2004), and Korea (Article 22, Korean Private International Law Act of 2001). And the same rule exists in Peru, where Article 2089 of the Civil Code contains a slightly more detailed rule based on the application of the situs law (Article 2088), which establishes that "tangible property in transit is considered to be located at the place of its definitive destination." It is also interesting to note that Peruvian law includes recognition of the autonomy of the parties concerning property in transit. Indeed, the parties "may submit the acquisition and loss of real rights over tangible goods in transit to the law that regulates the original legal act of the constitution or loss of such rights, or to the law of the place of shipment of the tangible goods." However, the validity of the choice made by the parties is limited, since it produces *inter partes* effects, which is probably an influence of the Swiss Private International Law Act (Article 104).

According to the third paragraph of Article 66 of the IADIP Draft, "Movable property subject to security is governed by the law designated by the special rules on the subject." Thus, it refers to the special legislation on the matter. In this regard, it is worth noting that Colombia has been a party to the UNIDROIT Convention on International Interests in Mobile Equipment (Cape Town Convention, 2001) since 2007.[44] According to this Convention, the law applicable to the creation and effects of international interests in airframes, aircraft engines and helicopters; railway rolling stock; and space assets (Article 2.3) is the law of the forum state (*lex fori*) (Article 5.3). Act No. 1676 of 2013 is also relevant, which includes the *lex rei sitae* rule concerning assets subject to security. According to its Article 83, "the law applicable to creation, third-party effectiveness, registration, priority, and enforcement shall be the law of the state in which the property that is the object of the security interest is located." This article also contains specific rules for certain situations that offer greater certainty, and thus serve the purpose of this Act, which consists of providing greater protection to the creditor.[45] Thus, the law of the place where the guarantor is located applies in case the property is used in more than one country (Article 83, second paragraph), and the law of the place where the registration is made, in case the property is subject to a special registration (Article 83, third paragraph).

Regarding the publicity of acts of creation, transfer, and extinction of property rights, Article 66 of the IADIP Draft states in its last paragraph that this "is governed by the law of the state where the formalities of such publicity are carried out." Note that this rule is conceived in broader terms so that it covers not only any type of property but also formalities of any kind.

Finally, it is worth highlighting that the specific conflictual rules of Article 66 of the IADIP Draft also have a bilateral approach, insofar as they do not limit themselves to ordering the application of Colombian law but allow the applicability of foreign law. They are, therefore, more flexible and modern than the general rule of Article 20 of the Civil Code, which, as mentioned above, was conceived in the nineteenth century and is still in force.

[44] Approved through Decree 4734-2007.

[45] Bejarano Guzmán (2023).

4.2 Intellectual Property

Article 90 contains the conflictual rule regarding intellectual property rights in the IADIP Draft. The first paragraph of this article establishes the *lex loci protectionis* rule as follows: "Rights relating to intellectual property are governed by the law of the state in which the intellectual property is claimed." In the absence of specific conflict-of-laws rules and since issues relating to contracts are dealt with separately, the *lex loci protectionis* rule would apply mainly to conflict of laws cases relating to non-contractual obligations.

The scope of the first paragraph thus embraces questions regarding the protection of intellectual property rights, as well as limitations and exceptions, such as duration, exhaustion of rights, and provisions on fair dealing in copyright. At first glance, the rule contained in the first paragraph of Article 90 leads to a territorial approach. However, an interpretation in that direction should be avoided as excessively formalistic—particularly in cases regarding copyright, the protection of which is not even subject to registration—and consideration should be given to the application of the law of the place where protection is sought, and not necessarily the *lex fori*.[46]

In the second paragraph, Article 90 deals with contractual issues. Here, the IADIP Draft clearly distances itself from a strict territorial approach and offers space for the freedom of choice by means of a remission to Section Two of Chapter Fourteen: "Contracts relating to intellectual property shall be governed by the provisions on contractual obligations of this Law."

4.3 Cultural Property

The international restitution of cultural property is considered in the IADIP Draft separately. Article 68 reflects that the advantages of using the *lex rei sitae* rule, e.g., legal certainty, predictability, are not uncontested regarding cultural property, since its special nature and great value.[47] This was considered by the Constitutional Court of Colombia in case No. T-3.402.625, in which the Court was asked whether the government is obliged to take the necessary actions so that 122 pre-Columbian gold sculptures are returned by Spain to Colombia. In cases of these kinds, notwithstanding underlying challenges, there is a tendency to prefer the application of the law of the place of origin of the property (*lex originis*). Thus, the 1991 Resolution by the

---

[46] Cfr. Metzger (2012).

[47] Fincham (2008), Jayme (1997), Siehr (2006a, b, 2015), Symeonides (2016), Wantuch-Thole (2015) and Wiese (2010).

Institute of International Law on "The International Sale of Works of Art from the Angle of the Protection of the Cultural Heritage" says in Article 2 that "The transfer of ownership of works of art belonging to the cultural heritage of the country of origin shall be governed by the law of that country." Article 3 of that Resolution goes further, stating that "The provisions of the law of the country of origin governing the export of works of art shall apply."

The *lex originis* rule is followed, for example, in Article 13 of Directive 2014/60/EU of the European Parliament and the Council, 15 May 2014, and in the national laws of Bulgaria and Belgium.[48] Furthermore, national courts in several countries have examined the use of the *lex originis* rule in several cases: for instance, in England, Attorney General of New Zealand v. Ortiz (1983) and Iran v. Barakat (2007);[49] in Italy, Ecuador v. Danusso (1982);[50] and in the United States (U.S.) v. McClain (1989) and U.S. v. Schultz (2002).[51]

In Article 68 of the IADIP Draft, the *lex originis* rule regarding the international restitution of cultural property is included as follows:

> If an object considered by a state to be part of its cultural heritage has left its territory in a manner that the law of that state considers illegitimate at the time of departure, the restitution requested by that state is governed by the law of that state or, at the choice of the latter, by the law of the state on whose territory the object is located at the time of the request for restitution.

In addition, Article 68 recognizes the rights of good faith possessors: "If the law of the state that considers the property to be part of its cultural heritage does not grant protection to the possessor in good faith, the latter may invoke the protection granted by the law of the state in whose territory the property is located at the time of the request for restitution." This shall be read together with Article 4 of the 1995 UNIDROIT Convention on Stolen or Illegally Exported Cultural Objects, to which Colombia is a party, when dealing with cases related to other states parties to this Convention,[52] and attention may be paid also to the rule proposed in Article 4, paragraph 2, of the above-mentioned 1991 Resolution of the Institute of International Law.

Finally, this rule refers to the property of cultural value to an Indigenous people or community that is returned from a foreign country to Colombia. In this regard, Article 68 of the IADIP Draft further states that the destination of such property "is

---

[48] International Private Law Code of Bulgaria (2005, modified in 2009), Article 70; International Private Law Code of Belgium (2004), Article 90 (Symeonides 2016; Wiese 2010).

[49] Gerstenblith (2009) and Wantuch-Thole (2015).

[50] Prott (2009) and Wiese (2010).

[51] Gerstenblith (2004).

Together with the use of the lex originis rule, in this matter, it is also considered the need for going beyond conflictual justice and seeking the satisfaction of material justice, which requires looking at the final result; cfr. Basedow (2017) and Symeonides (2001).

[52] Ratified since December 1, 2012.

governed by the rules of that people or community, unless the said people or community decides that it should be governed by the law of the state of which it is a part." Thus, this article recognizes the right of these peoples and communities to decide on such property, which is rooted in international legal instruments, as presented below.

4.3.1 Why Indigenous Cultural Property?

The rule on the restitution of property of cultural value to an Indigenous people or community, which is proposed in Article 68 of the IADIP Draft, acts as a complement at the national level to the only international private international law treaty on cultural restitution, i.e., the aforementioned 1995 UNIDROIT Convention on Stollen or Illegally Exported Cultural Objects that, as already said, was ratified by Colombia, and includes a regulation on this subject.[53] Although the 1995 UNIDROIT Convention does not contain a remission to the application of Indigenous law nor the law of the country of origin, it is worth noting that its Article 7, paragraph 2, allow return claims on illegally exported cultural objects that were "made by a member or members of a tribal or Indigenous community for traditional or ritual use by that community and the object will be returned to that community." This is contrary to the general rule that prevents claims on those objects that are legally exported at the time of the claim and those that were exported during the lifetime of their creator or for a short period thereafter.[54]

This kind of protection is framed by the recognition of Indigenous peoples' rights at the international level, ranging from the right to self-determination to cultural, health and labor rights. Such rights entered national legal systems through constitutional channels in the form of fundamental rights. Among all these rights, some are more directly related to the standards proposed by the IADIP Draft, which can be classified into two groups. The first group involves some rights that are basic to the protection of Indigenous peoples' ways of life, including living according to their own legal institutions. These rights are fundamental to the application of Indigenous rules, as stated in Article 68 of the Draft.

From the private international law perspective, it is relevant to consider the fact that "Indigenous legal systems represent particular social, cultural, and political dimensions of human interaction that define Indigenous peoples."[55] Regarding this, the UN Declaration contains "the right to maintain and strengthen their distinct political, legal, economic, social and cultural institutions" (Article 5), which is

---

[53] See Articles 3, 5, and 7. In its preamble, the Convention expresses concern about "the illicit trade in cultural objects and the irreparable damage frequently caused by it, both to these objects themselves and to the cultural heritage of national, tribal, Indigenous or other communities, and also to the heritage of all peoples, and in particular by the pillage of archaeological sites and the resulting loss of irreplaceable archaeological, historical and scientific information."

[54] Ochoa Jiménez (2019), p. 453.

[55] Anaya (2007), p. 3.

derived from the more general right to self-determination, in whose exercise they "have the right to autonomy or self-government in matters relating to their internal and local affairs" (Article 4). Additionally, the way in which the UN Declaration entails the right to access justice includes the consideration of their "customs, traditions, rules and legal systems" (Article 40). In similar terms, Article 8 of the ILO Convention states as follows: "In applying national laws and regulations to the peoples concerned, due regard shall be had to their customs or customary laws."

This Convention also understands that such a right presupposes Indigenous peoples' "right to retain their own customs and institutions," considering fundamental rights as the only limits, which also occurs within the framework of the UN Declaration (Article 46). Such rights are also included in the OAS Declaration.[56]

Before the adoption of this instrument, the main organs of the Inter-American human rights system, i.e., the Commission and the Court, developed an important jurisprudence that was especially triggered through the Court's decision in the Awas Tingni vs. Nicaragua case in 2001.[57] To a large extent, decisions of the Inter-American human rights organs deal with Article 21 of the American Convention on Human Rights (Pact of San José), which contains the human right to property of individuals, and interpret it considering that Indigenous peoples have a special relationship with their lands from which a collective right emerges.

According to Article 5 of the IADIP Draft:

> Provisions to protect the rights of Indigenous peoples or communities over the natural resources existing on their lands, traditional knowledge, the conservation of biological diversity, the sustainable use of resources, and plant varieties have the character of overriding mandatory rules.

The second group of rights of Indigenous peoples recognized at the international level directly relates to Article 5 of the IADIP Draft. Such rights are those that take into consideration the relationship of these peoples with the environment. This rule does not establish the direct application of Indigenous normative systems, but rather provisions aimed at protecting the rights of Indigenous peoples and communities. Specifically, Article 5 refers to rights related to "natural resources existing on their lands, traditional knowledge, the conservation of biological diversity, the sustainable use of resources and plant varieties."[58] In this regard, the following articles of

---

[56] See Articles VI, XIII (3), XXI (2), XXII.

[57] Mayagna (Sumo) Awas Tingni Community v. Nicaragua was decided by the Inter-American Human

Rights Court (IAHRC 2001). See also Yatama vs. Nicaragua (2005); Comunidad Moiwana vs. Surinam (2005); Comunidad Indígena Sawhoyamaxa vs. Paraguay (2006); Comunidad Moiwana vs. Surinam (2006); Comunidad Indígena Yakye Axa vs. Paraguay (2006); Pueblo Saramaka vs. Surinam (2008); Comunidad Indígena Xákmok Kásek vs. Paraguay (2010); Pueblo Indígena Kichwa de Sarayaku vs. Ecuador (2012); Pueblos Indígenas Kuna de Madungandí y Emberá de Bayano and their members vs. Panama (2014); Pueblo Indígena Xucuru and its members vs. Brasil (2018); Comunidades Indígenas Miembros de la Asociación Lhaka Honhat (Nuestra Tierra) vs. Argentina (2020).

[58] Although the protection of these rights may indirectly lead to the application of Indigenous norms. An example may be the environmental administrative norms that apply in Indigenous ter-

the UN Declaration can be highlighted: Article 25 (right to maintain spiritual relationship with their lands and other resources), Article 26 (right to lands and resources), Article 29 (right to the conservation and protection of the environment and the productive capacity of lands), Article 32 (right to determine and develop priorities and strategies for the development or use of their lands and other resources) and Article 31 (right to maintain, control, protect and develop their traditional knowledge), which is in relation to Article 24 (right to traditional medicine and health practices). Relevant provisions of the OAS Declaration are in Articles VI and XXV (rights to their lands, territories, and resources), in Article XXVIII (right to traditional knowledge associated with genetic resources), as well as in Article XIX (right to measures to mitigate adverse ecological, impacts of the implementation of development projects). The Convention of the International Labor Organization No. 169 on Indigenous and Tribal Peoples, ratified by Colombia through Act No. 21 of March 4, 1991 (ILO Convention), includes rights that take into consideration the relationship of these peoples with the environment are included in Part II (Articles 13–15). Additionally, Article 4 refers to measures for safeguarding the environment, and Article 7 establishes the right to decide on development that affects their lands.

The aforementioned rights have become part of Colombia's national legal system. Thus, according to Article 7 of the Political Constitution, "the State recognizes and protects the ethnic and cultural diversity of the Colombian nation." Such recognition extends to the language of the different ethnic groups (Article 10), to the protection of such diversity in educational processes (Article 68), to the definition of Indigenous territories as territorial entities (Articles 286, 329, 330), and to Indigenous jurisdiction (Article 246), as will be explained below.

The recognition of Indigenous peoples' rights in the Political Constitution of Colombia occurred hand in hand with the so-called neo-constitutionalism. This has made at least two specific contributions in this context, the first contribution being the possibility of including international instruments recognizing the rights of Indigenous peoples in the national legal system through the block of constitutionality,[59] which is contained in Article 93 of the Political Constitution of 1991: "International treaties and agreements ratified by Congress that recognize human rights … have domestic priority. The rights and duties mentioned in this Charter shall be interpreted in accordance with international treaties on human rights ratified by Colombia …" In this regard, Article 94 adds as follows: "The enunciation of the rights and guarantees contained in the Constitution and in international agreements in effect should not be understood as a negation of others which, being inherent to

ritories, according to which land use in Indigenous territories must be done following their own zoning and territorial planning, for which their own norms and procedures apply. This example is based on the Land Use Planning of the Department of Beni, in Bolivia; cfr. Department of the Beni Act, October 17, 2019, that approves the Land Use Planning of the Department of the Beni (PLUS—BENI), and Administrative Resolution 129/2020 of 2020 by the Audit and Social Control Authority for Forrest and Land of the Ministry of Environment and Water, that approves the Manual to Prepare Land Use Planning.

[59] Cfr. Constitucional Court of Colombia, Judgements No. SU-510/98 and No. T-606/01.

the human being, are not expressly mentioned in them." In addition, the recognition of the rights of Indigenous peoples by the Colombian Constitutional Court has taken place through copious decisions. Such decisions have made clear, for example, that the Indigenous community is a collective legal subject and not a mere accumulation of individual subjects who share common interests. In addition, the Constitutional Court expressly lists among the fundamental rights of Indigenous communities the right to communal land ownership, to participate in decisions and measures that could affect them, related to the extraction of natural resources in their territories,[60] as well as to the recognition and protection of traditional medicinal practices.[61]

4.3.2 Indigenous Peoples and Communities and Private International Law

The inclusion of the Indigenous cultural property found in Article 68 of the IADIP Draft unveils the relationship between Indigenous peoples and private international law. Today's private international law is called upon to respect the diversity of Indigenous normative systems. This role of private international law can find a valid foundation in the configuration of international human rights law, as well as in the way in which these rights have been absorbed by the Colombian national legal system.

It is undeniable that Indigenous peoples are holders of differentiated collective rights. At this point, it is worth recalling that collective rights are those that "affect an identifiable group of people"[62] linked together by pre-existing relationships.[63] Thus, the rights of Indigenous peoples are neither private rights nor diffuse rights, the latter being held by groups whose members are linked "only by the facts of a particular transaction or occurrence."[64] As noted above, Indigenous peoples' rights are included not only in international standards, such as the Declarations of the UN and the OAS on the Rights of Indigenous Peoples, but also in binding international instruments, especially the ILO Convention.

This has also occurred in decisions by the Inter-American Court of Human Rights. In the recognition of these rights in Colombia, the use of the term "Indigenous community" has a long tradition among both Indigenous and the state,[65] even though there are other ethnic groups in the country, namely, Afro-descendants, Raizal,

[60] Constitutional Court of Colombia, Judgement No. SU-510/98; see also Article 300 of the Political Constitution of Colombia.

[61] Constitutional Court of Colombia, Judgments No. C-377/94 and No. T-214/97; see Semper (2006), p. 765.

[62] González Mac Dowell, cited by Crawford (2020), p. 78.

[63] Weninger, cited by Crawford (2020), p. 78.

[64] Weninger, cited by Crawford (2020), p. 78.

[65] Semper (2006), p. 765.

Palenquero and Rrom. The IADIP Draft only contains rules relating to Indigenous peoples and communities, though.

Beyond discussions as to why or how legal pluralism in general can take place in this context, private international law is called upon to respect the diversity of Indigenous normative systems and the rights of Indigenous peoples and, more importantly, is particularly equipped to do so. Private international law is equipped with viewpoints and concrete legal mechanisms that can serve the configuration of a legal pluralism that, rather than confronting the control of the state in certain areas and confining the Indigenous to some thematic fragments or some territorial spaces, sees the relations of Indigenous peoples with state institutions in a general framework that is characterized by a certain horizontality.[66] This role of private international law is based on the aforementioned rights, which have been internationally recognized and incorporated into the Colombian national legal system.

Taking into account such rights, if a case relates to an Indigenous people or community, it may be necessary to consider the application of Indigenous rules and practices. If this issue is approached from the perspective of the general theory of private international law, this may take place *as if* Indigenous rules and practices were foreign law. In Latin American private international law codifications, the way foreign law must be applied is usually contained in a special rule.[67] The Inter-American Convention on General Private International Law Rules states in Article 2 that: "Judges and authorities of the States Parties shall enforce the foreign law in the same way as it would be enforced by the judges of the State whose law is applicable." In national codifications, a similar rule has been included, e.g., in the Civil and Commercial Code of Argentina (2014) (Article 2595), the Private International Law Act of Uruguay (2020) (Article 2), and the Civil Code of Peru (1984) (Article 2055). Following such a path, the IADIP Draft contains the following provision in Article 3: "The interpretation of the competent foreign law shall be made in accordance with the foreign law itself." Thus, if Indigenous rules and practices were considered *as if* they were foreign law, their interpretation had to be conducted in a way that is respectful of their customs and traditions of the peoples or communities involved.

However, it is worth making a brief clarification here, regarding the second paragraph of Article 3 of the IADIP Draft, which seems to be inapplicable in cases that involve an Indigenous people or community. Such a paragraph, which contains the so-called unknown legal institution, reads as follows:

> When the foreign law applicable to the case establishes institutions or procedures essential for its proper application not contemplated in Colombian law, the application of such law may be denied, provided that Colombian law does not have analogous institutions or procedures.

---

[66] Coyle (2020).

[67] Such a rule reflects the theory of juridical use (*uso jurídico*). See Goldschmidt (1990); Mosciati Olivieri (1993), p. 39.

One can find this rule, with an almost identical wording, in Article 3 of the Inter-American Convention on General Private International Law Rules. In this regard, one must bear in mind the cultural particularities of Indigenous peoples and communities, and the different ways in which they can distance themselves from state law. Thus, there can be cases in which it is not possible to find in state law institutions or procedures that are analogous to those of Indigenous peoples and communities. In such cases, the application of the unknown legal institution rule would mean refusing the consideration and application of Indigenous rules and practices, which would ultimately lead to the cancellation of Indigenous peoples' rights mentioned above and would go against the recognition of cultural diversity made in Article 7 of the Political Constitution, as already mentioned.

Another way of observing Indigenous peoples' rights from a private international law perspective is by considering that they are fundamental rights. As already mentioned, in Colombia, this is binding according to decisions of the Constitutional Court. In this sense, Article 6 of the IADIP Draft includes the criterion developed by the Supreme Court of Colombia, according to which fundamental rights are part of the public order: "A foreign law that is manifestly incompatible with fundamental rights shall not be applied." Thus, rights recognized to Indigenous peoples can also be part of the public order of Colombia and so impede the application of foreign law that undoubtedly goes against them.

5 Conflict Mobile

Article 67 of the IADIP Draft, which deals with mobile conflict cases, reads as follows: "The change of location of movable property does not affect the rights acquired under the law of the place where it was located at the time of its acquisition. However, such rights may be opposed to third parties only after the requirements of the law of the new situation have been fulfilled." This solution, based on the respect for vested rights, has historical roots in Latin America. The 1889 Treaty of Montevideo on International Civil Law includes such a rule in Articles 30 and 31, which also state the respect of the rights acquired according to the law of origin of the property.

6 Jurisdiction

The national procedural rules that are currently in force in Colombia do not refer to the competence of its national courts to decide on conflict of law cases, i.e., situations with relevant foreign elements. Because of the lack of such procedural norms, some authors[68] have argued that Article 28 of the Code of Civil Procedure, which addresses domestic—i.e., non-international—cases, might be interpreted extensively to also cover cross-border cases. Such an interpretation, nevertheless, does not eliminate the disadvantages linked to the lack of codified rules in this field, especially in view of the legal uncertainty that lies behind it. In this sense, the second paragraph of Article 32 of the IADIP Draft contains the *forum rei sitae* rule as follows: "Matters relating to rights in rem over real property located in Colombia are considered matters of exclusive jurisdiction." The first paragraph of the article clarifies that "The exclusive international jurisdiction of Colombian courts is of an exceptional nature, must be interpreted restrictively, and lacks jurisdiction over other matters that may arise with respect to the same subject." Article 30, for its part, regulates the competence of national courts regarding conflict of laws cases related to universal property: "Colombian courts will have jurisdiction to hear actions related to universal property if: 1. the domicile of the debtor is located in Colombian territory, or 2. assets that form an integral part of the universality are located in Colombia." In addition, the second paragraph of Article 95 entails the *forum rei sitae* rule in relation to statute of limitations, according to which extinctive prescription of actions "is governed by the law of the place where the property is located." Finally, it is worth mentioning that Article 29 of the IADIP Draft refers to international jurisdiction in intellectual property matters: "Colombian courts shall have jurisdiction to hear actions relating to the protection of intellectual property when the defendant is domiciled in Colombia or, in the absence of domicile, when the protection is invoked before them."

7 Final Remarks

The conflict of laws rule of Article 20 of the Civil Code of Colombia must be reviewed. It clearly includes, as has been seen, obsolete terms that, among other things, make the norm difficult to understand. Additionally, resorting to interpretation does not fully solve the underlying problem, which lies in the lack of clarity of its text and in its unilateral character. It thus limits the consideration of the application of a foreign legal system even when this would be the most appropriate in a specific case. Addressing this is needed, not only in terms of legal certainty but also in terms of justice.

While essentially maintaining the tradition included in the Colombian Civil Code currently in force, the IADIP Draft takes several steps forward. It not only includes rules relating to international jurisdiction but also clarifies how the applicable law is to be determined and considers developments in relation to different types of property, namely, property in transit, property subject to security, and intellectual property, as well as particular situations, such as mobile conflicts and

---

[68] Guerra Hernández (2016).

acquisitive prescription, and the international restitution of cultural property, including cultural property of Indigenous peoples and communities, the restitution of which represents nowadays one of the most sensible topics regarding the international restitution of cultural property.

References

Anaya J (2007) Indigenous law and its contribution to global pluralism. Indigenous Law J 6(1):3–12

Basedow J (2017) El Derecho de las sociedades abiertas. Ordenación privada y regulación pública en el conflicto de leyes. Legis, Bogota

Bejarano Guzmán R (2023) Garantías mobiliarias, Ámbito Jurídico. www.ambitojuridico.com/noticias/columnista-impreso/civil-y-familia/garantias-mobiliarias. Accessed 28 July 2024

Bonnemaison JL (2013) Curso de derecho internacional privado. Vadell Hermanos, Caracas

Cock Arango A (1952) Tratado de derecho internacional privado. Universidad Nacional de Colombia, Bogota

Delic A (2019) The role of comparative law in the development of modern private international law (1750–1914). In: Van Hule I, Lesaffer R (eds) International law in the long nineteenth century (1776–1914). Brill Nijhoff, Leiden, pp 186–213

Fincham D (2008) How adopting the lex originis rule can impede the flow of illicit cultural property. Columbia J Law Arts 32:11–150

Gerstenblith P (2004) From Steinhardt to Schultz: The McClain doctrine and the protection of archaeological sites. In: Richman J (ed) Legal perspectives on cultural resources. Altamira Press, Walnut Creek, pp 100–118

Gerstenblith P (2009) Schultz and Barakat: universal recognition of national ownership of antiquities. The DePaul University College of Law, Technology, Law & Culture research series paper no. 09-007, pp 21–48

Guerra Hernández VH (2016) Conflictos de jurisdicción y competencia en derecho internacional privado. In: García Matamoros L, Aljure Salame A (eds) Teoría general del derecho internacional privado. Temis, Bogota, pp 349–375

Hernández-Bretón E (2007) Mestizaje cultural en el derecho internacional privado de los países de la américa latina. Academia de Ciencias Políticas y Sociales, Caracas

Herrán Medina A (1959) Compendio de derecho internacional privado. Editorial Temis, Bogota

Jayme E (1997) Protection of cultural property and conflict of laws: the Basel Resolution of the Institute of International Law. Int J Cult Prop 6(2):376–378

Junker A (2017) Internationales Privatrecht. C. H. Beck, Munich

Lira Urquieta P (1981) Código Civil de la República de Chile. Introducción. In: Ministerio de Educación (ed) Obras completas de Andrés Bello, 2nd edn. Ministerio de Educación, Caracas, pp xiii–lxii

Lorenzen E (1919) Huber's de conflictu legum. Faculty Scholarship Series, Yale Law School Faculty Scholarship 4563:199–242

Martiny D (2012) Lex rei sitae as a connecting factor in EU private international law. IPRax 2:119–133

Mayorga F (2017) Codificación de la legislación en Colombia. Banco de la República. https://www.banrepcultural.org/biblioteca-virtual/credencial-historia/numero-148/codificacion-de-la-legislacion-en-colombia. Accessed 27 July 2024

Metzger A (2012) Intellectual property (IPL). Max-EuP 2012. https://max-eup2012.mpipriv.de/index.php/Intellectual_Property_(PIL). Accessed 28 July 2024

Niboyet JP (1951) Principios de derecho internacional privado. Editora Nacional, Mexico

Ochoa Jiménez MJ (2019) Conflict of laws and the return of indigenous peoples' cultural property: a Latin American perspective. Int J Cult Prop 26(4):437–456. https://doi.org/10.1017/S0940739119000341

Prott L (2009) Witnesses to history. Documents and writings on the return of cultural objects. UNESCO, Paris

Samtleben J (1982) La relación entre derecho internacional público y privado en Andrés Bello. Jurídica Anuario del Departamento de Derecho de la Universidad Iberoamericana 14:167–174

Samtleben J (2010a) Territorialitätsgrundsatz im Internationalen Privatrecht Lateinamerikas. In: Samtleben J (ed) Rechtspraxis und Rechtskultur in Brasilien und Lateinamerika. Shaker Verlag, Aachen, pp 344–369

Samtleben J (2010b) El principio de territorialidad en América Latina. In: Samtleben J (ed) Rechtspraxis und Rechtskultur in Brasilien und Lateinamerika. Shaker Verlag, Aachen, pp 370–403

Samtleben J (2010c) Internationales Privatrecht in Lateinamerika-Regionale Entwicklungen und nationale Kodificationen. In: Samtleben J (ed) Rechtspraxis und Rechtskultur in Brasilien und Lateinamerika. Shaker Verlag, Aachen, pp 431–443

Samtleben J (2014) Der Kleinstaat Uruguay als Zentrum des Internationales Privatrecht. In: Witzleb E, Ellger R, Mankowski P, Merck H, Remien O (eds) Festschrift für Dieter Martiny zum 70. Geburtstag. Mohr Siebeck, Tübingen, pp 567–594

Samtleben J (2018) Internationales Privatrecht in Panama-Eine neue Kodifikation in Lateinamerika. RabelsZ 82:52–135

Schellerer J (2016) Gutgläubiger Erwerb und Ersitzung von Kulturgegenständen. Mohr Siebeck, Tübingen

Semper F (2006) Los derechos de los pueblos indígenas de Colombia en la jurisprudencia de la Corte Constitucional. Anuario de Derecho Constitucional Latinoamericano II:761–778

Siehr K (2006a) Das IPR der Kulturgüter. MHB Yil 22:751–772

Siehr K (2006b) The beautiful one has come – to return. In: Merryman JH (ed) Imperialism, art and restitution. Cambridge University Press, New York, pp 114–134

Siehr K (2015) Private international law and the difficult problem to return illegally exported cultural property. Unif Law Rev 20:503–515

Story J (1846) Commentaries on the conflict of laws, foreign and domestic: in regard to contracts, rights, and remedies, and especially in regard to marriages, divorces, wills, successions, and judgments, 3rd edn. Charles and Brown, Boston

Symeonides S (2001) Material justice and conflicts justice in choice of law. In: Borchers P, Zekoll J (eds) International conflict of laws for the third millennium: essays in honor of Friedrich K. Juenger. Transnational Publishers, pp 125–140

Symeonides S (2016) Choice of law. Oxford University Press, New York

Tenorio O (1955) Lei de Introdução ao Código Civil Brasileiro (Decreto-lei n. 4.657, de 4 de setembro de 1942), 2nd edn. Borsoi, Rio de Janeiro

Valencia Zea A (2000) Derecho civil. Parte general y personas, vol I, 15th edn. Temis, Bogota

Wantuch-Thole M (2015) Cultural property in cross-border litigation. Turning rights into claims. De Gruyter, Berlin

Wiese V (2010) Der Bedeutungswandel der Situs-Regel im Internationalen Sachenrecht der Kulturgüter. In: Odendahl K, Weber P (eds) Kulturgüterschutz – Kunstrecht – Kulturrecht. Festschrift für Kurt Siehr zum 75. Geburtstag aus dem Kreise des Doktoranden- und Habilitandenseminars Kunst und Recht. Nomos Verlag, Baden-Baden, pp 83–100

Zapata A (2016) La ley aplicable al contrato internacional. In: García Matamoros L, Aljure Salame A (eds) Teoría general del derecho internacional privado. Temis, Bogota, pp 189–220

María Julia Ochoa Jiménez Dr. iur. and LLM from the University of Göttingen; Lawyer and Specialist in Intellectual Property from the Universidad de Los Andes; LLM, Universidad de Navarra; Research Fellow, University of Bonn, Alexander von Humboldt Foundation; Visiting Researcher, Max Planck Institute for Comparative and International Private Law; Professor, Universidad de Antioquia (2016–2022); Professor of Private International Law, Universidad Loyola.

International Intellectual Property Contracts in Colombia: Applicable Law and Dispute Resolution

Brenda Salas

Abstract In international contracts concerning intellectual property, the general principle is to resort to the autonomy of the parties' will. This means that the parties are free to determine both the law applicable to the contract and the means of dispute resolution. However, the question that arises in Colombia is how to determine the applicable law to the contract and the competent authority for conflict resolution when the parties have remained silent on these matters in an international contract concerning intellectual property. To this end, this chapter first analyzes the law applicable to the contract, then the competent authority for dispute resolution. Finally, it analyzes the regulation included in the Draft General Act on Private International Law for Colombia prepared by the *Instituto Antioqueño de Derecho Internacional Privado*.

1 Introduction

An international contract is a legally binding agreement usually intended to facilitate a cross-border commercial transaction.[1] An international contract is distinguished from a domestic contract by the fact that the legal relationship it creates transcends the boundaries of a single jurisdiction, as it involves connections with multiple state legal systems. The presence of a foreign element, whether objective—such as the place of contract formation—or subjective—such as the nationality or residence of a party—determines the international nature of the contract.[2]

[1] See Ortega Giménez (2022).

[2] Ibid.

B. Salas (✉)
Facultad de Derecho, Universidad Externado de Colombia, Bogotá, Colombia
e-mail: brenda.salas@uexternado.edu.co

M. J. Ochoa Jiménez, C. Madrid Martínez (eds.), *A Private International Law for Colombia*, Springer Textbooks in Law,
https://doi.org/10.1007/978-3-032-04106-7_12

In the business world, this legal framework is frequently used in various sectors to facilitate the commercialization of tangible and intangible assets. Particularly, intangible assets hold significant value in the marketplace. Examples include software, artistic and literary works, video games, trademarks, fashion designs, smartphone designs, and technological innovations that provide solutions to technical challenges.

The above has been profusely discussed in the context of international trade in goods and services. As a result, the Agreement on Trade-Related Aspects of Intellectual Property Rights (TRIPS) of the World Trade Organization (WTO) explicitly recognizes and regulates rights on creations that are products of human creativity, effort, and expertise.[3]

Intellectual creations are not excluded from the legal framework that applies to international contracts. The commercialization of these creations is governed by the principles of international contract law, such as good faith, *pacta sunt servanda*, due diligence, and party autonomy. Thus, contracts relating to intellectual property are often subject to the principle of autonomy of will.

The role of party autonomy in international contracts has been the subject of extensive doctrinal debate. This principle encompasses the parties' freedom to create, modify, and extinguish legal relationships, and to exercise their rights and powers.[4] The contract, as the embodiment of this autonomy, reflects the intentions of the parties through the agreed rights and obligations.

International contracts on intellectual property generally include standard provisions (e.g., title, parties, date, definitions, etc.) alongside two key clauses: choice of law and dispute resolution. The choice of law clause determines the applicable substantive law, while the dispute resolution clause establishes the mechanism for resolving potential disputes.[5]

The choice of law clause is essential in international contracts as it defines the applicable legal regime, ensuring compliance even in the absence of disputes. In case of conflicts, this clause streamlines dispute resolution by pre-determining the governing law, thus benefiting the parties who can choose a favorable legal framework. The dispute resolution clause further empowers the parties by allowing them to opt for either national courts or international arbitration, the latter often being a more efficient and cost-effective option.[6]

Though international contracts with foreign elements involving intellectual property generally rely on the principle of party autonomy, allowing the parties to choose the applicable law and dispute resolution mechanisms, a key question arises when the parties remain silent on these matters. This chapter addresses this question by analyzing the applicable law and the competent authority for dispute resolution. Attention is paid to the relevant solution proposed in the Draft General Act on

[3] World Trade Organization (n.d.).

[4] Alvarez (2021).

[5] Ortega Giménez (2016).

[6] Ibid.

Private International Law for Colombia prepared by the *Instituto Antioqueño de Derecho Internacional Privado* (IADIP) (hereinafter, "IADIP Draft General Act"). The chapter concludes with some final observations.

2 Applicable Law

As mentioned earlier, the applicable law in an international contract pertains to the legal framework that governs the contract, irrespective of any potential future disputes.[7] Several questions arise in this area. Primarily, do the parties have the autonomy to choose the applicable law to the contract, or does this authority rest with the legislative organs of each state? Furthermore, if the contract parties are silent, can the legislative organs of each state determine the applicable law?

Colombian scholars, such as Zapata and Monroy Cabra, advocate for party autonomy as the guiding principle in determining the applicable law to international contracts.[8] They emphasize the parties' freedom to choose the governing law rather than being bound by domestic law. Rojas Tamayo observes that, while the ability to choose the applicable law is generally accepted, its interpretation and conditions vary across legal systems. Some require an express choice, while others allow implicit or hypothetical choices. Additionally, some require a connection between the chosen law and the contract, while others mandate an international character for the contractual relationship.[9]

While it seems easy to answer in the affirmative the question concerning the freedom of the parties to choose the applicable law, answering the question concerning the case in which the parties remain silent appears more complex. The determination of the applicable law in such cases and the varying approaches taken by the different states will be explored further in what follows, particularly in relation to intellectual property.

2.1 Legal Approximation

The Colombian Commercial Code addresses this issue by stipulating that contracts concluded abroad but performed in Colombia are governed by Colombian law (*lex loci solutionis*).[10] Article 1238 reinforces this solution regarding commercial agency contracts, which are subject to Colombian laws if executed in Colombia, overriding any contrary provisions. Despite the challenges that such rules pose in constitu-

[7] Ochoa Jiménez et al. (2019).

[8] Ibid.

[9] Rojas Tamayo (2018).

[10] Article 869 of the Colombian Commercial Code. See also Dicey (1882).

tional terms, the Constitutional Court of Colombia recently confirmed their constitutionality.[11]

Although both provisions agree on the applicability of the law of the place of performance, there has been debate as to how the term "performance" should be interpreted. In addition, even when such regulation of the Commercial Code appears to operate across all international contracts, as Zapata notes, the rule raises a series of questions, as it:

> only refers to execution without mentioning other contractual characteristics such as the conclusion, nullity, or interpretation of the contract, among others. Therefore, it is possible that difficulties may arise in this respect for the interpretation of a contract, because if a contract is being analyzed for breach, its validity, or its conclusion, this rule is only proposed for contracts concluded abroad and whose performance takes place in Colombian territory, but on the other aspects, it does not allow elucidating an answer to this question.[12]

Furthermore, Article 20 of the Civil Code establishes that:

> property located in the territories, and those found in the States, in which the Nation has an interest or right of ownership, are subject to the provisions of this Code, even when their owners are foreigners and reside outside of Colombia. This provision shall be understood without prejudice to the stipulations contained in contracts validly concluded in a foreign country.

As can be seen, this rule of the Civil Code also stresses the territoriality of Colombian law when legal situations involve foreign elements. Whereas the last paragraph of Article 20 recognizes the possibility for the parties to define the contractual regime, thus consolidating the principle of party autonomy.

The aforementioned rules are provided by law in both the Commercial Code and the Civil Code. The question now is whether this solution can be extended to international contracts involving intellectual property.

2.2 *Solution for Intellectual Property Contracts*

As Werra states, contract law is a key component of the intellectual property ecosystem:

> contracts are the legal vehicles by which [intellectual property] rights can be lawfully used by third parties. Contracts are the essential tools by which [intellectual property] owners can monetize their rights. Making sure that contract law can perform these critical missions requires understanding the complex interactions between IP law and contract law.[13]

The strong territoriality of intellectual property rights is at the root of these complexities. These rights are valid only within the territory where protection is sought.

[11] Constitutional Court of Colombia, No. 385/20, 2023. Appeal against an order rejecting unconstitutionality complaint.

[12] Zapata (2016) cited by Jaimes (2022).

[13] Werra (2021).

This raises the question of the law that must apply in international contracts intended to be performed in several territories, especially when the parties have not chosen the applicable law.

In this regard, it is relevant to take into account that Colombia is a member state of the Andean Community of Nations. In accordance with the principle of supremacy that exists in Andean law, the rules of the Andean Community prevail—domestic law applies only when it does not oppose Andean law.

Colombian law on intellectual property comprises two distinct fields: copyright law and industrial property law. Copyright law safeguards the rights of authors of original works, while industrial property law protects new creations and distinctive signs used in commerce. Two Andean legal instruments contain the regulations that are relevant in this context: Andean Decision No. 351 of 1993, which addresses copyright and related rights, and Andean Decision No. 486 of 2000, which establishes a common regime for industrial property.

Given the high degree of specialization that characterizes intellectual property, it is appropriate to analyze separately the solutions provided by Andean Community law for both copyrights and industrial property, to evaluate their content in relation to the norms established by Colombian law at the domestic level.

2.2.1 Copyright (*Droit d'auteur*)

The Andean Decision No. 351 of 1993 upholds the principle of free will as a fundamental principle to determine the content of contracts, including respect for moral rights, the exploitation of economic rights, and the applicable law.

Article 29 specifically addresses this, stating that "Any transfer of economic rights, as well as authorizations or licenses for use, shall be understood to be limited to the forms of exploitation and other modalities expressly agreed upon in the respective contract." However, Decision No. 351 also stipulates that "The provisions relating to the assignment or licensing of economic rights and to the licenses for use of protected works shall be governed by the provisions of the domestic laws of the Member Countries," thereby imposing certain limitations on the extent of party autonomy.[14]

In this context, the granting and exploitation of economic rights are governed by domestic law. Colombian Acts No. 1450 of 2011 and No. 1955 of 2019, which govern this legal field, also contain the principle of party autonomy. This allows parties to freely transfer or license economic rights for the duration and within the territory they agree upon in their contract. They can choose a law other than Colombian law as the applicable rule, as it is implicitly allowed in Article 181 of Act No. 1955 of 2019, third paragraph, which refers to the transfer of economic rights (as part of copyrights) as follows:

[14] Article 30.

> [in agreements on economic rights] the lack of mention of the territorial scope limits [the transfer] to the country in which the transfer or license is made.

In relation to this rule, the question arises as to what constitutes the "country" where the transfer or license is made. This question stems from the fact that the law only refers to the transfer itself, leaving other aspects like the origin of the right or potential infringements unaddressed.

For illustrative purposes, let us consider a case in which a work of applied art is licensed in Peru, but the parties are silent on the territorial scope of the license. In such a scenario, under the rule cited above, Peruvian law would govern the license, since this is the jurisdiction where it is granted. This solution seems to be reasonable because Peru is one of the member countries of the Andean Community of Nations. However, if the transfer takes place in Argentina, the question arises as to whether Argentine law would be the applicable law. Or whether the solution should rather be sought in international treaties or domestic rules incorporating private international law. Other questions are linked to reciprocity or the relevance of the "national treatment" clause, among other aspects. In the absence of judicial decisions on the matter, it is necessary to look at how practice deals with this type of conflict.

Things are even more complex if such transfers occur in the digital realm, as it is unclear which law should apply to creations circulating on the internet when the parties have not specified the law governing the agreement. In this regard, it is important to note that online transfers require the prior express authorization of the author. In this regard, the question arises whether the aforementioned rule can encompass both analog and digital forms of exploitation. Colombian law does not appear to resolve these difficulties. Thus, unfortunately, there is no definitive legal answer yet. The solution may lie in the general rules of private international law, which so far are rather vague. In such a context, it is important to consider the content of international treaties on the subject, such as free trade agreements, where attention must be paid to the way in which reciprocity and the principle of national treatment are regulated. Also, here, the lack of judicial decisions leads us to take into account how questions around the applicable law are dealt with in practice.

Having considered challenges in the realm of copyright, the next section turns to examine the situation in the field of industrial property.

2.2.2 Industrial Property

Also in this field, the principle of party autonomy is recognized as the general rule. Specifically, in the context of patents, Article 56 of Andean Decision No. 486 states:

> A patent, whether granted or pending grant, may be transferred *inter vivos* or by succession. The transfer of a granted patent must be registered with the relevant national office, and failure to do so renders the transfer ineffective against third parties. The transfer must be in writing for registration purposes, and any person may request such registration.

This provision also applies to industrial designs, according to Article 133. A similar approach is taken in Article 161 regarding trademarks.

The Andean regulation is silent on the limits of party autonomy. It leaves open the question of how far the parties can go regarding the choice of law in international contracts on trademarks, patents, or designs. It appears that the parties have broad freedom to negotiate, except when it is a matter of public order and good customs. It follows that they may choose a law other than Colombian law.

The question remains as to which law applies when the parties are silent on the point in such contracts. Unlike copyright law, Colombian domestic law does not provide any criteria regarding industrial property rights. It is unclear whether Article 869 of the Colombian Commercial Code is applicable, according to which contracts concluded abroad but performed in Colombia are governed by Colombian law. The debate then centers on how to determine if a contract is "performed" in the country and what the term "performance" means in this context.[15]

Furthermore, it is important to note that industrial property rights are territorial: they are only valid within the jurisdiction where they are granted. Therefore, additional criteria for determining the applicable law in the absence of an explicit choice by the parties involve considering two distinct aspects. The first is the protective nature of industrial property rights and the purely contractual aspects of the relationship between the parties.[16] This distinction is particularly relevant in the context of technology transfer contracts, licenses, and assignments of rights.[17]

Due to the territorial nature of these rights, the applicable law to the contract seems to be that of the country where protection is sought. In both Colombia and Andean law, dispute resolution regarding patents, designs, or trademarks depends on the law of the country where the protection is invoked.[18]

In essence, the determination of applicable law varies between copyright and industrial property. Colombian law explicitly addresses the issue in the area of copyright, while it is silent in the field of industrial property, where protection is subject to the jurisdiction in which the application for protection is filed.

The IADIP Draft General Act proposes the following rule:

> Article 29: Colombian courts shall have jurisdiction to hear actions relating to the protection of intellectual property when the defendant is domiciled in Colombia or, in the absence of domicile, when the protection is invoked before Colombian courts.

The rule presents a broad framework for the protection of intellectual property. Such a framework encompasses various aspects, including the granting of rights in industrial property, the recognition of rights in copyright, and the infringement or denial of both.

Furthermore, the rule provides guidance for resolving intellectual property disputes, establishing the defendant's domicile as a key criterion for determining jurisdiction in cases of infringement or denial of rights. However, it also acknowledges

---

[15] Restrepo (2023).

[16] Guerrero (2010).

[17] Ibid.

[18] Ibid.

the principle of *lex loci protectionis*, stating that in the absence of a domicile, the authority of the jurisdiction where protection is sought will prevail.[19]

Now, Article 90 of the IADIP Draft states:

> Intellectual Property. Rights relating to intellectual property are governed by the law of the State in which the intellectual property is claimed. Contracts relating to intellectual property shall be governed by the provisions on contractual obligations of this Law.

From the text of the provision, two aspects can be observed. The first aims to reaffirm the territoriality of intellectual property; that is, to claim an intellectual property right, it will be necessary to have recognition of it in the territory where protection was sought, that is, for copyrights, patents, trademarks, or designs. The second leads to indicating that contracts relating to intellectual property will be governed by the provisions of the draft law on contractual obligations. This means that the parties are free to choose the applicable law, either totally or partially, for a part of the contract or the entire contract, or different laws of different states for all or part of the contract. It also indicates that in the absence of a choice of applicable law, the law of the place of performance of the obligation in question will apply.[20]

Nevertheless, in the interest of generating a harmonious interpretation of Articles 29 and 90 of the draft law concerning contractual obligations, and due to the specificity of intellectual property, it should be remembered that the claimant or the affected party in the contract has the alternative of bringing the action before the Colombian courts when the defendant is domiciled in Colombia. Otherwise, they must prove the intellectual property right duly recognized in Colombia so that the Colombian authorities are competent to analyze the violations, infringements, or disregard of intellectual property rights arising from the breach of contract.

The wording of the rule also prompts an analysis of another crucial aspect: the competent authority for dispute resolution.

3 Competent Authority to Resolve Disputes

The purpose of dispute resolution in this context is to resolve disputes arising from international intellectual property contracts. In this regard, the parties to the contract may determine the competent authority to resolve disputes arising from such contracts. This may involve the incorporation of a clause providing for international arbitration. Article 101 of Act No. 1563 of 2012 provides that an arbitral tribunal shall issue its decision in accordance with the legal rules chosen by the parties. That is, when the parties include in their agreement an arbitration clause to submit their legal relationship to arbitration. The law thus recognizes the principle of party autonomy as a decisive factor in the resolution of conflicts of law.[21]

---

[19] Guerrero (2010).

[20] Articles 73 and 79.

[21] Álvarez (2022).

The parties may also choose to submit any dispute to the national authorities of the country where the contract is to be performed. However, problems arise when the parties have not made an explicit choice. In such cases, Article 869 of the Colombian Commercial Code would again apply, and if the international contract is executed in Colombia, the Colombian courts would have jurisdiction, applying Colombian law.

The question then arises as to which authority is competent to resolve disputes arising from intellectual property issues. To answer this question, we must distinguish between disputes arising from copyright and those arising from industrial property.

*3.1 Copyright (***Droit d'auteur***)*

Andean Decision No. 351 of 1993 addresses procedural matters in Article 55. It provides that proceedings before the competent national authorities must comply with due process of law, ensuring procedural economy, celerity, equality of the parties, efficiency, and impartiality. It also guarantees the right of the parties to be informed of all procedural acts, with explicit exceptions.

From a procedural point of view, in cases where the parties have not designated a competent authority and the dispute arises within Colombia, jurisdiction will correspond to the national authorities. This is in accordance with Article 24 of the General Code of Procedure, which establishes that matters related to intellectual property, including copyrights, are within the jurisdiction of the civil courts or administrative authorities exercising judicial functions. Specifically, for copyright disputes, the *Dirección Nacional de Derechos de Autor* (National Copyright Office).

It is important to note that actions related to copyright law can be either criminal or civil in nature. Criminal actions are governed by the Colombian Criminal Code, enacted by Act No. 599 of 2000, specifically in Articles 270–272. On the other hand, civil actions fall under the jurisdiction of the ordinary courts. If a public entity is involved as a party, the matter would fall under the jurisdiction of the administrative courts.

It is essential to delimit which copyright disputes fall under the jurisdiction of the ordinary courts, an issue that has not been without controversy. Article 242 of Act No. 23 of 1982 states that "issues arising under this law, whether through the application of its provisions or as a consequence of legal acts and facts connected to copyright, shall be resolved by the ordinary courts." This provision implies that the civil jurisdiction will hear contentious cases concerning the direct application of Act No. 23 of 1982 or when the conflict stems from legal acts or facts related to copyright.[22]

[22] Bejarano Guzmán (2023).

The National Copyright Office has provided the following guidelines in relation to the protection of authors' rights:

> Authors have access to a variety of civil measures for the effective protection of their rights. The choice of judicial mechanism depends on the specifics of each case, the claims involved, and the impact on copyright, among other factors.
>
> These measures include:
>
> Precautionary procedures: Two types of precautionary procedures are applicable in copyright matters: those initiated with a lawsuit, as per Articles 244 and 246 of Law 23 of 1982, for the preventive seizure of works, productions, editions, copies, or proceeds from their sale or rental, including those from cinematographic, theatrical, musical, and similar shows. Precautionary measures without a lawsuit may also be sought, such as for the interdiction or suspension of a work.
>
> Executive processes: Executive processes can be initiated to enforce the fulfillment of an obligation related to an act or fact linked to copyright or related rights.
>
> Declaratory processes: Declaratory processes can be pursued in copyright matters to seek the imposition of a penalty, the judicial declaration of an existing but uncertain right, or the establishment of a new legal situation through a declaration.

In general, in these cases, the jurisdiction corresponds to the civil judges of the circuit, who act in a sole instance or the first instance, depending on the specific case. Following the decision, the parties may appeal before the Superior Court of the Judicial District of Bogota.

Having examined the copyright context, it is now worth considering the situation in the field of industrial property.

3.2 *Industrial Property*

Andean Decision No. 486 of 2000 establishes a mechanism to enforce industrial property rights. In cases of infringement, including patents, trademarks, and industrial designs, the holder of the rights may bring an action under Article 238, which states:

> The owner of rights protected under this Decision may bring an action before the competent national authority against any person who infringes his rights. He may also proceed against any person who engages in acts that indicate the imminence of an infringement.
>
> Where the domestic legislation of the member country permits, the competent national authority may institute the infringement proceedings provided for in the said legislation ex officio.

> In the case of joint ownership of rights, any of the joint owners may bring an action for infringement without the consent of the others being necessary, except where otherwise agreed between the joint owners.

This rule mandates that actions must be filed before the competent authority, which, in this context, encompasses both the ordinary jurisdiction and administrative authorities exercising judicial functions. The Colombian General Code of Procedure specifies in Article 19 that the civil circuit judges have jurisdiction, and in Article 24 designates the Superintendency of Industry and Commerce as the competent authority in its capacity as an administrative body with judicial powers.

In the field of industrial property, as in the field of copyright, there are various remedies and procedures for the protection of rights. These include attachment measures, declaratory actions, and enforcement proceedings related to trademarks, patents, or industrial designs.

Article 241 of Andean Decision No. 486 of 2000 provides as follows:

> The plaintiff or the party reporting the offense may apply to the competent national authority to have one or more of the following measures ordered, among others:
>
> (a) the cessation of the acts constituting the infringement;
> (b) indemnification for damages or prejudice;
> (c) withdrawal from commercial channels of the goods resulting from the infringement, including containers, packaging, labels, printed matter or advertising or other material, and also the material and means that mainly served for the commission of the infringement;
> (d) prohibition of the import or export of the goods, materials or means referred to in the foregoing subparagraph;
> (e) the award of ownership of the goods, materials or means referred to in subparagraph (c), in which case the value of the property shall be set against the amount of the indemnification for damages and prejudice;
> (f) the adoption of the necessary measures to ensure that the infringement does not continue or recur, including destruction of the goods, materials or means referred in subparagraph (c) or the temporary or permanent closure of the establishment of the defendant or accused; or
> (g) publication of the sentence handed down against the infringer and notification thereof, at the latter's expense, to all interested parties.
>
> In the case of goods bearing a false mark, the removal or elimination of the mark must be accompanied by measures designed to prevent such goods from entering commercial channels. In addition, such goods may not be cleared for re-exportation in the same State or placed under a different customs procedure.
>
> Exceptions may be established in cases duly characterized by the competent national authority, or when the express authorization of the owner of the trademark has been obtained.

Industrial property litigation mainly involves private parties, but public sector entities may also be parties to litigation. In these instances, the administrative courts have jurisdiction. Furthermore, the Constitutional Court has clarified that the Superintendency of Industry and Commerce also holds jurisdiction when an infringement action involves public entities.[23]

---

[23] Negative conflicts of competence between jurisdictions may arise between the Superintendence of Industry and Commerce and the First Section of the Council of State.

The provision proposed by the IADIP Draft General Act (Article 29, see *supra*) establishes two criteria for determining jurisdiction in Colombian courts: the domicile of the defendant and the law protecting the industrial property right. The rule suggests that the domicile of the defendant prevails, since it is the main criterion, with the protection law being applied only in the absence of domicile. This implies that, for Colombian courts to be considered competent, the corresponding industrial property right (trademark, design, or patent) must already be granted in Colombia, given the attributive nature of the registration. Therefore, if there is no registration in Colombia or the domicile of the defendant is not in Colombian territory, the matter may not be litigated in Colombia based on the proposed rule, except in the case of disputes over trade names and trade secrets, which do not require registration.

4 Conclusion

Intellectual property is a valuable asset in international trade, often embedded in various international contracts. Party autonomy typically governs such agreements, allowing parties to choose the applicable law and dispute resolution mechanism. However, a crucial question arises when parties remain silent on these matters: How are the applicable law and competent authority determined?

To answer this question, it is necessary to analyze how Colombian domestic law addresses this conflict in the context of intellectual property. Copyright law offers solutions, but industrial property law is less clear. For copyright, Colombian law specifies that the law of the place where the transfer or license is made will apply. Regarding dispute resolution, Colombian procedural rules clearly establish that if a copyright infringement or dispute arises in Colombia, Colombian authorities have jurisdiction. In industrial property, parties are free to choose the applicable law, but in the absence of such a choice, the *lex loci protectionis* principle applies, aligning with the registration-based system of industrial property. Regarding jurisdiction, the same principle applies to copyrights: Colombian authorities are competent to hear industrial property disputes arising in Colombia, provided that the right has been granted in Colombia.

In the absence of established case law on the subject, the resolution of these conflicts will probably be determined by the evolution of judicial practice. The debate is therefore still open.

The Draft General Law on Private International Law offers a potential framework for addressing conflicts involving the infringement of intellectual property rights. The broad language of the proposed rule, however, requires careful interpretation to determine its scope. Does it cover all forms of infringement, including contractual breaches and broader violations like piracy or counterfeiting? While the proposal entailed in the IADIP Draft General Act is a valuable contribution, its practical application will depend on how it is interpreted and implemented by Colombian authorities. The determination of the applicable law and the competent authority must remain a matter of party autonomy.

References

Alvarez JM (2021) Apuntes prácticos sobre la autonomía de la voluntad como punto de conexión en el derecho económico internacional. Universidad Externado de Colombia, Bogota

Álvarez PG (2022) Sobre la ley aplicable en los contratos internacionales. https://www.asuntoslegales.com.co/consultorio/sobre-la-ley-aplicable-en-los-contratos-internacionales-3353778. Accessed 29 Aug 2024

Bejarano Guzmán R (2023) Procesos declarativos, arbitrales y ejecutivos, 11th edn. Temis, Bogota

Dicey AV (1882) Conflict of law and bills of exchange. Am Law Rev 505 59(7) (Nov 1959):973–1025

Guerrero M (2010) Legislación aplicable a los contratos internacionales de transferencia de tecnología. Revista la Propiedad Inmaterial 14:141–193

Jaimes JP (2022) La ley aplicable al contrato de joint venture internacional a falta de elección por las partes. Universidad Externado de Colombia, Bogota

Ochoa Jiménez MJ, Carrillo Gamboa P, Zapata Flórez J (2019) La elección del derecho aplicable en el derecho internacional privado en Colombia. Estudios Socio-Jurídicos 21(1):91–120

Ortega Giménez A (2016) Los contratos de colaboración en el comercio internacional. Agencia comercial, distribución comercial, franquicia, joint-venture. Leyer, Bogota

Ortega Giménez A (2022) Guía práctica de contratación internacional. Libros Profesionales de Empresa ESIC, Madrid

Restrepo D (2023) Elección de la ley aplicable en contratos internacionales. https://www.asuntoslegales.com.co/consultorio/eleccion-de-la-ley-aplicable-en-contratos-internacionales-3597470. Accessed 27 Aug 2024

Rojas Tamayo D (2018) El derecho aplicable al contrato internacional. Universidad Externado de Colombia, Bogota

Werra J (2021) Contract law and intellectual property transactions: research perspectives. In: Motagnani ML, Calboli I (eds) Handbook of intellectual property research: lenses, methods, and perspectives. Oxford University Press, Oxford, pp 67–81

World Trade Organization (n.d.) TRIPS — Trade-Related Aspects of Intellectual Property Rights. https://www.wto.org/english/tratop_e/trips_e/trips_e.htm. Accessed 27 Aug 2024

Zapata A (2016) La ley aplicable al contrato internacional. In: García Matamorros L, Aljure Salame A (eds) Teoría general del derecho internacional privado. Universidad del Rosario Legis, Bogota, pp 189–217

Brenda Salas PhD and Master's in Private Law, University of Paris II Panthéon-Assas; Lawyer and Specialist in Intellectual Property, Universidad Externado de Colombia; Research Professor of Intellectual Property, Universidad Externado de Colombia.

Persons and Family

Natural Persons in Colombian Private International Law

Laura Victoria García Matamoros

Abstract This chapter focuses on the individual scope of the personal status. It first discusses its elements, particularly considering the private international law perspective. Furthermore, it presents the advantages and disadvantages of the criteria to determine the law that must be applied to cross-border situations. Finally, the chapter critically approaches the Colombian legal system, paying special attention to the current situation and to the solutions proposed by two recent law drafts: the Draft General Act on Private International Law for Colombia prepared by the *Instituto Antioqueño de Derecho Internacional Privado* in 2021 and the Draft Civil Code of Colombia presented by the *Universidad Nacional de Colombia* in 2023.

1 Introduction

Globalization and digital connectivity are leading today's world to an increasing internationalization of how individuals relate to each other. Such reality includes not only commercial or contractual relations, but also those areas that affect people as individuals, i.e., their personal existence and activities. These kinds of relations are no less complex and significant, and are also dealt with by private international law. To this end, this field resorts to the concept of personal status: "the set of institutions and material that are directly linked to the person, shaping his condition as a subject of law."[1] Within the realm of personal status, it is possible to distinguish between two main domains. The first is the individual personal status, which prescribes the legal status of individuals. The second is the family's personal status,

[1] Esplugues Mota et al. (2011), p. 257.

L. V. García Matamoros (✉)
Facultad de Jurisprudencia, Universidad del Rosario, Bogotá, Colombia
e-mail: laura.garcia@urosario.edu.co

M. J. Ochoa Jiménez, C. Madrid Martínez (eds.), *A Private International Law for Colombia*, Springer Textbooks in Law,
https://doi.org/10.1007/978-3-032-04106-7_13

which governs collective relationships between subjects. Among the latter, marriage and marital unions deserve particular attention.[2]

As with the law in general, it is essential that the rules that comprise these statutes can be revised and adapted with the regularity required by the evolving realities of human relations. In this regard, proposals that stimulate academic discourse on the potential updating of the laws that regulate this matter are always welcome. In this regard, two notable contributions have recently emerged in Colombia: the Draft General Act on Private International Law for Colombia prepared by the *Instituto Antioqueño de Derecho Internacional Privado* in 2021 (IADIP Draft), and the Draft Civil Code of Colombia prepared by the *Universidad Nacional de Colombia* in 2023 (UNAL Draft).[3] Both drafts contain relevant rules on this matter.

Accordingly, this chapter focuses on the fundamental aspect of personal status, namely its individual scope. To gain an understanding of this institution, it is first necessary to examine its elements, as well as some challenges that arise from the perspective of private international law. Subsequently, the advantages and disadvantages of the various criteria that determine the applicable rule in the event of a conflict of laws are presented. Finally, the current situation and perspectives in the Colombian legal system are analyzed to discuss a solution in light of the aforementioned drafts.

2 The Individual Personal Status: Elements and Issues

In essence, the status of the individual is the one that allows the legal system to individualize a person by emphasizing his or her unique character. In this regard, according to the national doctrine

> Conceptually, the natural person, a prototype of the subject of law, will always be special (species), because in an accurate legal and political technique he or she is someone without equal who deserves individual consideration even in those cases in which he or she is seen as an element of a whole… As each subject of Law—human or ideal—is different from another, it becomes necessary to know precisely who it is, if we want to allow him to exercise and defend his advantages or make him fulfill his obligations, we must have some mechanism to identify him.[4]

There is an interrelation with the attributes of personality—name, capacity, marital status, domicile, nationality, and patrimony—which are the legal categories that make a person unique to the law. Nevertheless, beyond the confines of academic discourse, it can be broadly asserted that the constituents of this individual status are, on the one hand, the capacity itself, given its intrinsic relevance, and, on the

[2] This subject is addressed in the following chapter.

[3] When this draft is mentioned, reference is made to the second version, which has no major substantive changes from the first version but does change the numbering of the articles.

[4] Medina Pabón (2017), pp. 605–606.

other hand, the status of the person, a comprehensive category that encompasses name and domicile.

Therefore, when a foreign element is present in legal relations concerning these aspects of individual status, it becomes essential to refer to private international law as a means of regulating conflicts of laws. Consequently, when examining these two elements, it is crucial to identify potential challenges that may emerge.

2.1 *Capacity*

Capacity consists of "the ability of a person to acquire rights and to enter into obligations."[5] In this category, a distinction is made between the capacity to enjoy and the capacity to exercise. The former is that which recognizes the subject as the holder of rights and obligations, while the latter refers to the possibility of exercising those rights and assuming those obligations directly, without the need for any mediation.

In this initial aspect, it is frequently the case that an individual possesses the nationality of State Y, maintains domicile in State X, and engages in legal transactions in additional jurisdictions. Consequently, an intrinsically personal aspect such as capacity is inevitably subject to the application of different laws. This is because, in the course of the individual's international activities, the question will eventually arise of how to determine the law governing the individual's capacity. This question can be answered in one of three ways: capacity should be governed by the law of the state where he or she is domiciled, by the law of his nationality, or by the law governing the legal act in question. Such conflicts can become even more complex when, for example, the three applicable laws establish discrepant criteria with respect to the determination of the adult age. This can result in a situation where an individual with the capacity to exercise in one jurisdiction lacks this in another jurisdiction.

2.2 *Status of Persons*

The second element of individual status is the status of persons, which is composed of the name and domicile.

The person's name encompasses the first name—or given name—and the surname. Both elements together form the identification of an individual:

[5] Constitutional Court of Colombia, Decision C-983, Nov. 13 of 2002.

> The name is the defining feature of human identity, conferring upon its bearer the right to use it in all private and public acts without hindrance. Conversely, there is an obligation to use it as a means of identifying oneself in legal proceedings.[6]

This legal institution introduces a certain degree of complexity when it comes to defining the applicable law, as it is situated within a complex web of legal categories from an international perspective. In addition to being an attribute of personality, it is also a human right, an indicator of the link with a family, and its assignment is further shaped by public order norms.

In this context, it is possible that the parents of an infant born abroad may exercise their right to choose the name they deem most appropriate for their child, despite the limitations imposed by public order regulations on the place of birth and the location of the civil registration. This leads to the question of which legislation will govern the naming of a person in a state that does not adhere to the same naming regulations. Furthermore, what are the consequences if an individual is baptized in contravention of the restrictions imposed by the law of their nationality and subsequently relocates to this country to establish their domicile, exercising their right to do so?

Regarding the domicile, this concept is defined as "that place in the national territory where, in accordance with the law, a person is located and where they act legally and exercise their rights and obligations."[7] In Colombia, the legal definition of domicile refers to the place of "residence accompanied, actually or presumptively, by the intention to remain there."[8] However, this criterion is not universally accepted and varies in each jurisdiction. Furthermore, the international components present additional challenges when determining the applicable law to ascertain a person's domicile.

As will be explained in the following section, domicile in itself is a rule of conflict in private international law and, in turn, is an attribute of personality that generates legal consequences such as, for example, determining the competent judge to define a dispute. This ambiguity is further compounded by the lack of a universally accepted definition of domicile. Consequently, an individual may be legally located in different jurisdictions according to the applicable laws, or even be legally unlocated. This lack of clarity gives rise to significant legal challenges.

From the delimitation of the elements that make up the individual personal status, together with examples of challenges that may arise in the light of private international law, the discussion will then turn to the various criteria that are employed to resolve conflicts of law, with particular attention paid to their relevance in the context of family personal status.

---

[6] Medina Pabón (2017), p. 623.

[7] Ibid., p. 688.

[8] Colombian Civil Code, Article 76.

3 Criteria for Determining the Applicable Law on Personal Status

In the field of private international law, the criteria for determining the applicable norm in the event of a conflict of laws concerned with personal relationships are defined as "factors of connection" or "points of contact." It is widely accepted in the doctrine that "at least three criteria for determining the applicable legal system for personal status in cases of external legal transactions: nationality, domicile, and habitual residence"[9] are fundamental. However, there is no unanimous agreement on which of these three criteria is the most suitable. In light of the continuing relevance of these three concepts, it is necessary to briefly address their advantages and disadvantages.

3.1 Nationality

Traditionally, nationality and domicile have been the predominant points of contact in resolving conflicts of laws concerning personal status. Nationality is understood as "the relationship or link between a legal subject and a state, which implies submission to its laws and receiving its protection, conferring additional advantages and rights, and imposing duties and obligations."[10] The criterion of nationality gained prominence with the nationalist ideas of Paolo Stanislao Mancini, who argued that "in the realm of international relations, individuals should be governed by their national law."[11] This perspective was embraced in various codes of continental Europe in the nineteenth century, influenced by the nationalist policies of the time.[12]

One advantage of this criterion is that it respects the cultural norms of foreigners by allowing the application of the laws of their home countries.[13] In our contexts of multiculturalism, this respect becomes increasingly significant, justifying the adoption of this approach and promoting the inclusion of diverse legal systems and respect for the cultural identity of foreigners. However, the application of this criterion does present certain challenges. In countries with high immigration rates, this criterion can be exclusionary and create a broad space for public policy exceptions. This is due to the difficulty faced by legal practitioners in applying foreign laws and potential contradictions between the law of the forum and the individual's national law.

[9] Rodríguez Benot (2010), p. 187.

[10] Medina Pabón (2017), p. 663.

[11] Boutin Icaza (2006), p. 46.

[12] Examples include the French Civil Code of 1804, the Portuguese Code of 1867, the Spanish Code of 1889, and the codes of Italy and Romania of 1865.

[13] See Rodríguez Benot (2010), p. 189.

Moreover, the social and cultural bond between the individual and their national law may diminish, rendering this law unsuitable for addressing the needs of proximity in the legal relationship. The situation becomes even more intricate for individuals fleeing persecution or those seeking to obtain the nationality of their host state but encountering obstacles due to rigorous requirements. In such instances, the nationality criterion may prove inadequate.

3.2 Domicile

Under Colombian legislation, the domicile has two fundamental elements: an objective component, which pertains to the geographical location of residence, and a subjective element, which concerns the intention to maintain a fixed abode in that particular place.[14] This legal point of contact permits an individual to "change the law governing their personal situation by their own private act, that is, by changing their domicile."[15] Accordingly, the system is based on individual autonomy and freedom, enabling a person who culturally identifies with a country other than their nationality to submit to the laws of that state without undergoing the bureaucratic processes typically associated with acquiring nationality. Thus, it acknowledges the possibility that an individual who does not identify with their country of origin may not be bound by the laws of their nationality. The rationale behind this legal framework is to prevent state interference in the personal affairs of any of its members who have left its territory and established themselves abroad.[16]

Nevertheless, this system is not without challenges. The subjective element of domicile renders it challenging to substantiate and gives rise to "interpretative controversies," in contrast to nationality, which is based on an objective criterion. Furthermore, the concept of domicile is not uniform across all states, which further complicates its application as a point of contact. Lastly, there is always the possibility that a change of domicile may be asserted to circumvent the applicable law of a particular case. In such cases, the claim of "fraud upon the law" may be asserted, which would render the change of contract invalid. However, this assertion would require a high level of evidentiary proof to be substantiated.

[14] See Medina Pabón (2017), p. 688.

[15] Wolff (2012), p. 99.

[16] Ibid.

3.3 Habitual Residence

In response to the criticisms and challenges that have arisen with regard to the criteria of nationality and domicile and building upon the work of the Hague Conference on Private International Law, the criterion of habitual residence has emerged as a viable alternative, often considered a "de facto domicile."[17] This criterion excludes the subjective element of domicile, namely the intention to remain in one's place of residence, which gives rise to various deficiencies. It instead focuses exclusively on the objective element. Therefore, habitual residence presents notable benefits as an integrative criterion. These include the prevention of disputes regarding the link between an individual and their nationality. It also facilitates the application of laws that are more familiar to the judge. Furthermore, it reduces the need for public policy exceptions. Finally, it eliminates the evidentiary difficulties associated with the concept of domicile, among other advantages.[18]

Nevertheless, this methodology also has inherent limitations. The removal of all subjective elements results in the individual being deprived of the freedom to determine the law that should govern their legal status. Furthermore, the cultural integration and acceptance inherent in the nationality system are diminished.

As can be observed, each of these points of contact presents advantages and challenges, rendering it impractical to exclusively favor one over the other in determining the applicable law for personal status. Consequently, the selection of these criteria is subject to variation following the internal legislation of states and the international treaties to which they are party.

In Anglo-Saxon countries, the application of the domicile criterion in matters of personal status is a prominent feature of the legal landscape. This practice is reflected in certain Inter-American treaties.[19] In contrast, countries in the continent of Europe, which have influenced the legislation of Latin American states, tend to favor the nationality criterion, sometimes combining it with domicile or certain aspects of family relations.[20] Nevertheless, there is an emerging tendency towards the incorporation of habitual residence as a connecting factor, either as the primary or alternative criterion in conjunction with nationality or domicile, as evidenced in the conventional texts of the European Union,[21] and as we shall see below in the different Latin American legislations.

[17] Kegel (1982), p. 257.

[18] See García Matamoros (2016), pp. 272–273.

[19] For example, the Civil Law Treaty of Montevideo of 1889.

[20] For example, as discussed in this chapter, Article 19 of the Colombian Civil Code provides for nationality as a criterion, however, Article 13 of Act No. 1 of 1976, amending Article 163 of the Civil Code, provides for the application of the law of the marital domicile for divorce, as will be discussed in the following chapter.

[21] See Cordero Álvarez (2023), pp. 254–274.

4 Colombian Conflicts of Law Rules on Natural Persons: Regulation and Prospects

4.1 Capacity

Capacity is a fundamental aspect of personal status, particularly about the individual, insofar as it is the power of the latter to acquire rights and contract obligations. In this regard, to validate this condition in the context of contemporary globalization, the Colombian legal system enshrines in Article 19 of the Civil Code the primary rule of conflict, which stipulates:

> Colombians resident or domiciled in a foreign country shall remain subject to the provisions of this Code and other national laws governing civil rights and obligations:
>
> 1. Concerning the status of persons *and their capacity* to carry out certain acts which are to have effect in one of the territories administered by the General Government, or in matters within the competence of the Union.
> 2. In obligations and rights arising out of family relations, but only in respect of their spouses and relatives in the cases mentioned in the preceding paragraph.

A preliminary examination of the rule suggests that, for Colombians, regardless of their place of residence, capacity is governed by national law. Nevertheless, several issues emerge in this context. First, it could be argued that the scope and effect of the rule in regulating international legal relations are null, as its factual assumption only contemplates what is applicable to Colombians. Nevertheless, a correct interpretation of the doctrine of private international law indicates that this article is written in unilateral terms, as is typical of the rules of conflict outlined in the internal legislation of states. These rules regulate the situation with respect to their nationals and not with respect to foreigners, within the framework of their sovereignty. Accordingly, a potential solution to this issue would be to bilateralize the rule, thereby encompassing the various factual assumptions. In light of the aforementioned, it can be posited that Article 19 of the Civil Code stipulates that the capacity of foreigners present in Colombia shall be governed by the law of their nationality.

The aforementioned rule remains ambiguous and complex, as it establishes a limitation to the competence of Colombian law, solely in matters where "acts that are to have effect in any of the territories administered by the general government" are carried out. A preliminary examination of the doctrine suggested that the rule applies to any type of act related to the status and capacity of Colombians. In this regard, Marco Gerardo Monroy offered a critique of this position, stating that "the interpreter cannot mutilate the law he or she interprets," particularly by eliminating the expression "certain acts" that is explicitly established in the rule.[22]

Similarly, the wording of the provision suggests that it applies to acts that have no effect on national territory but fall within the "competence of the Union," without

[22] Monroy Cabra (1999), p. 298.

specifying the situations to which it refers. In this regard, Aljure Salame (2011) points out that:

> The article does not explain what these acts are or which ones fall within national competence. First of all, the only reasonable interpretation of the expression "certain acts" is that it simply corresponds to those that have effects in Colombia and that the reference to national jurisdiction, in order not to be redundant and to maintain a useful effect, should refer to acts that do not have effects in the country, but are governed by our law in the aspects mentioned above.[23]

As evidenced by the preceding analysis, Article 19 of the Civil Code represents a complex, confusing, and challenging rule to apply in practice, which "actually leads to the fact that it is never known when Colombian law applies and when foreign law applies."[24] This ambiguity hinders the development of private international law in Colombia and generates uncertainty in private relations with international elements, which are becoming increasingly common in our country.

4.1.1 Comparative Perspective

Concerning the international conventions that Colombia has signed on this matter, it is noteworthy that the Treaty on Private International Law, which was signed with Ecuador in 1903, also accepts nationality as a point of contact, as set forth in Article 2 thereof.[25] In contrast, the 1889 Montevideo Treaty on International Civil Law establishes domicile as a criterion for the application of law[26] and also stipulates that "The change of domicile does not alter the capacity acquired by emancipation, age of majority, or judicial authorization" (Article 2). This not only establishes domicile as the predominant criterion, but also provides a solution to a possible mobile conflict, which arises due to the variable nature of the criterion of spatial connection. This is achieved by respecting the capacity to exercise acquired if a subject changes his domicile to a place where he or she would be considered lacking in such capacity.

It is similarly important to consider the legislation of neighboring and legally comparable countries to gain insight into the prevailing approaches to defining the applicable law in matters of capacity with foreign elements. In this regard, Ochoa and Zapata (2022) conclude that, after analyzing the laws of different Latin American countries, the preferred criterion for determining the applicable law in matters of personal status is that of domicile, which is defined as habitual residence.

---

[23] Aljure Salame (2011), p. 94.

[24] Caicedo Castilla (1967), p. 246.

[25] That article states as follows: "The status and legal capacity of persons shall be judged by their national law, even in the case of acts performed or property existing in the other country."

[26] Montevideo Treaty on International Civil Law of 1889, Article 1: "The capacity of persons is governed by their domicile."

The only exceptions to this are the laws of Colombia, Chile, Ecuador, and El Salvador, which adopt nationality.[27]

Indeed, the recently enacted Private International Law Act of Uruguay (2020) merits particular attention as it represents a significant advancement in the region. Article 20 establishes domicile as the point of contact, defining it as "habitual residence" as follows: "The capacity to practice of natural persons is governed by the law of their domicile. For the purpose of determining whether or not a person possesses capacity to exercise, the habitual residence is considered domicile."

Similarly, the 1998 Private International Law Act of Venezuela contemplated a significant change at that moment: replacing nationality with domicile, which is actually defined in terms of habitual residence,[28] as the point of contact to define the applicable law in matters of personal status,[29] among which is capacity.[30] The same provisions are reflected in Articles 2070[31] and 33[32] of the Peruvian Civil Code of 1984, which remains unchanged in the current reform project being discussed in that country.[33] As can be observed, the three systems under consideration (those of Uruguay, Venezuela, and Peru), in contrast to the regulation set out in the Civil Code of Colombia, are notable for their straightforward and unambiguous wording, a consequence of the updates they have undergone. Furthermore, they favor habitual residence as the point of contact in relation to capacity, rather than nationality or domicile in a strict sense.

In contrast, the 2014 Argentine Civil and Commercial Code of the Nation adopts the domicile connection as the point of contact that defines the applicable law in capacity matters, without defining it as habitual residence. This represents a continuity in the legislation that takes advantage of "the wise historical solutions of the matter since Froland, already adopted in the Argentine Civil Code, and those embodied in the jurisprudence and the Draft Code of Private International Law of

[27] See Ochoa Jiménez and Zapata Flórez (2022), pp. 556–561. Argentina, Bolivia, Brazil, Guatemala, México, Perú, República Dominicana, Uruguay, and Venezuela are the countries that adopt domicile as the point of contact.

[28] Private International Law Act of Venezuela, Article 11: (ESP) "El domicilio de una persona física se encuentra en el territorio del Estado donde tiene su residencia habitual."

[29] Maekelt et al. (2005), p. 655.

[30] Private International Law Act of Venezuela, Article 16: "The existence, status, and capacity of persons are governed by the law of their domicile."

[31] Peruvian Civil Code, Article 2070: "The status and capacity of the natural person are governed by the law of his domicile. The change of domicile does not alter the status or restrict the capacity acquired under the law of the previous domicile."

[32] Peruvian Civil Code, Article 33: "The domicile is constituted by the habitual residence of the person at a place."

[33] See Gobierno de Perú (2020) Anteproyecto de modificaciones del Decreto Legislativo N° 295 Código Civil. https://www.gob.pe/institucion/minjus/informes-publicaciones/429560-anteproyecto-de-modificaciones-del-decreto-legislativo-n-295-codigo-civil. Accessed on 4 July 2024.

2003"[34] and that, in the opinion of Argentine jurists, gives greater certainty than habitual residence.[35]

At the opposite end of the spectrum is the Civil Code of Chile, which states in Article 15 the primacy of the point of contact of nationality.[36] This is in alignment with the approach taken in Colombia, and the wording is strikingly similar to that used in both jurisdictions, employing the expressions "certain acts" and "must have effects." This may be perceived as unsurprising, given that the Colombian Civil Code is an inheritance of the Chilean one, as a point of reference for the jurist Andrés Bello. Additionally, neither of the two states has yet updated its rules. In any case, the draft update presented in 2020 by the Chilean Association of Private International Law[37] establishes in Article 26 that "a person is capable if he/she is capable according to the law of his/her habitual residence, the law of his/her nationality or the law of the place of celebration or granting of the respective legal act," including habitual residence in a complementary manner with other criteria, expanding the possibilities for a person's capacity. Likewise, the same rule prevents a possible conflict of mobility by respecting acquired rights, stating that "the capacity acquired according to the law of habitual residence or nationality shall not be lost by changing habitual residence or nationality, as the case may be."

In Spanish law, the criterion of nationality prevails in matters of capacity, as well as in matters of civil status, family rights and obligations, and inheritance (Article 9.1.I of the Civil Code), although habitual residence is accepted as an alternative criterion in some specific cases, such as in the case of dual nationality, neither of which is Spanish, or in the case of lack of Spanish nationality.[38]

4.1.2 The IADIP and UNAL Drafts

The IADIP Draft seeks to resolve the problems relating to the criterion of capacity arising from the wording of Article 19 of the Civil Code, which provides in Article 40 as follows:

> The existence, status and legal capacity of natural persons is governed by the law of the State of their domicile.

---

[34] Herrera (2013), p. 236.

[35] Ibid.

[36] Civil Code of Chile, Article 15: "Chileans, notwithstanding their residence or domicile in a foreign country, shall remain subject to the laws of their country that regulate civil obligations and rights. Concerning the status of persons and their capacity to execute certain acts, which are to have effect in Chile."

[37] See Universidad de Chile (2020) Decano de la Facultad de Derecho y Presidente de ADIPRI entregan Anteproyecto de Ley de Derecho Internacional Privado al Ministro de Justicia y Derechos Humanos. https://derecho.uchile.cl/noticias/168925/facultad-y-adipri-entregan-anteproyecto-de-ley-a-min-de-justicia. Accessed on 4 July 2024.

[38] See García Matamoros (2016), pp. 272–273.

> If the law governing the act for which capacity is to be determined prescribes special conditions as to the capacity of a person, that law shall be taken into account.

For its part, the UNAL Draft provides that the law governing the capacity of persons is the law of the domicile, as stated in Article 23: "The law of domicile that, at the time, the natural or natural person has, governs its scope, capacity, name and surname, absence and disappearance, without prejudice to the regulation of capacity in family matters ..."

Thus, in the first place, both stipulate that matters relating to personal status, in their individual aspect, are governed by domicile, which, in their respective articles,[39] is defined as habitual residence, i.e., they adopt the point of contact that the theory of International Law considers solves the criticisms and difficulties presented by the criteria of nationality and domicile, following the trend adopted, among others, by the legal systems of Uruguay, Peru, and Venezuela.

In this sense, the two drafts presented are right to take the concept of habitual residence as the point of reference for determining the law applicable to the aspects of the international legal relations of natural persons. On the one hand, they accept the criterion that already prevails in various legislations and, on the other, they establish a formulation in simple language and, in principle, free of abstractions.

However, Article 24 of the UNAL Draft provides that "The capacity to act shall be governed by the law of the place where it is exercised," without specifying whether this refers only to legal persons or also to natural persons, which may be in contradiction with the first provision of Article 23. In this sense, a person of 19 years of age, who is a minor in State A where he or she is domiciled, will not be able to enter into contracts under that law, but he or she could do so in State B, where the age of majority is 18 years, and such a transaction would in any case be valid also in State A, by the aforementioned provision, without the requirement of the age of majority for the acquisition of the capacity to act.

4.2 *Status of Persons*

As previously stated, the individual status of a person is constituted by two elements: his capacity and his status before the law. The former refers to those attributes that allow his identification, particularly through his name and domicile. It is crucial to acknowledge that in Colombia, civil status is primarily governed by Article 19 of the Civil Code, which establishes nationality as the primary reference point, despite the inherent complexities and challenges previously discussed.

---

[39] IADIP Draft, Article 11: "The domicile of a natural person is in the territory of the state in which he/she habitually resides with the intention of exercising his/her rights there."

UNAL Draft, Article 74: "Domicile is the habitual residence of a person in a given municipality or district."

Furthermore, it is crucial to acknowledge that states typically implement regulations to guarantee transparency and oversight of events and actions that may impact an individual's status. These regulations mandate the registration of civil status through public provisions, imposing penalties for failure to register pertinent acts. In Colombia, there are three primary types of civil registration: birth, marriage, and death.[40]

It is therefore established that in matters of registration, the applicable law in Colombia is that of the place where the event occurs, or the act is performed. These matters concern the status of persons before the law, including their existence and name, the formation of a family, and their disappearance. In this regard, as previously stated, both the IADIP Draft and the UNAL Draft establish that the status of the person shall be governed by the law of their domicile. However, this does not affect the provisions relating to registration, given the importance that each state ascribes to this matter. Indeed, even Article 79 of the UNAL Draft recognizes this, stipulating that "the civil status and other facts related to capacity must be proven before judges and public officials, through the respective registration in the civil registry."

4.2.1 Name

The name, which includes first name and surname, is regarded as an intrinsic aspect of the personality and, as such, is considered inalienable, imprescriptible, and unwaivable. Moreover, the right to possess a first and last name constitutes a fundamental human right, as evidenced by its recognition in numerous human rights treaties. The International Covenant on Civil and Political Rights guarantees children the right to have a name from birth,[41] while the American Convention on Human Rights establishes that everyone has the right to a first and last name, regulating its assurance through assumed names if necessary.[42] In this manner, international conventions establish that every individual is entitled to the fundamental right to their name. The UNAL Draft, as a comprehensive revision of the Civil Code, also incorporates the right to individuality and the name in Article 61.

In the context of conflict of laws in Colombia, recourse may be had again to Article 19 of the Civil Code, which establishes that the law applicable to the name is that of the nationality of the individual. This signifies that parents are at liberty to select the appellation of their offspring without legal constraints, even if it is unconventional or does not correspond to the child's biological sex, as has frequently been

[40] See Registraduría. Registro civil https://www.registraduria.gov.co/-Registro-civil-.html. Accessed on 26 May 2024.

[41] International Covenant on Civil and Political Rights, Article 24-2: "Every child shall be registered immediately after birth and shall have a name."

[42] American Convention on Human Rights, Article 18: "Every person has the right to a proper name and to the surnames of his parents or of one of them. The law shall regulate the manner of assuring this right for all, by means of assumed names, if necessary."

observed in the country.[43] Nevertheless, at the time of registration, the official may, through conscientious objection, decline to register any offensive expressions.[44] This legal freedom does not exist in all countries; for example, in New Zealand and Norway, there are prohibited names.[45]

This discrepancy can result in complications in terms of conflict of laws, particularly in instances where a child is born abroad and registered with a name that is not accepted upon their return to the country of origin.[46] In such cases, the applicable law could be determined by nationality, domicile, or habitual residence. However, the registration is subject to the law of the place where it is made, which may result in the denial of registration for names prohibited by immediate and necessary rules,[47] through conscientious objection or in disregard of such prohibitions of the applicable personal status law in less restrictive systems.

With regard to surnames, the order of these varies according to each country.[48] For example, in the United States and some European countries, it is customary to utilize a single surname, typically that of the father. In Brazil, the maternal surname is typically the primary designation, followed by the paternal. In Colombia, the order was the inverse of the Brazilian. However, Article 2 of Act No. 2129 of 2021 modified that rule and established that the order for the registration of surnames would be determined by mutual agreement or, in the absence of such an agreement, randomly by drawing lots.[49]

In this context, conflicts may emerge between the rules of conflict in matters of personal status and the rules of civil registration. These conflicts can give rise to complex situations for individuals, such as the existence of different names in different countries, which in turn gives rise to administrative and financial complications. In this regard, Article 43 of the IADIP Draft provides that a person's name and surname are to be governed, at their choice, by the law of the state of which they are

---

[43] See El Tiempo (2024) Los colombianos 'sin tocayo': los nombres más raros y únicos de Colombia, según la Registraduría https://www.eltiempo.com/cultura/gente/estos-son-los-sin-tocayo-los-nombres-mas-raros-y-unicos-de-colombia-segun-la-registraduria-3342627. Accessed on 07 July 2024.

[44] See El Espectador (2024) Nombres prohibidos en Colombia: los registradores se pueden negar a ponerlos https://www.elespectador.com/colombia/mas-regiones/estos-son-los-nombres-prohibidos-en-colombia-los-registradores-se-pueden-negar-a-ponerlos/. Accessed on 07 July 2024.

[45] See Peru.com (2013) The Telegraph: Estos son los nombres prohibidos alrededor del mundo http://peru.com/actualidad/internacionales/the-telegraph-estos-son-nombres-prohibidos-alrededor-mundo-noticia-157702. Accessed on 07 July 2024.

[46] See García Matamoros (2016), p. 280.

[47] Maekelt et al. (2005), pp. 337–356.

[48] Mantilla Rey (1996), p. 83.

[49] Act No. 2129 of 2021, Article 2: "Article 53 of Decree 1260 of 1970 is hereby amended to read as follows: In the Civil Registry of Birth, the first surname of the mother and the first surname of the father shall be registered as the surnames of the registered person, in the order decided by mutual agreement. If there is no agreement, the official in charge of keeping the Civil Registry of Birth shall resolve the disagreement by drawing lots, in accordance with the procedure established for such purpose by the National Civil Registry Office…."

a national or in which they are domiciled. This allows for the party's autonomy to choose the law that best suits their individual circumstances. However, it is important to note that this does not overcome the drawbacks with respect to registration. Conversely, the UNAL Draft, as previously referenced, stipulates in Article 23 that the law of domicile shall prevail.

Therefore, we can see that both proposals, with the slight difference in the IADIP Draft, converge in the law of domicile, again distancing itself from the current Colombian regulations that apply the law of the nationality of the individual in the aspects regarding the name and surname.

4.2.2 Domicile

As previously stated, the concept of domicile may be interpreted in different ways across legal systems. This underscores the necessity for each state to establish internal rules to determine the applicable law in the definition of domicile. However, this is an uncommon practice, and thus, in each system, the domestic law that defines this criterion will be applied. In the Colombian legal system, domicile is defined by Article 76 of the Civil Code as "the place of residence accompanied by the intention of remaining therein." In any case, given the difficulty in proving the subjective element of domicile, civil law establishes both negative and positive presumptions to determine the intent to remain.[50]

Furthermore, the current Civil Code establishes the presumption of domicile in the absence of a known domicile, which is presumed to be that of mere residence (Article 84). Additionally, the domicile of a child under parental authority is presumed to be that of the father, with the mother's domicile being disregarded, and the domicile of a person under guardianship or curatorship is presumed to be that of the respective guardian or curator (Article 88). Furthermore, it should be noted that the outdated provision stating that "the married woman follows the domicile of the husband" (Article 87) was revoked by Decree No. 2820 of 1974.

With regard to international conventions, the Treaty of Montevideo on International Civil Law of 1889, signed by Colombia, establishes a conflict rule on domicile, stating that the domicile of the person concerned determines the law that establishes the conditions for domicile.[51] This Convention also establishes that the domicile of parents, guardians, and curators is that of the state whose law governs the functions they exercise (Article 6), and that the domicile of incapacitated persons is that of their legal representatives (Article 7). Similarly, Article 8 provides that the domicile of the spouses is that established by the marriage and, failing that, that of the husband, and that "a woman who is legally separated shall retain the domicile of her husband unless she establishes another domicile." This reflects the

[50] Civil Code of Colombia, Articles 79 and 80.

[51] Montevideo Treaty on International Civil Law of 1889, Article 5: "The law of the place in which the person resides determines the conditions required for residence to constitute domicile."

social conceptions of the role of women at the time the Convention was issued. Finally, persons whose domicile is unknown are presumed to have their domicile in the place where they live (Article 9).

As noted above, the regional trend is to define domicile in terms of habitual residence (Uruguay, Venezuela, Peru), but some countries, such as Argentina and Chile, still maintain the classic definition of domicile, with its subjective component. Concerning the domicile of minors and incapacitated persons, both the private international law of Uruguay[52] and that of Venezuela[53] stipulate that it is the habitual residence, with the slight difference that, in the Uruguayan system, the domicile of a minor subject to parental authority is that of his parents, only in cases where they effectively exercise representation. About the marital domicile, Article 23 of the Uruguayan law defines it as the place "where the spouses live together" or where they have their own domicile. On the other hand, Article 12 of the Venezuelan law states that "the married woman has her own domicile, separate from that of her husband," which, while recognizing the independence of the woman in determining her domicile, does not make it appropriate to continue to define it in terms of the "married woman."

In this regard, both drafts under review define domicile in terms of habitual residence. Thus, Article 74 of the UNAL Draft states that "domicile is the habitual residence of a person in a given municipality or district." Article 11 of the IADIP Draft, for its part, states that "the domicile of a natural person is in the territory of the state in which he or she habitually resides intending to exercise his or her rights there." This last proposal raises concerns because, although it refers to the concept of habitual residence, it is complemented by a subjective aspect, the intention to exercise rights there, with the difficulties of proof that this usually entails. Regarding the marital domicile, the UNAL Draft defines it as the "common domicile of the spouses,"[54] while the IADIP Draft defines it in terms of the place where "they live together,"[55] in a similar way to the provision of the Uruguayan Law. Both drafts

[52] Private International Law Act of Uruguay of 2020, Article 16: "(Domicile of incapable natural persons). Minors subject to parental authority are domiciled in the State where their parents are domiciled when the latter exercise their representation. Otherwise, as well as when said parents are domiciled in different States, incapable minors are considered domiciled in the place of their habitual residence.

Incapacitated persons subject to guardianship, conservatorship or other equivalent protection mechanism are considered domiciled in the place of their habitual residence."

[53] Private International Law Act of Venezuela of 1998, Article 13: "The domicile of minors and incapable persons subject to parental authority, guardianship or curatorship is in the territory of the State where they have their habitual residence."

[54] UNAL Draft, Article 34: "The law of the common domicile of the spouses, conjugal domicile, applies in all matters relating to the rights and duties resulting from the marriage and to the causes of separation of bodies and property. If they have different domiciles, the law of the last conjugal domicile applies."

[55] IADIP Draft, Article 13: "Domicile of the spouses. The domicile of the spouses shall be that in which they live together, without prejudice to the right of each spouse to fix his/her domicile in the manner provided for in Article 11."

move away from the anachronistic views of referring to the domicile of the married woman and subordinating it to that of the husband.

In the case of minors and the elderly who are subject to assistance in the exercise of their legal capacity, not "incapacitated," in the terms of Act No. 1996 of 2019, the IADIP Draft states that their domicile will be the place where they have their habitual residence,[56] and that guardianship and other protective institutions will be governed by their domicile,[57] which recognizes greater autonomy for these subjects of protection. The UNAL Draft, on the other hand, opts for the domicile of the legal representative,[58] in accordance with the current provisions of the Civil Code and the provisions of the Treaty of Montevideo of 1889, which would be more appropriate since it is the legal representative through whom rights and obligations are exercised. However, in view of the provisions of the Act No. 1996, a mixed solution could be proposed. Thus, for minors, the domicile would be that of their legal representative, but limited to the exercise of such powers, while for adults subject to assistance, their domicile should be determined by their habitual residence.

5 Conclusion

The internationalization of relations between people implies the existence of complex legal situations with international elements that must be resolved by private international law as a regulator of conflicts of laws. In this sense, the three criteria identified by the doctrine to determine the law applicable to personal status are nationality, domicile, and habitual residence, all of which have advantages and disadvantages. However, the criterion of domicile has been the most criticized because its definition tends to change according to the legal system and because of the difficulties of interpretation and proof of the intention of permanence, a subjective aspect that characterizes it.

Thus, the criteria of nationality and habitual residence stand out, where the strength of the former, as a guarantee of the multicultural application of the law, can be a weakness of the latter in the same sense. Article 19 of the Colombian Civil Code, with the difficulties of application and interpretation that its wording creates, adopts the criterion of nationality to determine the applicable law. The complexity increases when we find international instruments, such as the Montevideo Treaty on

[56] IADIP Draft, Article 12: "The domicile of incapable persons shall be in the place where they have their habitual residence, under the terms of Article 11."

[57] IADIP Draft, Article 56: "Guardianship and other institutions for the protection of incapable persons are governed by the law of the domicile of the incapable person."

[58] UNAL Draft, Article 23: "… The domicile of the child or adolescent is subject to the law of the domicile of the legal representatives and, failing that, to the law of the domicile of the persons under whose effective care the child or adolescent is placed."

UNAL Draft, Article 76: "Incapacitated persons have the domicile of their legal representative, but if they are under the care of another person, they shall have the domicile of the latter …"

Civil Law of 1889, ratified by Colombia, which applies the criterion of domicile. In any case, as has been seen, that single article of the Civil Code prevails to regulate all aspects of personal status in its individual component.

The advantages of habitual residence as a point of reference are mainly that it eliminates the subjective component of the concept of domicile and avoids inappropriate interpretations of foreign laws, which are often unknown, as well as reducing the possibilities of applying the public policy exception. As we have seen throughout this chapter, it is clear that the current trend is to choose this criterion to define the vast majority of aspects of the individual component of personal status, either directly or through the concept of domicile, which is usually defined in terms of habitual residence.

In this sense, the various proposals of the academy to reform the rules of private international law in the country are well-received. Although there are slight differences in some sections of the drafts discussed, generally, they choose the criterion of habitual residence as the predominant one in these matters. In any case, there is the greatest consensus on the need to reform the current provisions, either through the enactment of a single law on the subject or through a comprehensive reform of the Civil Code. The first option may be more appropriate in that it does not require such a broad academic and legislative discussion on various issues, which in turn could lead to greater cohesion and coherence in the rules of private international law.

References

Aljure Salame A (2011) El contrato internacional. Legis and Universidad del Rosario, Bogota

Boutin Icaza G (2006) Derecho internacional privado. Maitre Boutin, Panama

Caicedo Castilla JJ (1967) Derecho internacional privado, 1st edn. Temis, Bogota

Cordero Álvarez CI (2023) Delimitación de la residencia habitual como principal criterio de competencia en el derecho europeo de familia y normas de aplicación en defecto de Estado miembro competente ante la reciente doctrina del TJUE. Desde un posible foro de la nacionalidad del demandado encubierto a supuestos claudicantes. Cuadernos de Derecho Trasnacional 15(1):254–274

Esplugues Mota C, Iglesias JL, Palao G (2011) Application of foreign law. Sellier, Munich

García Matamoros LV (2016) Estatuto personal. Los aspectos relacionados con el estatuto individual. In: García Matamoros LV, Aljure Salame A (eds) Teoría general del derecho internacional privado. Legis and Universidad del Rosario, Bogota, pp 267–284

Herrera M (2013) Breve reseña de la estructura y regulación de derecho internacional privado en el Proyecto de unificación del Código Civil y Comercial. Revista del Notariado 912:225–247

Kegel G (1982) Derecho internacional privado, 4th edn. Ediciones Rosaristas, Bogota

Maekelt T, Esis Villarroel I, Resende E (2005) Ley de derecho internacional privado comentada. Universidad Central de Venezuela, Caracas

Mantilla Rey R (1996) Recapitulación de derecho internacional privado, 1st edn. Universidad Nacional de Colombia, Bogota

Medina Pabón JE (2017) Derecho civil. Aproximación al derecho. Derecho de personas, 5th edn. Universidad del Rosario, Bogota

Monroy Cabra MG (1999) Tratado de Derecho internacional privado, 5th edn. Temis, Bogota

Ochoa Jiménez MJ, Zapata Flórez J (2022) Private international law rules regarding personal status in Colombia: a system in need of an overhaul. Anuario Mexicano de Derecho Internacional XXII:556–561
Rodríguez Benot A (2010) El criterio de conexión para determinar la ley personal: un renovado debate en derecho internacional privado. Revista Cuadernos de Derecho Transnacional 2(1):186–202
Wolff M (2012) Derecho internacional privado. Ediciones Coyoacán, Mexico

Laura Victoria García Matamoros Tenured Professor and former Dean of Law School, Universidad del Rosario: Ph.D. in Law Suma Cum Laude, Universidad Externado de Colombia; Postgraduate Studies in Private International Law, University of Paris 2. *The author would like to thank Cristian Fernando Barrios Almario, lawyer from Universidad del Rosario and research assistant, for his valuable support in literature review and editing of this chapter

Marriage and Marital Unions in Colombian Private International Law

Laura Victoria García Matamoros

Abstract This chapter first examines the international legal relationships that give rise to the formation of a family. It then analyzes the legal regulation of these aspects within the Colombian legal system. Subsequently, the chapter briefly discusses the relevant provisions of two proposals: the Draft General Act on Private International Law for Colombia, prepared by the *Instituto Antioqueño de Derecho Internacional Privado* in 2021, and the Draft Civil Code of Colombia presented by the *Universidad Nacional de Colombia* in 2023.

1 Introduction

The individual dimension of the personal status is just one aspect of it. The other aspect refers to "the situations and rights … arising from family relations,"[1] that is, its collective dimension. The advent of globalization and digital connectivity has also transformed these relationships, leading to the emergence of what are known as multinational families, which are becoming increasingly common around the world. Consequently, the study of these new kinds of families from the perspective of private international law has become crucial for understanding the current dynamics that arise in a world marked by cultural diversity.

The concept of family relations encompasses both the formation of the household, signified by the union of a couple, and its subsequent expansion, marked by the conception of children. This chapter will address the initial aspect, namely the celebration, consequences, and dissolution of marriage, as well as *de facto* marital unions.

[1] Mantilla Rey (1996), p. 96.

L. V. García Matamoros (✉)
Facultad de Jurisprudencia, Universidad del Rosario, Bogotá, Colombia
e-mail: laura.garcia@urosario.edu.co

M. J. Ochoa Jiménez, C. Madrid Martínez (eds.), *A Private International Law for Colombia*, Springer Textbooks in Law,
https://doi.org/10.1007/978-3-032-04106-7_14

This chapter first examines the international legal relationships that give rise to the formation of a family, before analyzing the legal regulation of these aspects within the Colombian legal system. Subsequently, two pertinent proposals are briefly discussed: the Draft General Act on Private International Law for Colombia prepared by the *Instituto Antioqueño de Derecho Internacional Privado* in 2021 (IADIP Draft), and the Draft Civil Code of Colombia prepared by the *Universidad Nacional de Colombia* in 2023 (UNAL Draft).[2]

2 The Family from an International Perspective

The emergence of multicultural families makes it necessary for private international law to address the conflicts of law that may arise in this area. This is so because states consider family matters to be of fundamental interest, making their regulation imperative. In this sense, this cultural interrelationship implies the convergence of different legal systems, which can either complement or exclude each other.

Differences can be found in the concept of the family itself. On the one hand, there is the concept of the married family, created by a legal act and based on monogamy, which prevails in Western society in general, including Colombia. On the other hand, some countries allow polygamy, where men who marry more than one woman. Similar divergences can be found regarding homoparental families, although it is true that more and more states are accepting them, such as Colombia, thanks to the rulings of its courts,[3] many countries still reject this family constitution.[4] While the disparities are more pronounced when there are different ways of understanding family relations, which some raise as a conflict of civilizations,[5] even in more similar legal systems, such as the European Union, "the discrepancies between states are great and reach the constitutional level."[6] As a result, the different views and regulations are the subject of discussion and need to be addressed from the perspective of private law.

Doctrine has identified three approaches to this phenomenon of the multicultural family: ethnocentrism, cultural relativism, and multicultural universalism.[7] The ini-

[2] When this draft is mentioned, reference is made to the second version, which has no major substantive changes from the first version but does change the numbering of articles.

[3] In accordance with Judgment No. C-577 of 2011 of the Constitutional Court, same-sex couples have been permitted to formalize their marital bond before a notary or judge of the Republic since June 20, 2013. In that decision, the Court recommended that Congress regulate the matter, but this recommendation was not acted upon. Consequently, the Court assumed the relevant powers in Judgment No. SU-214 of 2016, which definitively endorsed same-sex marriage and granted it equal legal recognition to that afforded to heterosexual couples.

[4] See CNN Español (2024).

[5] See Carrascosa González (2003), pp. 109–143.

[6] Arenas García (2020), p. 30.

[7] Carrascosa González (2003), pp. 109–143.

tial theory wholly prioritizes the authority of domestic legislation, effectively disallowing the implementation of foreign law, which can potentially give rise to discriminatory practices such as racism and xenophobia. In contrast, cultural relativism asserts that all cultures are equal and, consequently, that the legal system must recognize foreign law without distinction. This is also problematic when the foreign norm contravenes domestic imperative rights. Ultimately, multicultural universalism represents a moderate approach that acknowledges the primacy of domestic values and rights while facilitating the application of foreign laws, provided they do not contravene fundamental principles. This perspective is perceived to be reflected in Colombia's legal framework, which permits the recognition of foreign law through conflict rules and the invocation of the public order exception when foreign legislation is deemed to violate the fundamental principles of the state. Alternatively, in instances where direct and immediate police regulations are applicable, they may be invoked.[8]

On this final point, the Colombian legal system posits that "the fundamental nature and universal vocation of human rights necessitate their direct and immediate application to family relations, irrespective of their domestic or international character."[9] Consequently, the domestic legal system or the public order exception will be invoked when foreign norms contravene human rights and constitutional principles, including those of equality and freedom.

In the case of *de facto* families, several countries have had legal regulations in this field for some time now.[10] In Colombia, these unions have been subject to legal regulation since 1990,[11] conferring upon them the same legal effects as those associated with marriage. In Judgment C-075 of 2007, the Constitutional Court extended the aforementioned regulation to unions between same-sex couples. Subsequently, in Judgment C-456 of 2020, the Court indicated that the conferral of rights and prerogatives upon same-sex couples under the *de facto* marital union figure also entails the acceptance of the corresponding obligations and responsibilities.

This overview of international family law highlights significant challenges for private international law, arising from the varied perspectives inherent in domestic legal systems. In light of this context, the following analysis will focus on the current regulatory framework and proposed reforms regarding the subject in Colombia.

---

[8] Such considerations include the protection of overarching interests, including those pertaining to health, social interaction, and safety.

[9] Bouza Vidal (2007), p. 19.

[10] See Arenas García (2020), p. 30; Lema Tomé (2003), pp. 149–170.

[11] Act No. 54 of 1990.

3 The Colombian Conflicts of Law Rules on Marriage: Regulation and Prospects

Marriage is defined as "the legal institution that promotes and regulates the family organization derived from the union between a man and a woman for sexual satisfaction, mutual support, procreation, and child-rearing."[12] Despite its status as a personal statute, marriage is a legal act *intuitu personae*, a fact acknowledged by the Civil Code in Article 113, where it is referred to as "a solemn contract."

This legal act is examined from three perspectives: its celebration, the effects it produces, and its dissolution. Consequently, the regulation from the perspective of private international law must also respond to these three factors, as will be described below.

3.1 Celebration of Marriage

With the celebration, the marriage is born into legal life and produces the effects established by the law. In this section, the substantive requirements need to be distinguished from those of a formal nature.

Substantive requirements. The substantive requirements concern "those matters that are essential to the marriage and that consequently bind the person wherever they may be."[13] These are classified into two categories: positive and negative. The former pertains to the capacity of the contracting parties, as well as the expression of their will. This includes minimum age and the necessity for representation. The latter encompasses rules on undissolved ties and restrictions due to kinship.[14]

Article 19 of the Civil Code establishes the law of nationality as the applicable law in matters about the capacity and marital status of individuals,[15] encompassing the essential elements of marriage. It is noteworthy that both drafts dedicate provisions exclusively to clearly and directly stating the conflict rules that govern these matters. The UNAL Draft establishes that the applicable law is that of the place where the act is celebrated,[16] while the IADIP Draft proposes that it be that of the

[12] Medina Pabón (2018), p. 66.

[13] Adroher Biosca (1993), p. 71.

[14] Torrado (2020), pp. 53–71.

[15] For a more comprehensive examination of the rule in question, see the preceding chapter.

[16] Article 33 UNAL Draft: "The capacity of persons to contract marriage, the form of the act, its existence and validity are governed by the law of the place where it is celebrated …".

domicile of each party,[17] a concept that it defines as habitual residence.[18] Additionally, given that the residence of each spouse usually coincides when a couple marries, only one law will be applicable.

A comparative analysis reveals that Article 19 of the Civil Code aligns with Article 9 of the Treaty of Private International Law between Ecuador and Colombia of 1903,[19] whereas the UNAL Draft encompasses the stipulations outlined in Article 11 of the Treaty of International Law of Montevideo of 1889.[20] In contrast, the IADIP Draft incorporates the stipulations of Article 21 of the Venezuelan Private International Law Act.[21] In both instances, domicile is defined as habitual residence, which, as previously stated,[22] serves as a point of connection to address the conventional issues of domicile and nationality. It is important to note that, despite the absence of an invariable connection in the Venezuelan legal framework, doctrine has interpreted that it refers to the "domicile of each individual at the time of marriage."[23] This interpretation aligns with that of the IADIP Draft, which aims to prevent potential conflicts by establishing a consistent understanding of the law. This would be the same interpretation for the provision of the IADIP Draft, to prevent the emergence of mobile conflicts.

The requirements for the celebration of a marriage are, in turn, manifested in impediments to the application of foreign law. It is important to note that these impediments can be classified into two distinct categories. The first category comprises those of an intrinsic or unilateral nature, which primarily pertain to the following conditions: "age, capacity, and consent."[24] In other words, the former category comprises "those impediments that must be analyzed individually, separately concerning the subject."[25] The latter category, in contrast, encompasses the negative or bilateral impediments that refer to the conditions affecting the very constitution of the bond. These must be analyzed cumulatively, such as "those related to kinship of any type, the existence of a prior undissolved bond, and having committed the crime of homicide to obtain the status of widowhood."[26] However, this

[17] Article 45 IADIP Draft: "The law of the place of domicile of each of the contracting parties governs the capacity to contract marriage and the other substantive requirements for its celebration."

[18] Article 12 IADIP Draft: "The domicile of a natural person is in the territory of the State in which he habitually resides with the intention of exercising his rights there."

[19] Which establishes: "Legal capacity to contract marriage shall be judged by the national law of the parties."

[20] This provision states: "The capacity of persons to contract marriage, the form of the act and the existence and validity of the same, are governed by the law of the place where it is celebrated …"

[21] It establishes: "The capacity to contract marriage and the substantive requirements of marriage are governed, for each of the contracting parties, by the law of their respective domicile."

[22] See chapter Natural Persons in Colombian Private International Law.

[23] Barrios (2014), p. 248.

[24] Mantilla Rey (1996), p. 105.

[25] García Matamoros (2016), p. 291.

[26] Ibid.

distinction is not always clear, and many situations are difficult to fit into one of these two classifications, which makes the application of private international law complex.

In this context, a debate emerges when the applicable law to each contracting party in a marriage differs and encompasses a cause for impediment concerning the other. In the case of the current regulation, which contemplates nationality as the applicable rule, it is feasible, for example, that the couple has different nationalities and that the capacity to enter into marriage varies in each regulation. This could result in a person being capable according to his national law, but not according to the law of nationality of the other party. In the event of an intrinsic or unilateral impediment, the marriage will be considered fully valid, as each contracting party is subject to the laws of their respective nation. In contrast, the same does not occur in the case of negative or bilateral impediments since these conditions must concur and be applied cumulatively so that they must be valid in both legislations.

Regarding this matter of impediments, on the assumption that applicable law is the law of the domicile of each contracting party, understood as their habitual residence, as proposed by the IADIP Draft, difficulties of interpretation would be fewer when analyzing intrinsic or unilateral impediments, since, in general, the spouses share the same domicile, despite the existence of exceptions. Concerning the UNAL Draft, the aforementioned difficulties would be rendered moot, as the law of the place of celebration would remain constant for both contracting parties. This would wholly eliminate the possibility of applying two disparate legal systems to the substantive requirements. Furthermore, it would preclude the potential for modifications to arise from a resubmission or international public policy,[27] thereby considerably simplifying the procedure. Such a solution would significantly streamline the judicial authority's workload.

The UNAL Draft also establishes in Article 33 that "marriages celebrated in another State which are contrary to the norms of national public order shall not be recognized." The IADIP Draft, for its part, does not establish the exception specifically in the section on marriage, but rather provides for it in a general manner in Article 6, establishing the non-application of the foreign law when it is "incompatible with the fundamental principles of Colombian public order." In any case, although this concept refers to the "set of fundamental principles that embody the essence of the State,"[28] it would be more accurate to speak of the public order of private international law.[29] Similar observations have been made to the UNAL Draft, adding that this concept should not be confused with mandatory rules.[30]

About this conceptual precision, the Supreme Court of Justice, in the context of exequatur proceedings where the public policy exception applies, has stated that

[27] Barrios (2014), p. 251.

[28] Gutiérrez Castillo (2016), p. 127.

[29] Ibid., p. 126.

[30] See Universidad Externado de Colombia (2020).

"the concept to be adopted is that of 'international public order',"[31] and has explained that "not every divergence between foreign and national rules can serve as an excuse to prevent the exequatur of foreign judgments, but only those which are of a superlative gravity, because they violate the fundamental principles and values of the legal system or order."[32] In other rulings, it has added that to accept the contrary "would be to accept the public order exception as 'a simple pretext to facilitate the triumph of whimsical nationalisms', which would lead to the absurdity of allowing persons residing in Colombia to assume obligations abroad, knowing that they can violate them with impunity as long as they place themselves under the protection of their country's borders."[33]

In any case, although the proposals to legally enshrine this exception are valid, this does not mean that it is not currently applicable,[34] since marriage is an essential institution of the state and the judge cannot accept intolerable substantive conditions, such as the prohibition of marriage for ethnic reasons.[35] In this respect, European countries have been forced to face the reality of polygamous marriages in the face of migratory phenomena of individuals and families from countries where this type of marriage is permitted, but contrary to the principle of the monogamous family that prevails on the old continent. In this case, although the European authorities refuse to celebrate polygamous marriages, they have considered it necessary to recognize the attenuated effect of public order. This means that, under certain circumstances, such marriages should have legal effects so that, for example, the second wife, legally married according to the law of her country of origin, is not left unprotected.[36] This is a peculiarity of the European doctrine, since polygamous marriages "not only do not conform to the rules of the [European] legal system, but contradict essential principles of that system, and may nevertheless have effects in that system."[37]

Formal requirements. These are the formalities prior to and subsequent to the celebration of the marriage that guarantee its publicity, such as appearing before the competent authority and complying with the rules applicable to the ceremony itself, which regulate issues related to the place, time, presence of the parties and witnesses, among others.[38] In Colombia, these formalities vary depending on whether it is a catholic or civil marriage, the latter of which can be celebrated before a judge

[31] Supreme Court of Colombia, Civil Section. Judgment No. SC17371 of December 18, 2014, p. 7.

[32] Supreme Court of Colombia, Civil Section. Judgment No. SC879 of April 27, 2022, p. 20.

[33] Supreme Court of Colombia, Civil Section. Decision of July 27, 2011, rad. 2007-01956-00, p. 46.

[34] For example, Article 606 of the General Procedural Code establishes as a requirement for the recognition of a foreign judgment that "it does not oppose Colombian laws or other provisions of public order, except those of procedure." In addition, the Supreme Court of Justice constantly rejects exequatur requests for violations of fundamental principles of the country.

[35] See Mantilla Rey (1996), p. 110.

[36] See Loussouarn and Bourel (1996), pp. 295–301.

[37] See Arenas García (2020), p. 10.

[38] Adroher Biosca (1993), p. 13.

in accordance with the provisions of the General Code of Procedure, or before a notary in accordance with the provisions of Decree 2668 of 1988.

Currently, the Colombian legal system does not have a specific conflict rule on this matter, but, like most states, it establishes a series of clear, explicit, and mandatory requirements to which the celebration of marriage as a legal act must be subject. From the perspective of private international law, it is widely recognized and adopted by jurisdictions and treaties that these requirements must be fulfilled according to the principle of *locus regit actum*,[39] i.e., the application of the law of the place where the act takes place. This is provided for, for example, in Article 11 of the Civil Law Treaty of Montevideo of 1889.[40]

Referring to the form of the act, Article 115 of the Civil Code stipulates:

> The marriage contract is constituted and perfected by the free and mutual consent of the contracting parties, expressed before the competent official, in the form and with the solemnities and requirements established in this Code, and shall not produce civil and political effects if, in its celebration, these forms, solemnities, and requirements are violated.

Although this provision is not a conflict law rule in the strict sense, it establishes that the marriage must meet the specific requirements of the Code to be effective. On marriages validly contracted in another country, there is some doubt as to their validity in Colombian territory. In this regard, paragraph 2 of Article 20 of the Civil Code, although confusing, is relevant when it states that "this provision shall be understood without prejudice to the provisions contained in contracts validly celebrated abroad"; since marriage is a legal act, it can be concluded that the law of the place of celebration also regulates the formal aspects of marriages celebrated abroad. In conclusion, "all marriages celebrated in Colombia must have the formalities required by Colombian law, and marriages celebrated abroad must be subject to the law of the State in whose territory they are celebrated."[41]

On the proposals currently under consideration, both drafts acknowledge the principle of *locus regit actum* in their respective sections on legal acts. Consequently, the validity of the marriage is contingent upon the law of the place where the marriage is celebrated.[42] However, the IADIP Draft proposes a novel approach in this regard. It suggests that acts that meet the requirements of the place "governing the content of the act" or "the domicile of the grantor or the common domicile of the grantors" should also be considered valid. This is an attempt to align the legal framework with the realities of business transactions. However, it raises questions

[39] Ibid., p. 78.

[40] See supra note 20.

[41] Mantilla Rey (1996), p. 100.

[42] Article 29, UNAL Draft: "The conditions of existence and validity of legal transactions are governed by the applicable law of the place where they are perfected. The same law applies to the existence and proof of other legal acts unless otherwise provided by mandatory provisions."

Article 69, IADIP Draft: "Legal acts shall be valid as to their form, if they comply with the requirements established in any of the following legal systems: 1. that of the place of celebration of the act; 2. that which governs the content of the act; or 3. that of the domicile of its grantor or of the common domicile of its grantors."

regarding its implications for public institutions like marriage, which are subject to imperative norms, since the proposal allows for the selection of applicable law governing the form of a transaction, potentially circumventing mandatory rules.

Furthermore, the UNAL Draft proposes in Article 1667 the recognition of marriages celebrated abroad, provided that they are conducted before the relevant authorities and following the legal requirements of the country in question. For the marriage to be considered valid, it must be registered in the relevant registry. Similarly, the IADIP Draft, in Article 9, also establishes, but in a general sense, that a legal relationship validly constituted in a foreign state under the law of that state will be recognized in Colombia. In conclusion, it can be stated that the position is pacific concerning the fact that the form of the act must be governed by the law of the place of its celebration, except the IADIP Draft, which introduces a novel approach.

It is noteworthy that the rule of *locus regit actum* is not absolute, as evidenced by exceptions such as consular marriages. This marriage refers to that celebrated before a consular agent following its laws and not those of the country where the parties are physically located; its basis is found in Article 5, paragraph f, of the Vienna Convention on Consular Relations of 1982, which establishes as a consular function "to act as notary, civil registrar, and in similar functions and to exercise other functions of an administrative nature, provided they are not contrary to the laws and regulations of the receiving State." Each country establishes the conditions under which the celebration of this type of marriage is admitted, some jurisdictions limit it by the nationality of the parties and/or the compliance with the law of the country of the consulate.[43]

In Colombia, Article 1 of Act No. 266 of 1938 recognizes the validity of consular marriages, subject to the following conditions:

a) That the national law of the contracting parties authorizes this type of marriage;
b) That neither of the contracting parties is Colombian;
c) That the marriage celebrated does not contravene the provisions of the 7th, 8th, 9th, and 12th ordinals of Article 140 of the Civil Code and that of the 2nd ordinal of Article 13 of Law 57 of 1887; and
d) That the marriage is registered in the Registry of Civil Status within five days from the date of the celebration.

Conversely, the Colombian legal system does not explicitly confer jurisdiction upon its diplomatic missions abroad to officiate marriages of Colombian nationals. Therefore, if two Colombians residing abroad wish to marry, they shall be governed by the law of the place of celebration. This follows the guidance provided by the foreign affairs authority, which states, "If your intention is to marry abroad, you must verify with the entities of that country the corresponding requirements and procedures so that you can celebrate your marriage."[44] In this regard, the UNAL

[43] See Aguilar Benítez (2003).

[44] See Cancillería de Colombia (2024).

Draft is accurate in its assertion that diplomatic or consular agents should be granted the authority to officiate marriages of Colombians abroad.[45]

3.2 *Effects of Marriage*

Once a marriage is celebrated as a juridical act *intuitu personae*, the effects established by law are produced. These effects include a series of rights and obligations between the contracting parties, which can be either personal or patrimonial. Among the former, the primary effect is the establishment of the civil status of marriage. Additionally, there are the "main obligations derived from marriage which are more technically referred to as legal duties as fidelity, support and assistance, as well as cohabitation."[46] In the patrimonial aspects, there is the regulation regarding the matrimonial regime. Both effects, personal and patrimonial, also require recourse to the rules of private international law to solve the conflicts of laws that may arise.

The patrimonial effects. The patrimonial effects of marriage are contingent upon the existence and scope of the conjugal partnership between the spouses. If a marital relationship encompasses international elements, such as the presence of different nationalities, a change of the matrimonial domicile, or the acquisition of assets in disparate states, it becomes imperative to ascertain the applicable law that will regulate the rights and obligations of the spouses with respect to these matters.

Under Article 180 of the Civil Code, a conflict of law rule is established with respect to the matter in question, as follows:

> Article 180. The institution of marriage entails the creation of a conjugal partnership between the spouses, which is governed by the provisions set forth in Title 22, Book IV, of the Civil Code.
>
> Those who have married in a foreign country and are domiciled in Colombia, shall be presumed to have separate property, unless in accordance with the laws under whose rule they were married they are subject to a different property regime.

It is therefore established that couples who marry in a foreign country and then domicile in Colombia will be presumed to be separated from each other. This presumption of legal character is rebuttable, so it admits proof to the contrary that establishes that, under the law of the place of celebration, there is a different regime.

In addition to this, Article 1774 of the Civil Code stipulates that, in the absence of a written agreement, it shall be presumed that, by the mere fact of marriage, a conjugal partnership is contracted whose applicable law shall be "the provisions of this title." Accordingly, the prevailing conflict of law rule pertaining to the property implications of marriage stipulates that the governing law shall be that of the place

[45] Article 1668, UNAL Draft: "Colombians abroad may also celebrate marriages in accordance with the rules of this Code before Colombian diplomatic or consular agents."

[46] Medina Pabón (2018), p. 132.

of celebration. If the marriage is solemnized abroad, the presumption of separation of property shall apply.

In the case of marriages celebrated abroad, however, the condition of foreign nationality is also imposed, although this is not explicitly stated in the rule. This is the result of the Constitutional Court's interpretation of the constitutionality of Article 180, as examined in Judgment C-395 of 2002. The provision was alleged to violate the principle of equality by subjecting Colombians who marry abroad to different treatment than those who marry in Colombia. Specifically, it established a presumption of separation of property for those who marry abroad, which does not apply to those who marry in Colombia.

In that instance, the Court determined the constitutionality of the legislation in question, on the understanding that, given the fact that family relations are an integral aspect of civil status, the stipulations set forth in Articles 19 and 1774 of the Civil Code, i.e., the law of nationality, should apply to them. Consequently, the presumption of separation of property set forth in paragraph 2 of Article 180 would only be pertinent to marriages between foreigners. The Court thus affirmed that, "in the case of marriages between Colombian nationals or between a Colombian national and a foreigner, the Colombian civil law must be applied as a general rule, specifically the rules on conjugal partnership."[47]

The clarification of the vote by Judge Marco Gerardo Monroy Cabra[48] challenged this determination by asserting that "the property regime in marriage does not relate to the civil status and capacity of individuals."[49] In other words, the nationality law should not apply to these property matters, and the rule of *locus regit actum*, as stipulated in Article 180 of the Civil Code, should be applied. Consequently, the presumption of separation of property should apply universally, irrespective of whether one or both spouses are Colombian.

In any case, the Supreme Court of Justice has supported and approved the interpretation of the Constitutional Court, so it seems to be a settled issue. Recently, the Supreme ruled that "Colombians abroad, resident or domiciled, are not subject to foreign legislation in matters of civil status. Colombian law follows them wherever they are."[50] Position that reaffirms the determination established in Judgment SC7726-2014, which provided that:

> Although in other times there have been several discussions about the correct hermeneutics of the 2nd subsection of Article 180 idem, currently the debate has been overcome by considering this Corporation that: the harmonious and teleological interpretation of this provision allows to conclude that it covers only those marriages celebrated abroad in which foreigners participate.

---

[47] Constitutional Court of Colombia. Judgment No. C-395 of May 22, 2002.

[48] Which we have always regarded as the most accurate interpretation. See García Matamoros (2016), p. 296.

[49] Ibid.

[50] Supreme Court of Colombia, Civil Section. Judgment No. SC2502 of June 23, 2021, pp. 15–16.

On this point, the UNAL Draft establishes in its Article 36 that "the marriage of Colombians and foreigners celebrated in another country and who have their domicile or residence in Colombia shall be governed by the property regime established by this Code." In this way, it adopts a solution similar to the current Article 180 of the Civil Code, but it improves its clarity to indicate that the property aspects of the marriage celebrated abroad will be governed by Colombian law if one or both of the spouses are Colombian—jurisprudential position—but expressly adds as a condition that they have their domicile or residence in Colombia, so that if they do not, the law of the place of celebration would be applicable. In any case, since the UNAL Draft considers the principle of *locus regit actum* for the other aspects of marriage—capacity, form, existence, and validity[51]—it would be more consistent that this principle be unconditionally applicable also to the property regime to consolidate a unity of law applicable to all aspects of marriage.

Meanwhile, the IADIP Draft proposes that the spouses should choose the law applicable to both the patrimonial and the personal aspects, as follows:

> Article 47: Personal and property effects of marriage. The personal and property effects of marriage shall be governed by the law chosen by the spouses, who may choose between:
>
> 1. the law of the State in which the spouses or future spouses, or one of them, is domiciled; or
> 2. the law of the State of the nationality of one of the spouses or future spouses.
>
> The law applicable to the effects of the marriage under this Article shall apply to all property included in the property regime of the marriage, irrespective of the State in which it is situated.

This last paragraph legally proposes a sort of the theory *mobilia sequuntur personam,* which means "movable property follows the person," which is advantageous, for example, in inheritance matters, but in this case includes all types of property and seeks to unify the applicable law. In general terms, the proposal of this provision seeks to exclude the law of the place of celebration in favor of another chosen by the parties, which is an emerging trend in recent European legislation in this area,[52] and which generates much debate because "the regulation of the family has traditionally been a field of public order in which the social interest prevails over the individual, and therefore private autonomy should be limited to a minimum."[53] It is acknowledged that this option would serve to clarify the applicable law in these matters, which have been the subject of much controversy. However, even though we do not believe that in Colombia this patrimonial aspect should be considered of international public order to privilege national law, as mentioned above, we cannot lose sight of the fact that the institution of the family is of fundamental interest to the state and that this option "allows the 'deselection' of imperative norms of a

[51] See supra note 16.

[52] See González Beilfuss (2020).

[53] Lepin Molina (2022), p. 1238.

protective nature that seek to guarantee that this caregiving duties can be carried out."[54]

In any case, in the absence of a choice of applicable law, the IADIP Draft then establishes that it will be that of the common domicile or, if none, that of the last domicile they had.[55] This is the preferred solution in Latin America, since Article 41 of the Treaty of Montevideo of 1889 on International Civil Law,[56] Article 14 of the Treaty of Civil Law between Ecuador and Colombia,[57] and Article 22 of the Act of Private International Law of Venezuela[58] point in a similar direction.

Personal effects. These encompass all the rights and obligations that arise between spouses. These include the relationships of kinship and affinity with the other spouse's relatives by blood, as well as the legal duties of "fidelity, support and assistance, as well as cohabitation."[59]

Colombia does not have a specific conflict-of-law rule for the personal consequences of marriage; therefore, the conflict-of-law rule of Article 19 of the Civil Code applies, which means that the applicable law would be that of the parties' nationality. However, a broad interpretation of Articles 177 and 179 of the Civil Code[60] has led doctrine to suggest that in these matrimonial disputes, given the nature of the relationships involved, the conflict rule of Article 19 is applicable only if both spouses have the same nationality. Otherwise, the application of the law of the matrimonial domicile is preferred and, in the case of separation, Mantilla Rey advises considering the last common domicile, without the procedural requirement that one of the two maintain it, since this reflects a joint decision at a time when the marital relationship was consensual and accepted.[61]

In fact, this doctrinal position reflects an established tendency in international matters to recognize the matrimonial domicile as the point of reference for determining the applicable law. In this sense, Article 12 of the Treaty of Montevideo of

[54] Ibid., p. 112.

[55] Article 48, IADIP Draft: "In the absence of a choice of applicable law by the spouses, the effects of the marriage are governed by the law of the State of the common domicile; or, failing this, by the law of the State of their last common domicile.".

[56] The article provides: "In the absence of special capitulations, in all matters not provided for therein and in all matters not prohibited by the law of the place where the property is located, the relations of the spouses with respect to such property shall be governed by the law of the marital domicile that they have fixed by mutual agreement before the celebration of the marriage."

[57] It establishes: "In the absence of a marriage contract, the law of the matrimonial domicile governs the personal property of the spouses, regardless of the place where it is located or where it was acquired."

[58] The provision states: (ESP) "The personal and property effects of marriage are governed by the law of the common domicile of the spouses. If they have different domiciles, the law of the last common domicile shall apply ..."

[59] See supra note 47.

[60] Article 177 establishes the joint address of the home, and Article 179 allows the spouses, by mutual agreement, to determine the residence of the home and, in case of disagreement, gives such power to the judge.

[61] Mantilla Rey (1996), p. 115.

1889 on International Civil Law establishes that the personal rights and obligations arising from the marriage between the spouses are governed by the law of the matrimonial domicile and, in the event of a change, by the law of the new domicile; this provision is also included in the Treaty on International Private Law between Colombia and Ecuador.[62] Similarly, Article 22 of the Venezuelan Private International Law Act provides that the personal effects of the marriage shall be governed by the law of the common domicile of the spouses and, if different, by the law of the last common domicile.

This trend is taken up by the proposals under discussion. Article 34 of the UNAL Draft provides for the application of "the law of the common domicile of the spouses, the matrimonial domicile, in all matters relating to the rights and obligations arising out of the marriage" and, if different, the law of the last matrimonial domicile. However, strangely, it subjects the duties of cohabitation, fidelity, and support to the law of the country of residence. Although in most cases this applicable law would be the same, this is not always true, and it is therefore inconsistent to have two different points of reference for the same matter, again leaving aside the unity of law. On the other hand, the IADIP Draft introduces the abovementioned possibility of relying on the will of the parties and, in the event of their silence, takes up the previously mentioned trend.

Therefore, it is evident that the law of the matrimonial domicile should be applied to the personal effects of marriage, so it would be preferable for the drafts to point more directly to it, without the nuances commented upon, to update and generate clarity in Colombian legislation in this regard. This would leave aside the use of nationality as a point of contact or the resort to doctrinal interpretations when the spouses have different nationalities.

Furthermore, concerning the "provision of material elements necessary for a dignified life,"[63] specifically, maintenance—which is a contentious issue and falls under the duty of support between spouses—the Inter-American Convention on Support Obligations, to which Colombia is a party, stipulates in its conflict of laws rule the principle of favorability for the maintenance creditor. This principle mandates that the law most advantageous to the creditor should be applied, whether it is the law of the creditor's domicile or habitual residence, or that of the debtor.[64]

[62] Article 12 Treaty on International Private Law between Colombia and Ecuador: "The personal rights and duties that marriage produces between the spouses, and between them and their children, shall be governed by the law of the matrimonial domicile; but if this changes, they shall be governed by the laws of the new domicile."

[63] Medina Pabón (2018), p. 135.

[64] Article 6, Inter-American Convention on Support Obligations: "Maintenance obligations, as well as the status of maintenance creditor and maintenance debtor, shall be governed by whichever of the following legal systems is, in the opinion of the competent authority, more favorable to the interest of the creditor: a. The legal system of the State of the creditor's domicile or habitual residence; b. The legal system of the State of the creditor's domicile or habitual residence. a. the legal system of the State of the creditor's domicile or habitual residence; b. the legal system of the State of the creditor's domicile or habitual residence. The legal system of the State of the debtor's domi-

3.3 Dissolution of the Marriage

The dissolution of marriage encompasses what has been termed as "matrimonial crisis,"[65] which includes divorce, separation of bodies, and annulment. Divorce "affects the conjugal bond that exists between persons who have contracted a valid marriage, and proceeds according to predetermined grounds,"[66] whereas the separation of bodies, as outlined in Article 167 of the Civil Code, "does not dissolve the marriage, but suspends the life in common of the married parties." In contrast, nullity signifies "a primitive sanction of an exceptional nature, whose effect is, in principle, to render the marriage null and void from the perspective of the law, as if it had never been celebrated."[67] This also occurs in accordance with the specified grounds for nullity.

The dissolution phenomena raise the prior question[68] of the existence and validity of a marriage bond. Consequently, the conflict of law rules that govern the former are not necessarily the same as those that apply to the latter.[69]

The Civil Code contains in Articles 163 and 164, as amended by Articles 13 and 14 of Act 1 of 1976, the two unique rules governing the dissolution of marriages within the Colombian legal system. The first provision pertains to the divorce of a civil marriage that was solemnized abroad, whereas the second provision applies to divorces that were decreed abroad with respect to civil marriages that were solemnized in Colombia. In both cases, the law of the matrimonial domicile is the applicable law:

> Article 163. In the event of a civil marriage celebrated abroad, the divorce shall be governed by the law of the matrimonial domicile.
>
> For the purposes of this article, the term "matrimonial domicile" shall be understood to mean the place where the spouses live together. In the absence of such a domicile, the domicile of the defendant spouse shall be considered as such.
>
> Article 164. The divorce pronounced abroad, in relation to the civil marriage celebrated in Colombia, will be governed by the law of the matrimonial domicile and will not produce the effects of dissolution, provided that the cause is recognized by Colombian law and that the defendant has been personally notified or summoned in accordance with the law of his domicile. However, if the requirements of notice and summons are met, it may produce the effects of dissolution.

---

cile or habitual residence; b. The legal system of the State of the debtor's domicile or habitual residence."

[65] Jiménez Sánchez (2001), p. 241.

[66] Barrios (2014), p. 282.

[67] López Herrera (1970), p. 311.

[68] See Maekelt et al. (2005), pp. 247–288.

[69] See, for example, Article 8 of the Inter-American Convention on General Standards of Private International Law: "Preliminary, preliminary or incidental questions that may arise in connection with a main question need not necessarily be resolved in accordance with the law governing the latter."

It is observed that Article 163 defines the matrimonial domicile as the place where the spouses live together and, in the absence thereof, that of the defendant spouse. Furthermore, Article 164 stipulates that the effects of dissolution will not be produced unless the respective cause is admitted in the Colombian legal system and the defendant has been notified personally or summoned according to the law of their domicile. Furthermore, the aforementioned provision establishes that if only the latter requirement is met, the divorce may have the effects of a separation of bodies. Similarly, Article 13 of the 1889 Montevideo Treaty on International Civil Law establishes that the matrimonial domicile is applicable in these matters, provided that "the cause alleged is admitted by the law of the place where it was celebrated."

The proposals put forth by the IADIP Draft and the UNAL Draft stipulate that, in the majority of cases, the law of the matrimonial domicile shall be applicable in matters pertaining to the dissolution of marriage. In instances where the spouses have resided in different domiciles, the law of the last common domicile shall prevail.

The UNAL Draft establishes in Article 34 the aforementioned rule for the separation of bodies and property and in Article 35 the same for nullity and divorce. The same rule is retained in Article 1703 for the dissolution of a foreign marriage, but in such a case, it adds the procedural requirement that the defendant must maintain the last domicile of the couple or, if this is not possible, the applicable law will be that of the domicile of the defendant.[70] This rule is consistent with that set forth in Article 163 of the current Civil Code. Similarly, Article 1704 of the draft permits a spouse who resides or is domiciled in Colombia and who has entered into a marriage abroad to petition for a divorce in accordance with Colombian law, provided that the defendant is duly notified or summoned. This is intended to ensure the requisite procedural safeguards are in place.

As for the divorce of a Colombian marriage pronounced abroad, the UNAL Draft also sets the matrimonial domicile as the point of contact, taking up the initial part of Article 164 of the Civil Code, but leaving as the only requirement that the recognition procedure be fully complied with,[71] excluding the admission of the ground and the notification and summons, as well as the effects of separation of bodies when only the latter condition is complied with.

---

[70] Article 1703, UNAL Draft: "The divorce of a marriage with civil effects celebrated abroad will be governed by the law of the conjugal domicile, which is the previous common domicile, as long as the defendant keeps it and, in its absence, the law of the latter. The spouses whose marriage and divorce took place abroad, where they were domiciled, may prove in Colombia, where they have subsequently domiciled, their civil status as divorced, without requiring exequatur. Likewise, the spouse who subsequently to the divorce abroad resides or domiciles in Colombia, it will be sufficient to prove his/her marital status with the birth certificate and the certification of his/her single status or its equivalent."

[71] Article 1705, UNAL Draft: "Judicial divorce decreed abroad, with respect to a civil marriage celebrated in Colombia, shall be governed by the law of the marital domicile and shall not produce effects of dissolution unless it complies with the recognition procedure, according to the treaties in force or the procedural rules in force."

It is worth mentioning that the UNAL Draft aims to streamline the recognition of divorce decreed abroad, without always having to submit it to the exequatur process. In this sense, Article 1706 establishes that the Colombian marriage with divorce decreed abroad by mutual agreement, either by judicial, notarial, or other authority, may take effect in Colombia simply with its notarization in an authentic copy and its corresponding registration. It also eliminates the requirement of exequatur with respect to the divorce of a marriage celebrated abroad when both spouses or only one of them is subsequently domiciled in Colombia with a certificate indicating such marital status.[72]

In turn, the IADIP Draft also establishes the matrimonial domicile as the point of contact or, in its absence, that of the last common domicile.[73] However, Article 51 proposes a different rule for the nullity of the marriage, which shall be governed by "the law that regulates the cause of such nullity."

In any case, in matters pertaining to divorce, separation of bodies, and annulment, the exequatur process—that is, the recognition and approval of foreign judicial decisions—becomes crucial, as it is the judicial authorities who typically decree these dissolution figures. In this regard, the stipulations set forth for this process must be met, including the requirement of non-contradiction of public order, which, as previously stated, represents an exception that permits the non-application of foreign law. This requirement is explicitly stated in Article 606 of the General Procedural Code and in Article 2 of the Inter-American Convention on the Extraterritorial Effectiveness of Foreign Judgments and Arbitral Awards, which is the most significant treaty concluded by Colombia concerning the recognition and homologation process.

It is worth repeating that this public order refers to the public order of private international law, which implies that the refusal of the judgment should only occur under this assumption, i.e., only when fundamental principles of the legal system are violated. For example, the Supreme Court has rejected requests for exequatur of a foreign divorce decree for a period of separation of less than the two years provided for in the Civil Code, arguing that:

> If exequatur were granted, public order would be undermined, not only because the decree is based on a ground that is not recognized in any way in national law, but also because it would allow, without further ado, the mere unjustified lapse of time as a ground for divorce, all of which undermines the institution of the family, which is conceived by the superior norm as the fundamental nucleus of society, and against the integral protection that the state intends to guarantee by making the grounds for divorce exhaustive (Article 42 C.P.), in order to give it stability.[74]

Therefore, it is relevant to emphasize the already settled debate on the nature of the civil status of persons as an imperative rule, even though it has such a nature, this does not imply in any way that its modification by recognizing a foreign judgment

---

[72] See supra note 71.

[73] Article 50, IADIP Draft: "Divorce and separation are governed by the law of the state of the common domicile or, failing that, by the law of the state of the last common domicile."

[74] Supreme Court of Colombia, Civil Section. Judgment No. SC4101 of September 26, 2018, p. 12.

entails a violation of the international public order of the state (fundamental principles), otherwise, this would lead to rejecting foreign decisions regarding divorce and marriage annulment.[75]

3.4 Comments on the de facto *Marital Union*

Under Act No. 54 of 1990, the *de facto* marital union has been regulated and permitted in Colombia, wherein it is defined as a permanent and singular community of life formed by a man and a woman, without the necessity of being married. As previously mentioned, in Judgment C-075 of 2007, the Constitutional Court extended this figure to same-sex couples and later in Judgment C-456 of 2020, the Court indicated that granting rights to same-sex couples in *de facto* unions includes accepting corresponding obligations and responsibilities.

Although marriage and *de facto* conjugal union create a family that must be protected, the Constitutional Court has stated that these institutions are different "because the former creates a legal relationship with rights and obligations for the parties that are extinguished by divorce, annulment or death, while in the latter the relationship is born from the mere fact of cohabitation."[76] To understand this distinction, it should be noted that the birth of the *de facto* marital union is not a celebration as such, but, being a fact, it must be proven in a judicial proceeding, so the doctrine states that "the aspect of proving its existence must be governed, as in the case of marriage, by the law of the forum where its recognition is sought, accumulated with the laws of the country where the conjugal life took place and with the personal laws of the cohabitants."[77] That is to say, the law of the place where it is to be proved is applicable, in accordance with the law of the place where the marriage was contracted.

On its dissolution, the Constitutional Court has reiterated that "the sole will of one of its members is sufficient to terminate the *de facto* conjugal union."[78] The permanent partners are not obliged to remain in such a union, so, in principle, there is no debate about the law applicable to these matters. Once the *de facto* marital union is established, and regardless of the evidentiary issues, it is necessary to mention that the effects of the union are similar to those of marriage, for which we refer to the previous considerations.

---

[75] Debate that took place on the occasion of the decision of the Supreme Court of Justice, Civil Section, of August 3, 1995, rad. 4725, Judge Héctor Marín Naranjo, in which an exequatur was denied with respect to an adoption decreed in Venezuela for modifying the civil status, arguing reasons of public order. This consideration was reconsidered and corrected in a decision of November 5, 1996, Judge Carlos Esteban Jaramillo Scholss, rad. 6130, when granting the exequatur of a divorce decreed in Argentina. See García Matamoros (2016), pp. 298–299.

[76] Constitutional Court of Colombia. Judgment No. C-324 of September 23, 2021.

[77] Mantilla Rey (1996), p. 128.

[78] Constitutional Court of Colombia. Judgment No. C-239 of May 19, 1994.

Note that both proposals explicitly provide conflict-of-law rules on this matter. The UNAL Draft in its second version did introduce the provision on the law applicable to the *de facto* marriage, stating in Article 37 that it would be the law of the common domicile of the permanent partners.

In contrast, the IADIP Draft proposes a greater variety of conflict rules according to the nature of the matter. In this regard, Article 46 establishes the place of incorporation as the point of contact for capacity and substantive requirements, although for marriage it established the domicile; regarding personal and patrimonial effects, Article 49 establishes as applicable law the law of the place where the union is intended to be enforced, departing from the choice at will of the parties for marriage; finally, Article 52 of the IADIP Draft states that dissolution shall be governed by the law of the common domicile or, in its absence, by the law of the last common domicile. As can be observed, in the IADIP Draft, the rules regarding *de facto* unions are not similar to those governing marriage, which better addresses the differences of these two institutions by which a family is constituted, because while unions are a fact, marriage is a juridical act.

4 Conclusions

From the perspective of private international law, the institutions of marriage and *de facto* marital union are particularly complex. This is because they include a number of legal aspects pertaining to personal status, real status (in its property component), and contractual status (in the case of marriage). Furthermore, the aforementioned complexity is compounded in the context of a globalized and multicultural world. In this regard, the analysis conducted underscores the necessity for a comprehensive normative update in this domain in Colombia, given the shortcomings and deficiencies inherent in the prevailing Civil Code.

It is encouraging to observe that a variety of societal actors are proposing solutions and initiating discourse on the optimal incorporation of conflict-of-law rules into the Colombian legal system. As has been demonstrated, the two drafts exhibit both points of convergence and divergence, indicating that, despite the existence of discernible trends in other legal systems, the determination of applicable law in the family matters under discussion is not always straightforward, particularly given the diversity of legal scenarios encompassed.

While there are proposals that aim to enhance flexibility, as exemplified by the IADIP Draft concerning the matrimonial patrimony and personal effects, which strives to respond more effectively to contemporary dynamics, it is crucial to recognize that these family matters pertain to public order and necessitate the establishment of mandatory regulations in this domain. Moreover, it is preferable to favor a unity of law in those aspects that allow it, since, for example, it is not coherent, as proposed by the UNAL Draft, to apply two different laws to the same matter, such as the personal effects of marriage.

In any case, it is evident that the marital or common domicile represents the predominant point of contact in most of the aspects reviewed and is more decisive in the IADIP Draft. Furthermore, it is imperative to streamline the exequatur process, eliminating onerous requirements that impede the international recognition of decisions in this matter, as highlighted in the UNAL Draft. On the *de facto* marital union, it would appear that a differentiated treatment in the law applicable to its effects, in comparison with marriage, is the most appropriate course of action, particularly given the facts-based nature of its constitution and dissolution.

In conclusion, it is necessary to incorporate more precise rules that regulate the applicable law to the different aspects of the contemporary family in a clear, simple, and coherent manner from the perspective of private international law in Colombia. Moreover, it is imperative to recognize that these matters are not merely legally intricate; they are also socially and emotionally complex. Consequently, these academic deliberations are invaluable and essential for elucidating the subject matter and furnishing the Colombian legislature with the insights necessary for updating the country's regulatory framework.

References

Adroher Biosca S (1993) Forma del matrimonio y derecho internacional privado. Bosch, Madrid

Aguilar Benítez M (2003) El matrimonio consular. Boletín del Ministerio de Justicia 1937:825–850

Arenas García R (2020) Concepto y tratamiento del matrimonio en el derecho internacional privado. La Ley Derecho de Familia 26

Barrios H (2014) Instituciones de derecho de familia en la ley de derecho internacional privado venezolana. In: Guerra et al (eds) Derecho familiar internacional: metodología para su estudio, homenaje a Haydée Barrios. Diké and Universidad del Rosario, Medellin, pp 243–473

Bouza Vidal N (2007) Los problemas que plantea el derecho de familia y sucesiones en el derecho internacional privado. La Notaria 42:11–40

Cancillería de Colombia (2024) ¿En los consulados colombianos se pueden celebrar matrimonios? https://www.cancilleria.gov.co/faq/consulados-colombianos-pueden-celebrar-matrimonios. Accessed 3 June 2024

Carrascosa González J (2003) Nuevos modelos de familia y derecho internacional privado en el siglo XXI. Anales de Derecho 21:109–143

CNN Español (2024) ¿En qué países es legal el matrimonio homosexual? ¿Dónde fue legal primero? https://cnnespanol.cnn.com/2024/02/16/paises-legal-personas-del-mismo-sexo-matrimonio-igualitario-union-civil-orix/. Accessed 25 May 2024

García Matamoros LV (2016) Estatuto personal. Los aspectos relativos a las relaciones de familia. In: García Matamoros LV, Aljure Salame A (eds) Teoría general del derecho internacional privado. Legis and Universidad del Rosario, Bogota, pp 285–303

González Beilfuss C (2020) Reflexiones en torno a la función de la autonomía de la voluntad contractual en el derecho internacional de familia. Revista Española de Derecho Internacional 72(1):101–115

Gutiérrez Castillo VL (2016) El orden público en el derecho internacional privado. In: García Matamoros LV, Aljure Salame A (eds) Teoría general del derecho internacional privado. Legis and Universidad del Rosario, Bogota, pp 125–136

Jiménez Sánchez MA (2001) Procesos civiles de divorcio en la U.E.: El nuevo Reglamento Comunitario 1347/2000. Repercusión en nuestro actual sistema. In: Calvo Caravaca AL, Iriarte A (eds) Mundialización y familia. Colex, Madrid, pp 241–294

Lema Tomé M (2003) Matrimonio poligámico, inmigración islámica y libertad de conciencia en España. Migraciones Internacionales 2(2):149–170

Lepin Molina C (2022) La autonomía de la voluntad en el ámbito del derecho familiar. Actualidad Jurídica Iberoamericana 16:1236–1255

López Herrera F (1970) Anotaciones sobre Derecho de familia. UCAP, Caracas

Loussouarn Y, Bourel P (1996) Droit international privé. Dalloz, Paris

Maekelt T, Esis Villarroel I, Resende E (2005) Ley de derecho internacional privado comentada. Universidad Central de Venezuela, Caracas

Mantilla Rey R (1996) Recapitulación de derecho internacional privado, 1st edn. Universidad Nacional de Colombia, Bogota

Medina Pabón JE (2018) Derecho civil. Derecho de familia, 5th edn. Editorial Universidad del Rosario, Bogota

Torrado HA (2020) Derecho de familia. Matrimonio, filiación y divorcio, 4th edn. Legis and Universidad Sergio Arboleda, Bogota

Universidad Externado de Colombia (2020) Observaciones Críticas sobre el Proyecto de Código Civil presentado por la Universidad Nacional, pp 38–39. https://www.uexternado.edu.co/wp-content/uploads/2020/10/Concepto-Te%CC%81cnico-Observaciones-Cri%CC%81ticas-al-Proyecto-de-Co%CC%81digo-Civil-UNAL-Presentado-por-U-Externado.pdf. Accessed 2 June 2024

Laura Victoria García Matamoros Tenured Professor and former Dean of Law School, Universidad del Rosario; Ph.D. in Law Suma Cum Laude, Universidad Externado de Colombia; Postgraduate Studies in Private International Law, University of Paris 2. *The author would like to thank Cristian Fernando Barrios Almario, lawyer from Universidad del Rosario and reasearch assistant, for his valuable support in literature review and editing of this chapter.

International Family Law in Colombia

Gloria Rivera Ocampo

Abstract This chapter presents the main international treaties and instruments that make up Colombian international family law, particularly those that contain rules regarding child protection and international adoption, which refer to the general principles on this subject matter, i.e., safeguarding the best interest of the child, non-discrimination, and efficiency in legal processes. Reference is also made to the fact that the lack of regulation on other issues, such as surrogacy and post-mortem insemination, poses complex challenges for Colombian family courts.

1 Introduction

International family law has expanded considerably in Colombia in the last decade. Factors such as globalization, internet access, cultural exchange, Colombians seeking new opportunities abroad, the massive influx of migrants to the country,[1] and the absence of regulations in many areas have all significantly contributed to this growth.

Colombia is a party to several international conventions aimed at protecting children and families. Because some of such conventions have been adopted at the Hague Conference on Private International Law, it is worth noting here that, although Colombia has been admitted to this organization, this admission must still be formally accepted for such membership to be effective. In any case, some of the Hague conventions are among the important international treaties on international family law that are currently in force in Colombia, while other international instruments have been legally approved but not yet entered into force due to procedural issues, and others are still being discussed in Congress.

[1] Ministry of Tourism of Colombia (2024).

G. Rivera Ocampo (✉)
Facultad de Derecho y Ciencias Políticas, Universidad de Antioquia, Medellín, Colombia
e-mail: stella.rivera@udea.edu.co

M. J. Ochoa Jiménez, C. Madrid Martínez (eds.), *A Private International Law for Colombia*, Springer Textbooks in Law,
https://doi.org/10.1007/978-3-032-04106-7_15

This chapter presents the international conventions currently in force in the country and outlines some fundamental aspects of Colombian international family law. Pursuant to Article 93, paragraph 2, of the Colombian Political Constitution, the conventions in force that provide procedures to protect children and families internationally have been given the status of supra-constitutional rules, to the extent that they recognize human rights. This has been possible by means of the mechanism known as constitutional block (*bloque de constitucionalidad*). In this way, international conventions on this subject matter are at the top of the national legal system. In such a context, in general terms, the Colombian Constitutional Court has significantly contributed to the development of Colombian international family law by promoting the application of such conventions and treaties and creating an important case law. It has also provided valuable insights into areas of international family law not covered by treaties.

In this context, it is worth noting that the Convention on the Rights of the Child (1989), adopted by the United Nations General Assembly on November 20, 1989, and approved by the Colombian Congress in 1991, introduces the principle of the *best interests of the child*. This principle is internationally recognized and humanistic in nature, providing heightened protection to minors in need, and ensuring the development of healthy, free, and autonomous adults.

In addition, Decree No. 2737 of 1989 explicitly considers international family law treaties and conventions as guides for the interpretation and application of rules on the subject. In this way, these treaties, along with Article 93, paragraph 2, of the Colombian Political Constitution, have served as the basis for interpreting the Convention on the Rights of the Child. Further, Judgment No. C-574 of 1992 of the Colombian Constitutional Court prohibits the suspension or restriction of their application, even under states of exception.

This chapter is organized in the following manner. It first outlines the main international instruments of international family law, including conventions, covenants, and protocols. Then, it presents the conventions currently in force, followed by a review of Colombia's most significant cases lacking domestic regulation and requiring solutions from the perspective of private international law and comparative law.

2 International Instruments Adopted by Colombia as a Basis for International Family Law

The interconnections between international family law and human rights conventions are rooted in their content. These rights include the protection of individuals' physical and mental integrity, life, safety, and protection from discrimination based on race, gender, nationality, color, sexual orientation, ethnicity, religion, or disability. They also encompass individual rights such as privacy, freedom, and family rights. Under no circumstances can these rights be limited, suspended, or disregarded by the states. Human rights conventions allow for claims in court not only internationally but also in domestic courts, based on their protection as fundamental rights or directly through their recognition via constitutional block.[2] They additionally serve in this manner as an essential tool to fulfill the objectives of international family law in practice, i.e., to protect and support family members, especially minors, when they cross national borders.

2.1 Declarations

Among the international instruments that have a non-binding character, those adopted at the United Nations and the Organization of American States stand out, i.e., the American Declaration of the Rights and Duties of Man, adopted in Bogotá in April 1948, the Universal Declaration of Human Rights, adopted by the United Nations General Assembly on December 10, 1948, and the Declaration on the Rights of the Child, adopted by the United Nations General Assembly on November 20, 1959.

2.2 Treaties

The bilateral or multilateral agreements that have a binding nature include: the International Covenants on Economic, Social and Cultural Rights and on Civil and Political Rights, as well as the Optional Protocol to the latter (approved in Colombia by Act No. 74 of 1968), the American Convention on Human Rights, Pact of San José, signed at the Inter-American Specialized Conference on Human Rights in San José, Costa Rica, on November 22, 1969 (approved in Colombia by Act No. 16 of 1976), the Convention on the Rights of the Child, adopted by the United Nations General Assembly on November 20, 1989 (approved in Colombia by Act No. 12 of January 22, 1991), the Convention on the Elimination of All Forms of Discrimination against Women, adopted by the United Nations General Assembly on December 18, 1979 (approved in Colombia by Act No. 51 of 1981), the Convention No. 5, adopted by the International Labor Organization in 1919 at the First Conference on the Eradication of Child Labor, the Convention No. 138, promulgated in 1973 by the International Labor Organization (approved by Act No. 515 of 1999), the Convention No. 182, adopted by the International Labor Organization in 1999, along with Recommendation No. 90, which complements it regarding the worst forms of child labor (approved by Act No. 704 of 2001), the Convention on the Recovery Abroad of Maintenance, signed in New York on June 20, 1956 (approved by Act No. 471 of 1998, and declared constitutional by Judgement 305 of 1999 of the Constitutional Court of Colombia, 1999), the International Convention on the Elimination of All

[2] See Article 93, paragraph 2, of the Colombian Political Constitution.

Forms of Racial Discrimination, adopted by the United Nations General Assembly in Resolution 2106 (XX) on December 21, 1965 (approved by Act No. 22 of 1981), and the Convention No. 169, concerning Indigenous and Tribal Peoples in Independent Countries, adopted by the 76th Session of the International Labor Organization General Conference in Geneva in 1989 (approved by Act No. 21 of 1991).

2.3 *Protocols*

Protocols are complementary agreements to the international conventions and are intended to supplement them in relation to specific aspects. The following protocols are relevant in the Colombian context: the Optional Protocol on the Sale of Children, Child Prostitution, and Child Pornography (approved by Act No. 769 of 2002), the Protocol to Prevent, Suppress and Punish Trafficking in Persons, Especially Women and Children, adopted by the United Nations General Assembly on November 15, 2000 (approved by Act No. 800 of 2003, this protocol complements the Palermo Convention against Transnational Organized Crime), and the Optional Protocol to the Convention on the Rights of the Child on the Involvement of Children in Armed Conflict (approved by Act No. 833 of 2003).

3 International Family Treaties

The implementation of international family treaties currently in force is the responsibility of the Colombian Family Welfare Institute (ICBF). This is the country's central authority and interacts directly with the central authorities of the rest of the member states regarding the respective international instrument. Such treaties are the following: (1) the Hague Convention on Protection of Children and Cooperation in Respect of Intercountry Adoption, done on March 29, 1993 (approved by Act No. 265 of 1996), (2) the Hague Convention on the Civil Aspects of International Child Abduction, signed on October 25, 1980 (approved by Act No. 173 of 1994), (3) the Convention on the Recovery Abroad of Maintenance, signed in New York on June 20, 1956 (approved by Act No. 471 of 1988), and (4) the Inter-American Convention on Support Obligations, signed on July 15, 1989, in Montevideo, Uruguay (approved by Act No. 449 of 1998, and declared constitutional by the Constitutional Court through Judgment No. C-184 of 1999).

In addition, Colombia is committed to the application of the following international instruments which, although ratified, have not yet been implemented: the Inter-American Convention on Support Obligations, signed on July 15, 1989, in Montevideo, Uruguay (approved by the Congress of the Republic through Act No. 449 of 1998 and declared constitutional by the Constitutional Court through Judgment No. C-184 of 1999), the Inter-American Convention on International

Traffic in Minors, adopted in Mexico on March 18, 1994 (approved by Act No. 470 of August 5, 1998, which entered into force for Colombia on September 21, 2000, but has not yet entered into force for protocol reasons), the Inter-American Convention on the International Return of Children, signed in Uruguay on July 15, 1989 (approved by Act No. 880 of 2004, but the instrument of ratification has not been deposited), the Hague Convention on Jurisdiction, Applicable Law, Recognition and Enforcement, and Cooperation in Respect of Parental Responsibility and Measures for the Protection of Children, done on October 19, 1996 (it is pending to be submitted to the Congress of the Republic for the issuance of the approving act).

4 Treaties in Force and Their Implementation in Colombia

There are three conventions whose fundamental objective is the cooperation of the state parties aimed at the protection of children and the family at the international level, namely the Convention on Protection of Children and Cooperation in Respect of Intercountry Adoption, the Convention on the Civil Aspects of International Child Abduction, and the Convention on the Recovery Abroad of Maintenance. These international texts share the following common aspects, which facilitate interaction between the state parties and, consequently, the effective application of their rules.

4.1 General Considerations

Guiding Principles Some principles constitute a roadmap for action and define the criteria to be followed for the adequate implementation of the above conventions. The most relevant are the following:

(1) The best interest of the child. This fundamental principle prioritizes actions aimed at protecting minors and is enshrined in Article 44 of the Political Constitution of Colombia. It states that the family, society, and the state must assist and protect the child to guarantee their harmonious and integral development and the full exercise of their rights, as established in numerous national judgments. This principle is cross-cutting across the conventions in force and, due to its significance, will also apply to future conventions.
(2) Free of charge. This principle asserts that all actions related to the treaties and agreements in force must be provided at no cost. The state parties shall not receive any remuneration for carrying out these actions, resources, or means to fulfill the objectives of each agreement. In some states, there are penalties for officials who receive any form of benefit, and in Colombia, these penalties can range from disciplinary to criminal consequences.

(3) Speed. This principle is crucial in the development of international rules, as time is a factor that negatively impacts children benefiting from these rules. It is particularly important in international adoption, international return, and the international recovery of maintenance. The states must allocate all necessary resources to achieve the objectives of each convention; however, it is not sufficient for these resources to simply exist; they must be optimal and effective to achieve the best results in the shortest possible time.

Colombia accepts and applies these principles. However, there are some issues linked to the fact that the same entity—the Colombian Institute for Family Welfare (ICBF)—acts as both the central and intermediate authority for all the agreements being executed. This institution performs various functions at the local level and has been entrusted with this additional responsibility as the treaties have been adopted. This represents a significant difference in the outcomes of the application of the agreements in comparison to other states that have established public entities exclusively responsible for implementing them. This leads to a disadvantage in terms of results, allowing us to affirm that in Colombia, such principles are not always adequately upheld.

Legal Framework There is a framework formed by the rules that support and govern the agreements that are currently being implemented. These rules act as instruments to facilitate the application of the agreements: the Declaration of the Rights of the Child, proclaimed by the United Nations General Assembly in its Resolution 1368 (XIV) of November 20, 1959; the Convention on the Rights of the Child, adopted by the United Nations General Assembly on November 20, 1989, and in force for Colombia as of January 28, 1991, through Law 12 of January 22, 1991; rules by the central or intermediate authority; the Political Constitution of Colombia of 1991 (Articles 42, 44, 93, 94, 214, numeral 2); Act No. 12 of 1991, which approves the Convention on the Rights of the Child; Act No. 265 of 1996, which approves the Hague Convention on Protection of Children and Cooperation in Respect of Intercountry Adoption; Act No. 1098 of November 8, 2006, which contains the Childhood and Adolescence Code; Decree No. 2737 of 1989, which contains the Code of Minors; the Civil Code; Decree No. 2272 of 1989, which organizes family jurisdiction, creates certain judicial offices, and establishes other provisions; the General Code on Procedure Law; ICBF internal regulations; case law; and national and international doctrine.

Central Authority, Intermediate Authority, and Accredited Bodies Some administrative entities are appointed within each state party to the conventions or treaties to implement them. In line with the principle of celerity, their work extends beyond merely implementing the convention. They are also responsible for submitting periodic reports to the headquarters secretariat to identify and address shortcomings in the application of the corresponding convention. These entities communicate with one another to avoid delays in their procedures. Among their main activities are (1) cooperating and promoting collaboration between the competent authorities of their respective states to ensure the protection of children and achieve the other objectives of the convention; (2) providing information on their states' treaty legislation and other general information, such as statistics and forms; (3) informing each other about the operation of the agreement and, whenever possible, removing obstacles to its implementation; (4) responding, to the extent permitted by their state's law, to reasoned requests for information regarding a particular situation made by other central authorities or public authorities; and (5) taking appropriate measures, either directly or in cooperation with public authorities, to prevent improper financial gain in connection with the agreement and to avoid any practices contrary to the objectives of the agreement.

About the Procedure The three abovementioned conventions share the common feature of referring to direct intervention between the central authorities or authorized bodies during the administrative phase. This phase, which is defined by the nature of the entity as established by each convention, is characterized by its persuasive and conciliatory approach. However, the scope of this authority is not judicial. When the objectives of any agreement are not fulfilled, the respective authority must refer the matter to the competent family judge, leading to the direct intervention of the judicial authority in each country, and concluding the procedure with a decision on the merits. In the case of adoption, the judicial phase is mandatory; however, for the other two agreements, the process may conclude at the administrative phase.

Having reviewed the common aspects of the three agreements that were mentioned above, and which are currently being implemented, the main aspects of the most relevant international instruments are examined in what follows.

4.2 The Hague Convention on Protection of Children and Cooperation in Respect of Intercountry Adoption

Adopted by Colombia through Act No. 265 of 1996, the Hague Convention on Protection of Children and Cooperation in Respect of Intercountry Adoption has been designed to regulate international adoption and protect the interests of the minor involved. It is currently in force in 106 countries.[3] Its main purpose is to establish guarantees that ensure international adoptions occur in consideration of the best interests of the child and respect for the fundamental rights recognized by international law. The convention aims to create a system of cooperation among the contracting states to uphold these guarantees and, consequently, to prevent the abduction, sale, or trafficking of children.

The concept of adoption is defined in Article 88 of Decree No. 2737 of 1989 and Act No. 1098 of 2006. It is described as "a measure of protection through which, under the supreme supervision of the State, the paternal-filial relationship is

[3] More information is available at: https://www.hcch.net/es/instruments/conventions/status-table/notifications/?csid=763&disp=resdn Accessed on October 16, 2024.

irrevocably established between persons who do not have it by nature." Adoption serves as a mechanism to realize the child's right to have a family, and the entire institution is structured around the best interests of the child, whose rights take precedence over those of others. It also ensures the recognition in the contracting states of adoptions made in accordance with the convention, providing a family for children who do not have one.

Upon ratifying this convention, Colombia made the following declarations, which serve as additional conditions aimed at protecting the minors benefiting from international adoption:

> 2. In accordance with Articles 17, 21, and 28 of the Convention, the government of Colombia declares that only those children previously adopted according to an enforceable judgment may leave Colombian national territory.
>
> 3. In accordance with Article 22, paragraph 2, of the Convention, the Colombian government declares that the functions conferred upon the Central Authority under Articles 15 to 19 may also be performed in Colombia, to the extent permitted by the law and subject to the supervision of the competent authorities of Colombia, by the following institutions: …
>
> Only the above bodies, accredited in accordance with Article 22, paragraph 2, of the Convention, may, in addition to the Central Authority, perform in Colombia the functions referred to in Articles 15 to 19 of the Convention. No mention is made of Articles 20 and 21 because, under Colombian legislation on adoption, an adopted minor cannot leave the country until the judgment ordering the adoption has become final, as far as the adoption process takes place in Colombia only.
>
> 4. In accordance with Article 22, paragraph 4, of the Convention, Colombia declares that adoptions of children habitually resident in Colombia may only take place if the functions of the Central Authorities are performed in accordance with Article 22, paragraph 1, of the Convention.
>
> 6. The government of the Republic of Colombia reserves the right to withdraw the declarations made and to submit others to the depositary of the Convention, in accordance with Articles 22, 23, 25, and 45 of the Convention.

Since it started the implementation of this agreement, Colombia has identified itself as a provider country, characterized by a significant number of children with measures for the restoration of rights in the adoption process.[4] However, in June 2013, Colombia suspended the acceptance of applications for international adoption while it studied and readapted its internal model. In 2017, the suspension was lifted, allowing the receipt of applications from foreigners. Since then, international adoption has focused solely on children that the ICBF classifies as having special needs or as difficult to adopt,[5] according to its technical guidelines. Statistics from this

[4]The exceptional protective measures outlined in Act No. 1098 of 2006, the Childhood and Adolescence Code, apply within the process of restoring the rights of minors whose fundamental rights have been violated. This is considered an exceptional measure because it is only taken as a last resort when it is no longer possible to place the minor with their extended biological family.

[5]These are children with special conditions, illnesses, diagnoses, those over 12 years old, or those who are part of a sibling group who, for psychological reasons, should not be separated.

period show a significant change compared to international adoption: national adoption is now at the top, representing more than 50% of all adoptions.[6]

Regarding the development of adoption in Colombia, it can be stated that the process remains transparent. It is initiated through the central authority of the petitioning countries and culminates in Colombian territory with a judicial decision issued by the competent family judge.[7]

The Convention places significant burdens on the parties involved. First and foremost, minors eligible for national or international adoption must undergo an administrative process of Restoration of Rights. Adopters are required to compile a variety of documents, including identification, certificates, and medical opinions, which must be apostilled[8] and translated into Spanish if necessary. They then travel to Colombia to meet with the family defender, followed by the child's placement, an integration period, a judicial process, and administrative procedures for leaving the country.[9] This process culminates in post-adoption follow-up, which is the responsibility of the Central Authority of the adopting parents' country, requiring four reports at six-month intervals over two years after the local adoption decision.

Colombia faces various challenges in the international adoption process. Although the Convention allows for the adoption of children up to 16 years of age, this is not the typical age for adoption in Colombia. Another challenge is the lengthy waiting period for child placement, which can range from two to five years, depending on the adopters' position on the waiting list, with shorter wait times for children with special needs.[10]

Additionally, the integration period in Colombia is notably short, ranging from one to eight days between the child's placement with the adoptive parents and the evaluation by ICBF personnel. This short period is insufficient for meaningful integration, especially when the adoptive parents are in a foreign country, often residing in a hotel, and lacking familiarity with the family's routine. Language barriers and the absence of knowledge about the adopted child's background further complicate this process. These children often come from backgrounds of loss, separation, or abandonment, having just undergone a process of rights restoration due to parental abandonment or rights violations. Consequently, many adoptive parents may have

[6] In 2011, international adoptions represented 72% of total adoptions in Colombia. As of June 30, 2024, this proportion has decreased to 37%, according to the ICBF. See ICBF (2024).

[7] Matarazzo Briani (2016).

[8] More information about this at: https://www.hcch.net/es/instruments/conventions/specialised-sections/apostille Accessed on October 11, 2024.

[9] The adoptee must obtain the nationality of the adoptive parents before the embassy of their country, as they are required to leave Colombia under this nationality. If the adoptive parents' country does not allow dual nationality, the Colombian nationality will be temporarily deactivated until the adoptee decides to reactivate it.

[10] The ICBF maintains lists of children organized by age, along with an additional list for children with special needs. Prospective adoptive parents are classified into lists based on their age.

idealized their future child, only to face the harsh reality of their child's sadness and pain, which can be difficult to navigate.[11]

Furthermore, the 2018 Hague Report on International Adoption highlighted the surge in surrogate motherhood cases, an issue that has also affected Colombia. In these instances, the solution has often been to treat the adoption of the child as if it were a local adoption, thereby circumventing the regulations of the convention.

In conclusion, international adoption in Colombia has diminished in relevance over time. This decline is primarily attributed to the restrictions placed on foreigners regarding the lists of children with special needs, as well as the rise of assisted reproduction techniques, which have largely supplanted international adoption and shifted the focus towards local adoption.

4.3 *The Hague Convention on the Civil Aspects of International Child Abduction*

The Hague Convention on the Civil Aspects of International Child Abduction was incorporated into Colombian legislation through Act No. 173 of 1994 and was declared constitutional by the Constitutional Court in Judgment No. C-402-95 on September 7, 1995. It entered into force on March 1, 1996, with the ICBF designated as the central authority responsible for its implementation in Colombia, a role fulfilled through the Subdirectorate of Direct Interventions.

This convention aims to prevent the international transfer of minors by establishing close cooperation between the judicial and administrative authorities of the contracting states. This cooperation is founded on two key principles: first, the immediate return of the child to the environment from which he or she has been removed, and second, the effective respect for custody and visitation rights established in one of the contracting states.[12] The convention applies in cases where custody rights held by one parent are violated, without affecting the parental rights of either parent.[13] Its primary objective is to secure the immediate return of children wrongfully removed to or retained in any contracting state while enforcing the existing custody and visitation rights in one contracting state.

Colombia is acutely aware of this issue, which has become increasingly pronounced over time. A significant advantage is the access to this procedure through the ICBF, which has a presence throughout the country. Those seeking the return of

[11] I witnessed this situation while I was a trainee in the Master 2 in Private Law with a specialization in Family Law at the Association of Colombian Children in Toulouse, France—an association of parents of children adopted in Colombia—between 2007 and 2009.

[12] Resolution No. 1399 of 1998, issued by the General Directorate of the ICBF, which establishes the internal procedure for the application of the Hague Convention on international child abduction.

[13] Articles 3 and 4 of the Hague Convention, October 25, 1980.

a child must provide proof of filiation, effective custody,[14] and other pertinent information to facilitate the child's return to his or her habitual residence.[15]

The procedure begins with an administrative phase led by the ICBF as the central authority. When Colombia is the requesting country, the interested party must appear in person and submit the necessary documents to enable the ICBF to promptly contact the relevant authority in the requested country, where the minor is located or held. This authority is tasked with locating the minor and verifying that no grounds exist for his or her non-return[16] to the habitual residence. The ICBF will then undertake conciliatory and persuasive efforts to secure the child's return. It is important to note that this agreement does not address custody disputes between parents; its sole purpose is the return of the minor to his or her habitual residence.

The second phase is judicial, where a family judge intervenes to grant or deny the return of the child. It is crucial to understand that there are specific grounds outlined in the Convention that, if applicable, preclude its enforcement. These grounds include[17]:

a) the person, institution, or other body having the care of the person of the child was not actually exercising the custody rights at the time of removal or retention, or had consented to or subsequently acquiesced in the removal or retention; or
b) there is a grave risk that his or her return would expose the child to physical or psychological harm or otherwise place the child in an intolerable situation.

   The judicial or administrative authority may also refuse to order the return of the child if it finds that the child objects to being returned and has attained an age and degree of maturity at which it is appropriate to take account of its views.

According to the convention, wrongful removal is defined as a situation where there has been a violation of the right of custody assigned to an individual by the legislation of the state where the child habitually resided prior to his or her removal. This right must have been effectively exercised at the time of removal, allowing for proceedings to be initiated under the Convention to facilitate the child's effective return.

It is crucial to emphasize that the state party must provide the central authority of the country where the child is located with all available resources within its legal system to locate the child as quickly as possible, in accordance with the principle of celerity. In this regard, Interpol can play a fundamental and valuable role in locating minors. Importantly, it is not necessary to initiate a criminal proceeding for this assistance; a simple missing person report suffices.

[14] Through notarial testimony or by means of a judgment, public deed, conciliation deed, or private agreement between the parents.

[15] The basic concept of "habitual residence" centers on the *real integration* of an individual within a specific social and legal environment. In essence, "habitual residence" reflects the *genuine rootedness* of a person to a particular socio-legal context. IDIBE (2022).

[16] Refers to force majeure or fortuitous events, such as illness of the minor, and airspace closure, among others.

[17] Articles 12 and 13, Act No. 173 of 1994.

The administrative phase is governed by the provisions of the Agreement, aligned with Law 1008 of 2006, Law 1098 of November 8, 2006, the Code of Children and Adolescents, the Code of Minors, the Civil Code, and the General Code of Procedure. When Colombia is the requested country, the request must be submitted to the ICBF by the central authority of the child's habitual residence, and the procedure must be conducted in accordance with the terms of the Convention.

In practice, some difficulties have emerged in the application of the Convention in Colombia. Prior to 2006, when Law 1098 was enacted, the procedure was unclear, particularly regarding which judge had jurisdiction to handle the case. The lengthy duration of the restitution process has been highlighted in the case of Luciana, a girl of Colombian and Argentinian nationalities who was abducted by her mother and taken to Colombia. She was removed from school and lived nomadically in the southern part of the country for nearly 4 years to evade her mother's responsibility of returning her to her father in Argentina. The restitution was ultimately achieved, thanks to the father's resources.[18]

Additionally, there are concerns about the costs associated with the administrative phase, as the parent residing far from the child's location must have legal representation to participate effectively in the process while maintaining procedural balance. The use of the constitutional mechanism of tutela action that has been noted is often employed in these cases to halt the restitution orders issued by family judges, as exemplified by the Constitutional Court's Judgment No. 202 of 2018.

4.4 The Convention on the Recovery Abroad of Maintenance

The Convention on the Recovery Abroad of Maintenance was signed in New York on June 20, 1956, and incorporated into Colombian law through Act No. 471 of 1998, which was declared constitutional by Judgment No. C-305 of 1999 of the Constitutional Court. The instrument of ratification was deposited on November 10, 1999. The purpose of the convention is to facilitate the ability of individuals within the territory of one contracting state to obtain maintenance claims against another person subject to the jurisdiction of a different contracting state. This is achieved through the intervention of intermediary institutions and remitting authorities to address the legal and practical challenges associated with claiming this right. To this end, the convention establishes legal mechanisms that complement, rather than replace, other means available under domestic or international law.

The effective operation of the convention relies on the intermediary institutions and sending authorities that contracting states are obligated to designate. In Colombia, the Colombian Institute of Family Welfare (ICBF) serves as the intermediary institution, fulfilling this role through its Subdirectorate of Direct Interventions. The General Directorate of the ICBF is responsible for regulating the

[18] Séptimo Día (2018).

implementation of international treaties and conventions related to children and family matters. The Superior Council of the Judiciary has been designated as the referring authority, performing this function through its Administrative Chamber. This body issued Agreement No. 2207 on November 26, 2003, which regulates the procedure for receiving and transmitting maintenance applications abroad.

The procedure consists of two phases. First, an administrative phase where the Intermediate Authority acts as a conciliator to secure effective payment of the maintenance obligation. If this is unsuccessful, the case proceeds to the judicial phase, where the Family Judge will make the necessary decisions.

This Convention has some shortcomings, the following being the most relevant. (1) It does not specify who will be the competent authority, only mentioning the remitting authorities and intermediary institutions that may facilitate payment through the transaction, initiation, and execution of the procedure. (2) It fails to establish criteria for determining the applicable law. (3) Generally, it states that the applicable law shall be that of the respondent state. (4) It allows for requests for maintenance between individuals without regard to the cause giving rise to such obligations. (5) There is no enforcement procedure defined within the convention; this responsibility is left to the signatory states. (6) It contains a referral clause to the International Court of Justice for resolving interpretations or applications of the agreement (Article 16). (7) It includes a federal clause (Article 11). (8) There is no mechanism provided for locating the defendant. And (9) it does not address issues related to filiation as a component for the recovery of maintenance.

Overall, the convention is quite general. Despite this, Colombia has made progress in the gradual implementation of its provisions.

4.5 The Inter-American Convention on Support Obligations

The Inter-American Convention on Support Obligations was signed on July 15, 1989, in Montevideo, Uruguay. According to Article 1, its purpose is to determine the applicable law regarding maintenance obligations, as well as to establish competence and international procedural cooperation when the maintenance creditor and/or debtor has their domicile, habitual residence, assets, or income in another contracting state.

As of now, Colombia has not acceded to the convention. Nevertheless, the norm approving the convention is applicable within Colombian territory, and family defenders[19] operate in accordance with this convention, which addresses some gaps left by the previous agreement, particularly regarding the applicable law.

[19] Within the ICBF, they are the ones responsible for directing the process.

4.6 The Hague Convention on the International Recovery of Child Support and Other Forms of Family Maintenance

The Convention on the International Recovery of Child Support and Other Forms of Family Maintenance was adopted on November 23, 2007, and approved in Colombia through Act No. 2212 of 2022. This convention establishes the framework for the recognition and enforcement of decisions regarding maintenance, considering the habitual residence of the child, the respondent, and the creditor, as well as the authority's competence that issued the decision. Article 21 allows for the possibility of partial recognition of a decision, while Article 22 outlines the grounds for refusing recognition and enforcement, which include incompatibility with the public policy of the requested state, evidence of fraud in the proceedings, and the existence of an open judicial proceeding in the requested state, among others. Articles 23 and 24 detail the procedures for processing applications for recognition and enforcement through the central authorities, and Article 25 specifies the documents required to accompany these applications. The remaining articles provide additional details on the regulation and procedure for enforcing and recognizing maintenance decisions rendered by a contracting state.

The Convention's key contributions include the principle of non-discrimination and the adoption of effective measures for the international enforcement of maintenance rights. These measures encompass wage withholding, bank account attachment, deductions from social security benefits, property levies or forced sales, tax refund withholding, pension attachment, credit agency reporting, and the refusal, suspension, or withdrawal of various permits (e.g., driver's licenses[20]). Additionally, it promotes the use of mediation, conciliation, and other alternative dispute resolution methods to achieve voluntary compliance.

The Convention enhances cooperation between authorities, creating mechanisms for the recognition of judgments issued in one contracting state by another state where the minor has a habitual residence. It offers broader global coverage; notably, eleven states and one regional economic integration organization (European Union) have signed the convention, including the United States and Canada—countries that are not parties to the earlier instruments ratified by Colombia regarding maintenance and account for the highest number of requests for information and assistance in obtaining maintenance.

The central authority is tasked with gathering information on the creditor, alleviating the burden on the creditor, and ensuring the recognition and international enforcement of maintenance decisions, including outstanding payments. This authority facilitates access to relevant information regarding the debtor's or creditor's income and economic circumstances, including asset locations. Both debtors and creditors may submit applications, enabling protective measures such as garnishments or wage withholding to ensure the collection of maintenance. The

[20] Colombia does not apply this type of permit withdrawal measures.

convention guarantees access to justice and free legal assistance while establishing effective measures for the enforcement of maintenance decisions.

This represents a significant advancement in transnational maintenance recovery, enabling a much clearer and more efficient procedure before competent authorities.

5 Complex Unregulated Cases

To provide a clearer understanding of the dynamics surrounding surrogacy and assisted reproductive technologies in Colombia, it is essential to consider the discussions held by the Hague Conference on Private International Law. These discussions highlight the interplay between social changes, scientific advances in assisted reproduction, and the current lack of legal protection for biomedical practices in Colombia. This legal vacuum has opened avenues for new global trends, including post-mortem insemination and surrogate motherhood.[21]

Colombia is not immune to these practices. Indeed, family courts and the Constitutional Court have intervened to establish positions that permit them under specific conditions. However, concerns regarding these deliberate practices persist, necessitating regulation not only by local laws but also by norms of private international law.

Surrogate motherhood, or surrogacy, offers an alternative to traditional conception methods for genetic, social, or personal reasons. Currently, there is no specific legislation in Colombia that prohibits the establishment of surrogacy contracts. These contracts are atypical and governed by the autonomy of the private will of the parties involved—the surrogate mother and the biological parents—who negotiate and agree on the contract's terms and effects. While the expression of consent does not need to be in writing due to the consensual nature of the contract, it is advisable to document it, as medical procedures leading to conception typically commence once consent is given.

From a medical standpoint, surrogacy is described as a technique of assisted human reproduction, encompassing a range of biomedical methods designed to facilitate or substitute the natural biological processes involved in human procreation.

The primary challenge in Colombia lies in the absence of comprehensive legislation governing surrogacy, coupled with a burgeoning demand that has given rise to reproductive tourism in major cities.[22] This issue extends beyond mere regulation; it encompasses complex legal considerations regarding applicable laws, nationality, filiation, and the rights of children born through surrogacy and post-mortem

[21] Surrogacy, also known as surrogate motherhood, has been defined by legal doctrine as "the reproductive act that results in the birth of a child gestated by a woman under a pact or commitment to relinquish all rights over the newborn in favor of another woman who will be recognized as the child's mother." Constitutional Court, Judgment No. T-968 of 2009.

[22] GHL Hotels (2023).

insemination. While some countries have explicit regulations that either prohibit or permit surrogacy for altruistic or commercial purposes, foreigners often travel to Colombia from nations where surrogacy is banned, taking advantage of the existing regulatory gaps.

These challenges highlight the urgency of legislation on this subject matter in Colombia. Currently, three laws addressing surrogacy have been sent to Congress. However, the practice continues to proliferate in an uncontrolled manner.

References

GHL Hotels (2023) Turismo reproductivo, una esperanza de familia. https://www.ghlhoteles.com/blog/experiencias/turismo-reproductivo-una-esperanza-de-familia/. Accessed on 12 Oct 2024

ICBF (2024) Subdirección de Adopciones Programa de Adopción. https://www.//efaidnbmnnnibpcajpcglclefindmkaj/. https://www.icbf.gov.co/system/files/estadisticas_adopciones_a_junio_30_2024_0.pdf. Accessed on 12 Oct 2024

IDIBE (2022) Doctrina sobre la noción de "residencia habitual" a propósito de un divorcio keniata. https://idibe.org/derecho-internacional-privado/doctrina-la-nocion-residencia-habitual-proposito-divorcio-keniata/#:~:text=La%20idea%20b%C3%A1sica%20de%20la,concreto%20medio%20socio%2Djur%C3%ADdico. Accessed on 12 Oct 2024

Matarazzo Boriani SA (2016) La adopción en Colombia: un proceso judicial, psicológico y emocional. Reflexión a partir de una experiencia personal. Revista de Derecho Privado 31:409–427

Ministry of Tourism of Colombia (2024) Colombia registró un aumento en la llegada de turistas extranjeros durante el primer semestre de 2024. https://www.mincit.gov.co/prensa/noticias/turismo/aumento-en-la-llegada-de-turistas-extranjeros-2024#:~:text=De%20esta%20cifra%2C%20el%20total,el%20mismo%20mes%20de%202023. Accessed on 5 Oct 2024

Séptimo Día (2018) ¿Dónde está Luciana? La amarga disputa entre colombiana y argentino por su hija. https://www.youtube.com/watch?reload=9&v=NFv_5ZP6pQM. Accessed on 31 Oct 2024

Gloria Rivera Ocampo Lawyer; LLM in Private Law; PhD Candidate; Specialist in University Teaching; Professor, Faculty of Law and Political Sciences, University of Antioquia.

Commerce

Private International Law and Colombian Business Associations Law

Juan Antonio Gaviria

Abstract The intersection between Colombian business association law and private international law is dealt with in this chapter. For this purpose, it identifies the current issues in the international interaction of for-profit entities and their shareholders or partners, studying the former under a double angle or edge: both as juridical persons, and therefore subjects of rights and duties, and international contracts. This entails analyzing the legal rules determining which companies are domestic and foreign and the legal relevance of such a distinction. The chapter also makes some comments on the IADIP Draft General Act on Private International Act for Colombia regarding business association law.

1 Introduction

In Colombia, corporate law has been studied almost exclusively as a domestic area without in-depth analyses on business associations in particular whose purpose and relationships among its constituents happen and have effects in more than one country.[1]

This chapter intends to fill this void by summarizing the current legal rules on private international law applicable to both business associations incorporated in Colombia and shareholders agreements, identifying the main legal issues in such context, and critically commenting the Draft General Act on Private International Law for Colombia regarding its application to for-profit entities.

[1] This is a premise based on the best knowledge of the author. Since it is a negative affirmation, unprovable by definition, there is not any quote here.

J. A. Gaviria (✉)
Escuela de Derecho, Universidad EAFIT, Medellín, Colombia
e-mail: jgaviri5@eafit.edu.co

M. J. Ochoa Jiménez, C. Madrid Martínez (eds.), *A Private International Law for Colombia*, Springer Textbooks in Law,
https://doi.org/10.1007/978-3-032-04106-7_16

By focusing on juridical persons, this chapter leaves out of its scope any kind of joint ventures such as consortiums and partnerships which does not give rise to new legal entities. In the same connection, juridical persons are a broad term that needs to be narrowed before this chapter moves on. The analysis of public entities is excluded, with the text studying only private juridical persons. In this universe, the text focuses on for-profit entities, with any other type of non-for-profit juridical persons such as charities and cooperatives being out of its scope. Most for-profit entities are business associations, but some exceptions exist, such as private interest trusts. This chapter exclusively analyzes business associations. As used here and without limitation to, this term refers to corporations (in Spanish, *sociedad anónima*, or even other companies whose capital is divided into shares, such as *sociedad por acciones simplificada or SAS*, and *sociedad en comandita por acciones*), limited liability companies (in Spanish, *sociedad de responsabilidad limitada*, and also *sociedad en comandita simple*) and incorporated partnerships (in Spanish, *sociedad colectiva*).

To avoid the continuous repetition of the term "business association", the text alternates its use with the words: "companies" (synonymous here), corporations, and for-profit entities, keeping in mind that the latter two have a broader meaning but also that both terms are close to the definition of business associations since most companies have their capital divided into shares and are incorporated to invest assets in some business and, if turns lucrative, distributing dividends later on.

This text is divided into three sections. Section 1 applies private international law to Colombian business association law, identifying both the main issues and the rules in legal force. Section 2 comments on the IADIP Draft General Act on Private International Act for Colombia, regarding business associations. Section 3 makes some concluding remarks.

2 Private International Law and Colombian Business Association Law

Colombian Business Association rules related to private international law are not compiled in consecutive provisions being part of a specific code, law, or decree. On the contrary, there are only a few legal provisions dispersed alongside the different rules governing for-profit entities, such as the Commercial Code (Legal Decree No. 471 of 1971), Act No. 222 of 1995, and Act No. 1258 of 2008, the last one focusing on SAS.

Explicit legal rules with an international perspective in Book 2 on Business Associations of the Commercial Code are almost inexistent, reduced to a few provisions on foreign companies in Articles 469 to 497. Article 469 succinctly provides that any business association incorporated following the law of a country other than Colombia and with a legal seat abroad is a foreign one. The law mentions not one but two requirements for an entity to be foreign. Thus, both a company incorporated under the law of another country but with a legal seat in Colombia, a first case, and a corporation incorporated under Colombian law but with a legal seat out of its borders, a second case, are domestic legal entities. In practice however, most Colombian companies comply with both requirements: having been incorporated in this country and with a legal seat in one of its municipalities.[2]

Notice that, for local corporations, neither Article 110 of the Commercial Code nor Article 5 of the Act No. 1258 of 2008 explicitly orders that a business association has its domicile in Colombia. However, both Articles 112 of the Code and 5 of Act No. 1258 require the registration of the new legal entity in a Colombian Chamber of Commerce, the one having jurisdiction over the municipality that the bylaws provided for as its legal seat. Such Chamber would unlikely accept a legal seat outside Colombia. Thus, and regarding the law governing the internal affairs of a company, Colombian legal rules adopt the place of registration theory and not the real seat theory.[3]

Digressing into the differences between the place of registration and the real seat theories, the latter has the advantage of being closer to the reality of a company's businesses, but with the drawbacks of less predictability and the costs of moving the headquarters when shareholders intend to change the applicable law.[4] As place of registration theory's disadvantages, in turn, it may incentive shopping for places with lax corporate rules, with such location lacking any connection factor other than its legal domicile with a company's business.[5]

Coming back to Article 469 of the Commercial Code, what are the effects of being a foreign company under Colombian law? None, if such legal entity has no business in Colombia, or only infrequent commercial activities there. The effects only arise if the foreign company intends to carry out *permanent businesses* in Colombia. Article 474 mentions some professional activities that are legally categorized as permanents, without resolving the question whether the list is exhaustive. Simply stated, a permanent activity usually exists when the company abroad enters and performs for-profit contracts that requires its focus and a deployment of technological, financial, and human resources for a long while.

An investor intending to pursue permanent activities in Colombia needs to incorporate there either a branch (in Spanish, *sucursal*) or a subsidiary (a business association). In the first case, the branch is not a different juridical person from the investor, just its extension in another country. In other words, the foreign company is directly doing business in Colombia. Consequently, the branch does not limit the liability of the foreign company and, *prima facie*, lacks juridical standing to have rights and duties. In the second scenario, two companies exist, the parent abroad and the subsidiary in Colombia, although it is also possible that a majoritarian shareholder is absent, with several investors incorporating the new entity in this country.

---

[2] See generally Baum and Solomon (2021), p. 432.

[3] See generally ibid.

[4] See generally ibid.

[5] See generally ibid.

Besides the above-mentioned Commercial Code's rules governing branches of foreign companies, the legal rules on business associations with *express* references to private international law are almost nonexistent. Having said that, the implicit mentions and the intersections between private international law and Colombian business association law are multiple.

For instance, a Colombian for-profit entity has, of course, shareholders or partners. They may be individuals, trusts, or any kind of juridical persons.[6] Regardless of whether they are individual or legal entities, the shareholders may be foreigners and, therefore, international investors, subject to foreign exchange rules. On top of that, if a shareholder holds more than the 50% of the voting shares, it could be the parent company of the Colombian subsidiary, and of an entrepreneurial group composed of these two plus some other companies being managed as only one enterprise (Articles 260 and 261 of the Commercial Code). In such a case, the parent company shall file a document acknowledging such legal dominance over its subsidiary before the chamber of commerce having jurisdiction over the legal seat of the latter entity (Article 30 of Act No. 222 of 1995).

As another illustration, cash flows may go from other jurisdictions to Colombia (contributions to capital) or the other way around (dividends), with private international legal rules in general and foreign exchange regulations in particular governing them.

Needless to say, a company's bylaws bind all shareholders or partners. Additionally, some or all of them may enter into shareholders agreements, related either to the vote in general assemblies or to other matters. While the Commercial Code is silent on this topic, both Articles 70 of Act No. 222 of 1995 and 24 of Act No. 1258 of 2008 allow agreements among shareholders other than the bylaws themselves. These legal rules provides that a shareholder agreement shall have been filed at the company's headquarters in order to be legally binding to it.

According to the basic tenets of private international law, shareholders agreements are international ones if they have any foreign element or connection. This happens if at least two signatories have their establishment or place of business or if the agreement has effects in two or more countries. The former scenario is the most likely, especially in agreements binding many parties. The legal rules binding a company, i.e., the law of the country where its legal seat is, is the default law applicable to shareholders agreements; however, absent public policy or mandatory rules prohibiting any change, parties are free to choose a different set of legal rules governing their contract.

Indeed, Article 62 of Act No. 1563 of 2012—the Colombian Arbitration Statute—allows that. Such rule provides that arbitration is international whenever: (i) the parties have their domiciles in different countries at the formation of the contract, (ii) the place of compliance of the agreement is in two or more countries, or (iii) a controversy among the parties affects the interests of international trade. In turn,

[6] For SAS, see Articles 1 and 12 of Law 1258 of 2008.

Article 101 of the same law sets forth that an international arbitration tribunal shall decide based on the legal rules that the parties have freely chosen.

Notice that the law refers to international arbitrations but not to international contracts; as a result, the express freedom to agree on any governing law only exists if the parties provided an arbitration agreement to solve any dispute arising out the contract among them. Absent such arbitration and based on principles of international private law, such freedom may also exist, but there is not any Colombian legal rule explicitly referring to it.

As another illustration, some mergers and acquisitions, with a larger share when they are complex and larger, are international, involving companies and shareholders located or doing business in two or more countries. While Colombian corporate law is silent on international mergers, the Montevideo Convention, incorporated as Act No. 33 of 1992[7] seems to allow them by providing that the law where companies have their legal seats governs any relationships arising out of bylaws and its amendments. Mergers, and their reverse transactions, spin-offs, are amendments to a company's bylaws. In this connection, the doctrine of the Superintendence of Business Associations (in Spanish, *Superintendencia de Sociedades*) has accepted the legal feasibility of transborder mergers although stating that if the foreign company is the one receiving the assets and liabilities of one or more Colombian merged entities, it shall incorporate or keep a branch in Colombia in charge of carrying out the business purpose there.[8]

A third example of business associations' contracts that may have a foreign connection are the relationships between the company and their managers, that is, both the board of directors' members and the legal representatives. Needless to say, they may be foreigners, either as juridical persons or individuals. The international nature of such contracts is especially relevant whenever the legal liability of directors and officers and the applicable law are the main issues of a dispute between them and the company.

Indeed, not only the company. The so-called derivate action allows shareholders to sue, on behalf of the legal entity and even without its authorization, any director or legal representative that might have caused any damages to it. Such action, very common in the United States,[9] the United Kingdom,[10] and Asia,[11] had not been part of the Colombian legal landscape. However, and despite its possible contradiction with laws, which have a higher hierarchy, Decree 046 of 2024 allowed this derivative action in Colombia.[12] Needless to say, the derivate action makes more likely

---

[7] Inter-American Convention on General Rules on Private International Law, signed in Montevideo on May 9, 1979.

[8] See (Article 6.9.4 c) of the *Circular Básica Jurídica* and Opinion (*Oficio*) No. 220-16478 of August 30th, 1994).

[9] See Bainbridge (2015), pp. 207–209.

[10] See Davies and Worthington (2016), pp. 17-1 to 17-39.

[11] See Puchniak et al. (2012), p. 1.

[12] Paragraph 8 of Article 2.2.2.3.4 of Decree No. 1074 of 2015, as amended by Decree No. 046 of 2024.

that any conflict between a company and managers has an international connection. After all, and even if both parties are local, a shareholder filing a suit on behalf of the corporation may be a foreigner.

In turn and topics related to business association law, both insolvency law and tax law have provisions related to international private law. In the former case, Articles 85 to 116 of Act No. 1116 of 2006 governs the so-called trans-border bankruptcies. That is, insolvent companies, with assets, creditors and cash flows located in more than one country, intending either to renegotiate its liabilities with their creditors or to begin a receivership process. In this regard, Act No. 1116 acknowledges the likelihood of two or more insolvency processes taking place in different countries, facilitates cooperation among administrative and judicial authorities, and sets forth the requirements for the recognition and enforcement in Colombia of bankruptcy decisions taken abroad.

In the case of tax law, there is a myriad of legal rules applicable to business association transactions between parties located in different countries. To begin with, the term "permanent establishment" is of common usage in tax law. It refers to a permanent place of business in one country of a foreign investor triggering taxes or at least formal duties such as filing a tax return.[13] Such concept has been incorporated in Colombia, both in Article 20-1 of the Tax Statute (in Spanish, *Estatuto Tributario*) and in the Treaties for Avoid Double Taxation that are in legal force between Colombia and some other countries.[14]

As another example of a tax legal rule with effects both on corporate law and on private international law, Article 12-1 of Colombia Tax Statute defines companies with an effective or real seat in Colombia (in Spanish, *sede efectiva de administración*) as those entities which, despite being incorporated and having a legal seat abroad, have a C-suite taking the main business decisions in Colombia.[15] A foreign company with a tax real seat in Colombia continues being foreign for all legal effects save tax ones. Thus, the foreign corporation is regarded as a Colombian taxpayer; thereby, its world income, and not only its Colombian income, is taxed there (Article 12 of the Colombian Tax Statute).

Many other rules are in the triple intersection of tax law, corporate law, and private international law. Recounting and explaining all of them in depth is beyond the scope of this text. It suffices to mention in passing some other rules, such as treaties for avoid double taxation, that by definition are international, the withholding rates applicable to dividends paid from Colombian corporations to shareholders abroad or vice-versa and, of course, all the laws on transfer pricing.

Despite stating that the law applicable to a Colombian company is the local one, some debate arises, there or elsewhere, depending on the preferred theories

---

[13] See Evans Márquez (1999), pp. 16–17.

[14] See, e.g., Act No. 1082 of 2006, approving the treaty to avoid double taxation between Colombia and the Kingdom of Spain.

[15] See also Articles 12 and 20 of the Colombian Tax Code providing that national companies are taxed for its world income while foreign entities are taxed only for their income obtained in Colombia.

applicable to the legal entity as a juridical person different from its shareholders or partners.

Historically, corporations could only be incorporated after obtaining an authorization (charter) from the king, the Congress, or the President of a certain country.[16] In technical terms, once such permission was obtained, the company was chartered.[17] Under such antique view, a company was a creation of the State and, as such, inextricably connected to its law, without any margin for freedom of contract.[18] The State might even require some corporate purpose or activities.[19]

Nowadays, a charter is no longer required to incorporate a company. Save some entities such as financial institutions, whose crises may entail systemic risks, any individual—directly or through other juridical persons, solely or jointly with other investors—may incorporate a company in Colombia, without minimum capital and costs of registration. Under such regime, corporations could be viewed as the creation of its constituents, who infuse legal life to the new legal person without needing any previous authorization from the State other than the general laws.[20] Under this private-oriented view, freedom of contract would be greater than under the public law stance mentioned in the previous paragraph.

Finally, the nexus-contract theory is well-known.[21] Under it, the company is just a node where multiple relationships among its stakeholders converge. Thus, the purpose of incorporating a new legal entity is to reduce the transaction costs of such interactions. If the company were absent, the relationships among contributors of capital, creditors, suppliers, workers, customers, and the State itself having an international nature would follow the usual rules of private international law and, perhaps, the party autonomy principle. With the incorporation of the company, as a local entity, most of such relations turn into domestic ones, at least a pass-through approach, considering the corporation as just a medium, is taken.

[16] See, in the context of the United States, Winkler (2018), pp. 3–108.

[17] See ibid.

[18] See Dartmouth College v. Woodward 4 Wheat, 518; 4 L. Ed. 629 (1819) Chief Justice Marshall ("Corporation is an artificial being, invisible, intangible, and existing only in contemplation of law. Being the mere creature of law, it possesses only those properties which the charter of its creation confers upon it, either expressly or as incidental to its very existence.").

[19] See Winkler (2018), pp. 3–108.

[20] See Peari (2021), p. 25 ("Instead, corporations are now viewed as independent moral actors; their conduct is unrelated to the states of their creation and to the complex web of agreements within the corporate structure .... This vision of corporations conceptually separates corporations from the state that grants permission for incorporation (under the state-based fiction theory) and from the cluster of contracts that make up a corporation (under the nexus-contracts theory").

[21] See, e.g., Ayotte and Hansmann 2014, p. 1, and O'Kelley (2012), p. 1247.

3 The Draft of the General Act on Private International Law for Colombia and its Application to Business Associations

The *Instituto Antioqueño de Derecho International Privado* (IADIP) has proposed a draft of a general act on private international law, composed of ninety-seven articles. This section comments on some of the Draft's provisions related to business associations.

Article 2 provides "that judges and competent authorities shall apply *ex officio* the foreign law that is designated as applicable by the Colombian conflict of laws rules." After reading the proposed rule, a question jumped to my mind: When do Colombian judges or other authorities apply foreign law? Not frequently. After all, and under the place of incorporation rule that seems mandatory, Colombian companies are governed by Colombian law. Put it another way, and despite the wide scope for private autonomy that Act No. 1258 of 2008 gives for SAS, without referring to other more restrictive business association types, it does not seem possible that a company's bylaws provide that a law of a country different from Colombia will govern it. Thus, parties lack the freedom to choose the law governing the company relationships or *lex societatis*,[22] although some exceptions exist, as explained below.

But this premise focuses on a company as a juridical person. Save the case of a SAS with a single shareholder, it is also a contract giving rise not only to bylaws but to other kinds of agreements among its parties. These might be corporative in themselves (regarding their relationships as shareholders) or related to other type of contracts, such as a share purchase agreement.

It would be possible, therefore, that a judge or other authority has jurisdiction to settle a conflict among parties governed by a law foreign to Colombia. According to the above-mentioned Articles 62 and 101 of the Act No. 1563 of 2012, such a situation is more likely in international arbitration. Also, more logical. Parties may appoint arbitrators with expertise in corporate laws different from Colombian ones. Although unlikely, some Colombian judges might apply foreign laws. In such a case, they would possibly require, in addition to an official translation, some informed opinions from legal experts.

A second legal rule is the first paragraph of Article 4 of the IADIP Draft, providing that "notwithstanding the provisions of this Act, the judge shall apply the overriding rules of Colombian law which, according to this Act, must prevail even when a foreign law is competent".

Colombian legal rules on business associations may be either mandatory or default ones. Most of them do not explicitly say if they are the former or the latter. Anyway, it seems that some mandatory legal rules govern a company incorporated in Colombia and with a legal seat in one of its municipalities, such as complying with the legal procedures required for the entity being a legal person different from its shareholders or partners, having bylaws with the minimal content provided in Articles 110 of the Commercial Code or 5 of Act No. 1258 of 2008, and obtaining

[22] See Holderness (2018), p. 1.

the privilege of limited liability—unquestionably the most important company benefit—,[23] with the legal exceptions allowing third parties to request before a judge the piercing of the corporate veil,[24] On the topic of shareholders agreements, legal provisions requesting the contract to be filed at the company's headquarters in order to be legally binding to it seem also mandatory (Articles 70 of Act No. 222 of 1995 and 24 of Act No. 1258 of 2008). Similarly, and in accordance with the last paragraph of Article 24 of Act No. 222 of 1995, the rules on the legal liability of directors and officers do not seem waivable by contract (i.e., provisions clearing managers of legal liabilities indicated in such law are unenforceable). Thus, and as a paradigmatical example, bylaws cannot provide that managers are exempted from acting in good faith or that they may breach, without legal consequences, their duties of care and loyalty.

Nonetheless, in the context of international business transactions among shareholders, or between them and managers, and especially regarding SAS, legal restrictions should be the exception more than the rule. The principle of private autonomy shall prevail.

In this connection, a distinction shall be made between (i) matters related to contracts between a company and external parties, such as lenders, suppliers, employees, or consumers (extra corporate agreements), and (ii) transactions related to internal corporate affairs, such as those among shareholders or between the entity itself and its managers (intra corporate agreements).

The general rules of both contract law and private international law govern extra-corporate agreements. In them, the company is just a party to a contract. As an exception that proves the rule, some disputes arising out of these transactions may have a corporate content, such as creditors intending to pierce the veil to seize shareholders' assets. Save this exception, where Colombian law is mandatory if the entity is incorporated there, parties can freely choose the applicable legal rules to their international transactions. In other words, the party autonomy principle applies.[25]

Intra-corporate agreements, in turn, are corporate themselves. Examples of them are appointments of directors, legal representatives, and auditors, issuance of shares or dividends, compliance with legal capital, mergers, and bargaining over voting rights.[26]

The law of the country where a company is incorporated applies to its corporate internal affairs, in Colombia or everywhere if the theory of the legal seat applies,

---

[23] See Bainbridge and Henderson (2016), p. 1.

[24] Cfr. Rovira (2006), pp. 107–109 (distinguishing between public policy rules—in Spanish, *orden público*—and mandatory rules. The latter prohibits any agreement contravening them but, in contrast with the former, allow waiving or regulating the rights conferred. Rovira also states that there are few public policy corporate rules but many mandatory ones).

[25] See Baum and Solomon (2021), p. 387.

[26] See Peari (2021), p. 1.

without being possible to choose another law.[27] Here, the rules adhere to the legal seat as the single connecting factor.[28]

In any case, some exceptions to this restriction could arise. The issue here is whether parties incorporating a company, or amending its bylaws, may agree on a clause providing a different governing law, either from another country, a state or province within a country, or even an a-national law. *Prima facie*, under the restrictive Colombian law, the answer is no. Moreover, such choice would not be practical if all or most shareholders are Colombian, and the corporate purpose is to be carried out there.

Notwithstanding, if an international arbitration clause is provided, triggering Articles 62 and 101 of Act No. 1562 of 2012, these rules may trump corporate domestic rules; thereby, parties could freely choose the law governing their agreement. This would be especially useful in a company whose purpose is multinational per se and whose shareholders are nationals or have its domicile or place of business in several countries.[29] As another advantage of this freedom of choice, parties could select the most specialized, advanced, or better law, e.g., Delaware, England Law, etc., a mixture of law (*depeçage*, which could have more drawbacks than benefits[30]) or just a contract without governing law, just referring to international usages, Unidroit principles or some suggested model agreements that a commercial association has drafted.[31]

As a third rule triggering comments here, Article 7 of the IADIP's draft is about evasion of law or *fraus legis*. It provides that "the law designated by the conflict rule shall not apply when the essential principles of the law designated as applicable by the conflict rules has been artificially evaded".

Suppose a Country A's law requires a minimum capital to incorporate a company and, therefore, to limit their shareholders' legal liability before creditors, while a Country B's law lacks such requirements. Assume now that Z intends to do some

---

[27] See Reese and Kaufman (1958), p. 1118 (indicating that the rule subjecting a company to the place of incorporation's law is based on the notion that the state shall control an entity to which it had granted legal existence.

[28] See Baum and Solomon (2021), p. 387.

[29] See Peari (2021), p. 1 (suggesting to incorporate a choice-of-aw clause in the contract governing the internal affairs of a corporation, known as articles of association).

[30] For a case where depeçage turned problematic, see caso the Euro tunnel case, mixing English law and French law: Channel Tunnel Group Ltd. V Balfour Beatty Construction Ltd. (1993) A.C. 334 (H.L.) 347.

[31] The following is a real example of a choice of law in the corporate context. A Russian space scientist residing in the United States, a U.S. businessman and an Italian navy admiral incorporating a company in Delaware to commercialize old Soviet satellites, but with UK laws governing the agreement. Despite an arbitration provision, a dispute was litigated in Delaware for over a decade. See Reid v. Siniscalchi, No. 2874, 2018 WL 620475, at *1–2 (Del. Ch. Jan. 30, 2018) (alluding to the fictional lengthy case of Jardyce v. Jarndyce in Charles Dickens's novel Bleak House, Vice Chancellor Slights noted that "[a]s we approach the eleventh anniversary of the initiation of this action, Reid v. Siniscalchi has readily secured its place as a candidate for the Jarndyce award for interminable legal proceedings"). See also Baum and Solomon (2021), p. 387.

business in Country A but does not want, or cannot from a financial standpoint, make the minimal contribution required there. With the help of her lawyer, Z incorporates a company in Country B to exclusively do business in Country A. This could be categorized by Country A's authorities as illicit legal shopping, that is, an investor choosing Country B's laws to circumvent the more stringent Country A's laws without having any legitimate business purpose to prefer the former rules.

The facts summarized above were not fantasy. They gave rise to a controversy in the famous case C-212/97, Centros Ltd. v. Erhvervs-og Selskabsstyrelsen,

> 1999 E.C.R. I-01459, where Country A and Country B were, respectively, Denmark and the United Kingdom. The Court of International Justice settled the dispute holding that the incorporation of a company in the U.K. to do business in Denmark without complying with the corporate Danish laws requiring a minimum capital was a legitimate decision, based on the principle of free movement of corporations applicable in the European Union.[32]

Thus, the legislation applicable to a Union European's company is the law of its place of incorporation, and not the law of its real seat. Such legal rule gives more relevance to freedom of contract (the benefit) than to the effectiveness of control policies or restrictions in corporate laws (the cost).

Under this doctrine, and at least before Brexit, it was said that the United Kingdom was winning the European and even the global corporate law race, attracting companies through low incorporation costs and flexible legal rules such as the absence of minimum capital requirements or the requirement of employees' participation in management.[33] With the U.K. outside the European Union, this country has lost some European dominance, but it is still well-regarded as providing an efficient and convenient corporate law for international investors.[34]

In the United States, some corporate legal shopping is allowed. While some topics, such as securities law, are under the scope of federal law,[35] most of corporate law is state law. Under the doctrine of internal business affairs,[36] companies may elect the state of incorporation, whose laws will govern it, regardless of the real place of business. This is why many U.S. companies have their domicile in the tiny state of Delaware while operating elsewhere in the country or abroad.[37] Opinions

---

[32] See also Heymann (2019), p. 437.

[33] See Baum and Solomon (2021), p. 387.

[34] See ibid., p. 399 ("After Brexit, the ECJ's case law that protected companies incorporated in the U.K. but that have their real seat in another member state will no longer apply to U.K. companies because the United Kingdom became a 'third country', in terms of European Union law ... Even if the future dominance of the United Kingdom as a locus of incorporation is at risk after Brexit, U.K. law is still a popular choice for global M&A transactions, alongside Delaware").

[35] See, to take two illustrations, the Sarbanes-Oxley Act and Dodd-Frank Act.

[36] See Edgar v. MITE Corp., 457 U.S. 624, 645 (1982), CTS Corp. v. Dynamics Corporation of America, 481 U.S. 69, 90 (1987), and Section 302 of the Restatement (Second) of Conflicts of Law (1971). See also Coffee (2024), p. 1, https://www.law.com/newyorklawjournal/2024/03/20/the-internal-affairs-rule-is-under-attack-should-we-care/?slreturn=20240612144104

[37] See https://corplaw.delaware.gov/delawares-benefits-international-business/ ("Delaware does not require any business activities or offices to be located in Delaware, other than a registered agent. Owners and managers need not be U.S. citizens. Management and investors can vote or take

about the dominance of Delaware are mixed. Some scholars see it as the result of a race to the top, promoting legal innovations and continuous evolution,[38] and inducing states to enact rules protecting long-term investors.[39] Others, in contrast, view it as a race to the bottom that excessively relaxes legal rules in topics such as managers' discretion and liability,[40] triggering incentives to maximize managerial benefits at the expense of investors.[41]

Nonetheless, in cases outside of the EU's rules or the U.S. laws, artificially choosing a law of a country without a real business connection could be illicit shopping. Generally speaking, such practice is common in international public law, termed treaty shopping, as in the case of companies incorporating a shell company in a country with a wide web of tax treaties to take advantage of their benefits to maximize the bottom line of enterprises.[42]

In any case, corporate law shopping is very difficult under Colombian law. The reason is straightforward: Colombia is not a federal country but a unitary republic with a national business association law. There is no competition between company laws governing in different regions of Colombia and, as a result, corporate law is the same from south to north and west to east of the country, either in Bogotá, the capital, or in the smallest town. At the same time, and in contrast with tax law that allows some shopping, there are no significant international treaties regarding corporate law. Notice, in any case, that there is some competition between the SAS (Law 1258 of 2008) and the traditional business association types that the Commercial Code governs, a tournament where SAS has overwhelmingly prevailed.[43]

Having said that, some minor loopholes exist for some corporate legal shopping. For instance, a parent company located in one country and creating a shell subsidiary in another place, being the latter, the corporation entering into a contract with a local investor (e.g., a shareholder agreement) or merging a target entity (a triangular merger) with the dual objective of having the transaction governed by the law of the subsidiary and not of the parent company and, in the case of the merger, having the minority shareholders in the former place.

---

action by written consent from anywhere in the world, without the requirement of a formal meeting; this written consent may be made by electronic means").

[38] See New State Ice Co. v. Liebmann, 285 U.S. 262, 311 (1932), Louis Brandeis's dissenting vote ("It is one of the happy incidents of the federal system that a single courageous state may if its citizens choose, serve as a laboratory; and try novel social and economic experiments without risk to the rest of the country"). See also Baum and Solomon (2021), p. 391, n. 9.

[39] See Romano (1993), pp. 14–16. See generally Bainbridge et al. (2018), p. 1.

[40] See Weitzman (2022), p. 1.

[41] See Bebchuk (1992), p. 1458 and Bratton (1994), p. 403.

[42] See ibid., pp. 435–436 (reporting the results of interviews with practitioners in Mergers & Acquisitions, where the majority of interviewers said that the primary reasons to determine the place of incorporation of the merging company were based on tax law, being corporate grounds secondary, and concluding that contrary to common assumptions that corporate law incentives inter-jurisdictional competition for charters, "corporate law plays a relatively modest role in the incorporation decision").

[43] See Reyes (2018), p. 1.

In turn, Article 15 of the IADIP Draft provides that "the domicile of a legal entity is in the State where the principal place of business or professional activities of the legal entity is located." Thus, the project adopts the real seat theory,[44] and not the place of incorporation or legal seat theory.

According to well-known canons of interpretation and also with Article 10 of the Draft, Article 15 shall be read in harmony with Article 4, about overriding mandatory rules of Colombian law. After all, a Colombian company having its main place of business abroad does not make it a foreign corporation. As long as it continues having its legal seat in Colombia, the legal rules of this country still bind such a legal entity.

Nonetheless, the article of the draft might be relevant in dispute resolutions where a company with more than a place of business is either a plaintiff or a defendant. In such a case, for instance, the nature of arbitration (domestic or international) may depend on where the principal place of business is, which could be either the place of the parent company or the legal seat of the branch, among other options.[45]

Article 15 shall be read in connection with Article 18, setting forth that Colombian courts shall have jurisdiction to hear cases where the defendant, regardless of nationality, has its domicile in Colombia.

The topic of nationality of juridical persons is a contentious one, especially in an era where digital transactions are everywhere[46] and, in any case, beyond the scope of this article. Here, it is assumed that a company has the nationality of the country where it has been incorporated and has its legal seat.

In any cases, the issues arising out of Article 15 do not end there. What if there are several defendants, some domiciled in Colombia but others not? Also, what if the defendants form an entrepreneurial group with one parent entity or individual determining the business purpose of the whole? As to procedural matters, what happens if a subsidiary company is part of an arbitration agreement but not its parent company, located in another country, and which manages the former as a puppet or an alter ego entity?[47] The goal here is not to answer these open questions but just pose them to ignite further discussions and research.

Two final articles on the IADIP Draft related to company law are Article 24, on freely negotiated contracts, and Article 25, on asymmetric contracts. The project, besides making the distinction between these two kinds of agreements, gives more jurisdiction or leeway to Colombian courts in the second case under the assumption that doing so will be beneficial for the less-informed party, likely a consumer or, if an enterprise, a disadvantaged party.

This distinction, however, is problematic in business association law. Here, at least two kinds of contracts exist: these among shareholders and also agreements

---

[44] See Mereminskaya (2001), p. 145.

[45] See Cárdenas Mejía (2017), p. 1.

[46] See Baum and Solomon (2021), p. 387.

[47] See Article 37 of Law 1563 of 2012.

between the company itself and its managers. In the latter case, when is a contract an asymmetric one, and when not? Three scenarios could arise: (i) professional investors and professional managers, without any asymmetry, (ii) occasional investors and professional managers, with the asymmetry against the former, or (iii) sophisticated shareholders and amateur managers, as in the case of individuals expecting that managerial tasks take little time and being the asymmetry here in favor of officers. In any case, drafting a line separating sophisticated and freelance investors or managers is an uphill task.

Asymmetric cases may also arise in disputes between majority and minority shareholders, but these terms are diffuse or ambiguous, at best. Unquestionably, a corporation with a shareholder having 99% and another one with 1% is asymmetrical, but is not so clear when, to take just two illustrations, there are four shareholders each one with 25%, with three of them partially aligned, or one shareholder with 51% and the other with 49% with one shareholder agreement providing the vote on major decisions and protection the latter.

Many other issues may arise in further discussions. For now, it's time to close this chapter.

4 Concluding Remarks

Private international law is expansionary. After all, and setting aside the debate about it, legal globalization is part of the current landscape.[48] Thus, many contracts have a foreign element since either a party to the agreement has its domicile or its purpose is carried out in more than one country. Nonetheless, corporate law in a centralized country such as Colombia put some brakes on this expansion. The singularity of a company as a legal entity different from its shareholders and the fact that local mandatory laws govern the lion's share of its activities restricts the scope of private international law in this field.

This is not to say that private international law and corporate law, in the Colombian context, only intersect in a barren area or are a failed marriage. On the contrary, freedom of contract and the autonomy principle govern many agreements among shareholders, or among them and other stakeholders. In such cases, absent mandatory or public policy rules, parties can choose the governing law and also the procedures that would be triggered if a dispute arise, such as those on arbitration.

Regardless of the freedom of parties to international business associations contracts, the study of Colombian corporate law under the influx of private international law is still in its infancy. This chapter has posed some questions, left open on purpose, that can be the basis of further research.

[48] See, e.g., Muir Watt et al. (2019), p. 1.

References

Ayotte K, Hansmann H (2014) A nexus of contracts theory of legal entities. Int Rev Law Econ 42:1–12. https://doi.org/10.1016/j.irle.2014.10.001
Bainbridge SM (2015) Corporate law, 3rd edn. Foundation Press, New York
Bainbridge SM, Henderson MT (2016) Limited liability. A legal and economic analysis. Edward Elgar Publishing, Northampton
Bainbridge S et al (eds) (2018) Can Delaware be dethroned?: evaluating Delaware's dominance of corporate law. Cambridge University Press, Cambridge
Baum I, Solomon D (2021) The Least Uncomfortable Choice: Why Delaware and England Win the Global Corporate Law Race. S. C. L. Rev. 73:387-436
Bebchuk LA (1992) Federalism and corporation: the desirable limits of state competition in corporate law. Harv Law Rev 105:1435 ff
Bratton W (1994) Corporate law's race to nowhere in particular. Univ Toronto Law J 44:401 ff
Cárdenas Mejía JP (2017) El criterio de internacionalidad en la Ley 1563 de 2012, Comité Colombiano de Arbitraje: https://ccacolombia.org/articulo/2
Coffee Jr J (2024) The internal affairs rule is under attack! Should we care?, NY Law J, March 20, 2024. https://www.law.com/newyorklawjournal/2024/03/20/the-internal-affairs-rule-is-under-attack-should-we-care/?slreturn=20240612144104
Davies PL, Worthington S (2016) Principles of modern company law, 10th edn. Sweet & Maxwell, London, pp 17-1–17-39
Evans Márquez R (1999) Régimen jurídico de la doble tributación internacional. McGraw Hill, Caracas
Heymann J (2019) Freedom of establishment: one step closer to making a European Delaware possible? Free movement of corporations: Centros Ltd. V. Erhvers-og Selskabsstyrelsen. In: Muir Watt H et al (eds) Global private international law, adjudication without frontiers. Edwar Elgar Publishing, New York
Holderness C (2018) Equity issuances and agency costs: the telling story of shareholder approval around the world. J Financ Econ 129:415
Mereminskaya E (2001) Nacionalidad de las personas jurídicas en el derecho internacional. Revista de Derecho 18(1):145
Muir Watt H et al (eds) (2019) Global private international law, adjudication without frontiers. Edwar Elgar Publishing, New York
O'Kelley C (2012) Coase, knight, and the nexus-of-contracts theory of the firm: a reflection on reification, reality, and the corporation as entrepreneur surrogate. Seattle Univ Law Rev 35:1247
Peari S (2021) An Assessment of the US Rules Which Determine the Relevant Law Applicable to Corporations: A Suggestion For Reform. Delaware Journal of Corporate Law 45(3):469
Puchniak D et al (eds) (2012) The derivative action in Asia. Cambridge University Press, Cambridge
Reese W, Kaufman E (1958) The law governing corporate affairs: choice of law and the impact of full faith and credit. Colum Univ Law Rev 58:1118 ff
Reyes F (2018) La SAS, Sociedad por acciones simplificada, 4th edn. Legis, Bogota
Romano R (1993) The genius of American corporate law. American Enterprise Institute, pp 14–16
Rovira A (2006) Pactos de socios. Astrea, Buenos Aires
Weitzman H (2022) What's the matter with Delaware? How the first state has favored the rich, powerful, and criminal—and how it costs us all. Princeton University Press, Princeton
Winkler A (2018) We the corporations. How American business won their civil rights. Liveright Publishing Corporation, Nueva York

Juan Antonio Gaviria , PhD in Juridical Sciences and LL.M., American University, Washington College of Law; Tenured Professor, School of Law in Universidad EAFIT; Member of the Research Group Law and Power, Universidad EAFIT.

A New Beginning for Negotiable Instruments

Daniel Rojas-Tamayo

Abstract Colombian private international law on negotiable instruments is intriguing: very few rules in recent codes and legislation contrast with a rather extensive regulation in antique treaties. Despite both choice-of-law and substantial rules, there are only three rulings of the Colombian Supreme Court on the subject matter. In this context, the IADIP Draft on Private International Law for Colombia studied in this chapter seems to offer a satisfactory and necessary regulation. Furthermore, the IADIP Draft modernizes Colombian law in various manners, such as embracing a different connecting factor and introducing freedom of choice.

1 Introduction

The Draft General Act on Private International Law for Colombia prepared by the *Instituto Antioqueño de Derecho Internacional Privado* (IADIP) (hereinafter, "IADIP Draft") would bring a long-desired evolution for Colombian private international law. It could establish an adequate system for international private relations in Colombia and adopting it could profoundly change existing regulations in certain areas, as would be the case for negotiable instruments. The IADIP Draft devotes a chapter to these instruments.

The title of this chapter and its translation to English deserve a preliminary comment to avoid confusion. The English expression *negotiable instruments* may be translated into Spanish as *títulos valores* or as *instrumentos negociables*. Even though both concepts are close, they are not identical under Colombian law. According to the Colombian Commercial Code, the former is a broader concept and refers to negotiable instruments that represent both credits or merchandise (*lato sensu*), while the latter, as stated by Article 821, is a restricted concept and refers

D. Rojas-Tamayo (✉)
Facultad de Derecho, Universidad Externado de Colombia, Bogotá, Colombia
e-mail: daniel.rojas@uexternado.edu.co

M. J. Ochoa Jiménez, C. Madrid Martínez (eds.), *A Private International Law for Colombia*, Springer Textbooks in Law,
https://doi.org/10.1007/978-3-032-04106-7_17

only to negotiable instruments that have a credit content expressed in a currency (*stricto sensu*). This distinction is important for the characterization[1] of the instruments and the application of the provisions of the IADIP Draft.

The Colombian Commercial Code considers these instruments as commercial goods and regulates the different types of negotiable instruments lato sensu. This category includes bills of exchange (*letras de cambio*), promissory notes (*pagarés*), cheques, bonds (*bonos*), bills of landing (*cartas de porte* or *conocimientos de embarque*), invoices (*facturas cambiarias*), certificates of deposit (*certificados de depósito*) and pledge bonds (*bonos de prenda*).[2] The code establishes their characteristics and conditions and some aspects of the recovery proceedings.[3]

In addition, Colombia has several private international law rules on negotiable instruments latu sensu both in national codes and treaties. The analysis of the IADIP Draft must include all those provisions. Regarding the treaties, it is important to acknowledge that Colombia has participated in multiple conventions. On the one hand, Colombia signed two global conventions of the League of Nations: i) the Convention providing a Uniform Law for Bills of Exchange and Promissory Notes and ii) the Convention for the Settlement of Certain Conflicts of Laws in connection with Bills of Exchange and Promissory Notes.[4] On the other hand, Colombia took part in three regional conventions of the Organization of America States (hereinafter, "OAS"): (i) the Inter-American Convention on Conflict of Laws Concerning Checks, (ii) the Inter-American Convention on Conflict of Laws concerning Bills of Exchange, Promissory Notes, and Invoices and (iii) the Inter-American Convention on Contracts for the International Carriage of Goods by Road.[5] Unfortunately, Colombia signed all of these conventions but never ratified them.

---

[1] The Colombian Supreme Court of Justice has never ruled on the issue of characterization. Nevertheless, most Colombian authors consider that characterization must be conducted under *lex fori*. See, e.g., Calero Tafur (2016), p. 60; Monroy Cabra (2017), p. 275; Marín Fuentes (2021), p. 68. Colombian Law is in this matter like other important jurisdictions, see, e.g., Bucher and Bonomi (2004), para. 531; Symeonides (2016), p. 67; Audit and d'Avout (2018), para. 279; Fernández Rozas and Sánchez Lorenzo (2020), para. 101; Niboyet et al. (2023), para. 321.

[2] The Colombian Commercial Code gathered the provisions of several laws and codes that regulated the different types of negotiable instruments (Robledo Uribe 2021, p. 98); for example, the 1870 Colombian Maritime Commerce Code and Act No. 46 of 1923 on Negotiable Instruments. The latter act was inspired by the act on negotiable instruments of the United States of America (Londoño Hoyos 2021, p. 319). Instead, the Colombian Commercial Code was influenced by European authors (the Italian Vivante and the German Kuntze, see Pérez Vives (2021), pp. 101–102), and especially by the Uniform Law on Negotiable Instruments for Latin America prepared by the Mexican professor Ramón Cervantes Ahumada for the INTAL (Robledo Uribe 2021, p. 96).

[3] Articles 619 to 821.

[4] Both treaties were signed in Geneva, on June 7, 1930. Colombia was represented by Antonio José Restrepo Trujillo (1855–1933), a historian, author and politician from Antioquia of the late 1800s and early 1900s. It is worth noticing that these treaties were followed by two similar others on Cheques, signed in Geneva, on March 19, 1931, to which Colombia didn't take part.

[5] The first two conventions were signed in Panama, on January 30, 1975, and entered into force. The third convention, signed in Montevideo on May 15, 1989, didn't enter into force.

Finally, it is important to mention two additional elements that should be considered to analyze the chapter on negotiable instruments of the IADIP Draft. First, since its publication in 2021, very little information has surfaced about the objectives, the principles, and the rules of the IADIP Draft.[6] One may regret the absence of an explanatory memorandum, which would have been valuable to understand the IADIP Draft and the drafting choices made by its authors. For example, it could have clarified the sources of inspiration, the preference for certain connecting factors above others, and the reasons that justify the changes proposed to the existing rules. Second, the authors disagree on the importance of negotiable instruments in today's international trade. Some consider their legal framework still of interest,[7] while others affirm that their use in today's international trade has declined.[8]

Consequently, the analysis of the IADIP Draft must be preceded by examining the current regulation.

2 Current Regulation

As mentioned above, Colombia has private international law rules on negotiable instruments in national codes and international treaties. These rules differ in scope and method, so they deserve a separate analysis.

2.1 National Legislation

International negotiable instruments have a scarce legal framework in Colombian law. In fact, from both the legislative and the case law perspective, Colombian private international law has only a few rules that could be applied to negotiable instruments. The adoption of the IADIP Draft would only affect one provision in the Colombian Commercial Code. Moreover, the Colombian Supreme Court of Justice has never ruled on these provisions.

The Colombian Commercial Code, adopted in the 1970s, contains two provisions that could apply to international negotiable instruments: Articles 646[9] and 746.[10] The latter refers to the possibility of cashing a traveler's cheque at the issuer's

[6] The Institute held several conferences about the IADIP Draft, some of which are available at the Institute's social media platforms. The authors declared to have followed the Inter-American Commission, especially regarding cheches and bills of exchange.

[7] Geva and Peri (2020), para. 2.94.

[8] Hugo (2020), p. 244.

[9] "Instruments created abroad will be considered as negotiable instruments if they meet the minimum requirements established in the law governing their creation".

[10] "Traveler's checks shall be issued by the drawer at his own expense and shall be payable by his principal place of business or by the drawer's branches or correspondents at home or abroad.

main office, branches, or correspondents, wherever they may be. This provision should be considered a substantial rule of private international law that compels financial institutions in Colombia to pay a traveler's cheque issued abroad by its head office or one of its branches. Hence, it ensures the payment of foreign traveler's cheques.

In contrast, the characterization of Article 646 Colombian Commercial Code seems more problematic. It provides that any instrument issued abroad may be considered a negotiable instrument if it meets the conditions set out by the law that governed its creation. According to Marín Fuentes,[11] this provision is based on the traditional *locus regit actum* principle enshrined in Article 21 of the Colombian Civil Code.[12] Hence, negotiable instruments would be governed by the law of the state where they're issued.

At first glance, the Colombian Supreme Court of Justice seems to share this characterization. In the only decision to ever mention Article 646,[13] the Civil Chamber considered in the 1995 *Salzenstein* ruling that this Article was a choice of law rule.[14] In this decision, the Colombian Supreme Court of Justice distinguished two kinds of choice of law rules (or *normas de colisión* as she called them): (i) perfect or bilateral rules and (ii) remission rules. The latter kind, of which Article 646 would be an example, "defers the resolution of a conflict to foreign law.[15]"

The Colombian Supreme Court of Justice underlines an interesting nuance of Article 646. Indeed, this rule doesn't seem to simply provide for applying a law, whether local or foreign, designated by a connecting factor. In other words, it doesn't purely submit foreign negotiable instruments to the law of the place of their creation. Instead, it considers such instruments as negotiable if all the requirements of the law that governed its creation are fulfilled. For some authors, this kind of rule represents a different methodology, called *prise en consideration*, because instead of indicating the application of a law, they require the judge to consider a given content of a law designated by a given connecting factor.[16] One may even think that the expression "will be considered" in Article 646 encourages this characterization. Nevertheless, characterizing this provision as a special choice of law rule, remission or *prise en consideration* rule seems artificial.[17] Article 646 will inevitably compel judges to apply the law that governs the instrument's creation whenever the dispute is related to this act.

[11] Marín Fuentes (2021), p. 171.

[12] "Article 21. The form of public instruments shall be determined by the law of the country in which they are created ..."

[13] The book edited by Valencia Copete and Garcés Díaz (2008), which is considered one of the principal doctrinal sources in the matter, does not have any reference to a decision by the Colombian Supreme Court of Justice applying Article 646 of the Colombian Commercial Code.

[14] Colombian Supreme Court of Justice, Civil Chamber, August 3, 1995, exp. 4725, Gaceta Judicial T. CCXXXVII, vol. 1, pp. 299–305, 302.

[15] ibid.

[16] Mayer and Heuzé (2014), para. 144.

[17] In this sense, see Niboyet et al. (2023), para. 264.

This doesn't mean that this provision is a traditional choice of law rule founded in the *locus regit actum* principle. Certainly, Article 646 prescribes (only for negotiable instruments created abroad) the application of a foreign law eventually. But which law doesn't depend on the place of creation of the instrument as it should be following the above principle. In contrast, it commands the application of the law that governed the creation of the instrument, which may or may not be that of the place of creation, and it could well be Colombian law. For example, the parties could create a negotiable instrument abroad but according to Colombian law. So, according to Article 646, Colombian judges should apply Colombian law.

Furthermore, applying this rule seems difficult in practice because the identification of the place of creation of negotiable instruments could be uncertain. On the one hand, neither the indication of this place nor that of the law that governed its creation are requirements for the existence of these instruments under the Colombian Commercial Code.[18] On the other hand, in case the date and the place of creation are not mentioned, paragraph 4 of Article 621 provides that "the date and place of its transfer shall be deemed as such," which, in the event of an endorsement, could mean that there are various applicable laws or that the applicable law may change.

In any case, the *Salzenstein* ruling should not be considered a precedent on international negotiable instruments for two reasons. First, this ruling didn't truly apply Article 646 of the Colombian Commercial Code, which was only mentioned to illustrate the exceptions to the principle of territoriality. Second, the issue of the decision was the recognition of a Venezuelan judgement on the adoption of a Colombian citizen under foreign law.

Two other decisions are related to international negotiable instruments: the *Cuervo*[19] and *Camacho Roldán*[20] rulings. The origin of both rulings was unpaid bills of exchange. Nevertheless, these decisions aren't precedent either for several reasons. First, these rulings predate the current Colombian Commercial Code. Second, the Colombian Supreme Court of Justice ruled under Article 20 of the Colombian Civil Code as if the existence of the debts and their performance were to be determined in the application of the traditional *lex loci contractus* and *lex loci solutionis* choice of law rules for international contracts. Finally, the bills of exchange were only considered as evidence of the debts.

National legislation and case law don't adequately regulate international negotiable instruments. They are outdated. After all, they haven't evolved since the 1970s, when the Commercial Code entered into force, and insufficient because they only regulate some issues.

[18] See Articles 621, 671, 709, 713, 759, 760, 768, 769, 774, and 776 of the Colombian Commercial Code. Only numeral 8 of Article 754 implies, in the case of bonds, that there should be an indication of the place of creation.

[19] Colombian Supreme Court of Justice, December 15, 1900, Gaceta Judicial T. XV, No. 748–749, pp. 121–132.

[20] Colombian Supreme Court of Justice, December 17, 1902, Gaceta Judicial T. XVI, No. 791–792, pp. 49–59.

2.2 International Treaties

As mentioned, Colombia has participated in several supranational initiatives on negotiable instruments. Nevertheless, Colombia's only convention in force regulating this matter is the 1889 Montevideo Treaty on International Commercial Law. This treaty entered into force for Colombia in 1993 and is applicable when one of the parties is in Colombia and the other is in Argentina, Bolivia, Paraguay, Peru, and/or Uruguay, which greatly reduces its territorial scope. The 1889 Montevideo Treaty on International Commercial Law devotes the entire chapter IX to Bills of exchange. The nine provisions of this chapter[21] are mainly, but not exclusively, choice of law rules that may be applicable to other negotiable instruments.

Regarding the scope of the chapter, although all the provisions were conceived in view of bills of exchange, according to article 33[22] they can be applied to vouchers (*vales*) and promissory notes "insofar as they apply to them". It is worth noting that the Colombian Commercial Code doesn't use anymore the name "vouchers," which were considered equivalent to *pagarés* in Colombian law.[23] Therefore, the treaty would only apply to bills of exchange and promissory notes. However, the Colombian Commercial Code could facilitate an extension of the treaty's scope. Indeed, as the treaty does, Article 766 on certificates of deposit and pledge bonds, Article 771 on bills of landing, and Article 779 on invoices, defer to the regulation of the bill of exchange whenever it may be appropriate. Thus, the treaty could apply to these negotiable instruments by analogy.

Most of the treaty's provisions on bills of exchange are inspired by the *locus regit actum* principle. The angle adopted by the treaty consists of designating the applicable law to the acts related to negotiable instruments and not to these instruments themselves based on their location (*lex rei sitae*). These acts are in general governed by the law of the country where they take place.

In that sense, the form of the drawing, endorsement, acceptance, and protest is governed by the law of the country where each of these acts takes place (Article 26). In a relatively different manner, the principle inspires the rules of the first part of Article 27 and those of Articles 28, 29, and 32 of the 1889 Montevideo Treaty on International Commercial Law. The first rule provides that the law of the country where bills of exchange are issued applies to the relations between the drawer and the payee. According to the latter provisions, the obligations of the acceptor concerning the holder, the legal effects of the endorsement between endorser and endorsee, and of the acceptance by intervention are governed by the law of the country where the acceptance (Article 28), the endorsement (Article 29) or the intervention (Article 32) took place, respectively.

---

[21] Articles 26 to 34.

[22] "The provisions of this Title apply to vouchers, bills of exchange or commercial paper, insofar as they are applicable to them".

[23] Colombian Supreme Court of Justice, Civil Chamber, August 22, 1941, Gaceta Judicial T. LII, No. 1979, pp. 354–364, see Valencia Copete and Garcés Díaz (2008), p. 731.

Some authors considered that these rules don't address all the issues that may arise. For example, Caicedo Castilla affirmed that the treaty was silent regarding the relations between the holder and the drawee.[24] Nevertheless, Article 28, which designates the applicable law to the obligations of the drawee/acceptor, addresses part of those relations.

These rules are perfectly aligned with the trends of their time. In Colombian law, the *locus regit actum* principle was considered a reasonable exception to paragraph 3 of Article 20 of the Colombian Civil Code, which establishes the application of Colombian Law whenever the performance of a contract takes place in Colombia.[25] Moreover, since each act would be governed by the law where it takes place (autonomy theory[26]), which would eventually imply that multiple laws apply, the treaty is equally aligned with the ideas that inspired the Colombian Civil Code.[27] However, today, the application of such rules may seem artificial. Certainly, the acts could well take place online, raising the question of the localization of the place of the act, and any mention of a place could be misleading.

Even if the *locus regit actum* principle is the dominant trait, there are two exceptions in the 1889 Montevideo Treaty on International Commercial Law. First, the second part of Article 27 provides that the law of the country of the domicile of the drawee governs the relations between the drawer and the drawee. Second, per Article 31, the aval is governed by the law that governs the obligation that is guaranteed. The treaties adopted in Montevideo in 1940 abandoned this last rule.[28]

Finally, the 1889 Montevideo Treaty also has one substantial private international law rule and a rule on jurisdiction. The first one is ascertained in Article 30, which provides the severability of the rights originally acquired by the drawer and the acceptor to the greater or lesser extent of the obligations of the respective endorsers. The second is a classic jurisdiction rule inspired by the *actor sequitur forum rei* maxim. Article 34 provides that claims between parties involved in negotiating a bill of exchange must be brought in the courts of the domicile of the defendant.

As follows, the regulation of the treaty may lead to the application of multiple laws, and even if their scope didn't overlap, it would be a source of complications. Unfortunately, there is no trace of the application of the provisions of the 1889 Montevideo Treaty on International Commercial Law on bills of exchange by Colombian judges or courts. The 1889 Montevideo treaties on international commercial law and on international civil law have only been the subject matter of the C-276/93 ruling of the Colombian Constitutional Court,[29] which decided on their

[24] Caicedo Castilla (1960), p. 466.

[25] At the time of the adoption of the treaty, this principle or maxim was considered part of Colombian private international law on negotiable instruments, see Restrepo Hernández (1914), p. 466.

[26] Caicedo Castilla (1960), p. 462.

[27] Bello (1873), pp. 95 and 103.

[28] Caicedo Castilla (1960), p. 465.

[29] Colombian Constitutional Court, Full Chamber, July 12, 1993, No. C-276/93.

constitutionality. Sadly, the court restricted its opinion to issues of form related to the Colombian Congress's act of approval (*ley aprobatoria*) of the treaty.[30]

In summary, the current legislation is scarce and insufficient. The lack of provisions of the Colombian Commercial Code and the limited scope of the 1889 Montevideo Treaty on International Commercial Law are enough reasons to consider adopting a new regulation, such as the one proposed in the IADIP Draft.

3 The IADIP Draft General Act on Private International Law for Colombia

The IADIP Draft proposes four provisions (Articles 91 to 94) on negotiable instruments in Chap. 16. Although the sources of inspiration haven't been disclosed, it seems that the IADIP Draft is like the 1930 Geneva Convention for the Settlement of Certain Conflicts of Laws in connection with Bills of Exchange and Promissory Notes (hereinafter, "Geneva Convention"), the Swiss Federal Act on Private International Law and the National Civil and Commercial Code of Argentina.

It should be noted that one of the rules of the IADIP Draft is a substantial private international law rule. Article 92 enshrines the autonomy (severability) principle, which prevents the extension of the invalidity of one obligation according to its applicable law to the other obligations deriving from a single negotiable instrument whenever these obligations are valid under their applicable law. While this provision is close to the second paragraph of Article 2660 of the Argentinian Code, a similar principle can already be inferred from Article 627 Colombian Commercial Code. Nevertheless, this provision doesn't specify which connecting factor designates the applicable law.

The other provisions in Chap. 16 are choice-of-law rules. The IADIP Draft adopts various connecting factors, but the place of payment plays a key role.

3.1 *The Place of Payment*

In contrast to the Colombian Commercial Code and the 1889 Montevideo Treaty on International Commercial Law, the place of payment is the main connecting factor in the IADIP Draft. However, this factor will sometimes have a subsidiary role.

First, the place of payment is the principal connecting factor in two provisions of the IADIP Draft. On the one hand, according to Article 93, the law of the place of payment determines the procedures and time limits for acceptance, presentation for collection, payment, protest, and other diligences necessary to avoid the expiration

---

[30] This position was later abandoned, see Colombian Constitutional Court, Full Chamber, August 5, 1993, No. C-313/93.

of the right of the holder of the instrument. Despite some similarities with the Geneva Convention (Article 7) and the Argentinian Code (Article 2659), this rule is relatively original because it has a broader scope and a different connecting factor.

On the other hand, under Article 94, the same connecting factor determines the measures to be taken for theft, robbery, forgery, loss, destruction, or material disablement of the instrument. This provision has much more in common with Article 2661 of the code and, to a lesser extent, with Article 9 of the convention. The coincidence between the IADIP Draft and the Argentinian Code probably lies in a mutual source of inspiration: the Uniform Law on Negotiable Instruments for Latin America prepared by the Mexican professor Ramón Cervantes Ahumada for the *Instituto para la Integración de América Latina* (INTAL).[31]

This common ancestor may also explain the use of *theft* and *robbery* (*hurto* and *robo*) that appear both in the IADIP Draft and the code. Although in Colombian private law these terms are often used together, sometimes as synonyms,[32] it is noteworthy that robbery is not punishable conduct under Colombian criminal law nor mentioned by the Geneva Convention.

Second, the place of payment will also have a subsidiary role. According to Article 91, in the absence of a choice of law, the law of the place of payment shall apply to the circulation of credits, negotiable instruments, or other credit rights. Even if the provision doesn't provide for explicitly, the same rule should apply to the relations with third parties.[33] The IADIP Draft differs from the Swiss Act, its source of inspiration, in two elements. On the one hand, the IADIP Draft is a more concise version of Article 105.2 of the Swiss Act.[34] On the other hand, the connecting factor is different. Indeed, the Swiss Act favored the state of the pledgee's habitual residence.

The adoption of the IADIP Draft would have several consequences. First, it would constitute a solution to the legal gap in national legislation because its rules address issues that don't have any regulation in the Colombian Commercial Code. Second, the IADIP Draft would entail the existence of two different solutions in Colombian Law depending on the territorial scope of the 1889 Montevideo Treaty on International Commercial Law: if the treaty applies, each act related to a negotiable instrument would be governed by the law of the place where they take place and, if not, they would be governed by the law of the place of payment.

Furthermore, the new connecting factor would potentially favor applying a unique law to negotiable instruments. For Caicedo Castilla, this would mean the adoption of the unity theory,[35] although related to the place of payment instead of the place of creation, with some exceptions, that will be analyzed in the next section.

---

[31] Valencia de Urina (2013), p. 15.

[32] See Articles 1675, 2266, 2267, and 2268 Colombian Civil Code and 402 and 803 of the Colombian Commercial Code.

[33] Bucher and Bonomi (2004), p. 235.

[34] This paragraph was recently amended by the Federal Act of 25 September 2020 on the Adaptation of Federal Law to Developments in Distributed Ledger Technology.

[35] Caicedo Castilla (1960), p. 461.

Nevertheless, the place of payment raises some issues. First, most negotiable instruments are not required to indicate this place under the Colombian Commercial Code.[36] To this respect, paragraph 3 of Article 621 of the Colombian Commercial Code provides that, in the absence of such indication, the place of payment would be the place of domicile of the drawer. The place of payment could be inferred from other requirements in the case of bonds (Article 754), certificates of deposit (Article 759), pledge bonds (Article 760), bills of landing (Articles 768 and 769), and invoices of transport (Article 776). Second, the *Cuervo* and *Camacho Roldán* rulings show that the place of payment indicated in the instrument may be different from that where the payment is claimed. This could raise the question of which of the two should apply, encouraging the application of the *lex fori*.

Although the place of payment is key and undeniably one of its main features, the IADIP Draft proposes other connecting factors.

3.2 Other Connecting Factors

The IADIP Draft also uses other connecting factors regarding negotiable instruments. However, these will only have a limited application.

Above all, the IADIP Draft allows freedom of choice. This is undoubtedly its most important contribution to Colombian private international law and will take it closer to modern trends.[37] Paragraph 1 of Article 91, following Article 105.1 of the Swiss Act closely, allows the parties to choose the law that governs the pledging of claims, negotiable instruments, or other credit rights.

This provision is special for its scope. First, the rule also applies to credits in general. This broader scope implies that the IADIP Draft establishes a different solution than the 1889 Montevideo Treaty on International Civil Law. According to this treaty, credit rights are goods and are governed by the law of the country where they're situated (the traditional *lex rei sitae* rule embraced in Article 26), which is deemed to be the place of performance of the obligation to which they refer (Article 29). The coexistence of this treaty and the IADIP Draft would mean, as discussed above regarding the 1889 Montevideo Treaty on International Commercial Law, that freedom of choice would only be possible when the treaty does not apply.[38] The abandonment of the traditional *lex rei sitae* rule seems justified by the fact that credits are immaterial property not situated in a specific place.[39]

Second, the scope of the freedom of choice is limited. Indeed, Article 91 provides that the choice of law cannot be asserted against third parties. According to Bucher and Bonomi, "this choice of law does not concern the pledge contract, but

[36] See Articles 621, 671, 709, 713 and 774 of the Colombian Commercial Code.

[37] The freedom of choice is also authorized in contracts (Article 73) and torts (Article 85).

[38] On the freedom of choice in the Montevideo treaties, see Albornoz (2010), p. 32.

[39] Bucher and Bonomi (2004), p. 235.

the act by which the pledge right is constituted". In their view, this nuance explains why the choice does not affect third parties, even if it reduces the utility of the choice of law.[40] Finally, the broader scope also explains the absence of a provision on voluntary assignment in Sect. 2 (Contracts) of Chap. 14 (Obligations).

Furthermore, there are two hypotheses where the place of payment is complemented by another connecting factor. First, Article 93 designates subsidiarily the law of the place where the act is to be performed to govern the procedures and time limits for acceptance, presentation for collection, payment, protest, and other diligence necessary to avoid the expiration of the right of the instrument's holder. This means that the *locus regit actum* principle isn't completely abandoned by the IADIP Draft but has only a secondary role.

Second, Article 94 provides that, in the case of loss, theft, or destruction of negotiable instruments issued in series and publicly offered, the dispossessed holder must comply with the provisions of two different laws: on the one hand of the law of the place of payment, as mentioned above, and of the domicile of the issuer. The application of the latter seems perfectly reasonable, given the special characteristics of the instruments envisaged by this provision.

The proposal contained in the IADIP Draft (four provisions) may seem less thorough than the 1889 Montevideo Treaty on International Commercial Law (nine provisions). Certainly, some elements of negotiable instruments aren't explicitly dealt with in the IADIP Draft. For example, the form of negotiable instruments isn't even mentioned. Nevertheless, the categories regulated by the IADIP Draft, which are broader than those of the 1889 Montevideo Treaty, could include the ones that aren't directly mentioned. The choice of the place of payment as a connecting factor, despite the difficulties that it implies and the various exceptions, has some advantages that can perfectly justify the adoption of the IADIP Draft.

4 Conclusion

Existing regulations on negotiable instruments have some flaws. First, they are insufficient because they only regulate some issues or instruments. Second, they are outdated: the Colombian Commercial Code dates to the 1970s, and the Montevideo Treaty on International Commercial Law to the nineteenth century. Third, and most notably, their provisions haven't been applied, and only a few decisions of the Colombian Supreme Court of Justice could be of any use for issues related to negotiable instruments.

Therefore, adopting the IADIP Draft would be of great importance for Colombian private international law because it will establish a sufficient and modern regulation for negotiable instruments that could simplify international trade. The initiative of the Institute should not only be applauded but endorsed.

---

[40] ibid.

References

Albornoz M (2010) Choice of law in international contracts in Latin American legal systems. J Priv Int Law 6(1):23–58
Audit B, d'Avout L (2018) Droit international privé. LGDJ, Paris
Bello A (1873) Principios de derecho internacional. Garnier, Paris
Bucher A, Bonomi A (2004) Droit international privé. Helbing & Lichtenhahn, Basel
Caicedo Castilla JJ (1960) Derecho internacional privado. Temis, Bogota
Calero Tafur MA (2016) Calificaciones. Un problema sin solución ideal. In: García Matamoros LV, Aljure Salame AA (eds) Teoría general del derecho internacional Privado. Universidad del Rosario Legis, Bogota, pp 51–62
Fernández Rozas JC, Sánchez Lorenzo S (2020) Derecho internacional privado. Civitas Thomson Reuters, Cizur Menor
Geva B, Peri S (2020) International negotiable instruments. Oxford University Press, Oxford
Hugo C (2020) Negotiable instruments as instruments of payment in international trade. In: Research handbook on international commercial contracts. Edward Elgar, pp 244–261
Londoño Hoyos F (2021) Títulos-Valores en el nuevo Código de Comercio. In: 50 años del Código de Comercio. Tirant Lo Blanch, Bogota, pp 319–332
Marín Fuentes JL (2021) Derecho internacional privado: síntesis y análisis evolutivo. Ibáñez, Medellin
Mayer P, Heuzé V (2014) Droit international privé. LGDJ, Paris
Monroy Cabra MG (2017) Derecho internacional privado. Temis, Bogota
Niboyet M-L, de Geouffre de la Pradelle G, Fulli-Lemaire S (2023) Droit international privé. LGDJ, Paris
Pérez Vives Á (2021) Los títulos-valores en el nuevo Código de Comercio. In: 50 años del Código de Comercio. Tirant Lo Blanch, Bogota, pp 101–103
Restrepo Hernández J (1914) Derecho internacional privado. Imprenta de La Luz, Bogota
Robledo Uribe E (2021) Los "Títulos-valores" en el nuevo Código de Comercio. In: 50 años del Código de Comercio. Tirant Lo Blanch, Bogota, pp 95–100
Symeonides SC (2016) Choice of law. Oxford University Press, New York
Valencia Copete CJ, Garcés Díaz LR (2008) Derecho de los títulos valores. Universidad Externado de Colombia, Bogota
Valencia de Urina H (2013) Guía de clase. De los títulos valores. Universidad La Gran Colombia, Bogota

Daniel Rojas-Tamayo, PhD, University of Paris II Panthéon-Assas and Universidad Externado de Colombia; Associated Professor, Department of Civil Law, Universidad Externado de Colombia.

The *Lex Mercatoria* Method: Addressing International Private Cases Beyond Conflict of Laws

Néstor Raúl Londoño Sepúlveda

Abstract This chapter examines the use of *lex mercatoria* as a substitute legal system for transnational private conflicts. The l*ex mercatoria* is a set of *ad hoc*, international rules that originate from non-state entities and govern business transactions outside of the conventional conflict of law system. In international arbitration, for example, arbitrators frequently rely on it in the lack of clear national legal frameworks. These transnational rules continue to offer adaptable solutions in international trade, addressing legal gaps and enhancing both domestic laws and international treaties, despite criticism regarding their regulatory scattering. The chapter explores the development of the *lex mercatoria*, its origins, and its empirical application.

1 Development and Recognition of the *Lex Mercatoria*

In his 1973 book *Le Pluralisme des Méthodes en Droit International Privé*, Batiffol includes a type of material rule which he called "spontaneous rule" (*droit spontané*),[1] which is not created by the action of any government, state power, or the international community. The existence of this type of rules allows for the possibility of another method of regulating private international situations in addition to the conflict method and the application of conventional and supranational rules.

Batiffol noted that private relationships in international trade spontaneously created these rules. He established that such standards are, for example, model contracts, delivery conditions, general usages, etc. For him, these rules prevent the use

[1] Batiffol (1973), p. 107.

N. R. Londoño Sepúlveda (✉)
Facultad de Derecho, Universidad Pontificia Bolivariana, Medellín, Colombia
e-mail: nestor.londono@upb.edu.co

M. J. Ochoa Jiménez, C. Madrid Martínez (eds.), *A Private International Law for Colombia*, Springer Textbooks in Law,
https://doi.org/10.1007/978-3-032-04106-7_18

of the system for determining applicable law based on conflict rules. However, he acknowledges that these are not positive rules and that their existence challenges the traditional idea of rules of law produced by states.[2]

At this point, Batiffol's work gives rise to a new method, which has been identified by other authors as the *lex mercatoria*,[3] since it recognizes the existence of this spontaneous law, the enunciation of which had already been postulated by Clive Schmitthoff and Berthold Goldman.[4] It is a method that has mainly been in the hands of arbitrators and is based on a set of transnational rules. The academic sector was at first reluctant to recognize the existence of this third method since it does not identify a legal system of rules.[5]

The modern idea of the existence of a system of rules alien to state systems is linked to Berthold Goldman's *Frontières du Droit et Lex Mercatoria* of 1964. He uses the term *lex mercatoria* to refer to a set of norms that were appearing at the time in international trade operations, by virtue to the principle of party autonomy, such as the INCOTERMS (International Terms of Trade) and the rules relating to documentary credit, both instruments created by the International Chamber of Commerce (ICC).[6]

A few years later, in 1986, Goldman himself would define the *lex mercatoria* as "…a set of general principles and customary rules spontaneously referred to or elaborated in the framework of international trade, without reference to a particular national system of law."[7]

In 1964, Schmitthoff's *The Law of International Trade, Its Growth, Formulation and Operation* appeared. This work similarly acknowledges the existence of a universal custom used by businessmen and recognized as a source of law. This universal custom gave rise to a new *lex mercatoria*, which would be the beginning of a legal system independent from states.

Schmitthoff defined this modern *lex mercatoria* as an autonomous law, belonging to international trade and based on generally accepted standards of commercial conduct.[8] The author points out that this autonomous system has two main legal sources: international law and international trade customs. It states that the first source consists of a set of rules that are introduced into national legislation.

> ...consists of commercial practices, usages, or standards which are so widely used that businessmen engaged in international trade expect their contracting parties to conform with them and which are formulated by international agencies, such as the International Chamber of Commerce, the United Nations Economic Commission of Europe, or international trade associations.[9]

---

[2] Ibid., p. 122.

[3] Pereznieto Castro (2003), pp. 137, 140.

[4] Hatzimihail (2008), p. 174.

[5] Espinosa Pérez (2007), p. 12.

[6] Goldman (1964).

[7] Goldman (1986), pp. 113–125.

[8] Ibid., p. 139.

[9] Ibid., p. 149.

Ultimately, agree that the existence of this new system is partly due to international arbitration. This is a result of the fact that a normative system may function most effectively when it is controlled by arbitrators who are not obligated to protect a certain state policy. Therefore, it is imperative to address this legal phenomenon within a regulatory framework or agency specifically focused on private international law. This work seeks to elucidate the presence of a legal method that serves as an alternative approach for resolving international disputes, particularly those pertaining to commercial affairs.

2 The Sources of *Lex Mercatoria*

In its beginnings, the *lex mercatoria* was characterized by its legal sources. This is because it was necessary to identify the origin of this new set of rules that prescribed solutions to the problems of international trade, one of the characteristics of which was its ability to overcome legal barriers. On the one hand, this set of rules applied even to relations between countries with capitalist economies and those with communist-type state-planned economy systems. On the other hand, they overcame the differences between countries with legal systems of Roman-Germanic law and those of *common law*,[10] as the *lex mercatoria* implies a disengagement of local legal conceptions and their legal technicisms to provide neutral solutions that contribute to free international trade.[11]

In the definition of the contour of the modern *lex mercatoria*, the main reference is the work of Klaus Peter Berger (1999). In his book "The Creeping Codification of the New *Lex Mercatoria*,"[12] he shows the gradual process of creating or reproducing normative precepts. This process has resulted in the sources that are known today, and which allow for their easy consultation, interpretation, and application by legal operators, as well as the adoption of these as a set of written rules to regulate relations of private interest.

Among these sources are the UNIDROIT Principles on International Commercial Contracts,[13] which appeared for the first time in 1994 and which at that time was a "new form of international trade law" in the words of one of the main architects of these principles, Joaquim Bonell. The originality of these Principles is that they do not fit into any of the types of legal instruments used in international trade until that time, such as trade terms, model contracts, and clauses, international treaties, or national legislation.[14]

[10] Lowenfeld (1990), p. 133.

[11] Lando (1985), p. 748.

[12] Berger (2010).

[13] Brower and Sharpe (2004), p. 202.

[14] Joachim Bonell (1995), p. 1122.

Defining the *lex mercatoria* from this point of view, however, shows one of its alleged weaknesses: regulatory dispersion. This is one of the main criticisms that lead opponents to regard the *lex mercatoria* as a legal system applicable to international contracts. This regulatory dispersion is confusing in some cases, not because there are rules on a variety of topics that cover part of the problems—as is also the case—but because they regulate the same issues in different ways.

Examples of such redundancy of bodies of principles are in contrast to those produced by UNIDROIT;[15] with the Trans-Lex—a project led by Klaus Peter Berger, successor to the "Transnational Law Digest & Bibliography," which was managed by The Centre for Transnational Law at the University of Cologne, Germany, from October 2001 to March 2009[16]—and with the Principles of European Contract Law (PECL) sponsored by the European Parliament Commission on Contractual Law—headed by Professor Ole Lando of the Copenhagen School of Business, Denmark.[17]

It is such an academic astonishment that these bodies of principles in their day generate—since it was a true legal novelty—that this leads to Joachim Bonnel's work concentrating in large part on trying to understand what they are and why they are leading to providing an increasing number of solutions that are perceived as just.[18]

This is probably the most controversial of all concepts of the *lex mercatoria*,[19] since it approaches this legal phenomenon as if it were a system equivalent to national systems, as a kind of competitor,[20] or a global law or an expression of it.[21] Therefore, to determine whether the *lex mercatoria* is in itself a legal system, it is necessary to identify what are the characteristics of a legal order and to verify whether they can be established for the *lex mercatoria*.

For Gaillard, any system or legal system, to be such, must have four characteristics: integrity, structured character, ability to evolve, and predictability. This author conceives the right disconnected from power, because the *lex mercatoria* clearly does not emanate from an organization endowed with sovereignty and with the ability to impose decisions on individuals as states do.[22]

---

[15] International Institute for the Unification of Private Law. (2010). UNIDROIT Principles 2010. Retrieved from Unidroit.org: http://www.unidroit.org/instruments/commercial-contracts/unidroit-principles-2010.

[16] Center for Transnational Law - University of Cologne. Trans-Lex Principles. Retrieved from Trans-Lex.org: http://www.trans-lex.org/principles.

[17] Commission on European Contract Law (2002) The Principles of European Contract Law 2002 (Parts I, II, and III). Retrieved from Lexmercatoria.org: http://www.jus.uio.no/lm/eu.contract.principles.parts.1.to.3.2002.

[18] Joachim Bonell (1995), p. 1134.

[19] Schultz (2008), p. 686.

[20] Calvo Caracava and Carrascosa González (2012), p. 507.

[21] Le Goff (2006), p. 125.

[22] Gaillard (2001), p. 65.

However, it must be borne in mind that in the common law systems, law does not necessarily arise from written texts produced by a power invested in the ability to create rules. This is the case for the customary law, where the role of the state is reduced to recognizing its legal capacity if it meets certain conditions previously established by the judges or legislators.

For Schultz, it is necessary to start from the idea that legal systems have external and internal characteristics. The first is that it must have a sufficient structure and be independent of other systems. The latter refers to the quality of the rules that make it, such as its publicity, the predictability of decisions based on them, and its systematic nature.[23]

In essence, what this and other authors intend to do is to answer the question about what law is. The answer will depend on the schools of thought and authors who have tried to answer this question to explain the reality of social life. Therefore, each of these guidelines has its idea of what characterizes law. Depending on whether they are in favor of recognizing the power of the *lex mercatoria*, they will find that those elements that they attribute to their particular conception of what law is can or cannot be verified in the *lex mercatoria*.

Gaillard argues that, if the *lex mercatoria* is conceived as a list of sources, rules of private creation that regulate only certain aspects of commercial relations, these would hardly be sufficient in relation to the criterion of integrity of a legal system, so he proposes a methodological approach.[24] And that is logical, because the academic consensus about the conception of national law does the same, by resolving its internal gaps by means of a methodological proposal. Thus, the arbitrators will apply the *lex mercatoria* to find the solution to the case, even when its solution is not expressly envisaged. The rules for carrying out this task are not explained by the author, but it sheds light on the action of the arbitrators when applying the *lex mercatoria*, pointing out that such action in itself is not capricious, but obeys rules that are not clear enough.

In the context of private international law, this problem is even more serious, since each domestic legal system is supposed to be hermetic, when the judge of one state is called upon to apply the law of another state, the latter must be subject to the criterion that a judge should apply that foreign law as closely as possible to what the court from which the rule originates would do.[25] However, since the reference made by the conflict rules is considered integral, it would be assumed that when applying foreign law, the national court would have to apply the rules governing the problem of legal voids. This requires that such rules be invoked and proved, and this poses an additional problem: the likelihood that these rules do not exist, because that legal system does not have express rules to fill the voids in the law.

However, a legal system with all the solutions is nothing more than a claim since it cannot deny a national law its character as such. Thus, regarding foreign law, it

[23] Schultz (2008), p. 688.

[24] Gaillard (2001), p. 66.

[25] Calvo Caracava and Carrascosa González (2013), p. 482.

will be used on a trial on the assumption that it possesses hermetic fullness, although the rules used by the judge to fill the gaps come from the *lex fori*.

This leads us to a conclusion: a set of sources gives rise to an incomplete legal entity in itself, full of gaps and uncertainties. But this does not prevent it from being considered a legal system, provided that it has an internal methodology that produces a kind of internal closure and gives it autonomy.

3 Empirical Approach to the Scope of the *Lex Mercatoria*

Determining the actual dimension of the implementation of transnational rules requires addressing two fundamental issues. On the one hand, define the frequency with which the parties determine the application of these to their international relations. On the other hand, clarify the application of these by international arbitrators and national judges when resolving legal conflicts with elements of internationality.

The conduct of such research requires, however, a priori acceptance of certain limitations. On the one hand, the information available constitutes only a fraction of the totality of trade law decisions that are issued worldwide. This is because many judgments are confidential, as they have been agreed upon by the parties involved or so set by the policies of the institutions administering the arbitrations.

An empirical study conducted in 2004 by Christopher Drahozal of the University of Texas took as a sample the law covenants applicable to cases submitted to ICC arbitration between 2000 and 2003 and concluded that between 74% and 80% of such cases opted for a national law.[26]

Similarly, the ICC provides more recent information in this area. Thus, in their statistics on arbitration cases filed between 2007 and 2011, it is estimated that 85% of the parties chose the applicable law through a clause. Of the total of these contracts analyzed (3615),[27] 98% of the parties chose as applicable a national law, 1% the Vienna Convention on the International Sale of Goods, and with respect to the rest, 8 cases used the INCOTERMS, and 7 cases chose the UNIDROIT principles, among other instruments of international commercial law.[28]

Among the national laws chosen (about 3551 contracts analyzed), the laws of England and Wales (in 14% of cases), Swiss law (13%), French law (8%), German law (7%), State of New York law (5%), Brazilian law (3%), and Mexican law (2%) appear first.[29] This trend continues even today and can be seen in the current reports of the ICC Arbitration Court:

[26] Drahozal (2005), p. 539.
[27] Fry et al. (2012), p. 220.
[28] Ibid., p. 223.
[29] Ibid., p. 224.

> In 2023, 2% of all contracts relied upon included reference to rules or instruments other than national laws, such as the United Nations Convention on Contracts for the International Sale of Goods (CISG), the UNIDROIT Principles of International Commercial Contracts, "international laws and rules," amiable composition, and the ICC INCOTERMS.[30]

4 Resorting to the *Lex Mercatoria* in the Absence of Choice of Law

In cases where the parties have not explicitly or tacitly agreed on the governing law, the arbitrators will determine the necessary rules to resolve the issue without any influence from either side. This is mainly due to the authorization that arbitration regulations normally grant to arbitrators to determine the applicable law. This goes hand in hand with the fact that the arbitrators must exercise their powers to provide a prompt and effective solution to cases that are brought before them, offering a material solution to the case. In such situations, UNIDROIT principles have been used as a tool to provide answers to the disputes raised, as their regulatory premises are in line with the aspirations of order in international commercial relations.

An example of the use of the UNIDROIT principles as a rule applicable to a contract in the absence of choice by the parties is the 1995 ICC Law 7110 derived from an arbitration administered by the ICC.

In this case, the arbitral tribunal decided to apply the above-mentioned principles in the absence of explicit indication by the parties of the applicable law. The court highlighted the quality of the principles, their relationship with the 1980 Vienna Convention, and the clarity of its rules, which, by having the format of a restatement, facilitate the process of access and arbitral interpretation.[31]

This ICC Award 7110 has been cited in many other subsequent pages. Among them is highlighted the ICC Award 10422. It is based on a contract in which there is no explicit clause of law applicable to the parties, but in which they expressed the desire for a neutral settlement of the dispute. This leads arbitrators to apply the UNIDROIT principles, recognizing in them the quality of their legal formulations and solutions.

The reasons for using these principles are set out as follows:[32]

> Now, in the absence of an express indication as to the domestic law of a third country, the most appropriate solution in the case in which the parties express their desire for a neutral solution is to apply the general rules and principles of international contracts, the so-called *lex mercatoria*.

---

[30] ICC (2023). Dispute Resolution 2023 Statistics (2024). Retrieved from: https://iccwbo.org/wp-content/uploads/sites/3/2024/06/2023-Statistics_ICC_Dispute-Resolution_991.pdf. p. 13.

[31] Bulletin of the ICC International Court of Arbitration, 1999, vol. 10/2, p. 39.

[32] ICC International Court of Arbitration. (2001). ICC International Court of Arbitration 10422. Retrieved from UNILEX: http://www.unilex.info/case.cfm?id=957.

In this context, for questions concerning general contract law, reference can be made to the "UNIDROIT Principles of International Commercial Contracts" which represent—except for a few provisions (such as for example the provisions on hardship: see ICC Award N° 8873 of 1998, in Journal droit int., 1998, p. 1017)—a "restatement" of the rules that parties engaged in international trade consider to be consonant with their interests and expectations. This has been recognized in numerous arbitral awards in which the UNIDROIT Principles have been applied as an expression of the *lex mercatoria* or of international trade usages.

5 Application of the *Lex Mercatoria* as a Complementary Rule

Special material rules of conventional origin or instruments of uniform law contain formulas calling for the use of complementary sources when their text is insufficient to regulate the issue. This is the case in both the 1980 Vienna Convention and other legal instruments of conventional origin. This formula, which is set out below, has led to a debate around the space occupied by the UNIDROIT principles in these instruments, as well as the *lex mercatoria* in general.

Article 7.2 of the Vienna Convention of 1980 provides that: "Questions concerning matters governed by this Convention which are not expressly settled in it are to be settled in conformity with the general principles on which it is based or, in the absence of such principles, in conformity with the law applicable by virtue of the rules of private international law."[33] Defining what should be understood by these general principles referred to in Article 7.2 means defining the scope of UNIDROIT principles as a complementary instrument to this Convention.

The same rule appears in different international conventions, such as Article 7.2 of the UNIDROIT Convention on Agency in the International Sale of Goods (Geneva, 17 February 1983),[34] Article 4.2 de la UNIDROIT Convention on International Factoring (Ottawa, May 28, 1988),[35] Article 6.2 of UNIDROIT Convention on International Financial Leasing (Ottawa, May 28, 1988),[36] Article 7. United Nations Convention on the Assignment of Receivables in International Trade

[33] Hof van Cassatie, Bélgica (June 19, 2009). Retrieved from: http://cisgw3.law.pace.edu/cases/090619b1.html.

[34] International Institute for the Unification of Private Law. (1983). Convention on Agency in the International Sale of Goods. Retrieved from UNIDROIT.org: http://www.unidroit.org/instruments/agency.

[35] International Institute for the Unification of Private Law. (1988). UNIDROIT Convention on international factoring. Retrieved from UNIDROIT.org: http://www.unidroit.org/instruments/factoring.

[36] International Institute for the Unification of Private Law. (1988). UNIDROIT convention on international financial leasing. Retrieved from UNIDROIT.org: http://www.unidroit.org/instruments/leasing/convention-leasing.

(New York, 2001),[37] and Article 5.2 United Nations Convention on the Use of Electronic Communications in International Contracts (New York, 2005).[38]

The role of UNIDROIT principles as complementary to the 1980 Vienna Convention has been a subject of extensive debate. Such a controversy can also be understood in relation to other aforementioned conventions since they contain identical provisions.

Joachim Bonell explains that there is a tension between two extreme positions. On the one hand, those authors who indicate that the UNIDROIT principles complement the Convention based on the wording of Article 7.2, and, on the other hand, those who deny this possibility. My view—which may be seen as a third option between two extreme positions—is that only those aspects of the Convention that reflect the principles on which the Convention is inspired serve to complement its text.[39]

In the case Scafom International BV v. Lorraine Tubes SAS,[40] which was brought before the Belgian courts and was finally ruled on before the Court of Cassation of that country, a contract for the international sale of goods is dealt with. The parties had purchased steel pipes and, after the conclusion of the contract, a 70% increase in steel prices was presented. Given the huge economic variation, the seller tried to renegotiate the contract, but the buyer rejected it on the plan.

Given the situation, the Belgian court recognized a legal void in the 1980 Vienna Convention, in that it found that it did not regulate the excessive burdens that arose and rejected the application of French law made by the court of the second tier. The Belgian High Court concluded that the void had to be filled with the general principles of commercial law before resorting to the applicable national law.

The Court of Cassation then ruled that, based on Article 7.2 of the Convention, the void had to be filled by the UNIDROIT principles and referred to the provisions on excessive over-expenditure, which implies the right to request the renegotiation of the contract in the event of events that were not foreseen at the time of contracting and that are beyond the control of the subject. However, the court in Belgium orders the renegotiation of the contract in good faith, in cases of a change in the performance balance of the contracts.[41]

The ICC has also managed another arbitration, known as the chemical fertilizer case, identified under No. 8128 of 1995.[42] In this case, a contract was discussed between an Austrian seller and a Swiss buyer, which did not contain an applicable law pact. The court, based on its analysis of the case, concluded that the 1980 Vienna

---

[37] UNCITRAL (2001). Retrieved from: https://uncitral.un.org/en/texts/securityinterests.

[38] UNCITRAL (2005). United Nations Convention on the Use of Electronic Communications in International Contracts (New York, 2005). Retrieved from: https://uncitral.un.org/en/texts/ecommerce.

[39] Bonell (2009), pp. 100–117. p. 110.

[40] Hof van Cassatie and Bélgica (19 de junio de 2009).

[41] Ibid.

[42] ICC Arbitration Court (1995), Award 8128. Retrieved from: cisgw3.law.pace.edu/cases/958128i1.html.

Convention was applicable. In principle, several articles of the Convention were applied to the settlement of the case, but in the end, the buyer claimed interest in the seller's amounts due, owing to the cancellation of the contract.

Since Article 78 of the Convention did not establish the applicable interest rate, the arbitral tribunal found that an international rate such as LIBOR, applicable to interbank contracts in contracts on the London market, was applicable. The arbitral panel cites to justify its decision Articles 7.4.9 (2) of the UNIDROIT Principles and 4.507 (1) of the PECL Principles. Article 7.4.9 (2) of the Principles (1994 edition) states:

> The rate of interest shall be the average bank short-term lending rate to prime borrowers prevailing for the currency of payment at the place for payment, or where no such rate exists at that place, then the same rate in the State of the currency of payment. In the absence of such a rate at either place the rate of interest shall be the appropriate rate fixed by the law of the State of the currency of payment.[43]

The above-mentioned arbitration found that these two bodies of legislation corresponded to the principles set forth in Article 7.2 of the Convention. Consequently, it established the LIBOR rate plus 2% as the short-term credit rate for companies.

In France, the case SCEA des Beauches v. Société Teso Ten Elsen GmbH & CoKG reached the Grenoble Court of Appeal (Commercial Division). In this case, the buyer requested the seller to refund the money, as he considered that the value paid exceeded the invoiced value. In judging the case, the court considered that there was a principle that "payment must be made at the creditor's domicile, a rule to be extended to other international commercial contracts following Article 6.1.6 of the UNIDROIT Principles."[44]

As a general conclusion to the recent cases, it is clear that UNIDROIT principles have been used by judicial and arbitral courts as a complement to certain specific issues of the regulation of international contracts. For example, to define the interest rate to be applied to a monetary obligation,[45] or to determine the place where obligations are to be paid, such as the place of restitution, considering that they must follow the general principle of payment at the creditor's home.[46]

---

[43] The same rule appears in versions 2004, 2010, and 2016 of UNIDROIT Principles of International Commercial Contracts. Retrieved from: https://www.unidroit.org/instruments/commercial-contracts/.

[44] Cour d'appel de Grenoble, Francia (23 de octubre de 1996), también en Revue critique de droit international privé, 1997, 756.

[45] ICC Arbitration Court (1995), Award 8128, Unilex. China International Economic and Commercial Arbitration Commission, People's Republic of China (September 2, 2005). Retrieved from: cisgw3.law.pace.edu/cases/050902c1.html; Supreme Economic Court of the Republic of Belarus, Belarus (May 20, 2003); ICC Arbitration Court (1996) France, Award 8769. Retrieved from: www.unilex.info/case.cfm?pid=1&do=case&id=397&step=FullText; ICC Arbitration Court (1995) France, Award 8128, Journal du droit international, 1996, 1024 ss.; Internationales Schiedsgericht der Bundeskammer der gewerblichen Wirtschaft–Wien, Austria (June 15, 1994).

[46] Cour d'appel, Grenoble, France (October 23, 1996), also Revue critique de droit international privé, 1997, 756.

In addition, two arbitral decisions have been detected recognizing that UNIDROIT principles are practices of international trade that meet the conditions of the aforementioned article.[47] Accordingly, in accordance with such decisions, they would be implicitly incorporated into the contract.

ICC Award 9333 of 1988 particularly provides for the application of Section 7.4.9 of the UNIDROIT Principles with regard to the payment of an outstanding monetary obligation between the parties, recognizing that the contract does not exclude the possibility of collecting interest on amounts that have been delayed in payment. The jury therefore acknowledges that the collection of interest is the minimum compensation for the damage caused to the creditor, and recognizes that both the 1980 Vienna Convention and the UNIDROIT Principles accept it, thus constituting a use of trade incorporated into the contract.[48]

Particular attention is to be paid to the Venezuelan Supreme Court of Justice Rc. 000738 of 2014, which, after describing the role that the uniform use created by the ICC plays concerning the mercantile lex, recognizes that the law of that country's Private International Law orders the application of the commercial lex in Articles 30 and 31. Both precepts, which order the application of the *lex mercatoria* in the style of a conflict rule, expressly stipulate the following:

> Article 30. In the absence of a valid indication, contractual obligations are governed by the law with which they are most directly linked. The court will take into account all objective and subjective elements arising from the contract in determining that Right. It will also take into account the general principles of international commercial law accepted by international bodies.
>
> Article 31. In addition to the provisions of the preceding articles, the norms, customs, and principles of International Commercial Law, as well as generally accepted commercial practices and practices, shall apply, as appropriate, to fulfil the requirements of fairness and equity in the settlement of the particular case.

Consequently, the Tribunal decided to apply the UCP-500 to this particular case, in which Banque Artesia Nederland N.V., of the Netherlands, filed a lawsuit against Corp Banca, Banco Universal C.A. of Venezuela, for non-compliance with a document collection contract. The Venezuelan court notes:

> It follows from the quote that an important aspect of international banking activity, for the regulation of which, several rules have been created and accepted, which according to the will of the parties can be found or not included in the contract, and which have become, as is pointed out in the transcript, in something more than a collection of practices. Consequently, by giving the complainants the right to refuse to apply articles 30 and 31 of the International Private Law Act, as regards the commercial lex and the rules contained therein in banking matters, it is necessarily justified to declare the wrongful non-application.[49]

---

[47] International Commercial Arbitration Tribunal of the Chamber of Commerce and Industry of the Russian Federation (5 June 1997), Russia, Unilex. ICC Arbitration Court (1988), Switzerland (Award 9333), Unilex.

[48] ICC Arbitration Court (1988), Switzerland (Award 9333), Unilex.

[49] Tribunal Supremo de Justicia - Sala De Casación Civil (2014) Judgment No. RC.000738.

However, Venezuelan law is not the only one that requires consideration of international trade practices and customs. Other legislation uses formulas that call upon law enforcement to consider such criteria and therefore recognize the use of transnational rules. When such rules are effectively applied, they demonstrate their ability to provide appropriate solutions by indirectly recognizing their jurisdiction.

6 Application of the *Lex Mercatoria* as a Reference to the Solution Under National Law

Probably the most widespread trend in the use of UNIDROIT principles, which appears in decisions from both national judges and arbitrators, is to resort to principles as a way of supporting a particular legal solution based on national law. That is, the authority (the judge or arbitrator) takes the national law applicable to the contract—by mandate of the indirect method or the autonomy of the will—and establishes a theory about how it is applied and, to support that position, quotes the UNIDROIT principles showing how the solution proposed in the *lex causae* coincides with an enunciation of these principles.

Good examples of this use of UNIDROIT's principles are the 1998 ICC Award No. 9117 and the 1997 Award No. 8817.

In the ICC Award 9117[50] a substantiated international contract for the sale of goods between a seller from Russia and a buyer from Canada was analyzed. The seller delivered part of the goods before the expiry of the United States import license, delivering the remainder after its expiry. The buyer refused to pay the full price of the goods, arguing that the seller may have shipped the whole goods before the expiry of the license, and argued that he had violated the buyer's exclusive import duties in the United States.

Given this situation, the arbitral tribunal found that the parties did not choose the applicable law, so it was concluded that the 1980 Vienna Convention was applicable, and, where not covered by this text or the practices of international trade, the law of the Russian Federation would be applicable.

Regarding the UNIDROIT principles, the arbitral tribunal found that, although they were not directly applicable, it was informative to refer to them as they reflected a global consensus on the basic aspects of contract law. Accordingly, the Tribunal uses Articles 2.1.17—Integration Clauses and 2.1.18—Amendment in a particular form of the UNIDROIT principles, to confirm the rule of Article 29.2 of the Vienna Convention of 1980.

[50] ICC Arbitration Court (1988), Zürich (Award 9117), Unilex. Retrieved from: http://www.unilex.info/case.cfm?pid=2&do=case&id=661&step=Abstract.

On the other hand, ICC Award No. 8817 of 1997,[51] resolve a dispute concerning the distribution and sale of food products between a company from Denmark and another company from Spain. Since the contract concluded by the parties did not contain an applicable legal agreement, the arbitrators applied the Vienna Convention—particularly Article 9.1. This was confirmed by the referees by referring to Section 1.8 of the UNIDROIT Principles—called contradictory behavior or *venire contra factum proprium*—to indicate the binding nature of the practices established by the parties. Furthermore, the referees applied Article 77 of the Convention, confirmed by Article 7.4.8 of the UNIDROIT Principles, on the duty to mitigate the damage of the affected party.

In the judicial context, there are plenty of examples of national courts following this trend. Thus, the UNILEX database reports 240 cases in which national judges have used UNIDROIT principles—Russia with 51 cases, Spain with 30, Italy with 22, Ukraine with 20, the United Kingdom with 15, Australia, China, and Lithuania with 14 each, and the Netherlands with 12.[52]

For example, in Spain, the application of Article 7.3.1 of the UNIDROIT Principles and Article 8.101.1 of the PECL Principles was used as a reference to clarify when a serious breach of compliance is understood to result in a legal sanction under Spanish civil law. Accordingly, Article 7.3.1, particularly its paragraph 2b, constitutes the most cited article of the UNIDROIT principles by the Spanish Supreme Court.

In the case No. STS 2823/2014,[53] the court decides on the case Promedios, Exclusivas de Publicidad, S.L., v. Empresa Municipal de Transportes de Valencia, SLU. There was a contract between the two companies to operate advertising on the EMT buses for a period of four years, from 1 August 2006 to 31 July 2010. However, in April 2009, Promedios noted that there was a crisis in advertising investment and drops in their revenue that made it impossible to continue in the contract. In the face of this situation, he appeals to the courts for recognition of the "rebus sic stantibus" rule.

The tribunal rule:

> In this line, for the UNIDROIT Principles the unpredictability derives from the fact that events should not have been foreseen "by the disadvantaged party, nor that they fall within their sphere of control." The principles of European Contracting Law (EPL) configure it with regard to the fact that such change "could not reasonably be taken into account at the time of conclusion of the contract." In similar terms, the European Procurement Project, in relation to which this change "was not taken into account and cannot be expected to be taken into consideration" and, in short, our proposal for the Pre-Draft Modernisation Act.

The Spanish Supreme Court concludes that in 2006—the date on which the contract was concluded—the crisis of the magnitude that would arise in Spain afterward was

[51] ICC Arbitration Court (1997), Paris (Award 8817), Unilex. Retrieved from: http://www.unilex.info/case.cfm?pid=1&do=case&id=398.

[52] UNILEX (2024). Selected Cases by Court. Retrieved from: https://www.unilex.info/principles/cases/country/all.

[53] Cendoj: 28079110012014100324.

not foreseeable, a characteristic note of the figure enshrined in Article 6.2.2 of the UNIDROIT Principles.

Regarding Colombia, a limited number of judgments by courts of second instance and the Supreme Court of Justice have been found to have referred to UNIDROIT principles. Among others, the following were identified:

The Superior Court of Bogotá, the appeal body, in the decision of September 11, 2015,[54] ruled in the case Quibarca Colombia C.I. S.A. v. Algranel SA and SGS Colombia SA. This was initially brought before the District of Bogotá Civil Court 7 to recognize the existence of a deposit contract with Algranel and an audit contract with SGS. In this dispute, it was claimed that the defendants should be sentenced to pay damages for their non-compliance. The court notes that it is not possible to recognize the existence of a deposit contract, since the parties concluded a contract with multiple and varied obligations, governed by the parties' provisions, and states:

> Indeed, it is imperative to remember the principle that the parties are free to conclude a contract and to determine its content (UNIDROIT Principles 2010). Therefore, nothing prevents the parties from autonomously regulating their obligations, by resorting to the legal regulation that gives a set of rules to those contracts that are most common in trade, without anything preventing them from creating its own rules in accordance with the needs of the trade in goods.

The Court of Appeal concludes by pointing out that the parties can even subject their contract to the UNIDROIT principles, provided that it does not contradict Colombian mandatory rules.

Furthermore, the Supreme Court of Justice, the highest court in civil matters in Colombia, issued the judgment of 21 February 2012.[55] It studied a domestic case in which claimants were credited based on a variable index that depended on inflation rates, known as UPAC, which increased exorbitantly because of the inflationary processes that Colombia experienced in the 1990s. The case discussed the variation in the balance of the benefits of the parties, for which the court cited the UNIDROIT principles as a source to corroborate the assessments on the legal phenomenon that are recorded in Colombian law.

The Colombian Supreme Court, in its judgment of April 8, 2014,[56] concerning a case brought before Judge 12 Civil of the Medellin Circuit in the first instance, acknowledged a complaint for breach of an exchange contract. In this case, the court rejected all claims of the lawsuit, a decision that was confirmed by the Superior Court of Medellin. The central argument for the denial was that both parties violated the contract and, therefore, were not allowed to make mutual demands. The Supreme Court, in one of its paragraphs, finds:

---

[54] Tribunal Superior del Distrito Judicial de Bogotá Sala Civil de Decisión Bogotá, D.C. (September 11, 2015). File: 11001 31 03 007 2002 13327 01.

[55] Corte Suprema de Justicia, Sala de Casación Civil, February 21, 2012, File 11001-3103-040-2006-00537-01.

[56] Corte Suprema de Justicia, Sala de Casación Civil, April 8, 2014, File 0500131030122006-00138-01.

> The Vienna Convention of April 1, 1980, referring to a substantive breach, provides in its article 64 that the seller may declare the contract terminated if the breach of any of his obligations constitutes a "substantive contract breach." The compilation of UNIDROIT and the Principles of European Contract Law, do not ignore the right of contractual resolution.

In this case, therefore, the court considers that the complainant was entitled to terminate the contract on the basis of Colombian law and with the aforementioned instruments of *lex mercatoria*, but since in this case the claimant chose not to fulfill his obligations, it is concluded by the court that he was no longer allowed to claim the performance of the contract.

In a judgment of August 30, 2011, the Colombian Supreme Court of Justice examined the case of Mr. Luis v. Compañía Nacional de Microbuses Comnalmicros S.A. It was a claim for non-compliance with vehicle affiliation or linking contracts because they were terminated unilaterally. In the first instance, the Civil Court 3 of the Bogotá Decongestion Circuit declared the defendant's contractual civil liability. In the second instance, the Supreme Court of Bogota revoked the decision and denied the claims.

The Colombian Supreme Court recognizes the possibility of unilateral termination of contracts established in the 1980 Vienna Convention and the UNIDROIT Principles and proclaims:

> In the same sense, the UNIDROIT Principles on International Commercial Contracts, the third version adopted by its Board of Directors, establishes the right of a party to terminate the contract if the non-compliance of the counterparty constitutes an essential breach (Article 7.3.1.1) or, if, before the date of performance of the contract, there is certainty that the debtor will incur a substantial default, the creditor may settle it (Article 7.3.3), in which case "The right of a party to terminate the contract is exercised by notice to the other party" (Article 7.3.2.1).

Thus, the Court concludes: "Unilateral termination in any of the forms or modalities, cannot be exercised with abuse, or in bad faith, with the penalty of liability." Consequently, the Court upheld the second-instance judgment by finding that the defendant's behavior followed these precepts.

In the case Compañía Suramericana de Seguros S.A. v. Compañía Transportadora SA, of September 8, 2011,[57] the Supreme Court of Justice examined the case that was brought in first instance before the First Civil Court of the Bogota Decongestion Circuit, in which the insurer subrogated itself in the insured's rights for the damage in goods imported from the United States for the oil industry occurred during the shipping.

In the first instance, the defendant was held liable as a maritime agent, and compensation was ordered. In a second instance before the Supreme Court of Bogota, the judgment was confirmed, and the compensation increased. In this case, the relevance of the establishment of compensatory heights in the contract and whether these are admissible were discussed. The Supreme Court carries out the following analysis:

---

[57] Corte Suprema de Justicia, Sala de Casación Civil, September 8, 2011, File 11001-3103-026-2000-04366-01.

Recent regulations of international commercial law and new trends in the *lex mercatoria* affirm the widespread interest in regulating the conditions under which the parties can agree on the contractual liability regime. For example, Article 7.1.6 of the UNIDROIT Principles, 2010, according to which, a party may not invoke the limitation or exemption clause, in the event of a breach of an obligation, or if it allows a substantially different benefit from that reasonably due to the other party, or its implementation is manifestly unfair.

In this case, it was finally acknowledged that such contractual limits were in accordance with Colombian law and ruled on their recognition.

About this case, something else must be pointed out: the courts ignored the choice of law made by the parties to the contract of the United States law, the Carriage of Goods by Sea Act (COGSA), and applied Colombian law, because they had filed the lawsuit before the Colombian judges as if this entailed a submission to the laws of Colombia. This is a legal error that is relatively frequently committed by the Colombian courts: there is confusion about international jurisdiction and the law applicable to international contracts, a matter which in this case was not addressed in cassation since the appellant did not bring the respective claim against the second-instance judgment. This situation demonstrates the need for a rule in Colombia that properly regulates international private law.

As a conclusion of a review of judicial and arbitral decisions that somehow use UNIDROIT principles, it is clearly indicated that most of the time, such principles are used in both domestic and international cases. The function of the principles has essentially been to corroborate the legal content of decisions taken by judges or arbitrators, based on national substantive law. On other occasions, UNIDROIT principles have also been used to supplement international treaties applicable to private situations.

All this confirms the undeniable value of UNIDROIT principles as a concrete embodiment of fundamental ideas of international commercial law and, therefore, as a transnational instrument. By giving judges and arbitrators this function of corroboration, these courts are essentially acknowledging the value of these and consequently applying their underlying postulates.

However, it is important to clarify that UNIDROIT principles are not always welcomed. Particularly, the courts of common law systems sometimes use the principles to deviate completely from the rules set forth therein. An example of this is the case ruled by the Court of Appeal of South Wales (Australia) in 2009,[58] and many others.

[58] Supreme Court of New South Wales - Court of Appeal, Australia Franklins Pty Ltd v Metcash Trading Ltd NSWCA 407 (December 16, 2009). Retrieved from: http://www.austlii.edu.au/cgi-bin/sinodisp/au/cases/nsw/NSWCA/2009/407.html?stem=0&synonyms=0&query=cisg. "To a significant degree the approach to the construction and interpretation of contracts in the UNIDROIT Principles and the CISG reflects civil law principles: see Lord Hoffmann's comments in Chartbrook Limited v Persimmon Homes Limited [2009] UKHL 38; [2009] AC 1101 at 1119-20 [39]. This underlying difference in basal framework explains the brevity of the reference to the civil law by Lord Hoffmann in his discussion of the admissibility of pre-contractual negotiations in Chartbrook Limited v Persimmon Homes Limited at 1119-20 [39] and the absence of any such reference in

7 Concluding Analysis of the Methods of Implementing the *Lex Mercatoria*

First, transnational rules can be divided into general and special. The first are those aimed at regulating a wide range of relationships, such as those included in the UNIDROIT principles. This first type of sources, which could be called collections of contractual law principles, rival national laws as an alternative form of regulation of international contracts. The second type of sources, identified as special transnational contractual regulations, are standards specially designed for certain types of contracts or relationships, such as the UCP rules, which have received a very favorable reception in certain economic sectors.

Secondly, there is a strong distinction between the behavior of judges and arbitrators in relation to transnational rules, as regards the way in which they determine the rules applicable to international commercial relations. While national judges are conditioned to some extent by their local law, arbitrators, for their part, do not necessarily have to consider local laws or substantive issues of the place of execution of the verdict.

8 Conclusions

As identified in this chapter, the use of the *lex mercatoria* has the following modalities:

(a) Cases presented to national judges

(i) *Lex mercatoria* as a primary rule by legal mandate

In each country, there may be rules governing the application of international trade practices and customs, in the absence of choice by the parties. This is the case with Venezuelan law—Articles 30 and 31 of its Law on Private International Law. This is reflected in the case Rc. 000738 of 2014, resolved by the Supreme Court of Venezuela. Thus, transnational rules apply to the case as the main rule because an indirect rule so orders.

This form of application is still anecdotal, as practices and customs normally play a supplementary role to the other applicable legal order.

(ii) *Lex mercatoria* as the main rule chosen by the parties

Whether due to conflict autonomy or material autonomy, parties can choose—and often they do so—a national regulatory order for the regulation of their contracts. Sometimes, however, the parties do not choose a specific body of law or national law applicable to their relationship, but only transnational rules. In this regard, there have been some cases in which the contractual clauses and

Lord Mance's restatement of the principles of interpretation of a legal document in Sigma Finance Corporation [2009] UKSC 2 at [9]-[11]."

transnational rules chosen by the parties have been sufficient for the judges to provide a solution to the dispute, without identifying national or general transnational standards applicable to the case.

(iii) *Lex mercatoria* as a subsidiary rule of applicable law

In this form of application, three variants are distinguished. Firstly, transnational rules are complementary to an international instrument, as established in the various international treaties mentioned. In them, the creator of the international standard fills the gaps therein by invoking the application of parameters of the *lex mercatoria*. Secondly, transnational rules are used to supplement national laws if gaps persist or there is no response in national law or applicable rules. Thirdly, transnational rules may also appear as a subsidiary rule of applicable national law, as is the case in Colombia under the mandate of Article 7 of the Commercial Code.

(iv) *Lex mercatoria* as a standard for confirming, supplementing, or rejecting interpretations in the light of applicable law

This constitutes one of the most important uses of general rules for transnational trade. Through this form of application, judges use transnational rules of a general nature as a form of integration of international commercial law.

Thus, the judges are acknowledging the authority of these rules, not because they are binding, but because in most of the cases recorded, they have offered solutions that have been considered under national rules applicable to international commercial relations.

It can then be pointed out that when the judge bases his solution on transnational rules, really, he is using them because of their compatibility with his internal system.

The reception that transnational rules have had, in most cases, reflects a serious effort to consolidate and identify appropriate solutions for international trade and therefore demonstrates the persuasive authority they possess in certain instruments, particularly the UNIDROIT principles.

(b) Cases presented to international arbitration

(i) *Lex mercatoria* as the main rule chosen by the parties

When parties choose arbitration as a means of settling disputes, their party autonomy is undeniable, since, thanks to the international arbitral regulations, they have the freedom to determine the applicable legal rules. Although, as has been shown, it is not usual for parties to determine a general instrument of *lex mercatoria* as the law applicable to their contract.

In any case, the use of general instruments is a useful option for those seeking an accessible system of rules to regulate private relations. These provide a clear framework of work, with solutions that have been accepted in most cases as appropriate by referees, judges, and arbitrators around the world.

(ii) *Lex mercatoria* as the main rule chosen by the arbitrators as appropriate in the absence of the parties' choice of law

When the parties do not choose the system of rules applicable to their legal relationship, the arbitrators are empowered to choose the rules of law that they consider most appropriate to govern the matter. This is because it is established in the most important current arbitration rules, to which arbitrators in the development of their resolution activity must be subject.

This has led some arbitrators, in the absence of a standard selected by the parties, to opt for a transnational instrument of general scope, particularly when the parties have incorporated INCOTERMS or the UCP rules as described in their contract, or even when parties have not said anything about it.

The choice of these instruments is explained by the fact that it is precisely the arbitrators who recognize the capacity of these rules to provide solutions that are compatible with the regulation of the most widespread commercial conduct, without the need to refer to a specific national law.

(iii) *Lex mercatoria* as a primary standard as an internationally recognized custom

Commercial arbitration rules usually require arbitrators to take account of trade customs and practices. This means that in many cases, even before examining the applicable law, the arbitrators have decided to apply rules arising from transnational norms, particularly UNIDROIT principles, since they recognize that they constitute practices and customs of international trade.

(iv) *Lex mercatoria* as a standard of reference

Like judges, arbitrators have repeatedly used transnational rules to confirm or interpret national rules applicable to the cases presented to the international arbitration tribunals.

References

Batiffol H (1973) Le pluralisme des méthodes en droit international privé. Martinus Nijhoff Publishers, Hague

Berger KP (2010) The creeping codification of the new *lex mercatoria*, 2nd edn. Kluwer Law International, London

Bonell MJ (2009) The CISG and the UNIDROIT principles of international commercial contracts. Two complementary instruments. Int Law Rev Wuhan Univ, 100–117

Brower CN, Sharpe JK (2004) The creeping codification of transnational commercial law: an arbitrator's perspective. Virginia J Int Law Assoc, 200–221

Bulletin of the ICC International Court of Arbitration (1999) 10(2):39 ff

Calvo Caracava AL, Carrascosa González J (2012) Contratos internacionales (I): competencia judicial y ley aplicable. In: Calvo Caracava AL, Carrascosa González J, Derecho del comercio internacional. Constitución y Leyes, Madrid, pp. 477–726

Calvo Caravaca AL, Carrascosa González J (2013) Derecho internacional privado. Comares, Granada

Drahozal CR (2005) Contracting out of national law: an empirical look at the new law merchant. Notre Dame Law Rev 523–552
Espinosa Pérez, C. A. (2007). La *Lex Mercatoria*: el verdadero derecho de los negocios internacionales. Derecho Privado Universidad de los Andes:5–30
Fry J, Greenberg S, Mazza F (2012) The secretariat's guide to ICC arbitration. ICC, Paris
Gaillard E (2001) Transnational law: a legal system or a method of decision making. Arbitr Int 59–71
Goldman B (1964) Frontières du droit et *lex mercatoria*. Archives de Philosophie du Droit.
Goldman B (1986) General principles of law—the *lex mercatoria*. In: Lew IJD (ed) Contemporary problems in international arbitration. Martinus Nijhoff Publishers, Dordrecht, pp 113–125
Hatzimihail NE (2008) The many lives and faces of *lex mercatoria*: history as genealogy in international business law. Law Contemp Probl 169–190
Joachim Bonell M (1995) The UNIDROIT principles of international commercial contracts: Why? What? How? Tulane Law Rev 1121–1147
Lando O (1985) The *lex mercatoria* in international commercial arbitration. Int Comp Law Q 747–768
Le Goff P (2006) Global law: a legal phenomenon emerging from the process of globalization. Indiana J Glob Legal Stud 119–145
Lowenfeld AF (1990) *Lex mercatoria*: An arbitrator's view. Arbitr Int 133–150
Pereznieto Castro L (2003) Derecho internacional privado, parte general. Oxford University Press, Mexico
Schultz T (2008) Some critical comments on the juridicity of *lex mercatoria*. Yearb Priv Int Law 667–710

Néstor Raúl Londoño Sepulveda . Doctor Cum Laude in Law, Universidad de Zaragoza; Lawyer, Universidad Pontificia Bolivariana; Research Professor and Member of the Research Group GRID, Universidad Pontificia Bolivariana.

MIX
Papier aus verantwortungsvollen Quellen
Paper from responsible sources
FSC® C105338

If you have any concerns about our products,
you can contact us on
ProductSafety@springernature.com

In case Publisher is established outside the EU,
the EU authorized representative is:
Springer Nature Customer Service Center GmbH
Europaplatz 3, 69115 Heidelberg, Germany

Printed by Libri Plureos GmbH
in Hamburg, Germany